# A BIBLIOGRAPHY OF THE HISTORY OF WALES

# A BIBLIOGRAPHY

OF THE

# HISTORY OF WALES

PREPARED BY

THE HISTORY AND LAW COMMITTEE
OF THE BOARD OF CELTIC STUDIES
OF THE UNIVERSITY OF WALES

*Second edition*

CARDIFF
UNIVERSITY OF WALES PRESS
1962

*First edition, 1931*
*Second edition, 1962*

WILLIAM LEWIS (PRINTERS) LTD., CARDIFF

# PREFACE

In 1926 the Guild of Graduates of the University of Wales, which has an honourable record in the publication of works illustrating Welsh culture, established a 'Welsh History Section' with Mr. (now Sir) Ifan ab Owen Edwards as secretary. In 1927 the Section decided to produce a Bibliography of Welsh History. Its compilation was the work of scholars within and outside the University and the editors were Dr. R. T. Jenkins and Professor William Rees (the first holders of the chairs of Welsh History at Bangor and Cardiff). The volume was published by the University of Wales Press Board in 1931 and the costs were met with the aid of grants from the Guild and the Thomas Ellis Memorial Fund. The Bibliography was designed to meet the needs, not only of school teachers and research students, but also of those who were generally interested in the history of Wales.

During the past thirty years the Bibliography has served the purposes for which it was intended; but the same period has seen great development in the study of the subject. The University has established chairs of Welsh History: the learned societies which were at work in 1931 have continued their labours: new county and other historical societies, each with its *Transactions,* have been founded: the Board of Celtic Studies has produced an impressive series of volumes in its History and Law Series: the Press Board of the University has published works of historical and literary scholarship in a steady stream. It has been clear for some years that a revised edition of the Bibliography was needed.

The initiative came, again, from the Guild of Graduates. In 1953 the Guild suggested to the Board of Celtic Studies that the History and Law Committee of the Board should undertake the revision, the Guild to subscribe towards the cost of publication. The Board approved the proposal and the History and Law Committee, through a sub-committee, planned the pattern and scope of the work and chose contributors for the various sections. A first draft was ready by the end of 1956. It was not possible to find a single editor who was free to take sole responsibility for the final arrangement of the material; the History and Law Committee therefore invited those of its members who lived in Bangor to prepare the final draft. They were: Professor A. H. Dodd, Mr. E. Gwynne Jones (Librarian of the College), Mr. J. Gwynn Williams, and myself as Chairman. This committee recast and expanded the material, working on the principle that the revised Bibliography should serve the scholarly needs of historians generally, and that it should include material published up to December 31, 1958.

Those who contributed the various sections are listed at the close of this preface; they include a number who assisted in the production of the first edition. Co-operative works of this kind are indebted to the many who have shared in the task; but they owe special debts of gratitude to particular individuals. The then secretary of the History and Law Committee, Professor David Williams of Aberystwyth, set the work fairly on its course, and his successor in that office from 1956, Professor Glanmor Williams of Swansea, ensured that the efforts of the team of contributors were co-ordinated from the outset. Mr. E. Gwynne Jones, as secretary of the final editorial committee, was responsible for the labour of embodying its decisions in successive drafts, and his bibliographical knowledge was of the greatest value. Dr. Elwyn Davies, Secretary of the University Council, gave freely of his experience and the resources of the University Registry in the task of reproducing drafts for the History and Law Committee. Perhaps the greatest single debt is owed to Mr. Ieuan M. Williams of the University Press Board. With the full co-operation of Dr. Elwyn Davies he has prepared and checked the final manuscript, guided it through the press, and prepared the index. His contribution is the greater because much of it has been made after he left the Press Board to take up new duties as Director of Extra-Mural Studies at University College, Swansea. His efficiency, patience, and unfailing courtesy, have smoothed the path of all who have been concerned with the project.

GLYN ROBERTS,
*Chairman of the History and Law Committee*
*of the Board of Celtic Studies.*

# LIST OF CONTRIBUTORS

Section A.  The National Library of Wales. Through Dr. Thomas Parry
and Mr. E. D. Jones, Librarians.
Dr. Iorwerth C. Peate, Welsh Folk Museum, St. Fagans.

Section B.  Mr. G. P. Ambrose, Training College, Caerleon.
Professor E. G. Bowen, University College, Aberystwyth.
Sir Goronwy Edwards, University of London.
Mr. E. D. Jones, National Library of Wales.
Mr. E. Gwynne Jones, University College, Bangor.
Mr. F. Price Jones, University College, Bangor.
Mr. J. F. Jones, The Museum, Carmarthen.
Mr. T. I. Jeffreys Jones, Coleg Harlech.
Mr. J. D. K. Lloyd, Garthmyl, Montgomeryshire.
Sir Frederick Rees, St. Mellons, Cardiff.
Professor William Rees, University College, Cardiff.
Mr. Melville Richards, University of Liverpool.
Royal Commission on Ancient Monuments in Wales and
Monmouthshire. Through Mr. A. H. A. Hogg, Secretary.
Professor Glanmor Williams, University College, Swansea.
Mr. W. Ogwen Williams, University College, Bangor.

Section C.  Dr. H. N. Savory, National Museum of Wales.

Section D.  Professor E. G. Bowen, University College, Aberystwyth.
Professor T. Jones Pierce, University College, Aberystwyth.
Mr. Melville Richards, University of Liverpool.
Sir Ifor Williams, University College, Bangor.

Section E.  Sir Goronwy Edwards, University of London.

Section F.  Mr. John Griffiths, University of Liverpool.
Professor T. Jones Pierce, University College, Aberystwyth.

Section G.  Professor Glyn Roberts, University College, Bangor.
Professor Glanmor Williams, University College, Swansea.

Section H.  Mr. J. Martin Cleary, St. Joseph's Secondary School, Wrexham.
Professor A. H. Dodd, University College, Bangor.
Dr. Thomas Richards, University College, Bangor.

Section J.  Professor R. T. Jenkins, University College, Bangor.
Professor Glyn Roberts, University College, Bangor.
Mr. R. O. Roberts, University College, Swansea.
Mr. J. Gwynn Williams, University College, Bangor.

Section K.  Mr. Aled Eames, University College, Bangor.
Mr. T. I. Ellis, Aberystwyth.
Mr. Gwynedd Pierce, University College, Cardiff.
Professor David Williams, University College, Aberystwyth.

# CONTENTS

*Page*

# LIST OF ABBREVIATIONS

| | |
|---|---|
| *Agric. Hist. Rev.* . . . | Agricultural History Review. |
| *Amer. Hist. Rev.* . . . | American Historical Review. |
| *Antiq. Jnl.* . . . . | Antiquaries' Journal. |
| *Arch. Camb.* . . . | Archaeologia Cambrensis. |
| *Arch. f. Celt. lex.* . . | Archiv für Celtische Lexikographie. |
| *Arch. Jnl.* . . . . | The Archaeological Journal. |
| Bangor Welsh MSS. Soc. . | Bangor Welsh Manuscript Society. |
| *B.B.C.S.* . . . | Bulletin of the Board of Celtic Studies, University of Wales. |
| Brit. Rec. Soc. . . | British Record Society. |
| *Bull. Inst. of Hist. Res.* . . | Bulletin of the Institute of Historical Research. |
| *Caerns. Hist. Soc. Record Ser.* . | Caernarvonshire Historical Society Record Series. |
| *Camden Misc.* . . . | Camden Miscellany. |
| *Camden Soc.* . . . | Camden Society. |
| *Carm. Antiq.* . . . | The Carmarthen Antiquary. |
| *Cath. Rec. Soc. Pubns.* . | Catholic Record Society Publications. |
| *Cylch. Cymd. Hanes M.C.* . | Cylchgrawn Cymdeithas Hanes Methodistiaid Calfinaidd. |
| D.N.B. . . . | Dictionary of National Biography. |
| *Econ. Hist. Rev.* . . | Economic History Review. |
| *Efryd. Cath.* . . | Efrydiau Catholig. |
| E.H.R. . . . | English Historical Review. |
| *Flints. Hist. Soc. Pubns.* . | Flintshire Historical Society Journal and Publications. |
| Flints. Hist. Soc. Rec. Ser. . | Flintshire Historical Society Record Series. |
| *Hist. Mag. of Prot. Episc. Church* | Historical Magazine of the Protestant Episcopal Church. |
| *Hist. Soc. Church in Wales Pubns.* | Publications of the Historical Society of the Church in Wales. |
| *Jnl. Brit. Arch. Assoc.* . . | Journal of the British Archaeological Association. |
| *Jnl. Hist. Soc. Church in Wales* . | Journal of the Historical Society of the Church in Wales. |
| *Jnl. Mer. Hist. and Rec. Soc.* . | Journal of the Merioneth Historical and Record Society. |
| *Jnl. R. Anthrop. Inst.* . | Journal of the Royal Anthropological Institute. |
| *Jnl. Rom. Stud.* . . | Journal of Roman Studies. |
| *Jnl. Royal Soc. Arts* . | Journal of the Royal Society of Arts. |
| *Jnl. Welsh Bibl. Soc.* . | Journal of the Welsh Bibliographical Society. |
| *Mons. Rev.* . . . | Monmouthshire Review. |
| *Mont. Coll.* . . . | Montgomeryshire Collections. |
| n.d. . . . . | No date of publication given. |
| n.p. . . . . | No place of publication given. |
| N.L.W. . . . | National Library of Wales. |
| *N.L.W. Jnl.* . . . | Journal of the National Library of Wales. |
| *P.D. Review* . . . | Powell Duffryn Review. |
| P.R.O. . . . | Public Record Office. |
| *Procs. Brit. Acad.* . . | Proceedings of the British Academy. |
| *Procs. Brit. Arch. Assoc.* . | Proceedings of the British Archaeological Association. |
| *S. Wales and Mon. Rec. Soc. Pubns.* | South Wales and Monmouth Record Society Publication. |
| *Shrop. Arch. and Nat. Hist. Soc.* | Shropshire Archaeological and Naturalists' Historical Society. |
| *Traf. Cymd. Hanes Bed.* . . | Trafodion Cymdeithas Hanes Bedyddwyr Cymru. |

| | | |
|---|---|---|
| *Trans. Angl. Antiq. Soc.* . . | . | Transactions of the Anglesey Antiquarian Society and Field Club. |
| *Trans. Caerns. Hist. Soc.* . . | . | Transactions of the Caernarvonshire Historical Society. |
| *Trans. Caradoc Field Club* | . | Transactions of the Caradoc and Severn Valley Field Club. |
| *Trans. Cardiff Nat. Soc.* . . | . | Transactions of the Cardiff Naturalists' Society. |
| *Trans. Cards. Antiq. Soc.* | . | Transactions of the Cardiganshire Antiquarian Society. |
| *Trans. Carms. Antiq. Soc.* | . | Transactions of the Carmarthenshire Antiquarian Society and Field Club. |
| *Trans. Cymmr.* . . | . | Transactions of the Honourable Society of Cymmrodorion. |
| *Trans. Denbs. Hist. Soc.* . . | . | Transactions of the Denbighshire Historical Society. |
| *Trans. Hist. Soc. Lancs and Chesh.* | | Transactions of the Lancaster and Cheshire Historic Society. |
| *Trans. Neath Antiq. Soc.* | . | Transactions of the Neath Antiquarian Society. |
| *Trans. Rads. Soc.* . . | . | Transactions of the Radnorshire Society. |
| *Trans. R.H.S.* . . | . | Transactions of the Royal Historical Society. |
| *Trans. Shrops. Arch. Soc.* | . | Transactions of the Shropshire Archaeological Society. |
| *U.C.N.W.* . . . | . | University College of North Wales. |
| *Univ. of Birmingham Hist. Jnl.* . | . | University of Birmingham Historical Journal. |
| *W. Wales Hist. Rec.* . | . | West Wales Historical Records. |
| *Y Cymmr.* . . . | . | Y Cymmrodor. |
| *Zeitschrift f. Celt. phil.* . | . | Zeitschrift für Celtische Philologie. |

# SECTION A

## GENERAL HISTORY

Much historical material is embodied in the theses presented for higher degrees of the University of Wales; typewritten lists are available in the National Library of Wales at Aberystwyth, in the libraries of the constituent colleges of the University of Wales at Aberystwyth, Bangor, Cardiff, and Swansea, and in the University Registry at Cardiff. For theses other than those of the University of Wales, the Thesis Supplement of the *Bulletin of the Institute of Historical Research* should be consulted.

### I. BIBLIOGRAPHIES

For bibliographies of special subjects or of special periods see under the appropriate sections below.

See also Report of the Royal Commission on land in Wales and Monmouthshire: bibliographical, statistical, and other miscellaneous memoranda, being appendices to the report (No. 2971).

1. AP GWYNN, ARTHUR, and LEWIS, IDWAL (eds): Subject index to Welsh periodicals. Vol. i, 1931. Cardiff, 1933. In progress.

2. Archaeological bulletin for the British Isles. Council for British Archaeology. London, 1940–9; continued as Archaeological bibliography for Great Britain and Ireland, 1950. In progress.

3. ASHTON, CHARLES: Llyfryddiaeth Gymreig y bedwaredd ganrif ar bymtheg. London, 1908; additions by LEWIS, IDWAL, in *Jnl. Welsh Bibl. Soc.*, vi, 6, 1949; vii, 1, 1950; viii, 4, 1957.

4. BALLINGER, JOHN, and JONES, JAMES IFANO (eds): Catalogue of printed literature in the Welsh Department of the Cardiff Free Library. Cardiff, 1898.

5. Bibliotheca Celtica. A register of publications relating to Wales and the Celtic peoples and languages. Aberystwyth. Series 1 and 2, 11 vols., 1909–38; series 3, vol. i, 1954. In progress.

6. BONSER, WILFRID: Anglo-Saxon and Celtic bibliography for A.D. 450 onwards. 2 vols. London, 1957.

7. DAVIES, WILLIAM LLEWELYN: Welsh books entered in the Stationers' Company's registers. Part I, 1554–1660; part II, 1660–1708. *Jnl. Welsh Bibl. Soc.*, ii, 5 and 6, 1921.

8. Id.    Short-title list of Welsh books. Part I, 1546–1640; part II, 1641–1680; part III, 1681–1700. Ibid., ii, 5, 6, and 7, 1921.

9. GROSS, CHARLES: Sources and literature of English history from the earliest times to about 1485. 2nd edn. London, 1915.

**10.** HUGHES, WILLIAM JOHN: Wales and the Welsh in English literature. Wrexham, 1924.

> Contains a bibliography of topographical works; see also TUCKER, NORMAN: Travellers and tourists of bygone days. Proceedings of the eighteenth conference of library authorities in Wales and Monmouthshire in 1951.

**11.** JONES, JAMES IFANO: A history of printing and printers in Wales and Monmouthshire to . . . 1923. Cardiff, 1925.

**12.** MILNE, A. TAYLOR (ed.): Writings on British history. Royal Historical Society. London.

> 1934 (published 1937)
> 1935 (published 1939)
> 1936 (published 1940)
> 1937 (published 1949)
> 1938 (published 1951)
> 1939 (published 1953)
> 1940-5 (published 1958). In progress.

> See also the annual bulletin of historical literature published by the Historical Association.

**13.** ROWLANDS, WILLIAM: Llyfryddiaeth y Cymry. Ed. Daniel Silvan Evans. Llanidloes, 1869.

## II. GENEALOGY AND FAMILY HISTORY

Valuable genealogical matter is contained in Reports on Manuscripts in the Welsh language (No. 116), in the Catalogue of the Manuscripts relating to Wales in the British Museum (No. 109 (4) ), in Y Bywgraffiadur Cymreig (No. 106), and in The Dictionary of Welsh Biography (No. 107).

**14.** BUCKLEY, JAMES: Genealogies of the Carmarthenshire sheriffs. 2 vols. Carmarthen, 1910-13.

**15.** CLARK, GEORGE THOMAS: Limbus patrum Morganiae et Glamorganiae, being the genealogies of the older families of the lordships of Morgan and Glamorgan. London, 1886.

**16.** CUST, ALBINIA LUCY: Chronicles of Erthig on the dyke. 2 vols. London, 1914.

**17.** EVANS, ARTHUR LESLIE: The story of Sker House. Privately printed. Port Talbot, 1956; repr. 1957.

**18.** EVANS, GWENLLIAN NESTA: Presaddfed, 1800-1873. *Trans. Angl. Antiq. Soc.*, 1953.

**19.** GREEN, FRANCIS: Old county families of Dyfed: the Wogans of Boulston, Merrion, and Somersetshire. *Y Cymmr.*, xv and xvi, 1902-13.

**20.** Id.    (ed.): Genealogies of Cardiganshire, Carmarthenshire, and Pembrokeshire families. *West Wales Hist. Rec.*, ii and iii, 1911-13.

**21.** Id.  The Barlows of Slebech. Ibid., iii, 1912–13.

**22.** Id.  The Musgraves of Llanina. Ibid., iv, 1914.

**23.** Id.  Walter of Roche Castle. Ibid., v, 1915.

**24.** Id.  The Wogans of Pembrokeshire. Ibid., vi and vii, 1916–18.

**25.** Id.  The Dyers of Aberglasney. Ibid., vii, 1917–18.

**26.** Id.  The Stepneys of Prendergast. Ibid., vii, 1917–18.

**27.** Id.  Harries of county Pembroke. Ibid., viii, 1919–20.

**28.** Id.  Stedman of Strata Florida. Ibid., viii, 1919–20.

**29.** Id.  Lloyd of Danyrallt. Ibid., viii, 1919–20.

**30.** Id.  Scurlock of Carmarthen. Ibid., ix, 1920–3.

**31.** Id.  Scourfield of New Moat. Ibid., ix, 1920–3.

**32.** Id.  The Pictons of Poyston. Ibid., x, 1924.

**33.** Id.  Bowen of Roblinston and Camrose. Ibid., xi, 1926.

**34.** Id.  The Fortunes of Leweston. Ibid., xii, 1926.

**35.** Id.  Cuny of Welston and Golden. Ibid., xii, 1927.

**36.** Id.  Symins of Martell and Llanstinan. Ibid., xiv, 1929.

**37.** Id.  and HIGGON, CATHERINE OCTAVIA: The Tuckers of Sealyham. Ibid., viii, 1919–20.

**38.** Id.  and id.: The Edwardes of Sealyham. Ibid.

**39.** GLENN, THOMAS ARTHUR: The family of Griffith of Garn and Plasnewydd in the county of Denbigh. London, 1934.

**40.** GRIFFITH, JOHN EDWARDS: Pedigrees of Anglesey and Caernarvonshire families. Horncastle, 1914.

**41.** HANMER, JOHN LORD: A memorial of the parish and family of Hanmer in Flintshire. London, 1876.

**42.** HEMP, WILFRID JAMES: Presidential address [to the Cambrian Archaeological Association, Nefyn, 1955]. *Arch. Camb.*, 1956.
On early heraldry and heraldic monuments in North Wales.

**43.** HUGHES, GARFIELD HOPKIN: Y Dwniaid [Cydweli]. *Trans. Cymmr.*, 1941.

**44.** JENKINS, DAVID: The Pryse family of Gogerddan. *N.L.W. Jnl.*, viii, 1953–4.

**44A.** JENKINS, ROBERT THOMAS: Some pages in the history of Pant Glas, Ysbyty Ifan. *Trans. Caerns. Hist. Soc.*, 1949.

**44B.** Id.  More Vaughans of Pant Glas. Ibid., 1950.

**45.** JONES, EMYR GWYNNE (ed.): History of the Bulkeley family (N.L.W. MS. 9080 E). *Trans. Angl. Antiq. Soc.*, 1948.

**46.** JONES, ENID SOPHIA (Lady Clement Jones): Trevors of Trevalyn and their descendants. Privately printed, 1955.

**47.** JONES, EVAN DAVID: The family of Nannau (Nanney) of Nannau. *Jnl. Mer. Hist. and Rec. Soc.*, ii, 1953.

**48.** JONES, FRANCIS: The squires of Hawksbrook. *Trans. Cymmr.*, 1937.

**49.** Id.     Griffith of Penybenglog. Ibid., 1938.

**50.** Id.     Two border families [Edwards of Kilhendre and Morall of Kenston]. Ibid., 1948.

**51.** Id.     An approach to Welsh genealogy. Ibid.

**52.** JONES, GWILYM PEREDUR: Rhos and Rhufoniog pedigrees. *Arch. Camb.*, 1925.

**53.** Id.     Notes on some non-dynastic Anglesey clan-founders. *Trans. Angl. Antiq. Soc.*, 1923 and 1924.

**54.** KENRICK, W. BYNG: Chronicles of a Nonconformist family: the Kenricks of Wynne Hall, Exeter, and Birmingham. Birmingham, 1932.

**55.** LEWIS, RICE: A breviat of Glamorgan, 1596–1600. Ed. William Rees. *S. Wales and Mon. Rec. Soc. Pubn.*, iii, 1954.
> Transcript, with notes, of a document in the National Library of Wales; mainly genealogical.

**56.** LLOYD, JOHN: Bedwenni, Llandderfel. *Jnl. Mer. Hist. and Rec. Soc.*, ii, 3, 1955.

**57.** LLOYD, JOHN DAVIES KNATCHBULL: Six glass armorial shields in Meifod church. *Mont. Coll.*, lii, 1951–2.

**58.** LLOYD, JACOB YOUDE WILLIAM: History of the princes, the lords marcher, and the ancient nobility of Powys Fadog. 6 vols. London, 1881–7.

**59.** LLOYD, WILLIAM VALENTINE (ed.): Pedigrees of Montgomeryshire families . . . selected about the year 1711–12 from Lewis Dwnn's original visitation by . . . John Rhydderch. *Mont. Coll.* supp., 1888.

**60.** MEYRICK, SAMUEL RUSH (ed.): Heraldic visitations of Wales (by Lewys Dwnn). 2 vols. Llandovery, 1846.

**61.** MOSTYN, Lord, and GLENN, THOMAS ARTHUR: History of the family of Mostyn of Mostyn. London, 1925.

**62.** MYDDELTON, WILLIAM MARTIAL: Pedigree of the family of Myddelton of Gwaynynog, Garthgynan, and Llansannan, all in the county of Denbigh. Privately printed. Horncastle, 1910.

**63.** NICHOLAS, THOMAS: Annals and antiquities of the counties and county families of Wales. 2 vols. London, 1872.

**64.** OWEN, HENRY: Old Pembroke families. London, 1902.

**65.** PHILLIPS, JOHN ROLAND: Memoirs of the ancient family of Owen of Orielton, county Pembroke. London, 1886.

**66.** PINK, WILLIAM DUNCOMBE: Notes on the Middleton family of Denbighshire and London, etc. Privately printed, 1891.

**67.** POWELL, ANTHONY DYMOKE: Notes on some individual Powells and ap Howells on the Radnor-Hereford border in the 16th century. *Trans. Rads. Soc.*, xvii, 1957.

**68.** [ROBERTS, ASKEW]: Wynnstay and the Wynns, a volume of varieties, put together by the author of the Gossiping guide to Wales. Oswestry, 1876.

**69.** ROBERTS, GLYN: The Glynnes and the Wynns of Glynllifon. *Trans. Caerns. Hist. Soc.*, 1948.

**70.** STEEGMAN, JOHN: Portraits from Welsh houses. Vol. i, Houses in North Wales. Nat. Museum of Wales. Cardiff, 1957.

**71.** THOMAS, DANIEL LLEUFER: Iscennen and Golden Grove. Ed. A. J. Richard. *Trans. Cymmr.*, 1940.

**72.** TUCKER, NORMAN: Wynne of Trofarth and Coed Coch. *Procs. Llandudno, Colwyn Bay and District Field Club*, xxvii, 1954.

**73.** Id.　　Marle Hall [Llangystennin, Caerns.]. *Trans. Caerns. Hist. Soc.*, 1957.

**74.** UNWIN, MARY: Chambres of Plas Chambres and Llysmeirchion. *Trans. Denbs. Hist. Soc.*, 1954.

**75.** VAUGHAN, HERBERT MILLINGCHAMP: The Millingchamps of Cardigan. *W. Wales Hist. Rec.*, v, 1915.

**76.** WILLIAMS, JOHN: Llyfr Baglan, 1600–7. Ed. J. A. Bradney. London, 1910.

**77.** WILLIAMS, JOHN GWYNN: Sir John Vaughan of Trawscoed, 1603–1674. *N.L.W. Jnl.*, viii, 1954.

> An account of the rise of the Crosswood estate, Cardiganshire.
>
> See also HOWELLS, JOHN MARTIN: The Crosswood estate, 1547–1947. *Ceredigion*, iii, 1, 1956.

78. WRENCHE, W. G.: Wrenche (Pransiaid) and Radcliffe of Glamorgan. Privately printed. [Cardiff], 1956.

79. WYNN, SIR JOHN: The history of the Gwydir family. Ed. Daines Barrington. London, 1770; 2nd edn published in Daines Barrington's Miscellanies, London, 1781; 3rd edn by Angharad Llwyd, Ruthin, 1827; 4th edn by Askew Roberts, Oswestry, 1878; 5th and latest edn by John Ballinger, Cardiff, 1927.

80. WYNNE, R. O. F.: The Wynne family of Melai and Garthewin. *Trans. Denbs. Hist. Soc.*, 1956.

81. YORKE, PHILIP: The royal tribes of Wales. Wrexham, 1799; ed. Richard Williams, Liverpool, 1887.

### III. BIOGRAPHICAL DICTIONARIES, ETC.

82. ALLEN, JAMES: Notes on the sheriffs of Pembrokeshire, 1541–1899. Tenby, 1900.

83. BREESE, EDWARD: Kalendars of Gwynedd. London, 1873.

> Contains lists of sheriffs, lords lieutenant, members of parliament, and constables of castles. See also: Public Record Office. List of sheriffs for England and Wales. Lists and Indexes No. IX, 1898.

84. Catholic Encyclopaedia. 16 vols. New York, 1907–14.

85. Dictionary of national biography. Ed. Leslie Stephen and Sidney Lee. 63 vols. London, 1885–1900; also, supplementary vols with index and epitome.

86. HOWSE, WILLIAM HENRY: High sheriffs of Radnorshire, 1541–1900. *Trans. Rads. Soc.*, xxv, 1955.

87. LLOYD, JOHN YOUDE WILLIAM: The sheriffs of Denbighshire (1541–1700). *Arch. Camb.*, 1869–70.

88. LLOYD, WILLIAM VALENTINE (ed.): The sheriffs of Montgomeryshire . . . from 1540–1639. First published in *Mont. Coll.*, ii–vi and ix, 1869–73, 1876; Lloyd continued the series to 1658 in ibid., xxvii, 1893.

89. PARRY, EDWARD: A list of the names and residences of all the high sheriffs of the county of Denbigh from . . . 1541 down to . . . 1906. n.p. [1906].

### REGISTERS OF UNIVERSITIES, INNS OF COURT, AND SCHOOLS

The universities and schools listed below were those normally frequented by Welshmen, particularly during the 16th–18th centuries. For a comprehensive list of registers, see JOHNSON, MARJORIE: Bibliography of registers (printed) of the universities, inns of court, colleges, and schools of Great Britain and Ireland. *Bull. Inst. of Hist. Research*, ix, 1931.

UNIVERSITIES :

### Cambridge

**90.** Alumni Cantabrigienses. A bibliographical list of all known students, graduates, and holders of office . . . to 1900. Ed. J. and J. A. Venn. 10 vols. Cambridge, 1912–54.

### Oxford

**91.** Alumni Oxonienses . . . 1500–1714. Ed. J. Foster. 6 vols. Oxford, 1888–92.

**92.** EMDEN, ALFRED BROTHERSTON: A biographical register of the University of Oxford to A.D. 1500. 2 vols. Oxford, 1957–8.

INNS OF COURT :

### Gray's Inn

**93.** Register of admissions . . . 1521–1889. Ed. J. Foster. London, privately printed, 1889.

### Inner Temple

**94.** Students admitted . . . 1547–1660. London, privately printed, 1887.

### Lincoln's Inn

**95.** Records . . . admissions, 1429–1893. 2 vols. London, 1896.

### Middle Temple

**96.** Middle Temple bench book . . . a register of benchers . . . from the earliest records to the present times. Ed. A. R. Ingpen. London, 1912.

**97.** Catalogue of notable Middle Templars, with brief biographical notices. Ed. J. Hutchinson. London, 1902.

**98.** Register of admissions . . . from the fifteen century to the year 1944. Ed. H. A. C. Sturgess. 3 vols. London, 1949.

> See also ROBERTS, RICHARD ARTHUR: Caernarvonshire and the Middle Temple. *Trans. Caerns. Hist. Soc.*, 1956.

SCHOOLS:

### Shrewsbury School

**99.** Regestum Scholarium, 1562–1635. Admittances and readmittances. Ed. E. Calvert. Shrewsbury, [1892].

**100.** Register, 1636–1664. Ed. J. E. Auden. Shrewsbury, 1917.

**101.** Register, 1734–1908. Ed. J. E. Auden. Oswestry, 1909.

### Westminster School

**102.** The record of old Westminsters. A biographical list of all those who are known to have been educated at Westminster School from the earliest times to 1927. Ed. G. F. Russell and Alan H. Stenning. 2 vols. London, 1928.

> See also PRYCE, ARTHUR IVOR: Westminster School and its connection with North Wales prior to the Victorian era. *Trans. Angl. Antiq. Soc.*, 1932.

**103.** WILLIAMS, WILLIAM RETLAW: The parliamentary history of the principality of Wales from the earliest times to the present day, 1541–1895. Brecknock, 1895.

**104.** Id.    The history of the Great Sessions in Wales, 1542–1830, together with the lives of the Welsh judges. Brecknock, 1899.

**105.** WOOD, ANTHONY: Athenae Oxonienses. Ed. Philip Bliss. 4 vols. Oxford, 1813–20.

**106.** Y bywgraffiadur Cymreig hyd 1940. Gol. Syr John Edward Lloyd, R. T. Jenkins, a Syr William Llewelyn Davies. Llundain, 1953.

**107.** The dictionary of Welsh biography down to 1940. Eds Sir John Edward Lloyd, R. T. Jenkins, Sir William Llewelyn Davies, and Miss Margaret Beatrice Davies. London, 1959.
     Contains a complete list of earlier biographical dictionaries.

### IV. SOURCES AND CALENDARS OF SOURCES

For a list of calendars and texts published by Government, national, and regional record societies, etc., see MULLINS, E. L. C.: Texts and calendars: an analytical guide to serial publications. Royal Hist. Soc. London, 1958.

For general articles relating to Welsh sources the following are useful: HALL, HUBERT: The diplomatics of Welsh records, *Trans. Cymmr.*, 1900–1; id.: The foreign aspect of Welsh records, *Y Cymmr.*, xxii, 1909; id.: Welsh local records, *Trans. Cymmr.*, 1914–15; ROBERTS, RICHARD ARTHUR: Public records relating to Wales, *Y Cymmr.*, x, 1889; LLOYD, JOHN EDWARD: The Welsh chronicles (No. 1164). See also Nos. 113, 114 and 2723.

**108.** BOWEN, IVOR: The statutes of Wales. London, 1908.

**109.** Cymmrodorion Record Series:

(1) The description of Penbrokshire, by George Owen of Henllys. Ed. Henry Owen. 4 vols. London, 1902–36.
     See also CHARLES, BERTIE GEORGE: The second book of George Owen's Description of Pembrokeshire. *N.L.W Jnl.*, v, 1947–8.

(2) The court rolls of the lordship of Ruthin or Dyffryn-Clwyd, of the reign of King Edward the First . . . Ed. R. Arthur Roberts. London, 1893.

(3) Gildae de excidio Britanniae, liber de paenitentia, accedit et lorica Gildae (Gildas: the ruin of Britain, fragments from lost letters, the penitential, together with the lorica of Gildas). Ed. Hugh Williams. 2 vols. London, 1899–1901.

(4) A catalogue of the manuscripts relating to Wales in the British Museum. Compiled and edited by Edward Owen. 4 vols. London, 1900–22.
     See also Catalogue of additions to the manuscripts in the British Museum . . . 1841–1845. London, 1850 (Nos. 14,866–15,089: manuscripts presented by the governors of the Welsh school and by the Cymmrodorion Society).

(5) The black book of St. David's: an extent of all the lands and rents of the lord bishop of St. David's made . . . in 1326. Ed. J. W. Willis-Bund. London, 1902.

(6) The episcopal registers of the diocese of St. David's, 1397 to 1518. 3 vols. London, 1917–20.

(7) A calendar of the public records relating to Pembrokeshire. Ed. Henry Owen. 3 vols. London, 1914–18.

(8) A calendar of the register of the Queen's Majesty's council in the dominions and principality of Wales and the marches, 1569–71. Ed. Ralph Flenley. London, 1916.

(9) Walter Map's 'De nugis curialium'. Trans. Montague R. James, with historical notes by John Edward Lloyd. Ed. E. Sidney Hartland. London, 1923.

(11) The first extent of Bromfield and Yale, A.D. 1315. Ed. T. P. Ellis. London, 1924.

(12) The Welsh port books (1550–1603), with an analysis of the customs revenue accounts of Wales for the same period. Ed. E. A. Lewis. London, 1927.

(13) Ministers' accounts for west Wales, 1277–1306. Part I, text and translation. Ed. Myvanwy Rhys. London, 1936.

110. DAVIS, G. R. C.: Medieval cartularies of Great Britain: a short catalogue. London, 1958.

111. DUGDALE, WILLIAM: Monasticon Anglicanum. 3 vols. London, 1665–73; best subsequent edn by J. Cayley, H. Ellis, and B. Bandinel. 8 parts. London, 1817–30; reprinted 1846.
> The material relating to Wales is found in parts III–VI. It is of considerable value also for political history, especially for the period of the Norman conquest and the settlement of the marches.

112. ELLIS, HENRY (ed.): Original letters illustrative of English history. 2nd series, 4 vols., London, 1827; 3rd series, 4 vols., London, 1846.

113. GALBRAITH, VIVIAN HUNTER: An introduction to the use of the public records. Oxford, 1934.

114. GIUSEPPI, MONTAGUE SPENCER: A guide to the manuscripts preserved in the Public Record Office. 2 vols. London, 1923–4.

115. HADDAN, ARTHUR WEST, and STUBBS, WILLIAM (eds): Councils and ecclesiastical documents relating to Great Britain and Ireland. 3 vols. (4 parts). Oxford, 1869–78.
> The first volume is especially important for Welsh history.

**116.** Historical Manuscripts Commission. Reports on manuscripts in the Welsh language. Ed. J. Gwenogvryn Evans. London, 1898–1910.

> For Welsh material in the series generally, see Guide to the reports of the Royal Commission on Historical Manuscripts. Part I : Topographical, London, 1914; Part II : Index of persons, 2 vols., London, 1935 and 1938.

**117.** JONES, OWAIN and WILLIAMS, EDWARD, and [PUGHE], WILLIAM OWEN: The Myvyrian archaiology of Wales. London, 1801–7; later edn, Denbigh, 1870.

> To be used with caution; see WILLIAMS, GRIFFITH JOHN: Iolo Morganwg (No. 710).

**118.** National Library of Wales: Calendars of deeds and documents: Vol. i, The Coleman deeds. Ed. Francis Green. Aberystwyth, 1921.

**119.** Id.　　Vol. ii, The Crosswood deeds. Ed. Francis Green. Aberystwyth, 1927.

**120.** Id.　　Vol. iii, The Hawarden deeds. Ed. Francis Green. Aberystwyth, 1931.

**121.** Id.　　Catalogue of MSS. Vol. i, Additional MSS. in the collections of Sir John Williams. Aberystwyth, 1921.

**122.** Id.　　Calendar of the Wynn (of Gwydir) papers, 1515–1690. Aberystwyth, 1926.

**123.** Id.　　Handlist of manuscripts in the National Library of Wales. 2 vols. and index vol. Aberystwyth, 1943–51. In progress.

**124.** Id.　　Clenennau letters and papers in the Brogyntyn collection. Part I. Ed. T. Jones Pierce. Aberystwyth, 1947.

**125.** OWEN, GEORGE: The taylors cussion. Facsimile. Ed. E. M. Pritchard. London, 1906.

**126.** PARRY, EDWARD: Royal visits and progresses to Wales. London, 1850.

> Contains transcripts of many important documents.

**127.** Placita de quo warranto temporibus Edw. I, II, and III, etc. *Record Commission.* London, 1818.

**128.** RYMER, THOMAS (ed.) : Foedera, conventiones, litterae, etc. 20 vols. London, 1704–35; 2nd edn, 17 vols. London, 1727–9; 3rd edn, 10 vols. The Hague, 1739–45; new edn (1069–1383), 4 vols. (7 parts). *Record Commission.* London, 1816–69.

> For an abstract of the various editions, see HARDY, THOMAS DUFFUS: Syllabus of documents in Rymer's Foedera. 3 vols. *Rolls Series.* London, 1869–85.

**129.** The Record of Caernarvon. Ed. Henry Ellis. *Record Commission.* London, 1838.

> A collection of fourteenth and fifteenth century documents relating to the principality of North Wales, including *quo warranto* proceedings. Described by R. W. Banks in *Arch. Camb.*, 1873.

**130.** University of Wales: Board of Celtic Studies. History and Law Series:

(1) A catalogue of Star Chamber proceedings relating to Wales. Ed. Ifan ab Owen Edwards. Cardiff, 1929.

(2) Calendar of ancient correspondence concerning Wales. Ed. J. Goronwy Edwards. Cardiff, 1935.

(3) An inventory of early Chancery proceedings concerning Wales. Ed. E. A. Lewis. Cardiff, 1937.

(4) Exchequer proceedings (Equity) concerning Wales. Henry VIII—Elizabeth. Ed. Emyr Gwynne Jones. Cardiff, 1939.

(5) Littere Wallie, preserved in Liber A in the Public Record Office. Ed. J. Goronwy Edwards. Cardiff, 1940.

(6) Brut y Tywysogyon (Peniarth MS. 20). Gol. Thomas Jones. Caerdydd, 1941.

(7) The Welsh Assize Roll (1277–1284). Ed. J. Conway Davies. Cardiff, 1940.

(8) A review of the records of the Conway and the Menai ferries. By Henry Rees Davies. Cardiff, 1942.

(9) Vitae sanctorum Britanniae et genealogiae. Ed. A. W. Wade-Evans. Cardiff, 1944.

(10) Correspondence and minutes of the S.P.C.K. relating to Wales, 1699–1740. Ed. Mary Clement. Cardiff, 1952.

(11) Brut y Tywysogyon, or the Chronicle of the Princes (Peniarth MS. 20 version). A translation into English by Thomas Jones. Cardiff, 1952.

(12) A survey of the duchy of Lancaster lordships in Wales, 1609–1613. Ed. William Rees. Cardiff, 1953.

(13) Records of the Court of Augmentations relating to Wales and Monmouthshire. Ed. E. A. Lewis and J. Conway Davies. Cardiff, 1954.

(14) Calendar of Salusbury correspondence, 1553–c.1700. Ed. W. J. Smith. Cardiff, 1954.
   See review by R. Geraint Gruffydd in *Trans. Cymmr.*, 1954.

(15) Exchequer proceedings concerning Wales *in tempore* James I. Ed. T. I. Jeffreys Jones. Cardiff, 1955.

(16) Brut y Tywysogyon or the Chronicle of the Princes (Red Book of Hergest version). Ed. Thomas Jones. Cardiff, 1955.

(17) Acts of Parliament concerning Wales (1714–1901). Ed. T. I. Jeffreys Jones. Cardiff, 1959.

**131.** WILLIAMS, WILLIAM RETLAW (ed.): Old Wales. 3 vols. Tal-y-bont, Brecks., 1905–7.

## V. HISTORIES

### (a) General

**132.** BOWEN, EMRYS GEORGE: Wales: a study in geography and history. Cardiff, 1941; 5th impression, Cardiff, 1952.

**133.** Id. (ed.), *et al.*: Wales: a physical, historical, and regional geography. London, 1956.

**134.** BRIDGEMAN, GEORGE THOMAS ORLANDO: History of the princes of South Wales. Wigan, 1876.

**135.** CAMDEN, WILLIAM: Britannia, sive florentissimorum regnorum Angliae, Scotiae, Hiberniae chorographica descriptio. London, 1586; 6th edn (enlarged), 1606; first English trans. by Philemon Holland, London, 1610; trans. (enlarged) by Richard Gough. 3 vols. London, 1789.

**136.** CROSSLEY-HOLLAND, PETER (ed.): Music in Wales. London, 1948.

**137.** DAVIES, DAVID J.: The economic history of South Wales prior to 1800. Cardiff, 1933.

**138.** DODDRIDGE, JOHN: The history of the ancient and modern estate of the Principality of Wales. 1630; later edn, London, 1714.

**139.** EDWARDS, JOHN GORONWY: Hanesyddiaeth Gymreig yn yr ugeinfed ganrif. *Trans. Cymmr.*, 1953.

**140.** EDWARDS, OWEN MORGAN: Wales. London, 1901; 2nd edn, 1927.

**141.** JENKINS, ROBERT THOMAS: Yr apêl at hanes. Wrecsam, 1930.

**142.** JONES, E. ALFRED (ed.): Memorials of old North Wales. London, 1913.

**143.** JONES, GLYN PENRHYN: Y gwahanglwyf yng Nghymru. *Y Traethodydd*, 1958.

**144.** LLOYD, JOHN EDWARD: A history of Wales from the earliest times to the Edwardian conquest. 2 vols. London, 1911; 3rd edn., 1939.

> See also id.: Rulers of Wales. In Handbook of British chronology. Ed. F. M. Powicke. London, 1939.

**145.** O'RAHILLY, CECILE: Ireland and Wales, their historical and literary relations. London, 1924.

> For a brief general discussion of the relations between Wales and Brittany, see A. H. DODD: Wales and Brittany. *Procs. Llandudno, Colwyn Bay, and District Field Club*, 1949.

**146.** PARRY, THOMAS: Hanes llenyddiaeth Gymraeg hyd 1900. Cardiff, 1944; 3rd edn, Cardiff, 1953; English trans. by Harold Idris Bell: A history of Welsh literature, Oxford, 1955.

**147.** PEATE, IORWERTH CYFEILIOG: Cymru a'i phobl. Caerdydd, 1931.

**148.** PIERCE, THOMAS JONES: Wales: history. Chambers's Encyclopaedia. 1950, and later edns.

**149.** POWEL, DAVID: The historie of Cambria. London, 1584, etc.

> The nucleus of this work was a translation, by Humphrey Lhuyd, of Brut y Tywysogion (No. 1164). Powel made additions from other sources, and continued the story down to the reign of Elizabeth I. His work was reissued in 1697 by William Wynne, with further additions derived mainly from the notes of the seventeenth century Welsh antiquary, Robert Vaughan (d. 1667). This revised version subsequently appeared in several editions, the last in 1832. It was the standard work on Welsh history for more than two centuries and is the ultimate source of a great many of the 'traditional views' of medieval Welsh history. A reprint of Powel's original edition was issued for J. Harding, London, 1811.

**150.** PRYSE, THOMAS (Carnhuanawc): Hanes Cymru (hyd 1282). Crughywel, 1842.

**151.** REES, JAMES FREDERICK: Studies in Welsh history. Cardiff, n.d.

**152.** Id. Of Welsh history and historians. Annual B.B.C. lecture (Welsh Home Service). British Broadcasting Corporation. Cardiff, 1951.

**153.** Report of the Departmental Committee appointed . . . to enquire into the position of the Welsh language. London, 1927.

> The report is published under the title, Welsh in Education and life. A translation into Welsh by G. J. Williams was issued the same year. The historical introduction, pp. 1–81, is a good sketch of the cultural history of the language.

**154.** RHŶS, JOHN, and BRYNMOR-JONES, DAVID: The Welsh people, etc. London, 1900; 4th edn, 1906.

> Based largely on the historical sections of the report of the Royal Commission on land in Wales and Monmouthshire (No. 2723).

**155.** RICHARDS, ROBERT: Cymru'r Oesau Canol. Wrecsam, 1933.

**156.** WARRINGTON, WILLIAM: The history of Wales in nine books. 2 vols. London, 1786; 4th edn, Brecon, 1823.

**157.** WILLIAMS, ALBERT HUGHES: An introduction to the history of Wales. Vol. i. Prehistoric times to 1063, Cardiff, 1941; vol. ii. The Middle Ages. Part I, 1063–1284. Cardiff, 1948.

**158.** Id. The background of Welsh history. Cardiff, [1950].

**159.** WILLIAMS, DAVID: A history of modern Wales. London, 1950.

> See also his article on Wales in Chambers's Encyclopaedia, 1950 and later edns.

**160.** WILLIAMS, GRIFFITH JOHN: Traddodiad llenyddol Morgannwg. Caerdydd, 1948.

**161.** Id.      Traddodiad llenyddol Dyffryn Clwyd a'r cyffiniau. *Trans. Denbs. Hist. Soc.*, i, 1952.

**162.** WILLIAMS, JANE (Ysgafell): A history of Wales. London, 1869.

> Ends at 1603. One of the best of the older general histories of Wales.

**163.** WILLIAMS, WILLIAM LLEWELYN: The making of modern Wales. London, 1919.

**164.** WOODWARD, B. B.: The history of Wales from the earliest times to its final incorporation with the kingdom of England. 2 vols. London, 1853; 1 vol. London, 1859.

**165.** WYNNE, WILLIAM: The history of Wales. London, 1697.

> Revised version of Powel's Historie (No. 149). On the editor, see JENKINS, ROBERT THOMAS: William Wynne and the history of Wales. *B.B.C.S.*, vi, 2, 1932.

### (b) Ecclesiastical

General works only are listed below. Ecclesiastical works belonging to specific periods will be found under the relevant sections. See also HADDAN, ARTHUR WEST, and STUBBS, WILLIAM (eds): Councils, etc. (No. 115); and section A VII (*b*) for a list of historical journals.

**166.** EDWARDS, ALFRED GEORGE (Archbishop of Wales): Landmarks in the history of the Welsh Church. London, 1912.

**167.** EDWARDS, CHARLES: Hanes y ffydd yng Nghymru, sef penodau xvi, xviii, a xix o'r Ffydd ddi-ffuant. Gol. Hugh Bevan. Caerdydd, 1948.

**168.** GRIFFITHS, EDWARD: Historical handbook to the Presbyterian Church of Wales, 1735–1905. Wrexham, n.d.

**169.** HIRSCH-DAVIES, JOHN EDWIN DE: A popular history of the Church in Wales. London, 1911.

**170.** Id.      Catholicism in mediaeval Wales. London, 1916.

**171.** HUGHES, JOHN: Methodistiaeth Cymru. 3 vols. Gwrecsam, 1851–6.

**172.** JAMES, JAMES SPINTHER: Hanes y Bedyddwyr yng Nghymru. 4 vols. Caerfyrddin, 1893–8.

**173.** JAMES, JOHN WILLIAMS: A Church history of Wales. Ilfracombe, 1945.

**174.** JONES, DAVID AMBROSE: History of the Church in Wales. Carmarthen, 1926.

**175.** Jones, Hugh: Hanes Wesleyaeth yng Nghymru. 4 vols. Bangor, 1911–13.

**176.** Newell, Ebenezer Josiah: A history of the Welsh Church to the dissolution of the monasteries. London, 1895.

**177.** [Powicke, Frederick Maurice]: Wales: lists of bishops. In Handbook of British chronology. Royal Hist. Soc. London, 1939.

**178.** Rees, Thomas: History of Protestant Nonconformity in Wales. London, 1861; enlarged edn, 1883.

**179.** Id.    and Thomas, John: Hanes eglwysi Annibynol Cymru. 4 vols. Liverpool, 1871–5; vol. v by John Thomas. Dolgellau, 1891.

**180.** Richards, Thomas: Hanes yr achos. *Llafar*, 1951; enlarged version in *Traf. Cymd. Hanes Bed.*, 1952–3.
   A survey of sources.

**181.** Roberts, John: Methodistiaeth Galfinaidd Cymru. *Darlith Davies*, 1930. Llundain, 1931. (English abbreviated version: The Calvinistic Methodism of Wales. Caernarvon, 1934.)
   See also review by R. T. Jenkins in *Y Traethodydd*, 1932.

**182.** Stubbs, William: Registrum sacrum Anglicanum. 2nd edn. Oxford, 1897.

**183.** Thomas, Joshua: Hanes y Bedyddwyr yng Nghymru. Caerfyrddin, 1778.

**184.** Welsh Church Congress (Llandrindod). Handbook. 1953.

### (c) Education

### (i) General

**185.** Carlisle, Nicholas: A concise description of the endowed schools in England and Wales. 2 vols. London, 1818. Vol. ii (pp. 921–69): Wales.

**186.** Griffiths, Griffith Milwyn: Education in the diocese of St. Asaph. *N.L.W. Jnl.*, vi, 1949–50.

**187.** Id.    Further notes on education in the diocese of St. Asaph. Ibid., vii, 1951–2.

**188.** Jones, Evan John: History of education in Wales. Vol. i [from the time of the Druids till the tenth century]. Wrexham, 1931.

**189.** Id.    Addysg yng Nghymru yn yr oesau canol. *Yr Haul*, 1940.

**190.** Id.    Education in Wales during the middle ages. Inaugural lecture at University College, Swansea, 1947. Oxford, 1949.

**191.** KNIGHT, LEWIS STANLEY: Welsh cathedral schools to 1600 A.D. *Y Cymmr.*, xxix, 1919.

**192.** Id.      Welsh schools from A.D. 1000 to A.D. 1600. *Arch. Camb.*, 1919.

**193.** Id.      The Welsh monasteries and the education of later mediaeval Wales. Ibid., 1920.

**194.** Id.      Welsh independent grammar schools to 1600. Newtown, 1926.

**195.** WATSON, FOSTER: The English grammar schools to 1660: their curriculum and practice. Cambridge, 1908.

### (ii) Individual schools

This sub-section does not include works on nineteenth century elementary schools, which will be found in section K IV.

**196.** ANON.: Christ's College, Brecon: its past history and present capabilities considered. London, 1853.

**197.** BARBER, H., and LEWIS, HENRY: The history of Friars school, Bangor. Bangor, 1901.

> See also No. 216 below and CLARKE, M. L.: The Elizabethan statutes of Friars school, Bangor. *Trans. Caerns. Hist. Soc.*, 1955.

**198.** BULKELEY-OWEN, FANNY MARY CATHERINE ('Gwenrhian Gwynedd'): The founder and first trustees of Oswestry grammar school. Oswestry, n.d.

**199.** BRADNEY, JOSEPH ALFRED: A history of the free grammar school in the parish of Llantilio-Crosseny in the county of Monmouth. London, 1924.

**200.** CAMPBELL, M. COLNEY: Some records of the free grammar school of Deythyr in the county of Montgomery, 1690–1900. *Y Cymmr.*, xliii, 1932.

**201.** CARR, CATHERINE: The spinning wheel: City of Cardiff high school for girls, 1895–1955. Cardiff, 1955.

**202.** GRIFFITHS, GRIFFITH MILWYN: Ruabon grammar school. *N.L.W. Jnl.*, ix, 1955–6.

**203.** HOWSE, WILLIAM HENRY: School and bell: four hundred years of a Welsh grammar school [Presteign]. Halesowen, 1957.

**204.** JENKINS, ROBERT THOMAS: A sketch of the history of Bala grammar school, 1713–1893. *Jnl. Mer. Hist. and Rec. Soc.*, i, 3, 1951.

**205.** Id.      Further notes on Bala grammar school. Ibid., ii, 1, 1953.

**206.** JONES, E. MADOC: The free grammar school of Beaumaris. *Trans. Angl. Antiq. Soc.*, 1922.

**207.** JONES, WILLIAM BELL: The Hawarden grammar school. *Flints. Hist. Soc. Pubns.*, 1916–17.

**208.** LEIGHTON, RACHEL: Rise and progress: the story of the Welsh girls' school [London and Ashford]. London, 1950.

**209.** MORGAN, J.: David Hughes, founder of Beaumaris free school. Caernarvon, 1883.

**210.** Id. Coffadwriaeth am Henry Rowlands . . . sylfaenydd ysgol Bottwnog. Bangor, 1910.

**211.** NEWCOMBE, RICHARD: Memoir of Dr. Gabriel Goodman, with some account of Ruthin school. Ruthin, 1825.

**212.** OLDHAM, J. BASIL: A history of Shrewsbury school, 1552–1952. Oxford, 1952.

**213.** OSBORNE-JONES, D. G.: Edward Richard of Ystradmeurig, with the story of his school and its associations under its successive masters, 1734–1934. Carmarthen, 1934.

**214.** PARRY, GRUFFYDD: Hanes ysgol Botwnnog. *Trans. Cymmr.*, 1957.

**215.** PRITCHARD, JOHN: Hanes yr ysgol sir ym Mrynrefail. Caernarfon, 1940.

**216.** ROBERTS, GLYN; WILLIAMS, WILLIAM OGWEN, and EAMES, ALED: A history of Friars School [Bangor], 1557–1957. *The Dominican* [magazine of Friars School]. Fourth centenary number, 1957.

**217.** SAMUEL, DAVID: Ysgol Llanymddyfri. Caernarfon, n.d.

**218.** T[HOMAS], D. J. (ed.): Swansea grammar school, 1682–1932. Special number of the Swansea Grammar School magazine issued on account of the celebration of the 250th anniversary of the foundation of the school, July 27, 1932.

**219.** WILLIAMS, ALBERT HUGHES: Dr. Richard Parry ac ysgol Ruthun. *Llên Cymru,* ii, 1953.

**220.** Id. The origins of the old endowed grammar schools of Denbighshire. *Trans. Denbs. Hist. Soc.*, ii, 1953.

**221.** WILLIAMS, JOHN: David Hughes, M.A., and his free grammar school at Beaumaris. Beaumaris, 1833; repr. 1864; repr. and ed. with additions by Vaughan Bowen, Leeds, 1933.

**222.** WRIGHT, ARTHUR: The history of Lewis' School, Pengam, with some remarks upon the family of Lewis of the Van, Glamorgan, and a chapter upon Hengoed School. Newtown, 1929.

#### (d) Military (Regimental) history

**223.** ATKINSON, C. T.: The South Wales Borderers, 24th Foot, 1689–1937. Cambridge, 1937.

**224.** BROUGHTON-MAINWARING, ROWLAND: Historical records of the Royal Welch Fusiliers [1689–1889]. London, 1889.

**225.** CARY, A. D. L., McCANCE, STOUPPE, HUDSON, GERALD C., and WARD, C. H. DUDLEY: Regimental records of the Royal Welch Fusiliers, late the 23rd Foot (1689–1918). 4 vols. London, 1921–9.

**226.** HARRISON, R. J.: The Royal Montgomeryshire Regiment of Militia. *Mont. Coll.,* xvii, 1884.

**227.** OWEN, HUGH JOHN: Merioneth volunteers and local militia during the Napoleonic wars. Dolgelley, 1934.

**228.** PARFITT, G. ARCHER: Military history of Radnorshire. *Trans. Rads. Soc.,* xxvi, xxvii, and xxviii, 1956, 1957, and 1958.

**229.** PARRY, LL. E. S., and FREEMAN, B. F. M.: Historical records of the Denbighshire Hussars Imperial Yeomanry from their formation in 1795 till 1906. Wrexham, 1909.

**230.** SKAIFE, E. O.: A short history of the Royal Welch Fusiliers. London, etc., 1927.

**231.** THOMAS, HOWEL: The story of the Royal Welsh Fusiliers. London, 1916.

**232.** TIPPING, H. AVRAY: The story of the Royal Welsh Fusiliers. London, n.d.

**233.** WARD, C. H. DUDLEY: History of the Welsh Guards. London, 1920.

**234.** WILLIAMS-WYNN, CHARLES WATKIN: The rise and progress of the Volunteers in Montgomeryshire [1803–77]. *Mont. Coll.,* xiii, 1922.

### VI. SOCIAL CUSTOMS, CRAFTS, ETC.

#### (a) General

**235.** JONES, ANNA MARIA: The rural industries of England and Wales: a survey. Vol. iv, Wales. Oxford, 1927.

**236.** OWEN, BOB: Diwydiannau coll ardal y ddwy afon—Dwyryd a Glaslyn. Liverpool, 1943.

**237.** PARRY-JONES, DANIEL : Welsh country upbringing. 2nd edn. London, 1949.

**238.** PEATE, IORWERTH CYFEILIOG: Guide to the collection of Welsh bygones. Cardiff, 1929.

**239.** Id.     Y crefftwr yng Nghymru. Aberystwyth, 1933.

**240.** Id.     Welsh folk industries. *Folklore,* 1933.

**241.** Id.     Diwylliant gwerin Cymru. 2nd edn. Cardiff, 1943.

**242.** Id.     Two Montgomeryshire craftsmen. *Mont. Coll.,* xlviii, 1943-4.

**243.** Id.     Welsh folk crafts and industries. 2nd ed. Cardiff, 1945.

REES, ALWYN DAVID: Life in a Welsh countryside (No. 769).

**244.** WADDINGTON, HILARIE MARGARET: Games and athletics in bygone Wales. *Trans. Cymmr.,* 1953.

### (b) Agricultural implements and transport

**245.** FOX, [SIR] CYRIL FREDERICK: Sleds, carts, and waggons. *Antiquity,* 1931.

**246.** PAYNE, FFRANSIS GEORGE: Yr aradr Gymreig. Cardiff, 1954.
See also id. The plough in ancient Britain. *Arch. Jnl.,* 1946.

**247.** PEATE, IORWERTH CYFEILIOG: Some aspects of agricultural transport in Wales. *Arch. Camb.,* 1935.

### (c) Ships, boats, and fishing

**248.** COATES, J. F.: Swansea Bay pilot boats. *The Mariner's Mirror,* 1944.

**249.** CRESTON, R. Y.: Les Celtes et la mer: coracles et corrachs. Brest, 1956.

**250.** DAVIS, F. M.: An account of the fishing gear of England and Wales. 3rd edn. London, 1937.

**251.** HORNELL, JAMES: British coracles and Irish corraghs. London, 1938.

**252.** HUGHES, HENRY: Immortal sails: a story of a Welsh port [Portmadoc] and some of its ships. London, [1946].
Review by J. Glyn Davies in *Trans. Cymmr.,* 1945.

**253.** LLOYD, ROBERT JOHN HERBERT: The Mumbles oyster skiffs. *The Mariner's Mirror,* 1954.

**254.** Id.     Aberystwyth fishing boats. Ibid., 1955.

**255.** Id.     Tenby fishing boats. Ibid., 1958.

**256.** MATHESON, COLIN: Wales and the sea fisheries. Cardiff, 1929.

MORGAN, D. W.: Brief Glory. (No. 720).

**257.** PEATE, IORWERTH CYFEILIOG: Severn eel-traps. *Man,* 1934.

**258.** THOMAS, DAVID: Hen longau a llongwyr Cymru. Bilingual. Cardiff, 1949.
> Review by J. Glyn Davies in *Trans. Cymmr.,* 1948.

**259.** Id.　　Hen longau sir Gaernarfon. Caernarfon, 1952.
> See also MORRIS, THOMAS EDWARD: Llongau ym Mhorthmadog, 1828. *Yr Arweinydd,* 1940.

**260.** VALE, EDMUND: Fixed engines. *Out of Doors,* ii, 4, 1949.
> A study of North Wales fish weirs.

### (d) Clock making

**261.** PEATE, IORWERTH CYFEILIOG: John Tibbott, clock and watch maker. *Mont. Coll.,* xlviii, 1943–4.

**262.** Id.　　Clock and watch makers in Wales. Cardiff, 1945.

**263.** Id.　　John Tibbott's inventions. *Mont. Coll.,* li, 1949–50.

### (e) Embroidery and Quilting

**264.** FITZRANDOLPH, MAVIS: Traditional quilting, its story and its practice. London, 1954.

**265.** PAYNE, FFRANSIS GEORGE: Samplers and embroideries in the National Museum of Wales. Cardiff, 1939.

### (f) Iron work

**266.** AYRTON, MAXWELL, and SILCOCK, ARNOLD: Wrought iron and its decorative use. London, 1929.
> Includes a chapter on the Welsh smiths.

**267.** EDWARDS, IFOR: Robert Davies of Croes Foel, Bersham. *Trans. Denbs. Hist. Soc.,* vi, 1957; vii, 1958.

**268.** PEATE, IORWERTH CYFEILIOG: A Caernarvonshire inventor (John Williams, 'Ioan Madog'). *Y Cymmr.,* xlii, 1931.

**269.** Id.　　The Powis castle gates. *Mont. Coll.,* xlvii, 1941–2.

### (g) Medal making

**270.** PEATE, IORWERTH CYFEILIOG: Welsh society and eisteddfod medals and relics. Cardiff, 1938.

### (h) Milling

**271.** PEATE, IORWERTH CYFEILIOG: Traethawd ar felinyddiaeth. *B.B.C.S.,* viii, 1935–7.

### (i) Musical instruments

**272.** ANDERSON, OTTO: The bowed-harp. London, 1930.
> Includes a chapter on the *crwth.*

**273.** CROSSLEY-HOLLAND, PETER: Secular homophonic music in Wales in the middle ages. *Music and Letters*, 1942.

Id.    Music in Wales (No. 136).

**274.** GRIFFITH, ROBERT: Llyfr cerdd dannau. Caernarvon, n.d.

**275.** MORRIS, WILLIAM MEREDITH: British violin makers, classical and modern. London, 1904.

**276.** PEATE, IORWERTH CYFEILIOG: Welsh musical instruments. *Man*, 1947.

**277.** Id.    Telynau Cymru. *Allwedd y Tannau*, 1953.

**278.** WILLIAMS, JOHN LLOYD: Y tri thelynor. London, 1944.

#### (j) Pottery

**279.** BARTON, K. J.: The Buckley potteries: excavations at Prescot's pottery, 1954. *Flints. Hist. Soc. Pubns.*, xvi, 1956.

#### (k) Printing

JONES, JAMES IFANO: A history of printing and printers in Wales and Monmouthshire to . . . 1923 (No. 11).

#### (l) Textiles

**280.** CRANKSHAW, WILLIAM P.: Report on a survey of the Welsh textile industry made on behalf of the University of Wales. Cardiff, 1927.

**281.** DRAGE, GILBERT: Wool and handloom weaving. Presteigne, 1948.

**282.** PEATE, IORWERTH CYFEILIOG: A north Cardiganshire woollen yarn factory. *Y Cymmr.*, xxxix, 1928.

#### (m) Woodwork

**283.** EDWARDS, RALPH, and PEATE, IORWERTH CYFEILIOG: Welsh furniture from Tudor to Georgian times. Catalogue of an exhibition. Cardiff, 1936.

**284.** EVAN-THOMAS, OWEN: Domestic utensils of wood, 16th to 19th centuries. London, 1932.

**285.** PEATE, IORWERTH CYFEILIOG: Welsh piggins. *The Connoisseur*, 1930.

**286.** Id.    Some Welsh wood-turners and their trade. In Studies in regional consciousness and environment. Oxford, 1930.

**287.** Id.    Welsh furniture. *Apollo*, 1936.

**288.** Id.    Some Welsh light on the development of the chair. Ibid., 1938.

**289.** PINTO, EDWARD H.: Treen, or small woodware throughout the ages. London, 1949.

> Discusses Welsh material.

**290.** TWISTON-DAVIES, [SIR] LEONARD, and LLOYD-JOHNES, HERBERT JOHNES: Welsh furniture: an introduction. Cardiff, 1950.

## VII. HISTORICAL JOURNALS, ETC.

### (a) County, local, and regional

**291.** Aberafan and district Historical Society. Transactions. 1925–8.

**292.** Anglesey Antiquarian Society and Field Club. Transactions. 1913 ff. Index of publications from 1911 to 1938 in 1938 vol.

**293.** Brecknock Society. Transactions (and Records of the Brecknock Museum). 1928–9. See also Brycheiniog.

**294.** Brycheiniog (published by the Brecknock Society). 1955 ff.

**295.** Bye-Gones relating to Wales and the border counties. 1871–1919.

**296.** Caernarvonshire Historical Society. Transactions. 1939 ff.

**297.** Caradoc and Severn Valley Field Club. Transactions. 1893 ff.

**298.** Cardiff Naturalists' Society. Report and Transactions. 1867 ff.

**299.** Cardiganshire Antiquarian Society. Transactions [and Archaeological Record]. 1909–39; continued as Ceredigion. 1950 ff.

**300.** Carmarthenshire Antiquarian Society and Field Club. Transactions (*now* The Carmarthen Antiquary). 1905 ff.

**301.** Cheshire Sheaf, The, being local gleanings historical and antiquarian relating to Cheshire, Chester, and North Wales. 1878 ff.

**302.** Chester and North Wales Archaeological and Historic Society. Journal. 1849 ff.

**302A.** Cymru Fu. Notes and queries relating to North Wales and the border counties. London and Cardiff, 1889–92.

**303.** Denbighshire Historical Society. Transactions. 1952 ff.

**304.** Flintshire Historical Society. Journal and publications. 1911–25, 1952 ff.

**305.** Gower, Journal of the Gower Society. 1948 ff.

**306.** Lancaster and Cheshire Historic Society. Transactions. 1848 ff.

307. Liverpool Welsh National Society. Transactions. 1885–1912.

308. Llandudno, Colwyn Bay and district Field Club. Proceedings. 1906 ff.

309. Merioneth Historical and Record Society. Journal. 1950 ff.

310. Montgomeryshire Collections, The. The Transactions of the Powysland Club. 1868 ff. (*Formerly* Collections Historical and Archaeological relating to Montgomeryshire.)

311. Morgannwg. Transactions of the Glamorgan Local History Society. 1957 ff.

312. Neath Antiquarian Society. Transactions. 1930 ff.

313. Northern Flintshire. 1913.

314. Radnorshire Society, The. Transactions. 1931 ff.

315. Shropshire Archaeological Society. Transactions. 1878 ff.

316. South Wales and Monmouth Record Society. Publications. 1932 ff.

317. West Wales Historical Records. 1910–29.

318. Woolhope Naturalists' Field Club, The. Transactions. 1851 ff.

### (b) Religious

319. Annibynwyr Cymru, Cymdeithas Hanes. See Y Cofiadur.

320. Bathafarn: Cylchgrawn yr Eglwys Fethodistaidd yng Nghymru. 1946 ff.

321. Bedyddwyr Cymru, Cymdeithas Hanes. Trafodion. 1906 ff.

322. Church in Wales, Historical Society of the. Journal. 1949 ff.

323. Cofiadur, Y: Cylchgrawn Cymdeithas Hanes Annibynwyr Cymru. 1923 ff.

324. Efrydiau Catholig. 1946 ff.

325. Methodistiaid Calfinaidd, Cymdeithas Hanes. Cylchgrawn. 1916 ff.

326. St. Peter's Magazine. Cardiff. 1921 ff.

### (c) General

327. Aberystwyth Studies. 1912 ff.

328. Archaeologia Cambrensis, 1846 ff; index vols., 1846–84, 1884–1900.

**329.** Bulletin of the Board of Celtic Studies, University of Wales. 1921 ff.

**330.** Cymmrodor, Y (magazine of the Honourable Society of Cymmrodorion). 1877 ff.

**331.** Cymmrodorion, Honourable Society of. Transactions. 1893 ff.

**332.** National Library of Wales. Journal. 1939 ff.

**333.** Welsh Bibliographical Society. Journal. 1910 ff.

### (d) Miscellaneous

Many Welsh journals have devoted a varying amount of space to historical matters. Included in this section are the most important examples.

**334.** Beirniad, Y (gol. J. Morris-Jones). 1911–20.

**335.** Cambrian Journal, The. 1854–64.

**336.** Cambrian Quarterly Magazine and Celtic Repertory, The. 1829–32.

**337.** Cambrian Register, The. 1795–1818.

**338.** Cambro-Briton, The. 1819–22.

**339.** Cymru (gol. O. M. Edwards). 1891–1927.

**340.** Geninen, Y (gol. John Thomas, 'Eifionydd'). 1883–1928.

**341.** Llên Cymru. 1950 ff.

**342.** Llenor, Y (gol. W. J. Gruffydd a T. J. Morgan). 1922-51.

**343.** Traethodydd, Y. 1845 ff.

**344.** Wales (ed. O. M. Edwards). 1894–7.

**345.** Welsh Outlook, The. 1914–33.

**346.** Welsh Review, The (ed. Gwyn Jones). 1939–48.

# SECTION B

## *TOPOGRAPHY AND LOCAL HISTORY*

### I. GENERAL TOPOGRAPHY

**347.** BLACKWELL, HENRY: Bibliography of local and county histories. Old Welsh Chips. Brecon, 1886.

BOWEN, EMRYS GEORGE: Wales: a study in geography and history (No. 132).

Id. (ed.), *et al.*: Wales: a physical, historical, and regional geography (No. 133).

**348.** CARLISLE, NICHOLAS: A topographical dictionary of the dominion of Wales. London, 1811.

**349.** CARR, HERBERT REGINALD CULLING, and LISTER, GEORGE: The mountains of Snowdonia. 2nd edn. London, 1948.

**350.** CATHRALL, WILLIAM: History of north Wales. 2 vols. Manchester, 1828.

**351.** COOKE, GEORGE ALEXANDER: Topographical and statistical description of North Wales. n.d., *c.* 1830.

**352.** FOX, CYRIL FREDERICK: The boundary line of Cymru. Sir John Rhŷs Memorial Lecture. *Procs. British Acad.*, xxvi, 1940.

**353.** Id.     The personality of Britain. 4th edn. Cardiff, 1943.

**354.** Id.     Offa's dyke: a field survey of the western frontier-works of Mercia in the seventh and eighth centuries A.D. London, 1955.

**355.** FULLARTON, ANDREW: Parliamentary gazetteer of England and Wales. London, 1840–4.

**356.** GROSE, FRANCIS: The antiquities of England and Wales. New edn. 8 vols. London, 1783–7. Vol. vii, Wales.

**357.** GRUFFYDD, WILLIAM JOHN: North Wales and the marches. About Britain series, No. 7. London, 1951.

**358.** Id.     South Wales and the marches. Ibid., No. 6. London, 1951.

**359.** HOWE, GEORGE MELVYN: Wales from the air: a survey of the physical and cultural landscape. Cardiff, 1957.

**359A.** JONES, P. THORESBY: Welsh border country. London, 1938.

HUGHES, WILLIAM JOHN: Wales and the Welsh in English literature (No. 10).

**360.** LEWIS, SAMUEL: A topographical dictionary of Wales. 2 vols. London, 1833; 4th edn., 1849.

**360A.** LEWIS, ELUNED and PETER: The land of Wales. London, 1937 and later edns.

**361.** LHWYD, EDWARD: Parochialia. *Arch. Camb.* supplements, 1909–11.
  See also EMERY, FRANK VIVIAN: A new reply to Lhwyd's Parochial Queries (1696): Puncheston, Pembrokeshire. *N.L.W. Jnl.*, x, 4, 1958. Id.: A map of Edward Lhwyd's 'Parochial Queries in order to a geographical dictionary, etc.' of Wales (1696). *Trans. Cymmr.*, 1958.

**362.** LOWE, WALTER BEZANT: The heart of northern Wales. Privately printed. 2 vols. Llanfairfechan, 1912 and 1927.

**363.** NORTH, FREDERICK JOHN: Sunken cities. Cardiff, 1957.

**364.** Id.  The river scenery at the head of the vale of Neath. Cardiff, 1930.

**365.** Id.  CAMPBELL, BRUCE, and SCOTT, RICHENDA: Snowdonia. *The New Naturalist.* London, 1949.

**366.** PENNANT, THOMAS: A tour in Wales, 1770–? 1773. London, 1778–81. Tours in Wales, 3 vols., London, 1810; ed. John Rhŷs, 3 vols., Caernarvon, 1883.

**367.** REES, WILLIAM: Bibliography of . . . the municipal history of Wales and the border counties. *B.B.C.S.*, ii and iii, 1925–6.

**368.** SAYCE, RODERICK URWICK: The old summer pastures: a comparative study. *Mont. Coll.*, liv, 1955–6.

**369.** STEERS, JAMES ALFRED: The coastline of England and Wales. Cambridge, 1946.

**370.** TRUEMAN, ARTHUR ELIJAH: The scenery of England and Wales. London, 1938.

## II. MAPS AND ATLASES

For county maps and atlases see under various shires.

**371.** DAVIES, MARGARET: Wales in maps. Cardiff, 1951. 2nd edn, Cardiff, 1958.

**372.** HOWEL, J. PRYSE: Agricultural atlas of Wales. Ordnance Survey. Southampton, 1921.

**373.** Map of Britain in the dark ages. South sheet. Ordnance Survey. Chessington, 1939.

**374.** Monastic Britain. South sheet. Ordnance Survey. Chessington, 1950.

**375.** NORTH, FREDERICK JOHN: The map of Wales. *Arch. Camb.*, 1935.

> Also reprinted by the National Museum of Wales. A very important survey, and the only one of its kind.

**376.** Id.   Humphrey Lhwyd's maps of England and Wales. *Arch. Camb.*, 1937.

**377.** PARSONS, E. J. S.: The map of Great Britain *c.* 1360, known as the Gough map. Oxford, 1958.

**378.** REES, WILLIAM: South Wales and the border in the fourteenth century. Ordnance Survey. Southampton, 1933.

**379.** Id.   An historical atlas of Wales. Cardiff, 1951.

**380.** Roman Britain. 3rd edn. Ordnance Survey. Chessington, 1956.

> See also MARGARY, IVAN DONALD: Roman roads in Britain. 2 vols. London, 1955–7 (Wales and the marches are treated in vol. ii); and NASH-WILLIAMS, VICTOR ERLE: The Roman frontier in Wales (No. 1129).

## III. ARCHITECTURE

### (a) General

The following standard works have relevance to Wales: BERESFORD, M. W., and ST. JOSEPH, J. K. S.: Medieval England: an aerial survey, Cambridge, 1958; SALZMAN, LOUIS FRANCIS: Building in England down to 1540: a documentary history, Oxford, 1952; TOUT, THOMAS FREDERICK: Medieval town planning: a lecture in *Collected Papers*, iii, Manchester, 1934.

**381.** H.M. Ministry of Works (formerly Office of Works and Buildings).

> Illustrated regional guides to ancient monuments under ownership or guardianship of the Ministry. Vol. iv, South Wales and Monmouthshire, by Sir Cyril Fox, London, 1938, 1954; vol. v, North Wales, by Lord Harlech, London, 1948, 1954. For official guides to individual monuments (abbeys, castles, etc.) see sectional list No. 27 issued by H.M.S.O.; these guides are not referred to in the sections devoted to the shires.

**382.** Royal Commission on ancient monuments in Wales and Monmouthshire: Inventories of the ancient monuments. In progress.

> Volumes already published deal with the following counties: Montgomery (1911), Flint (1912), Radnor (1913), Denbigh (1914), Carmarthen (1917), Merioneth (1921), Pembroke (1925), Anglesey (1937), Caernarvon: East (1956).
>
> The earlier volumes, up to and including Pembroke, require revision.
>
> So far the only border county for which an inventory has been published is Herefordshire. See Royal Commission on Historical Monuments, England: Herefordshire. Vol. i, South West. London, 1931.
>
> Consult also *Arch. Camb., Y Cymmr.,* and *Trans. Cymmr.*; other journals of historical and antiquarian societies (see under A VII); COLVIN, H. M.: A biographical dictionary of English architects, 1660–1840, London, 1954 (see index of places); GUNNIS, G. R.: A dictionary of British sculptors, 1660–1851, London 1953 (see index of places); KNOOP, DOUGLAS, and JONES, GWILYM PEREDUR: A note on the mason in Wales (No. 1413); NEAVERSON, E.: Medieval quarrying in north-eastern Wales. *Flints. Hist. Soc. Pubns.*, xiv, 1953–4; SHILLABER, CAROLINE: Edward I, builder of towns, *Speculum*, viii, 1933.

## (b) Military

**383.** BARNET, CEFNI: Carmarthen castle, the chamberlain's hall. *Trans. Carms. Antiq. Soc.*, xxvi, 1936.

**384.** BROWN, R. ALLEN: English medieval castles. London, 1954.

**385.** Id.       Royal castle-building in England, 1154–1216. *E.H.R.*, lxx, 1955.

**386.** CLARK, GEORGE THOMAS: Mediaeval military architecture. 2 vols. London, 1884.
> The best general work. But see the criticisms in ARMITAGE, E. S.: The early Norman castles of the British Isles, London, 1912; and ROUND, JOHN HORACE, in *E.H.R.*, xxvii, 1912.

**387.** EDWARDS, JOHN GORONWY: Edward I's castle-building in Wales. Sir John Rhŷs Memorial Lecture, 1944. *Procs. British Acad.*, xxxii.

**388.** HEMP, WILFRID JAMES: The castle of Ewloe and the Welsh castle plan. *Y Cymmr.*, xxix, 1928.

**389.** HUGHES, HENRY HAROLD: The Edwardian castle and town defences at Conway. *Arch. Camb.*, 1938.
> With plans.

**390.** KING, D. J. CATHCART, and PERKS, J. CLIFFORD: Llangibby castle. *Arch. Camb.*, 1956.

**391.** KNOOP, DOUGLAS, and JONES, GWILYM PEREDUR: Castle building at Beaumaris and Caernarvon in the early fourteenth century. *Trans. Quatuor Coronati Lodge*, xlv, 1932.

**392.** Id.       and id.: The repair of Beaumaris town wall, 1536–8. *Trans. Angl. Antiq. Soc.*, 1935.

**393.** NEAVERSON, E.: Mediaeval castles in North Wales: a study of sites, water supply and building stones. Liverpool, 1947.
> See also id.: The building stones of Harlech castle and Cymmer abbey. *Arch. Camb.*, 1949.

**394.** OMAN, CHARLES WILLIAM CHADWICK: Castles. Published by Great Western Railway Company. London, 1926.

**395.** O'NEIL, BRYAN HUGH ST. JOHN: The castles of Wales. In A hundred years of Welsh archaeology. Cambrian Archaeological Association. Centenary volume. Gloucester, 1946.

**396.** Id.       Castles: an introduction to the castles of England and Wales. H.M. Stationery Office. London, 1953.

**397.** SIMPSON, WILLIAM DOUGLAS: Harlech castle and the Edwardian castle plan. *Arch. Camb.*, 1940.

**398.** TAYLOR, ARNOLD JOSEPH: Usk castle and the Pipe Roll of 1185, with a note on an expense account of 1289. *Arch. Camb.*, 1947.

**399.** Id.    A note on Walter of Hereford, builder of Caernarvon castle. *Trans. Caerns. Hist. Soc.*, 1948.

**400.** Id.    The birth of Edward of Caernarvon and the beginnings of Caernarvon castle. *History*, xxxv, 1950.

**401.** Id.    Master James of St. George. *E.H.R.*, lxv, 1950.

**402.** Id.    Building at Caerphilly in 1326. *B.B.C.S.*, xiv, 1952.

**403.** Id.    Building at Caernarvon and Beaumaris in 1295–6. Ibid., xv, 1952–3.
> Contains documents supplementing those given by J. G. EDWARDS: Edward I's castle-building (No. 387).

**404.** THOMPSON, ALEXANDER HAMILTON: Military architecture in England in the middle ages. London, 1912.

**405.** TOY, SIDNEY: The castles of Great Britain. London, 1953.
> Reviews by A. J. Taylor in *Antiq. Journal*, 1954; and W. Douglas Simpson in *E.H.R.*, 1954.

**406.** WALKER, RONALD FRANCIS: Carew castle. *Arch. Camb.*, 1956.

### (c) Ecclesiastical

For a general background see ADDLESHAW, GEORGE WILLIAM OUTRAM, and ETCHELLS, FREDERICK: The architectural setting of Anglican worship, London, 1948 (on the arrangement of church interiors and their furnishing since the Reformation); BOAS, T. S. R.: English art, 1100–1216, vol. iii in the Oxford History of English Art, Oxford, 1953; BOND, FRANCIS: Gothic architecture in England [London, 1906] (for the cathedrals and Cwm-hir and Strata Florida abbeys see index of illustrations and places); BRIEGER, PETER: English art, 1216–1307, vol. iv in the Oxford History of English Art, Oxford, 1957 (chapter xiii on the Edwardian castles); CLARKE, BASIL F. L.: Church builders of the 19th century, London, 1938; CROSSLEY, FRED, and RIDGEWAY, MAURICE, H.: The English abbey: its life and work in the middle ages, London, 1935; GRAHAM, ROSE: An essay on English monasticism, Historical Assoc. pamphlet No. 112, London, 1939; KNOWLES, DAVID, and ST. JOSEPH, J. K. S.: Monastic sites from the air (No. 875); WEBB, GEOFFREY: Architecture in Britain in the middle ages, The Pelican History of Art, Harmondsworth, 1956.
See also section B VIII below.

**407.** CAROE, A. D. R.: Porth-y-twr, St. David's. *Arch. Camb.*, 1954.

**408.** CAROE, WILLIAM DOUGLAS: Recent excavations at St. David's; bishop Houghton's (1361–1389) cloister. Ibid., 1934.

409. CLARKE, MARTIN L.: Bangor cathedral, 1700–1828. *Trans. Caerns. Hist. Soc.*, 1952.

410. CROSSLEY, FRED H., and RIDGEWAY, MAURICE H.: Screens, lofts and stalls situated in Wales and Monmouthshire. Ibid., 1943–52, 1957.

411. GLYNNE, SIR STEPHEN R.: The older Welsh churches (1824–74). London, 1903; repr. from *Arch. Camb.*, 1884–1902.

412. HAGUE, DOUGLAS B.: Capel Newydd, Llangian (Caerns.). *Arch. Camb.*, 1956.

413. Id.     Rug chapel, Corwen. *Jnl. Mer. Hist. and Rec. Soc.*, iii, 2, 1958.

414. Id.     Maesyronen Independent chapel, Glasbury (Radnor). Ibid.

415. HEMP, WILFRID JAMES: Llangwnadl church. *Arch. Camb.*, 1956 (Miscellany).

416. HUGHES, HAROLD, and NORTH, HERBERT L.: The old churches of Snowdonia. Bangor, 1924.

417. NEAVERSON, E.: The older building stones of St. Asaph cathedral. *Arch. Camb.*, 1945.

418. Id.     The building stones of the churches in the vale of Clwyd. Ibid., 1948.

419. NORTH, FREDERICK JOHN: The stones of Llandaff cathedral. Cardiff, 1957.

420. RICHARDS, ROBERT, and LLOYD, R. G.: The old church of Llandanwg. Ibid., 1935.

421. Id.     The church of St. Mary, Llanfair-juxta-Harlech. Ibid., 1936.

422. TAYLOR, ARNOLD JOSEPH: The greater monastic houses. In A hundred years of Welsh archaeology (No. 395; i.e. under O'NEIL: The castles of Wales).

### (d) Domestic

The following standard works have some relevance to Wales: CROSSLEY, FRED H.: Timber building in England from early times to the end of the seventeenth century, London, 1951; LLOYD, NATHANIEL: A history of the English house from primitive times to the Victorian period, London, 1931; repr. 1949.

423. ALLEN, A. ROMILLY: Old farmhouses with round chimneys near St. David's. *Arch. Camb.*, 1902.

424. BARNWELL, E. LOWRY: Domestic architecture of south Pembrokeshire. *Arch. Camb.*, 1867.

**425.** DAVIES, D. ERNEST: Llanina [Cardiganshire]. *Trans. Cards. Antiq. Soc.*, i, 4, 1914.

**426.** Id.      Wern Newydd [Cardiganshire]. Ibid., ii, 1915.

**427.** DAVIES, WILLIAM LLEWELYN, and JONES-ROBERTS, KATE WINIFRED: Pengwern, Ffestiniog. *Jnl. Mer. Hist. and Rec. Soc.*, i, 3, 1951.

**428.** FOX, AILEEN: Dinas Noddfa, Gellygaer Common, Glamorgan. *Arch. Camb.*, 1937.

**429.** Id.      Early Welsh homesteads on Gelligaer Common, Glamorgan. Ibid., 1939.

**430.** FOX, [SIR] CYRIL FREDERICK: Peasant crofts in north Pembrokeshire. *Antiquity*, 1937.

**431.** Id.      A settlement of 'platform' houses, Dyrysgol, Radnorshire. *Arch. Camb.*, 1939.

**432.** Id.      The round-chimneyed farm-houses of northern Pembrokeshire. In Aspects of archaeology in Britain and beyond (No. 1150).

**433.** Id.      Three 'round-gable' houses in Carmarthenshire. *Arch. Camb.*, 1951.

**434.** Id.      A country house of the Elizabethan period in Wales; Six Wells, Llantwit Major, Glamorganshire. Cardiff, National Museum of Wales, 1941.

**435.** Id.      and FOX, AILEEN: 'Platform' house-sites of South Wales type in Swydd Buddugre Malienydd, Radnorshire. *Arch. Camb.*, 1948.

**436.** Id.      and LORD RAGLAN: Monmouthshire houses: a study of building techniques and small house-plans in the fifteenth to seventeenth centuries. Part I, Medieval houses; part II, Sub-medieval houses, *c.* 1550–1610; part III, Renaissance. Cardiff, National Museum of Wales, Welsh Folk Museum, 1951–4.

**437.** GRESHAM, COLIN A.: Platform houses in north-west Wales. *Arch. Camb.*, 1954.

**438.** Id.      and HEMP, WILFRID JAMES: Rhiwlas. Ibid., 1955.

**439.** Id.      and id.: Lasynys. *Jnl. Mer. Hist. and Rec. Soc.*, iii, 1, 1957.

**440.** HAGUE, DOUGLAS B.: Pontysgarwyd, Montgomeryshire. *Mont. Coll.*, liv, 1, 1955.

**441.** Id.      Brogynin, Trefeirig. *Ceredigion*, ii, 4, 1955.

**442.** Id.      Penrhyn castle, Caernarvon. I. *Country Life*, July 14, 1955.

4

**443.** Id.      The bishop's palace, Gogarth, Llandudno, Caernarvonshire. *Trans. Caerns. Hist. Soc.*, 1956.

**444.** Id.      Some light on the site of the palace of Aberffraw. *Trans. Angl. Antiq. Soc.*, 1957.

See also JONES, GLANVILLE REES JEFFREYS: The site of Llys Aberffraw. Ibid.

**445.** Id.      Giler, Cerrig y drudion, Denbighshire. *Trans. Denbs. Hist. Soc.*, 1958.

**446.** Id.      Plas Chambres. Ibid.

**447.** HARLECH, LORD: Glyn Cywarch. *Jnl. Mer. Hist. and Rec. Soc.*, i, 1, 1949.

**448.** HEMP, WILFRID JAMES: Early timber work at Henblas, Llandderfel, and Penarth Fawr, Llanarmon. *Arch. Camb.*, 1942.

**449.** Id.      Ty Nant, Llandrillo (Merioneth). Ibid., 1950, pp. 84–6.

**450.** Id.      and GRESHAM, COLIN A.: Park, Llanfrothen, and the unit system. Ibid., 1942.

**451.** HOGG, ALEXANDER HUBERT ARTHUR: A 14th century house-site at Cefn-y-fan near Dolbenmaen, Caernarvonshire. *Trans. Caerns. Hist. Soc.*, 1954.

**452.** HUGHES, HAROLD, and NORTH, HERBERT L.: The old cottages of Snowdonia. Bangor, 1908.

**453.** HUSSEY, C.: Penrhyn castle, Caernarvon. II and III. *Country Life*, July 21 and 28, 1955.

**454.** Id.      Plas Newydd, Anglesey. Ibid., November 24 and December 1, 1955.

**455.** Id.      Plas Brondanw, Merioneth. Ibid., September 12, 1957.

**456.** Id.      Garthewin, Denbighshire. Ibid., February 13, 1958.

**457.** KNOOP, DOUGLAS, and JONES, GWILYM PEREDUR (eds): The Carreglwyd building account, 1636. *Trans. Angl. Antiq. Soc.*, 1934.

**458.** LEACH, G. B.: Excavations at Hen Blas, Coleshill Fawr, near Flint. *Flints. Hist. Soc. Pubns.*, xvii, 1957.

**459.** LLOYD, THOMAS ALWYN: The Georgian period in Welsh building. *Arch. Camb.*, 1957.

LOWE, WALTER BEZANT: The heart of northern Wales (No. 362).

**460.** LLOYD-JOHNES, HERBERT: The lesser country houses of Cardiganshire. *Ceredigion*, ii, 1952–5; iii, 1, 1956. In progress.

Voelallt, Green-grove, Penybont (Tregaron), Strata Florida, Ffos y Bleiddiaid, Plâs Llangoedmor, Llanina.

461. MONROE, L.: Plas Ucha, Llangar, Merioneth. Ibid., 1933.

462. MORRIS, BERNARD: Medieval platform sites in east Gower. *Gower*, vii, 1954.

463. PEATE, IORWERTH CYFEILIOG: The Welsh house: a study in folk culture. *Y Cymmr.*, xlvii; 3rd edn, Liverpool, 1946.

464. Id.      The cruck truss: a reassessment. *Folk-Liv* (Stockholm), 1957–8.

465. SMITH, PETER: Corsygedol. *Jnl. Mer. Hist. and Rec. Soc.*, ii, 4, 1956.

466. Id.      Coldbrook House. *Arch. Camb.*, 1957.

### (e) Miscellaneous

467. CRASTER, O. E.: A medieval limekiln at Ogmore castle, Glamorgan. *Arch. Camb.*, 1950.

468. DUNNING, GERALD CLOUGH: A medieval beacon at Merthyr Mawr, Glamorgan. Ibid., 1937.

469. JERVOISE, E.: The ancient bridges of Wales and western England. Written on behalf of the Society for the Protection of Ancient Buildings. London, 1936.

470. WAILES, REX: Tide mills of England and Wales. *Trans. Newcomen Soc.*, xix, 1938–9.

## IV. PLACE-NAMES

Indexes to notes in the following should be consulted: MORGAN, THOMAS JOHN: Y treigladau a'u cystrawen, Caerdydd, 1952; WILLIAMS, IFOR: Cyfranc Lludd a Llevelys, Bangor, 1910; id.: Canu Aneirin, Caerdydd, 1938; id.: Canu Llywarch Hen, ail argraffiad, Caerdydd, 1953; id.: Pedeir keinc y Mabinogi, ail argraffiad, Caerdydd, 1951.

471. BALLINGER, JOHN, and PHILLIPS, DAVID RHYS: Llyfryddiaeth enwau lleoedd. A short bibliography of place-names. *Trans. Cymmr.*, 1925–6.

472. CHARLES, BERTIE GEORGE: Old Norse relations with Wales. Cardiff, 1934.

> See also PATERSON, DONALD ROSE: Scandinavian influence in the place-names and early personal names of Glamorgan, *Arch. Camb.*, 1920. Id.: The Scandinavian settlement of Cardiff, ibid., 1921. Id.: The pre-Norman settlement of Glamorgan, ibid., 1922. Id.: Early Cardiff, Exeter, 1926.

473. Id.      Non-Celtic place-names in Wales. London, 1938.

474. DAVIES, ELWYN (ed.): Rhestr o enwau lleoedd (A gazetteer of Welsh place-names). Cardiff, 1957; 2nd edn, 1958.

**475.** ELLIS, DEWI MACHRETH: A study of the place-names in Montgomeryshire. *Mont. Coll.,* xliv, 1936; xlv, 1938.

**476.** EKWALL, EILERT: The concise Oxford dictionary of English place-names. 3rd edn; repr. Oxford, 1951.

> The addenda to this edition have notes on Monmouthshire place-names. See also id.: English river-names. Oxford, 1928. Contains references to Welsh river-names.

**477.** FORSTER, MAX: Der flussname Themse und seine Sippe . . . Munich, 1941.

**478.** JACKSON, KENNETH HURLSTONE: On some Romano-British place-names. *Jnl. Rom. Stud.,* xxxviii, 1948.

**479.** Id.    Language and history in early Britain. Edinburgh, 1953.

**480.** JONES, ARTHUR GRAY: The place-names of Ebbw Vale (Monmouthshire). Llandysul, n.d.

**481.** JONES, THOMAS: The place-names of Cardiff. *S. Wales and Mon. Rec. Soc. Pubn.,* ii, 1950.

**482.** JONES, TOM: A bibliography of monographs on the place-names of Wales. *B.B.C.S.,* v, 3, 1930.

**483.** LLOYD, JOHN EDWARD: Welsh place names, a study of some common name-elements. *Y Cymmr.,* xi, 1890.

> Id.    History of Wales (No. 144).
>
> Contains valuable notes on Welsh place-names.

**484.** LLOYD-JONES, JOHN: Random remarks on place-names [principally in North Wales]. *Trans. Angl. Antiq. Soc.,* 1920.

**485.** Id.    Enwau lleoedd. *Y Geninen,* xliii, 1925.

**486.** Id.    Enwau lleoedd Sir Gaernarfon. Caerdydd, 1928.
> See review by W. J. Gruffydd in *Y Llenor,* vii, 1928.

**487.** NORTH, FREDERICK JOHN: Place-names and early maps. *Antiquity,* xv, 1941.

**488.** OWEN, HUGH: Military place-names in Wales. *Trans. Angl. Ant q. Soc.,* 1933.

**489.** RICHARDS, GRAFTON MELVILLE: Place-names of North Wales. In A scientific survey of Merseyside. Brit. Assoc. for the Advancement of Science. Liverpool, 1953.

**490.** Id.    The study of place-names. *Mont. Coll.,* liv, 1956.

> The description of Penbrokshire (No. 109 (1)).
>
> Contains extensive notes on place-names by Egerton Phillimore.

**491.** THOMAS, RICHARD JAMES: Cyfatebiaeth rhwng enwau-lleoedd Cymraeg a Saesneg. *B.B.C.S.*, vii, 1933–5.

**492.** Id.      Celtic place-names formed from animal-head names. *Arch. Camb.*, 1934.

**493.** Id.      Enwau afonydd â'r olddodiad *-wy. B.B.C.S.*, vii, 1933–5; viii, 1935–7.

**494.** Id.      Enwau afonydd a nentydd Cymru. Caerdydd, 1938.
> See review by Sir Ifor Williams in *Y Traethodydd*, 1938.

**495.** WILLIAMS, IFOR: Rhai enwau lleoedd yn Ninbych. *Jnl. Welsh Bibl. Soc.*, v, 1941 (with English abstract: Place-names in the Denbigh district).

**496.** Id.      Enwau lleoedd. *Cyfres Pobun*, v. Lerpwl, 1945.

**497.** Id.      Glasinfryn. *Trans. Caerns. Hist. Soc.*, 1948.

**498.** Id.      Commentary on individual names in RICHMOND, IAN ARCHIBALD, and CRAWFORD, OSBERT GUY STANHOPE: The British section of the Ravenna cosmography, III. *Archaeologia*, xciii, 1949.

## V. PERSONAL NAMES

**499.** LLOYD, JOHN EDWARD: The personal name-system in Old Welsh. *Y Cymmr.*, ix, 1888.

**500.** LLOYD-JONES: Enwau Cymraeg. *Y Geninen*, xliv, 1926.

**501.** MORRIS, T. E.: The re-naming of Welshmen. *Trans. Cymmr.*, 1901–2.

**502.** Id.      Welsh surnames in the border counties of Wales. *Y Cymmr.*, xliii, 1932.

**503.** NASH-WILLIAMS, VICTOR ERLE: The early Christian monuments of Wales. Cardiff, 1950.
> Notes on personal names.

**504.** RHŶS, JOHN: [Many notes on personal names in various epigraphical studies: see bibliography in MORRIS-JONES, JOHN: Sir John Rhŷs. Sir John Rhŷs Memorial Lecture. *Procs. Brit. Acad.*, London, 1925.]

**505.** WILLIAMS, IFOR: The personal names in the early inscriptions [in Anglesey]. In An inventory of the ancient monuments in Anglesey. Royal Commission on Ancient Monuments in Wales and Monmouthshire. London, 1937.

## VI. THE SHIRES

See publications of county record offices, e.g. BEVAN-EVANS, M.: Guide to the Flintshire record office, 1955; ELSAS, MADELINE: The Glamorgan county record office, *Archives*, iii (1950); WILLIAMS, WILLIAM OGWEN:

An introduction to the county records, Caernarvon, 1950; id.: Guide to the Caernarvonshire record office (No. 554); and reports of county archivists and record committees from the various shires, e.g. Carmarthen (1953), Flint (1952), Glamorgan (1947 ff.), Merioneth (1954 ff.), and Monmouth (1905, 1939 ff.).

### (a) Anglesey

See *Transactions of the Anglesey Antiquarian Society and Field Club* (A VII, No. 292).

A review of the records of the Conway and the Menai ferries (No. 130 (8)).

**506.** EVANS, GWENLLIAN NESTA: Social life in mid-eighteenth century Anglesey. Cardiff, 1936.

**507.** Id.     Religion and politics in mid-eighteenth century Anglesey. Cardiff, 1953.

**508.** HUGHES, OWEN: Hanes plwyf Trefdraeth. Bangor, 1903.

**509.** JONES, BOBI: Crwydro Môn. Llandybie, 1957.

JONES, EMYR GWYNNE (ed.): History of the Bulkeley family (No. 45).

**510.** JONES, GLANVILLE REES JEFFREYS: Some medieval rural settlements in North Wales. Institute of British Geographers, Transactions, 1953.

**511.** Id.     The distribution of medieval settlement in Anglesey. *Trans. Angl. Antiq. Soc.,* 1955.

**512.** LLWYD, ANGHARAD: History of the island of Anglesey. Ruthin, 1832.

**513.** OWEN, HUGH: The plea rolls of Anglesey (1509–1516). Supplement to *Trans. Angl. Antiq. Soc.,* 1927.

**514.** Id.     Hanes plwyf Niwbwrch ym Môn. Caernarfon, 1952.

**515.** OWEN, NICHOLAS: History of the island of Anglesey. London, 1775.

**516.** PIERCE, THOMAS JONES: Medieval settlement in Anglesey. *Trans. Angl. Antiq. Soc.,* 1951.

**517.** Id.     (ed.): An Anglesey crown rental of the sixteenth century. *B.B.C.S.,* 1940.

**518.** ROWLANDS, HENRY: Mona Antiqua. 2nd edn. London, 1766.

**519.** SKINNER, JOHN: Ten days tour through the isle of Anglesey, December, 1802. *Arch. Camb.* supplement, 1908.

**520.** WILLIAMS, E. A.: Hanes Môn yn y XIX ganrif. Llangefni, 1927.

**521.** [WILLIAMS, JOHN]: Historia Bellomarisei, or the history of the town and burrough of Beaumaris, *c.* 1669. *Arch. Camb.* supplement, 1917, pp. 275–306.

**522.** WILLIAMS, JOHN: History of Berw [1861]. Supplement to *Trans. Angl. Antiq. Soc.*, 1915.

**523.** WILLIAMSON, OWEN: Hanes Niwbwrch. Lerpwl, n.d.

**524.** [WRIGHT, THOMAS (ed.)]: Anglesea. *Arch. Camb.*, 1881.

### (b) Brecknock

See *Transactions of the Brecknock Society* and *Brycheiniog* (A VII, Nos. 293, 294).

**525.** GRIGSON, GEOFFREY: The camps of Y Pigwn. *Country Life*, December 1, 1955.

**526.** JONES, THEOPHILUS: History of the county of Brecknock, vol. i, 1805; ii, 1809; repr. Brecon, 1898; repr. Glanusk edn, 4 vols., 1909–30.

**527.** LLOYD, JOHN: Historical memoranda of Breconshire. 2 vols. Brecon, 1903, 1904.

**528.** POOLE, EDWIN: The illustrated history and biography of Brecknockshire. Brecon, 1886.

**529.** REES, WILLIAM: The mediaeval lordship of Brecon. *Trans. Cymmr.*, 1915–16.

**530.** Id.   The charters of the boroughs of Brecon and Llandovery. *B.B.C.S.*, ii, 1923–5.

### (c) Caernarvonshire

See *Transactions of the Caernarvonshire Historical Society* (A VII, No. 296); also *Proceedings of the Llandudno, Colwyn Bay, and District Field Club* (A VII, No. 308).

**531.** AMBROSE, WILLIAM ROBERT: Hynafiaethau, cofiannau, a hanes presennol Nant Nantlle. Pen-y-groes, 1872.

A review of The records of the Conway and the Menai ferries (No. 130 (8)).

**532.** BAKER, A., and BAKER, H.: Plas Mawr, Conway. London, 1888.

**532A.** DAVIES, D. T. (gol.): Hanes eglwysi a phlwyfi Lleyn. Pwllheli, 1910.

**533.** HALL, EDMUND HYDE: A description of Caernarvonshire (1809–11). Ed. Emyr Gwynne Jones. *Caerns. Hist. Soc. Record Series*, No. II. Caernarvon, 1952.

**534.** HEMP, WILFRID JAMES: Conway castle. *Arch. Camb.* 1941.
> But see now TAYLOR, ARNOLD JOSEPH: Conway castle and town walls. Ministry of Works official guide-book. H.M.S.O., London, 1956.

HUGHES, HENRY: Immortal sails: a story of a Welsh port (No. 252).

**535.** HUGHES, HUGH DERFEL: Hynafiaethau Llandegai a Llanllechid. Bethesda, 1866.

**536.** JONES, GWILYM PEREDUR, and OWEN, HUGH (eds): Caernarvon court rolls, 1361–1402. *Caerns. Hist. Soc. Record Series*, No. I. Caernarvon, 1951.

**537.** JONES, HARRY LONGUEVILLE, with JONES-PARRY, T. L. D.: Arvona Mediaeva. *Arch. Camb.*, 1847–9, 1855–7.
> On Aberdaron, Bodwrda, Bardsey, Beddgelert, Clynnog, etc.

**538.** JONES, JOHN ('Myrddin Fardd'): Gleanings from God's acre; within the hundred of Lleyn and commot of Eifionydd. Pwllheli, 1903.

**539.** JONES, ROBERT ISAAC ('Alltud Eifion'): Y 'Gestiana', sef hanes Tre'r Gest a phlwyfi Ynyscynhaiarn a Threflys. Tremadog, 1892.

**540.** JONES, WILLIAM HENRY: Old Karnarvon: a historical account of the town of Carnarvon, etc. Carnarvon, 1882.

LOWE, WALTER BEZANT: The heart of northern Wales (No. 362).

**541.** O'NEIL, BRYAN HUGH ST. JOHN: Criccieth castle, Caernarvonshire. *Arch. Camb.*, 1944.

**542.** OWEN, EMYR HYWEL, a THOMAS, ELFED: Atlas Sir Gaernarfon: hanes a daearyddiaeth. Caernarfon, 1954.
> See also section B II.

**543.** OWEN, NICHOLAS: Caernarvonshire. London, 1792.

**544.** PARRY, GRIFFITH TECWYN: Llanberis: ei hanes, ei phobl a'i phethau. Caernarfon, 1908.

**545.** PEERS, CHARLES REED: Carnarvon castle. *Trans. Cymmr.*, 1915–16.

**546.** ROBERTS, GLYN: Borough records at Caernarvon. *B.B.C.S.*, vi, 1, 1931.

**547.** Id.    Caernarvon borough records. *Jnl. Welsh Bibl. Soc.*, iv, 7–8, 1936.

**548.** ROBERTS, WILLIAM: Dau can mlynedd o hynafiaeth a chrefydd yn ardal Nant Nanhoron (Lleyn). Caernarfon, [1953].

**549.** ROWLANDS, EDWARD DAVID: Dyffryn Conwy a'r Creuddyn. Lerpwl, 1948.

**550.** STALLYBRASS, BASIL: Recent discoveries at Clynnog-fawr (church). *Arch. Camb.,* 1914.

> See also BLIGHT, J. T.: St. Beuno's chest (at Clynnog Fawr). Ibid., 1868.

THOMAS, DAVID: Hen longau Sir Gaernarfon (No. 259).

**551.** TOY, SIDNEY: The town and castle of Conway. *Archaeologia,* lxxxvi, 1937.

> Illustrated with plans and photographs.

**552.** WILLIAMS, ROBERT: History and antiquities of the town of Aberconwy. Denbigh, 1835.

**553.** WILLIAMS, WILLIAM: Observations on the Snowdon mountains. London, 1802.

**554.** WILLIAMS, WILLIAM OGWEN: Guide to the Caernarvonshire Record Office. Caernarvon, 1952.

**555.** Id. (ed.): Calendar of the Caernarvonshire quarter sessions records. Vol. i, 1541–58. Caernarvon, 1956.

> The introduction, published separately under the title Tudor Gwynedd (Caernarvon, 1958), is particularly valuable.

**556.** WYNNE, JOHN: Sir a thref Caernarfon fel yr oeddynt ac fel y maent yn 1860. Caernarfon, 1861.

### (d) Cardiganshire

See *Transactions of the Cardiganshire Antiquarian Society* continued as *Ceredigion* (A VII, No. 299).

**557.** BALLINGER, JOHN: Gleanings from a printer's file. Aberystwyth, 1928.

**558.** DAVIES, D. J.: Hanes, hynafiaethau, ac achyddiaeth Llanarth Henfenyw, Llanllwchaiarn, a Llandysilio-gogo. Caerfyrddin, 1875; ail arg. 1930.

**559.** DAVIES, DAVID REES, a ZABETH, S. CLEDLYN: Hanes Llanwenog; y plwyf, a'i bobl. Aberystwyth, 1939.

**560.** DAVIES, EVAN: Hanes plwyf Llangynllo. Llandysul, 1905.

**561.** EDWARDES, EVAN: Byr hanes am blwyf Nantcwnlle. Aberystwyth, 1930.

**562.** EDWARDS, JOHN GORONWY: The early history of the counties of Carmarthen and Cardigan. *E.H.R.*, xxxi, 1916.

**563.** ELLIS, THOMAS IORWERTH: Crwydro Ceredigion. Llandybie, 1952.

**564.** EVANS, GEORGE EYRE: Aberystwyth and its court leet, etc., 1690–1900. Aberystwyth, 1902.

**565.** Id.      Cardiganshire: a personal survey of some of its antiquities, chapels, churches, fonts, plate and registers. Aberystwyth, 1903.

**566.** Id.      Lampeter. Aberystwyth, 1905.

**567.** HORSFALL-TURNER, ERNEST RICHMOND: Walks and wanderings in county Cardigan. Privately printed, n.d.

**568.** HUGHES, HENRY HAROLD: Aberystwyth castle: excavations carried out in the year 1903. *Arch. Camb.*, 1904. See also ibid., 1931, 1946.

**569.** HUGHES, JOHN: A history of the parliamentary representation of the county of Cardigan. Aberystwyth, 1849.

**570.** JONES, EMRYS: Tregaron, a Welsh market town. *Geography*, March, 1950.

**571.** KING, D. J. CATHCART: The castles of Cardiganshire. *Ceredigion*, iii, 1956.

**572.** LEWIS, FRANK ROBERT: A short history of the church of Llanbadarn Fawr, Cardiganshire. Aberystwyth, 1937.

**573.** Id.      The history of Llanbadarn Fawr, Cardiganshire, in the later middle ages. *Trans. Cards. Antiq. Soc.*, xiii, 1938.

**574.** Id.      Lewis Morris and the parish of Llanbadarn Fawr, Cardiganshire, in 1755. *Arch. Camb.*, 1938.

**575.** LEWIS, M. GWYNETH: The printed maps of Cardiganshire, 1578–1900, in the National Library of Wales: a descriptive list with a tabular index. *Ceredigion*, ii, 4, 1955.

**576.** LEWIS, WILLIAM J.: Ceredigion: atlas hanesyddol. Aberystwyth, 1955.

**577.** LLOYD, JOHN EDWARD: Aberystwyth. *Arch. Camb.*, 1931.

**578.** Id.      The story of Ceredigion (400–1277). Cardiff, 1937.

**579.** MEYRICK, SAMUEL RUSH: History and antiquities of the county of Cardigan. 1st edn, London, 1808; latest edn, Brecon, 1907.

Ministers' accounts for West Wales, 1277 to 1306 (No. 109 (13)).

**580.** REES, DAVID C.: Tregaron: historical and antiquarian. Llandysul, 1936.

**581.** REES, WILLIAM (ed.): Ministers' accounts (General Series), bundle No. 1158, No. 3 (Public Record Office): Accounts of the ministers for the lands of the Crown in West Wales for the financial year 1352–3. *B.B.C.S.*, x, 1939–41.

**582.** SANDERS, IVOR JOHN: The boroughs of Aberystwyth and Cardigan in the early fourteenth century. *B.B.C.S.*, xv, 1952–4.

**583.** WRIGHT, F. J.: Norman earthworks near Aberystwyth. *Aberystwyth Studies,* i, Aberystwyth, 1912.

### (e) Carmarthenshire

See *Transactions of the Carmarthenshire Antiquarian Society and Field Club* (now *The Carmarthen Antiquary*) (A VII, No. 300); also *West Wales Historical Records* (A VII, No. 317).

A survey of the duchy of Lancaster lordships in Wales, lordship of Kidwelly, 1609–13 (No. 130 (12)).

**584.** BRIGSTOCKE, THOMAS E.: St. Peter's church, Carmarthen. 5th edn, Carmarthen, 1934.

**585.** BRUNKER, JOHN: Llan Egwad. Carmarthen, 1937.

BUCKLEY, JAMES: Genealogies of the Carmarthenshire sheriffs (No. 14).

**586.** CURTIS, MARY: The antiquities of Laugharne, Pendine, and their neighbourhoods. Norwich, 1871; 2nd edn, London, 1880.

**587.** DANIEL-TYSSEN, J. R.: Royal charters and historical documents relating to the town and county of Carmarthen and the abbeys of Talley and Tygwyn-ar-Daf, 1201–1590. Ed. A. C. Evans. Carmarthen, 1876.

**588.** DAVID, E. AWELRYDD: Guide to Laugharne and Pendine. Carmarthen, 1904.

**589.** DAVIES, ANEIRIN TALFAN: Crwydro sir Gâr. Llandybie, 1955.

**590.** DAVIES, ETHEL M.: The story of Llandefeilog parish. Carmarthen, 1953.

**591.** DAVIES, WILLIAM ('Gwilym Teilo'): Llandeilo Vawr and its neighbourhood, past and present. Llandilo, 1858.

**592.** Id.    Caio a'i hynafiaethau. Caernarvon, 1862.

EDWARDS, JOHN GORONWY: The early history of the counties of Carmarthen and Cardigan (No. 562).

593. EVANS, ALCWYN CARYNI: Local historic lore. 106 printed sheets, with description of Carmarthen in Elizabethan times. Carmarthen, n.d.

594. EVANS, EVAN LEWIS (ed.): Braslun o hanes Pontarddulais a'r cylch. Llandysul, 1949.

595. EVANS, GRUFFYDD: The story of the ancient churches of Llandovery. *Trans. Cymmr.*, 1911–12.

596. Id.     Carmarthenshire gleanings (Kidwelly). *Y Cymmr.*, xxv, 1915.

597. Id.     The story of Newcastle-Emlyn. Ibid., xxxii, 1922.

598. INNES, JOHN: 'Old Llanelly'. Cardiff, 1902.

599. JENKINS, DAN: Cerddi ysgol Llanycrwys, ynghyd a hanes plwyf Llanycrwys. Llandysul, 1934.

600. JENKINS, DAVID: Abergwili and its parish church. Carmarthen, 1936.

601. JENKINS, J.: A short history of Llangunnor church. Carmarthen, 1937.

602. Id.     Llanarthney: the parish, its people and places. Carmarthen, 1939.

603. JONES, DANIEL E.: Hanes plwyfi Llangeler a Phenboyr. Llandysul, 1899.

604. JONES, DAVID DAVEN: A history of Kidwelly. Carmarthen, 1908.

605. LLOYD, JOHN EDWARD (ed.): A history of Carmarthenshire. 2 vols. Cardiff, 1935 and 1939.

606. LODWICK, MALCOLM and EDITH: The story of Carmarthen. Carmarthen, [1954].

607. MATTHEWS, ARTHUR WAIGHT: Index of Carmarthenshire rentals and surveys, etc. *Trans. Carms. Antiq. Soc.*, x, 1914–15.

608. MEE, ARTHUR: Carmarthenshire notes. 3 vols. Vol. i (1889), Llanelly; vol. ii (1891), Carmarthen; vol. iii (1891), Llanelly and Carmarthen.

609. Id.     Llanelly parish church. Llanelly, 1888.

610. Id.     The Carmarthenshire miscellany. Vol. i, Carmarthen and London, [1892].

611. MORGAN, T. M.: The history and antiquities of the parish of Newchurch. Carmarthen, 1910.

**612.** PRICE, FRED S.: History of Llansawel. Swansea, 1898.

**613.** Id.    History of Caio. Swansea, 1904.

REES, WILLIAM (ed.): Ministers' accounts . . . West Wales (No. 581).

**614.** ROBERTS, EDWARD, and PERTWEE, H. A.: St. Illtyd's church, Pembrey: its history and architecture. Swansea, 1898.

**615.** ROBERTS, GOMER MORGAN: Hanes plwyf Llandybie. Caerdydd, 1939.

**616.** SAMUEL, W.: Llandilo, present and past. Carmarthen, 1868.

**617.** SPURRELL, WILLIAM: Carmarthen and its neighbourhood. 2nd edn. Carmarthen, 1879.

**618.** TREHERNE, GEORGE G. T.: Notes on the dedication of the church in honour of St. Margaret Marlos. London, 1904.

**619.** Id.    Eglwys Cymmin: the story of an old Welsh church. Carmarthen, 1918.

**620.** WATERS, ERNEST J.: The lordship of Llanstephan, its castle, church, and charities. Carmarthen, 1943.

**621.** WATERS, WILLIAM: A history of Llanstephan. Carmarthen, 1881.

**622.** WOOD-GRIFFITHS, J. H.: Golden Grove and Jeremy Taylor. Carmarthen, 1950.

### (f) Denbighshire

See *Denbighshire Historical Society Transactions* (A VII, No. 303).

CUST, ALBINIA LUCY: Chronicles of Erthig on the Dyke (No. 16). 1914.

**624.** DAVIES, ELLIS: The prehistoric and Roman remains of Denbighshire. Cardiff, 1929.
See also short appendix in Id.: The prehistoric and Roman remains of Flintshire (No. 657).

**625.** DODD, ARTHUR HERBERT: Welsh and English in east Denbighshire. *Trans. Cymmr.*, 1940.

**626.** Id.    (ed.): A history of Wrexham. Wrexham, 1957.

**627.** EVANS, HUGH: Cwm Eithin. Lerpwl, 1931.
English translation by E. Morgan Humphreys: The Gorse Glen. Liverpool, 1948.

**628.** GRIMES, WILLIAM FRANCIS: Holt, Denbighshire; the works-depot of the twentieth legion at Castle Lyons. *Y Cymmr.*, xli, 1930.

**629.** HEMP, WILFRID JAMES: Denbigh castle. Ibid., xxxvi, 1925.

**630.** HUGHES, HUGH ELLIS (ed.): Eminent men of Denbighshire. Liverpool, 1946.

**631.** JONES, FRANK PRICE: The story of Denbighshire through its castles. Denbigh, 1951.

**632.** JONES, GWILYM PEREDUR (ed.): The extent of Chirkland (1391–3). Liverpool, 1933.

**633.** JONES, JAMES IDWAL: An atlas of Denbighshire. Denbighshire Education Committee, 1951.

JONES, ENID SOPHIA: Trevors of Trevalyn and their descendants (No. 46).

**634.** LERRY, GEORGE GEOFFREY: The collieries of Denbighshire, past and present. Wrexham, 1946.

LLOYD, JOHN YOUDE WILLIAM: The sheriffs of Denbighshire (1541–1700) (No. 87).

**635.** MAHLER, MARGARET: Chirk castle and Chirkland. London, 1912.

**636.** MYDDELTON, WILLIAM MARTIAL (ed.): Chirk castle accounts, 1605–66. Privately printed, 1908.

**637.** Id. (ed.).　　Chirk castle accounts, 1666–1753. Manchester, 1931.

**638.** NEWCOMBE, RICHARD: An account of the castle and town of Denbigh. Denbigh, 1829.

**639.** Id.　　An account of the castle and town of Ruthin. Ruthin, 1836.

**640.** PALMER, ALFRED NEOBARD: Town, fields, and folk of Wrexham in the reign of James I. Wrexham, 1883.

**641.** Id.　　The Welsh settlements east of Offa's Dyke during the 11th century. *Y Cymmr.*, x, 1890.

**642.** Id.　　A history of the parish church of Wrexham. Wrexham, 1886.

**643.** Id.　　A history of the older Nonconformity of Wrexham. Wrexham, 1888.

**644.** Id.　　The history of the town of Wrexham. Wrexham, 1893.

**645.** Id.　　The thirteen country townships of the old parish of Wrexham. Wrexham, 1903.

**646.** Id.    A history of the old parish of Gresford in the counties of Denbigh and Flint. Reprinted from *Arch. Camb.*, 1903–5.

**647.** Id.    The town of Holt in county Denbigh. Reprinted from *Arch. Camb.*, 1906–10.

PARRY, EDWARD: A list of the names and residences of all the high sheriffs of the county of Denbigh from . . . 1541 down to . . . 1906 (No. 89).

**648.** [ROBERTS, ASKEW]: Wynnstay and the Wynns. Oswestry, 1876.

**649.** SIMPSON, W. T.: An account of Llangollen. Birmingham. 1827.

The court rolls of the lordship of Ruthin or Dyffryn Clwyd of the reign of king Edward I (No. 109 (2)).

The first extent of Bromfield and Yale, A.D. 1315 (No. 109 (11)).

**650.** TUCKER, NORMAN: Colwyn Bay, its origin and growth. Colwyn Bay, 1953.

**651.** VINOGRADOFF, PAUL, and MORGAN, FRANK: Survey of the honour of Denbigh, 1334. London, 1914.
See also USHER, GWILYM ARTHUR: A survey of the honour of Denbigh in 1334 (translation of the part of the extent dealing with the township of Llewenny). *Trans. Denbs. Hist. Soc.*, 1954.

**652.** WILLIAMS, ALBERT HUGHES: The early history of Denbighshire —an outline. Cardiff, 1950.

**653.** WILLIAMS, JOHN ('Glanmor'): Ancient and modern Denbigh. Denbigh, 1856.

**654.** Id.    The records of Denbigh and its lordship. Wrexham, 1860.

**655.** WILLIAMS, OWEN: Bibliography of the county: part 2, historical and topographical sources. Wrexham, 1937. New and enlarged edn, Denbighshire County Library, Ruthin, 1951.

### (g) Flintshire

See *Flintshire Historical Society Journal and Publications* (A VII, No. 304) and *Northern Flintshire* (A VII, No. 313).

**656.** BEVAN-EVANS, MYRDDIN: Thomas Pennant and Downing. *Flints. Hist. Soc. Pubns.*, xiv, 1953–4.

**657.** DAVIES, ELLIS: The prehistoric and Roman remains of Flintshire. Cardiff, 1949.

**658.** EDWARDS, JOHN GORONWY: Flintshire since 1801. *Flints. Hist. Soc. Pubns.*, xv, 1954–5.

HANMER (JOHN LORD): A memorial of the parish and family of Hanmer (No. 41).

**659.** HARRIES, EDWARD RHYS: Bibliography of the county of Flint. Part I (biographical sources). Mold, 1953.

**660.** LLOYD, JOHN EDWARD: Flintshire notes: Flint and Mold. *Arch. Camb.*, 1940.

MOSTYN (LORD) and GLENN, THOMAS ARTHUR: History of the family of Mostyn of Mostyn (No. 61).

**661.** PENNANT, THOMAS: The history of the parishes of Whiteford and Holywell. London, 1796.

**662.** POOLE, J.: Gleanings from the histories of Holywell, Flint, St. Asaph, and Rhuddlan. Holywell, 1831.

**663.** TAYLOR, HENRY: Historic notices of Flint. London, 1883.

**664.** WILLETT, R.: Memoir of Hawarden. Chester, 1822.

### (h) Glamorgan

See *Transactions of the Aberafan and District Historical Society* (A VII, No. 291); *Report and Transactions of the Cardiff Naturalists' Society* (ibid., No. 298); *Morgannwg* (ibid., No. 311); *Transactions of the Neath Antiquarian Society* (ibid., No. 312); *Publications of the South Wales and Monmouth Record Society* (ibid., No. 316); and *Gower* (ibid., No. 305). See also under Glamorgan in the Catalogue of printed literature in the Welsh department of the Cardiff Free Library (No. 4).

**665.** BIRCH, WALTER DE GRAY: A descriptive catalogue of Penrice and Margam MSS. Series I–IV. London, 1893–5.
> See additional typewritten lists to this material in the National Library of Wales.

**666.** CHAPPELL, EDGAR LEYSHON: History of the port of Cardiff. Cardiff, 1939.

**667.** Id.      Old Whitchurch: The story of a Glamorgan parish. Cardiff, 1945.

**668.** CLARK, GEORGE THOMAS: The manorial particulars of the county of Glamorgan. *Arch. Camb.*, 1877–8.

**669.** Id.      The land of Morgan, being a contribution towards the history of the lordship of Glamorgan. London, 1883.

Id.      Limbus patrum Morganiae et Glamorganiae, etc. (No. 15).

**670.** Id.     The signory of Gower. *Arch. Camb.,* 1893–4.

**671.** Id.     (ed.): Cartae et alia munimenta quae ad dominium de Glamorgan pertinent. 2nd edn. 6 vols. Cardiff, 1910.

**672.** CORBETT, JOHN STUART: Glamorgan. Ed. D. R. Paterson. Cardiff, 1925.

**673.** DAVIES, JOHN DAVID: A history of west Gower. 4 vols. Swansea, 1877–94.

**674.** DILLWYN, LEWIS WESTON: Contributions towards a history of Swansea. Swansea, 1840.

**675.** EVANS, CYRIL J. O.: Glamorgan, its history and topography. Cardiff, 1938.

EVANS, EVAN LEWIS (ed.): Braslun o hanes Pontarddulais (No. 594).

**676.** GEORGE, THOMAS NEVILLE: The geology, physical features, and natural resources of the Swansea district. Social and economic survey of Swansea and district. Pamphlet No. 1. Cardiff, 1939.

**677.** GRANT-FRANCIS, GEORGE (ed.): Charters granted to the chief borough of Swansea, the seigniory of Gower, 1215–1837. London, 1867.

**678.** Id.     and BAKER, CHARLES: Surveys of Gower and Kilvey. *Arch. Camb.* supplements, 1861, 1864, 1870.

**679.** GRAY, THOMAS: The buried city of Kenfig. London, 1909.

**680.** GRIMES, WILLIAM FRANCIS: Early man in Cardiff district. Nat. Assoc. of Head Teachers: *The book of Cardiff.* Oxford, 1937.

**681.** HAGUE, DOUGLAS B.: Notes on Swansea castle. *Gower,* x, 1957.

**682.** JAMES, LEMUEL HOPKIN: Old Cowbridge. Cardiff, 1922.

**683.** JONES, DAVID WATKIN ('Dafydd Morganwg'): Hanes Morganwg. Aberdâr, 1874.

JONES, THOMAS: The place-names of Cardiff (No. 481).

**684.** JONES, WILLIAM HENRY: History of Swansea and of the lordship of Gower from the earliest times to the fourteenth century. Vol. i. Carmarthen, 1920.

**685.** Id.     History of the port of Swansea. Carmarthen, 1922.

**686.** MATTHEWS, JOHN HOBSON (ed.): Cardiff records, materials for a history of the county borough. 6 vols. Cardiff, 1898–1911.

5

**687.** MERRICK, RICE: A booke of Glamorganshires antiquities. 1st edn, ed. Sir Thomas Phillipps, Middle Hill, 1825; 2nd edn, ed. J. A. Corbett, London, 1887.

**688.** NICHOLAS, THOMAS: The history and antiquities of Glamorganshire and its families. London, 1874.

> A reprint of the Glamorganshire portion of Annals and antiquities of the counties . . . of Wales (No. 63).

**689.** NICHOLL, LEWIS D.: The Normans in Glamorgan, Gower, and Kidweli. Cardiff, 1936.

NORTH, FREDERICK JOHN: The stones of Llandaff cathedral (No. 419).

**690.** PATERSON, DONALD ROSE: The Scandinavian element in Glamorgan. *Arch. Camb.*, 1920–2.

**691.** Id.     Early Cardiff. Exeter, 1926.

**692.** PHILLIPS, DAVID RHYS: History of the vale of Neath. Swansea, 1925.

**693.** PHILLIPS, S.: The history of the borough of Llantrisant. Bristol, 1866.

**694.** Id.     and REES, WILLIAM: The story of the Lower Borowes of Merthyrmawr (with map). *S. Wales and Mon. Rec. Soc. Pubn.*, i, [1949].

**695.** RANDALL, HENRY JOHN: Bridgend: the story of a market town. Newport, 1955.

**696.** REES, WILLIAM: The lordship of Cardiff. *Trans. Cardiff Naturalists' Soc.*, lxiii, 1932.

**697.** Id.     Caerphilly castle: a history and description. Cardiff, 1937.

**698.** Id.     Cardiff, its history. Nat. Assoc. of Head Teachers: *The book of Cardiff*. Oxford, 1937.

**699.** RICHARD, ARTHUR JOHN: Kenfig castle. *Arch. Camb.*, 1927.

**700.** RICHARDS, JOHN: The Cowbridge story: history and anecdotes of the ancient borough. Bridgend, 1956.

**701.** ROBERTS, GLYN: The municipal development of the borough of Swansea to 1900. Social and economic survey of Swansea and district. Pamphlet No. 2. Cardiff, 1940.

**702.** SEYLER, CLARENCE ARTHUR: The early charters of Swansea and Gower. *Arch. Camb.*, 1924–5.

703. SHEPHERD, CHARLES FREDERICK: St. Nicholas. Cardiff, 1934.

704. Id.    Annals of St. Fagans. Cardiff, 1936.

705. TAYLOR, GLEN A.: The development of Neath. *Trans. Neath Antiq. Soc.*, 1937–9.

706. THOMPSON, HERBERT METFORD: Cardiff. Cardiff, 1930.

707. WILKINS, CHARLES: The history of Merthyr Tydfil. Merthyr Tydfil, 1867.

708. WILLIAMS, DAVID TREVOR: Gower: a study in linguistic movements and historical geography. *Arch. Camb.*, 1934.

709. Id.    The economic development of Swansea and of the Swansea district to 1921. Social and economic survey of Swansea and district. Pamphlet No. 4. Cardiff, 1940.

710. WILLIAMS, GRIFFITH JOHN: Iolo Morganwg. Y gyfrol gyntaf. Caerdydd, 1956. In progress.
> Important historically in view of Iolo Morganwg's distortions.

### (i) Merioneth

See *Journal of the Merioneth Historical and Record Society* (A VII, No. 309).

711. DAVIES, DAVID: Ardudwy a'i gwron. Blaenau Ffestiniog, 1914.

712. DAVIES, WILLIAM LLEWELYN: Phylipiaid Ardudwy. *Y Cymmr.*, xlii, 1931.

713. Id.    (ed.): Memoirs of Samuel Holland. Mer. Hist. Soc. Extra Publication, series I, no. 1, 1952.

714. ELLIS, THOMAS IORWERTH: Crwydro Meirionnydd. Llandybie, 1954.

715. ELLIS, THOMAS PETER: Merioneth notes. *Y Cymmr.*, xxxviii, 1927.

716. Id.    The story of two parishes: Dolgelley and Llanelltyd. Newtown, 1928.

717. GRIFFITHS, GRIFFITH MILWYN (ed.): A report of the deanery of Penllyn and Edeirnion. Mer. Hist. Soc. Extra Publication, series I, no. 3 (*The Merioneth Miscellany,* I), 1955.

718. JONES, FRANCIS WYNN: Godre'r Berwyn. Cardiff, 1953.

719. JONES, E. ROSALIE: History of Barmouth. Barmouth, 1909.

720. MORGAN, DAVID WILLIAM: Brief glory: the story of a quest. Liverpool, 1948.

**721.** MORRIS, R. PRYS: Cantref Meirionydd. Dolgellau, 1890.

**722.** OWEN, HUGH JOHN: Echoes of old Merioneth. Dolgelley, [1946].

**723.** Id.      Treasures of the Mawddach. Bala, 1950.

**724.** PEERS, CHARLES REED: Harlech castle. *Trans. Cymmr.,* 1921–2.

**725.** ROBERTS, GOMER: Atgofion amaethwr. Ed. Cadwaladr Bryner Jones. Mer. Hist. Soc. Extra Publication, series I, no. 2, 1954.

**726.** VAUGHAN, ROBERT: Sketch history of Merionethshire. *Cambrian Register,* 1795.

**727.** WILLIAMS, GRIFFITH JOHN: Hanes plwyf Ffestiniog. Wrexham, n.d. [1882?].

### (j) Monmouthshire

See *South Wales and Monmouth Record Society Publications* (A VII, No. 316).

**728.** ANDREWS, J. H.: Chepstow: a defunct seaport. *Geography,* April, 1955.

A survey of the duchy of Lancaster lordships in Wales (No. 130 (12)).

**729.** BRADNEY, JOSEPH ALFRED: A history of Monmouthshire. 4 vols. London, 1904–33.

**730.** CLARK, ARTHUR: Story of Pontypool. Pontypool, 1951; repr. 1958.

**731.** COLLINS, WILLIAM JOHN TOWNSEND: Monmouthshire writers: a literary history and anthology. Newport, 1945.

**732.** COXE, WILLIAM: A historical tour through Monmouthshire. 1st edn, 1801; recent edn, Brecon, 1901.

**733.** DAVIES, EBENEZER THOMAS: History of the parish of Mathern. Chepstow, 1950.

**734.** Id.      An ecclesiastical history of Monmouthshire. Part I (medieval). Risca, 1953.

**735.** DAVIES, LEONARD TWISTON: Men of Monmouthshire. 2 vols. Cardiff, 1933.

**736.** DAVIS, HENRY JOHN: The rise and progress of Newport (Monmouthshire). London, 1891.

**737.** DAWSON, JAMES WILLIAM: Commerce and custom: a history of the ports of Newport and Caerleon. Newport, 1932.

**738.** DICKER, J. J.: Life in Hewelsfield and Brockweir during the sixteenth century. Chepstow, 1950.

**739.** ELLIS, THOMAS IORWERTH: Crwydro Mynwy. Llandybie, 1958.

**740.** EVANS, CYRIL J. O.: Monmouthshire: its history and topography. Cardiff, [1954].

**741.** FARR, GRAHAME E.: Chepstow ships. Chepstow Society and Monmouthshire branch of the Historical Association, 1954.

**742.** GRAHAM, ROSE: Four alien priories in Monmouthshire. *Jnl. Brit. Arch. Assoc.* Vol. 35, 1929.

**743.** HOEY, RICHARD: Short history of the Bedwellty district. Pontypool, 1951.

**744.** JONES, BRYNMOR PIERCE: From Elizabeth I to Victoria: the government of Newport (Mon.), 1550–1850. Newport, 1957.

**745.** JONES, THOMAS: Rhymney memories. Newtown, 1938.

**746.** KING, D. J. CATHCART, and PERKS, J. CLIFFORD: Llangibby castle. *Arch. Camb.*, 1956.

**747.** MARSH, JOHN FITCHETT: Annals of Chepstow castle or six centuries of the Lords of Striguil, etc. Ed. Sir John Maclean. Exeter, 1883.

**748.** REES, WILLIAM: Mediaeval Gwent. 7 maps. *Jnl. Brit. Archaeol. Assoc.*, 1929.

**749.** TAYLOR, ARNOLD JOSEPH: Usk castle and the Pipe Roll of 1185, with a note on an expenses account of 1289. *Arch. Camb.*, 1947.

**750.** WATERS, IVOR: Chepstow parish records. Chepstow Society, 1955.

**751.** Id.      Inns and taverns of the Chepstow district. Chepstow, 1949.

**752.** Id.      About Chepstow. Chepstow, 1952.

**753.** WILLIAMS, DAVID: History of Monmouthshire. London, 1796.

### (k) Montgomeryshire

See *Montgomeryshire Collections* (A VII, No. 310).

**754.** CHITTY, LILY FRANCES: Subsidiary castle sites west of Shrewsbury. *Trans. Shrops. Arch. Soc.,* liii, 1949.

**755.** CLARK, GEORGE THOMAS: The castle of Montgomery: notes upon its structure and history. *Mont. Coll.*, x, 1877.

**756.** Id.     The castle of Dolforwyn. Ibid.

**757.** Id.     The moated mounds of the upper Severn. Ibid.

**758.** ELLIS, THOMAS IORWERTH: Crwydro Maldwyn. Llandybie, 1957.

**759.** GRIFFITHS, WILLIAM ARTHUR: Our vanishing lesser landmarks. *Mont. Coll.*, liv, 1955-6.

**760.** HAMER, EDWARD, and LLOYD, HOWEL WILLIAM: History of the parish of Llangurig. London, 1875.

**761.** HORSFALL-TURNER, ERNEST RICHMOND: Municipal history of Llanidloes. Llanidloes, 1908.

**762.** HUGHES, HENRY HAROLD: Llanerfyl reliquary and reredos. *Arch. Camb.*, 1932.

**763.** JONES, WILLIAM: Statistical account of the parishes of Llanerful, Llangadvan, and Garth-beibio in Montgomeryshire. Ed. Walter Davies. *Cambrian Register*, 1796.

LLOYD, WILLIAM VALENTINE (ed.): The sheriffs of Montgomery-shire . . . 1540-1639 (No. 88).

**764.** O'NEIL, BRYAN HUGH ST. JOHN: The castle and borough of Llanidloes. *Mont. Coll.*, xliii, 1933-4.

**765.** Id.     Excavations at Breiddin hill camp, Montgomeryshire, 1933-5. *Arch. Camb.*, 1937.

**766.** Id.     Excavations at Ffridd Faldwyn camp, Montgomery, 1937-9. Ibid., 1943.

**767.** Id.     and FOSTER-SMITH, ALFRED HENRY: Montgomery town wall. Ibid., 1940. See also revision by A. J. Taylor: Montgomery town wall. Ibid., 1947.

**768.** OWEN, C. E. VAUGHAN: An Arwystli note-book. *Mont. Coll.*, liv, 1955-6.

**769.** REES, ALWYN DAVID: Life in a Welsh countryside: a social study of Llanfihangel yng Ngwynfa. Cardiff, 1950.

**770.** RICHARDS, ROBERT: The medieval castles of north Montgomery-shire: a topographical survey. *Mont. Coll.*, xlvii, 1942; xlviii, 1943-4.

**771.** ROWLANDS, B. BENNETT: History of Newtown. Newtown, 1914.

**772.** SYLVESTER, DOROTHY: The rural landscape of eastern Montgomery-shire. *Mont. Coll.*, liv, 1955-6.
     On the open-field system.

**773.** WILLIAMS, RICHARD: Montgomeryshire worthies. 2nd edn. Newtown, 1894.

### (l) Pembrokeshire

See *West Wales Historical Records* (A VII, No. 317).

A calendar of the public records relating to Pembrokeshire (No. 109 (7)).

ALLEN, JAMES: Notes on the sheriffs of Pembrokeshire, 1541–1899 (No. 82).

**774.** BARONIA DE KEMEYS. *Arch. Camb.* supplement. London, 1862.

**775.** BOAKE, E. J.: Report on the excavation of the chapel of St. Justinian, St. David's. *Arch. Camb.*, 1926.

**776.** CARÖE, A. D. R.: Porth-y-tŵr, St. David's. *Arch. Camb.*, 1954.

**777.** CLARK, GEORGE THOMAS: The earls, earldom, and castle of Pembroke. *Arch. Camb.*, 1859–61. Also published separately, Tenby, 1880.

**778.** FENTON, RICHARD: A historical tour through Pembrokeshire. London, 1811; repr. Brecon, 1903.

**779.** FREEMAN, E.: A vanished Welsh port (Solva). *Country Life*, June 17 1954.

**780.** LAWS, EDWARD: The history of Little England beyond Wales. London, 1888.

**781.** KING, D. J. CATHCART, and PERKS, J. CLIFFORD: Castell Nanhyfer, Nevern (Pemb.). *Arch. Camb.*, 1951.

**782.** LOCKLEY, RONALD MATHIAS: Pembrokeshire. London, 1957.

OWEN, GEORGE: The taylors cussion (No. 125).

**783.** PETERS, ELIZABETH E.: The history of Pembroke Dock. London, 1905.

**784.** PHILLIPS, JAMES: The history of Pembrokeshire. London, 1909.

**785.** PHILLIPS, JOHN ROLAND: History of Cilgerran. London, 1867.

**786.** PHILLIPS, J. W., and WARREN, FRED J.: The history of Haverfordwest. Haverfordwest, 1914.

**787.** REES, JAMES FREDERICK: The story of Milford. Cardiff, 1954.

The description of Penbrokshire, by George Owen (No. 109 (1)).

**788.** THOMAS, FLORA: The builders of Milford. Haverfordwest, 1920; repr. 1952.

WALKER, RONALD FRANCIS: Carew castle (No. 406).

**789.** WILLIAMS, ERNEST LLWYD: Crwydro sir Benfro. Llandybie, 1958.

#### (m) Radnor

See *Transactions of the Radnorshire Society* (A VII, No. 314).

**790.** HOWSE, WILLIAM HENRY: Radnorshire. Hereford, 1949.

**791.** LLOYD, JOHN: A collection of miscellaneous papers relating to the history of the county of Radnor. London, 1900.

**792.** OWEN, EDWARD: The parish church of New Radnor at the period of the Reformation. *Arch. Camb.*, 1918.

**793.** WILLIAMS, JONATHAN: General history of the county of Radnor. 1st edn, Tenby, 1859; 2nd edn, Brecon, 1905.

#### (n) The Border

See *Transactions of the Caradoc and Severn Valley Field Club* (A VII, No. 297), *The Cheshire Sheaf* (ibid., No. 301), *Journal of the Chester and North Wales Archaeological and Historic Society* (ibid., No. 302), *Transactions of the Lancaster and Cheshire Historic Society* (ibid., No. 306), *Bye-Gones relating to Wales and the border counties* (ibid., No. 295), *Transactions of the Shropshire Archaeological Society* (ibid., No. 315), *Transactions of the Woolhope Naturalists' Field Club* (ibid., No. 318), and *Collectanea Archaeologica* (communications made to the British Archaeological Association), vol. i, London, 1862, which contains several useful articles on border history, as do vols. xvii (1861) and xxiv (1868) of the *Journal* of the Association.

**794.** AUDEN, THOMAS: Shrewsbury: a historical and topographical account. London, 1905.

**795.** BANNISTER, ARTHUR THOMAS: History of Ewias Harold. Hereford, 1902.

**796.** Id.    Herefordshire and its place in English history. Hereford, 1912.

**797.** BARRACLOUGH, GEOFFREY: The earldom and county palatine of Chester. *Trans. Hist. Soc. Lanc. and Chester*, ciii, 1951; repr., Oxford, 1953.

**798.** BULKLEY-OWEN, FANNY MARY KATHERINE ('Gwenrhian Gwynedd'): History of Selattyn parish. Oswestry, n.d. [*c.* 1900]; repr. from *Trans. Shrop. Arch. Soc.,* ii, iii, and iv, 1892 ff.

**799.** CATHRALL, WILLIAM: The history of Oswestry. Oswestry, 1855.

**800.** CLIVE, ROBERT HENRY: Documents connected with the history of Ludlow and the lords marcher. London, 1841.

**801.** DUNCUMB, JOHN: Collections towards the history and antiquities of the county of Hereford. 4 vols. Hereford, 1804–92. Hundred of Grimsworth (vols. iii and iv) by W. H. Cooke. Continuation volumes: Hundred of Huntington by M. G. Watkins, Hereford, 1897; Hundred of Radlow by M. G. Watkins, Hereford, 1902; Hundred of Wormelow, upper division, by J. H. Matthews, Hereford, 1912.

**802.** EARWAKER, JOHN PARSONS: East Cheshire past and present, or a history of the hundred of Macclesfield in the county palatinate of Chester, from original sources. 2 vols. London, 1877–80.

**803.** EYTON, ROBERT WILLIAM: Antiquities of Shropshire. 12 vols. London, 1854–60.

**804.** FORREST, HERBERT EDWARD: Some old Shropshire houses and their owners. Reprinted privately from *Trans. Shrop. Arch. Soc.* and *Trans. Caradoc Field Club*, 1924.

**805.** GALBRAITH, VIVIAN HUNTER, and TAIT, JAMES: Herefordshire domesday, *c.* 1160–1170. *Pipe Roll Soc.*, lxiii, 1950.

**806.** Herefordshire, its natural history, archaeology and history, etc. Centenary volume of the Woolhope Club. Gloucester, 1954.

**807.** LEIGHTON, STANLEY: Records of the corporation of Oswestry. *Trans. Shrop. Arch. Soc.*, 1879–83.

**808.** ORMEROD, GEORGE: The history of the county palatinate and city of Chester. 2nd edn. Ed. Thomas Helsby. 3 vols. London, 1875–82.

**809.** OWEN, HUGH, and BLAKEWAY, JOHN BRICKDALE: History of Shrewsbury. 2 vols. London, 1825.

**810.** PAGE, WILLIAM, and DOUBLEDAY, HERBERT ARTHUR (eds): Herefordshire. Vol. i. Victoria County Histories. London, 1908.

**811.** Id.  Shropshire. Vol. i. Victoria County Histories. London, 1908.

**812.** PALMER, ALFRED NEOBARD: History of ancient tenures of land in the marches of North Wales. Wrexham, 1885; 2nd edn (in collaboration with Edward Owen—it does not, however, supersede the first), 1910.

**813.** PHILLIPS, THOMAS: History and antiquities of Shrewsbury. Shrewsbury, 1779.

**814.** SHONE, WILLIAM: Prehistoric Cheshire. London and Chester, 1911.

**815.** SLACK, WALTER JOHN: The lordship of Oswestry, 1393–1607. Shrop. Arch. Soc. Shrewsbury, 1951.

**816.** SYLVESTER, DOROTHY, and NULTY, GEOFFREY: The historical atlas of Cheshire. Chester, 1958.

**817.** VARLEY, WILLIAM JONES: The hill-forts of the Welsh marches. *Arch. Jnl.*, cv, 1948.

**818.** Id.      and JACKSON, JOHN WILFRED: Prehistoric Cheshire (with distribution maps by Lily F. Chitty). Chester, 1940.

**819.** WARD, ARTHUR WALBURGH: A guide to the Shropshire records. Salop City Council. Shrewsbury, 1952.

**820.** WHITFIELD, JOHN ROGER WEBB: The lordship of Cause, 1540–1. *Trans. Shrop. Arch. Soc.*, liv, 1951–2.

**821.** WRIGHT, THOMAS: The history of Ludlow and its neighbourhood. London and Ludlow, 1852.

## VII. DIOCESES

See also the relevant subsections on ecclesiastical history in other sections.

The history of the diocese of Monmouth before 1921 is included in that of Llandaff; that of the diocese of Swansea and Brecon before 1923 in that of St. David's.

### (a) General

**822.** DAVIES, JAMES CONWAY: The records of the Church in Wales. *N.L.W. Jnl.*, iv, 1945–6.

**823.** Id.      (ed.): Episcopal acts and cognate documents relating to Welsh dioceses, 1066–1272. 2 vols. *Hist. Soc. Church in Wales Publications.* No. 1 and Nos. 3 and 4. Cardiff, 1948 and 1953.

HIRSCH-DAVIES, JOHN EDWIN DE: A popular history of the Church in Wales (No. 169).

JAMES, JOHN WILLIAMS: A Church history of Wales (No. 173).

NEWELL, EBENEZER JOSIAH: A history of the Welsh Church (No. 176).

**824.** THOMPSON, ALEXANDER HAMILTON: The Welsh medieval dioceses. *Jnl. Hist. Soc. Church in Wales*, i, 1947.

### (b) Individual dioceses

#### Bangor

CLARKE, MARTIN L.: Bangor cathedral, 1700–1828 (No. 409).

HAGUE, DOUGLAS B.: The bishop's palace, Gogarth, Llandudno (No. 443).

**825.** HUGHES, WILLIAM: Bangor. *S.P.C.K. Diocesan Histories.* London, 1911.

**826.** Id.    Recollections of Bangor cathedral. London, 1904.

**827.** PRYCE, ARTHUR IVOR: The diocese of Bangor in the sixteenth century. Bangor, 1923.

**828.** Id.    The diocese of Bangor during three centuries (seventeenth to nineteenth inclusive). Cardiff, 1929.

**829.** Id.    Records at the diocesan registry of Bangor. *B.B.C.S.*, x, 1941.

**830.** WILLIS, BROWNE: A survey of the cathedral church of Bangor. London, 1721.

### Llandaff

**831.** BIRCH, WALTER DE GRAY: Memorials of the see and cathedral of Llandaff. Neath, 1912.

**832.** BRADNEY, JOSEPH ALFRED, and RICKARDS, RICHARD: Llandaff records. 5 vols. Cardiff and London, 1905–14.
> Includes a digest of parish records and the Acts of the bishops of Llandaff.

**833.** GREEN, CHARLES ALFRED HOWELL (Archbishop of Wales): Notes on churches in the diocese of Llandaff. 3 parts. Aberdare, 1906–7.

**834.** Id.    The chapter of Llandaff cathedral, 1561–1668. *Y Cymmr.*, xxxi, 1921.

**835.** JONES, EVAN DAVID: The book of Llandaff. *N.L.W. Jnl.*, iv, 1945–6.

**836.** NEWELL, EBENEZER JOSIAH: Llandaff. *S.P.C.K. Diocesan Histories.* London, 1902.

NORTH, FREDERICK JOHN: The stones of Llandaff cathedral (No. 419).

**837.** OLLIVANT, ALFRED: Some account of the condition of the fabric of Llandaff cathedral. London, 1857; 2nd edn with plates, 1860.

**838.** THOMAS, LAWRENCE: The reformation in the old diocese of Llandaff. Cardiff, 1930.

**839.** Id.    The fall and rise of a cathedral. *Friends of Llandaff Cathedral Annual Report*, v, 1938.

**840.** WILLIS, BROWNE: Survey of the cathedral church of Llandaff. London, 1719.

### St. Asaph

**841.** EVANS, DAVID LEWIS: Llyfr Coch Asaph. *N.L.W. Jnl.*, iv, 1945–6.

**842.** GRIFFITHS, GRIFFITH MILWYN: A St. Asaph 'register' of episcopal acts, 1506–1571. *Jnl. Hist. Soc. Church in Wales*, vi, 1956.

NEAVERSON, E.: The older building stones of St. Asaph cathedral (No. 417).

**843.** THOMAS, DAVID RICHARD: St. Asaph. *S.P.C.K. Diocesan Histories.* London, 1888.

**844.** Id.    History of the diocese of St. Asaph. New edn. 3 vols. Oswestry, 1908–13.

**845.** WILLIS, BROWNE: A survey of the cathedral church of St. Asaph. 2nd edn. Wrexham, 1801.

### St. David's

**846.** BAKER, THOMAS: Diocese of St. David's: particulars relating to endowments of livings. 4 vols. Carmarthen, 1907.

**847.** BEVAN, WILLIAM LATHAM: St. David's. *S.P.C.K. Diocesan Histories.* London, 1889.

**848.** DAVIES, JAMES CONWAY: The black book of St. David's. *N.L.W. Jnl.*, iv, 1946.

**849.** EMMANUEL, HYWEL DAVID: A fragment of the register of Stephen Patryngton, bishop of St. David's. *Jnl. Hist. Soc. Church in Wales*, ii, 1950.

**850.** Id.    Early St. David's records. *N.L.W. Jnl.*, viii, 1954.

**851.** EVANS, GEORGE EYRE: Abergwili, the episcopal chapel. *Trans. Carms. Antiq. Soc.*, xxiv, 1933.

**852.** Id.    The records of St. David's diocese. Ibid.

**853.** Id.    Parochial records [at Abergwili palace]. Ibid., xxv, 1934.

**854.** Id.    Acts of the bishops of St. David's, 1203–1484. Ibid., xxix, 1939.

**855.** JONES, WILLIAM BASIL, and FREEMAN, EDWARD AUGUSTUS: The history and antiquities of St. David's. London, 1856.
See also catalogue published by Cardiff Public Library. Cardiff, 1927.

**856.** MORGAN, WALTER THOMAS: The consistory courts in the diocese of St. David's, 1660–1858. *Jnl. Hist. Soc. Church in Wales*, vii and viii, 1957 and 1958.

**857.** MORGAN, W. E. T.: St. David's and Swansea diocese. *Trans. Woolhope Naturalists' Field Club,* 1932 (1935).

**858.** RADFORD, COURTENAY ARTHUR RALEGH: The palace of the bishops of St. David's at Lamphey, Pembrokeshire. *Arch. Camb.,* 1938.

The black book of St. David's (No. 109 (5)).

See also DAVIES, JAMES CONWAY: The black book of St. David's (No. 848).

The episcopal registers of the diocese of St. David's, 1397–1518 (No. 109 (6)).

**859.** WILLIAMS, GLANMOR: The second volume of St. David's registers, 1554–64. *B.B.C.S.,* xiv, 1950–52.

**860.** WILLIAMS, WILLIAM MOSES, and JONES, IDWAL: An inventory of records at the palace of Abergwili. Ibid., ix, 1937-9.

**861.** WILLIS, BROWNE: Survey of the cathedral church of St. David's. London, 1717.

**862.** YARDLEY, EDWARD: Menevia sacra. *Arch. Camb.* supplement, 1927.

## VIII. RELIGIOUS ORDERS AND HOUSES

### (a) General

See GILYARD-BEER, R.: Abbeys: an introduction to the religious houses of England and Wales. H.M.S.O. London, 1958. See also section G III (*b*) (ii).

**863.** BACKMUND, NORBERT: Monasticon Praemonstratense: id est historia circariarum atque canoniarum candidi et canonici ordinis Praemonstratensis. Tom. i and ii. Straubing, 1949–52.

See under Talley below.

**864.** BEBB, WILLIAM AMBROSE: Machlud y mynachlogydd. Aberystwyth, 1937.

**865.** CANIVEZ, JOSEPH M.: Statuta capitulorum generalium ordinis Cisterciensis. 8 vols. *Bibliothèque de la Revue d'Histoire Ecclesiastique.* Fascs. ix–xiv B, 1933–41.

**866.** COOKE, A. M.: The settlement of the Cistercians in England. *E.H.R.,* viii, 1893.

**867.** CRONIN, JOHN M.: St. Francis of Assisi and Wales. *St. Peter's Magazine,* Cardiff, 1926, p. 290.

**868.** DAVIES, JAMES CONWAY: Dominicans in Wales. *N.L.W. Jnl.,* iii, 1945.

**869.** DONELEY, JAMES S.: Changes in the grange economy of English and Welsh Cistercian abbeys. *Traditio*, x, 1954.

DUGDALE, WILLIAM: Monasticon Anglicanum (No. 111).

**870.** ELLIS, THOMAS PETER: The Welsh Benedictines of the terror. Newtown, 1936.

**871.** GRAHAM, ROSE: English ecclesiastical studies. London, 1929.

Id.      Four alien priories in Monmouthshire (No. 742).

**872.** JANAUSCHEK, L.: Origines Cistercienses. Tomus i. Vienna, 1877.
See index s.v. Wallia.

**873.** KNOWLES, DAVID: The monastic order in England. Cambridge, 1940.

**874.** Id.      The religious orders in England. 2 vols. Cambridge, 1950, 1955.

**875.** Id.      and ST. JOSEPH, J. K. S.: Monastic sites from the air. Cambridge, 1952.

**876.** Id.      and HADCOCK, R. NEVILLE: Medieval religious houses: England and Wales. London, 1953.
See also additions and corrections in *E.H.R.*, lxxii, 1957, pp. 60–87.

**877.** LEWIS, FRANK ROBERT: The religious orders in medieval Wales. *The Month,* February, 1938.

**878.** Id.      The racial sympathies of the Welsh Cistercians. *Trans. Cymmr.,* 1938.

**879.** LITTLE, ANDREW GEORGE: Studies in English Franciscan history. Manchester, 1917.
For individual houses see DUGDALE, WILLIAM: Monasticon Anglicanum (No. 111), and TANNER: Notitia Monastica (No. 885); and for the Welsh friars see EASTERLING, RUTH C.: The friars in Wales, *Arch. Camb.*, 1914; and OWEN, EDWARD: The fate of the structures of Conway abbey and of Bangor and Beaumaris friaries (No. 888).

**880.** Id.      A guide to Franciscan studies. *Helps for Students of History.* No. xxiii, 1920.

Monastic Britain. South sheet (No. 374).

**881.** O'SULLIVAN, JEREMIAH F.: Cistercian settlements in Wales and Monmouthshire, 1140–1540. New York, 1947.

Records of the Court of Augmentations relating to Wales (No. 130 (13)).

**882.** PANTIN, WILLIAM ABEL (ed.): Documents illustrating the activities of the general and provincial chapters of the English black monks, 1215–1540. Camden Soc. 3rd series, xlv, xlvii, liv, 1931, 1933, and 1937.

**883.** REES, WILLIAM: A history of the order of St. John of Jerusalem in Wales and on the Welsh border. Cardiff, 1947.

**884.** RICHARDS, ROBERT: The Cistercian abbeys of Wales, with particular reference to Denbighshire. *Trans. Denbs. Hist. Soc.*, 1952.

**885.** TANNER, THOMAS: Notitia monastica: an account of all abbeys, etc., in England and Wales. London, 1744; later edn (with additions) by J. Nasmith, Cambridge, 1787.

### (b) Individual houses

Ministry of Works guides to the following houses should be consulted: Basingwerk, Buildwas Abbey, Cymmer, Strata Florida, Talley, Tintern, Ewenny Priory, Margam, and Valle Crucis.

### Aberconway

**886.** ELIAS, THOMAS: The history and associations of the abbeys and convents of the vale of Conway and district. *Procs. Brit. Archaeol. Assoc.,* 1898.

**887.** GRESHAM, COLIN A.: The Aberconway charter. *Arch. Camb.*, 1939.

**888.** OWEN, EDWARD: The fate of the structures of Conway abbey and Bangor and Beaumaris friaries. *Y Cymmr.*, xxvii, 1917.

**889.** Register and chronicle of the abbey of Aberconway. *Camden Misc.,* i, 1847.

### Bangor

OWEN, EDWARD: The fate of the structures of Conway abbey and Bangor and Beaumaris friaries (No. 888).

**890.** ROBERTS, GLYN: The Dominican friary of Bangor. In A history of Friars school [Bangor], 1557–1957 (No. 216).

### Basingwerk

**891.** JONES, ARTHUR: Basingwerk abbey. In Historical essays in honour of James Tait. Ed. J. G. Edwards, V. H. Galbraith, and E. F. Jacob. Manchester, 1933.

### Brecon

**892.** BANKS, RICHARD W.: Cartularium prioratus S. Iohannis Evangelistae de Brecon. *Arch. Camb.*, 1882–3; repr. London, 1884.

**893.** MORGAN, GWENLLIAN ELIZABETH FANNY: Brecon cathedral, formerly the priory church of St. John the Evangelist. Privately printed, 1935.

## Cardiff

**894.** CRONIN, JOHN M.: The ancient Benedictine priory in Cardiff. *St. Peter's Magazine,* Cardiff, 1923 (p. 247).

> See also ibid., 1922 (December).

**895.** Id.     Cardiff Grey Friars, 1280–1538. Cardiff, 1924; 2nd edn, 1929.

**896.** Id.     Cardiff Black Friars. *St. Peter's Magazine,* Cardiff, 1925 (pp. 130, 162, 194, 226, 258, 302, 322).

**897.** REES, WILLIAM: The priory of Cardiff and other Tewkesbury possessions in Glamorgan. *S. Wales and Mon. Rec. Soc. Pubns.,* ii, 1950.

**898.** Id.     (ed.): The houses of the friars at Cardiff and Newport: the first financial accounts after the suppression (1538–9). Ibid., iv, 1957.

## Cardigan

**899.** PRITCHARD, EMILY M.: Cardigan priory in the olden days. London, 1904.

> See also MALDEN, H. E.: The possessions of Cardigan priory by Chertsey abbey; a study in some medieval forgeries. *Trans. R.H.S.,* series II, v, 1911.

## Carmarthen

**900.** OWEN, GERAINT DYFNALLT: The extent and distribution of the lands of the priory of St. John's at Carmarthen. *Carm. Antiq.,* i, 1941.

**901.** PHILLIPS, THOMAS (ed.): Cartularium S. Johannis Baptistae de Carmarthen. Cheltenham, 1865.

> See also *Arch. Camb.* supplement, 1879. Original documents.

## Cwm Hir

**902.** DAY, ERNEST HERMITAGE: The Cistercian abbey of Cwm Hir. *Arch. Camb.,* 1911.

**903.** WILLIAMS, STEPHEN WILLIAM: The Cistercian abbey of Cwm Hir, Radnorshire. *Trans. Cymmr.,* 1894–5.

> See also REES, WILLIAM JENKIN: Account of Cwm Hir abbey, *Arch. Camb.,* 1849; and BANKS, RICHARD W.: Notes to the account of Cwm Hir abbey, Radnorshire, ibid., 1888.

## Cymer

ELLIS, THOMAS PETER: The story of two parishes (No. 716). Chapter viii, The founding of Cymer abbey.

**904.** OWEN, HUGH: The romance of the chalice and paten of Cymer abbey. *Jnl. Mer. Hist. and Rec. Soc.,* ii, 3, 1955.

**905.** WILLIAMS-JONES, KEITH: Llywelyn's charter to Cymer abbey in 1209. *Jnl. Mer. Hist. and Rec. Soc.,* iii, 1, 1957.

### Denbigh

**906.** EVANS, WILLIAM ABRAHAM: The Salusburys of Llewenni and the Carmelite friary in Denbigh. *Trans. Denbs. Hist. Soc.*, 1955.

### Ewenni

**907.** DAVIES, JAMES CONWAY: Ewenni priory: some recently-found records. *N.L.W. Jnl.*, iii, 1943–4.

**908.** TURBERVILLE, J. P.: Ewenni priory. London, 1901.

**909.** WELSH, C. E.: An early charter of Ewenni priory. *N.L.W. Jnl.*, x, 1957–8.

### Grace Dieu

**910.** OWEN, EDWARD: Documents relating to the dissolved monastery of Grace Dieu. *S. Wales and Mon. Rec. Soc. Pubns.*, ii, 1950.

### Llanfaes

**911.** BLOXAM, MATTHEW HOLBECHE: Some account of the friary of Llanvaes, near Beaumaris. *Arch. Camb.*, 1875.

**912.** JONES, H. LONGUEVILLE: Llanfaes friary. Ibid., 1855.

OWEN, EDWARD: The fate of the structures of Conway abbey and Bangor and Beaumaris friaries (No. 888).

### Llantarnam

**913.** EMMANUEL, HYWEL DAVID: A document relating to the monastery of Caerleon *alias* Llantarnam. *N.L.W. Jnl.*, v, 1947–8.

### Llanthony

**914.** LOVEGROVE, EDWIN WILLIAM: Llanthony priory, Monmouthshire. *Arch. Camb.*, 1947.

**915.** ROBERTS, GEORGE: Llanthony priory, Monmouthshire. Ibid., 1846.

### Margam

**916.** BIRCH, WALTER DE GRAY: A history of Margam abbey. London, 1897.

Id.　　Catalogue of Penrice and Margam MSS. (No. 665).

See also CLARK, GEORGE THOMAS: Contribution towards a cartulary of Margam. *Arch. Camb.*, 1867–8.

**917.** EVANS, ARTHUR LESLIE: Margam abbey. Port Talbot, 1958.

**918.** GRAY, THOMAS: Notes on the granges of Margam abbey. *Jnl. Brit. Archaeol. Assoc.*, n.s., ix, 1903.

### Monmouth

**919.** CLARKE, BASIL FULFORD LOWTHER: St. Mary's church, Monmouth. *Notes on churches and abbeys, No. 59, S.P.C.K.,* 1936.

**920.** MARCHEGAY, PAUL: Chartes . . . du Prieuré de Monmouth. Bibliothèque de l'Ecole des Chartes, xl. Paris, 1879.

### Neath

**921.** BIRCH, WALTER DE GRAY: A history of Neath abbey. London, 1902.

**922.** FRANCIS, GEORGE GRANT: Original charters and materials for the history of Neath and its abbey (1129–1747). Swansea, 1845.

**923.** LEWIS, DAVID: Notes on the charter of Neath abbey. *Arch. Camb.,* 1887.

**924.** SUTTON, THOMAS S.: Neath abbey. Ibid., 1887.

**925.** THOMAS, C. STANLEY, and TAYLOR, FRANK E.: Neath abbey, 1130–1938. Neath, 1939.

### Pen-rhys

**926.** ANON.: Pen-rhys, 1179–1538. Catholic Truth Soc. (Welsh province). Cardiff, n.d.

**927.** CRONIN, JOHN M.: Our Lady of Penrhys. *St. Peter's Magazine,* Cardiff, 1927 (p. 139).
> See also ibid., 1923, p. 187.

**928.** EDWARDS, THOMAS CHARLES, and WILLIAMS, GRIFFITH JOHN: Pen-rhys: y cefndir hanesyddol, and Atodiad o gerddi. *Efryd. Cath.,* v, 1951.

### Slebech

**929.** CHARLES, BERTIE GEORGE: The records of Slebech. *N.L.W. Jnl.,* v, 1947–8.

**930.** JONES, FRANCIS: Sir Rhys ap Thomas and the knights of St. John. *Carm. Antiq.,* ii, 1951.

**931.** Id.     Some Slebech notes. *N.L.W. Jnl.,* vii, 1951–2.

**932.** MORRIS, BRINLEY LLEWELYN (ed.): The Slebech story. Haverfordwest, n.d. [1948].
> See especially the contribution by Ewart O. T. Lewis.

**933.** REES, J. R.: Slebech commandery and the knights of St. John. *Arch. Camb.,* 1897–9; repr. London, 1900.

> REES, WILLIAM: A history of the order of St. John of Jerusalem in Wales and on the Welsh border (No. 883).

## St. Dogmael

**934.** PRITCHARD, EMILY M.: History of St. Dogmael's abbey. London, 1907.

**935.** VAUGHAN, HERBERT MILLINGCHAMP: The Benedictine abbey of St. Mary at St. Dogmael's. *Y Cymmr.*, xxvii, 1917.

### Strata Florida

**936.** BOWEN, EMRYS GEORGE: The monastic economy of the Cistercians at Strata Florida. *Ceredigion,* i, 1950–1.

**937.** DAVIES, JAMES CONWAY: A papal bull of privileges to the abbey of Ystrad Fflur. *N.L.W. Jnl.,* iv, 1945–6.

**938.** PIERCE, THOMAS JONES: Strata Florida abbey. *Ceredigion,* i, 1950–1.

**939.** POWELL, SAMUEL MORRIS: Pilgrim routes to Strata Florida. *Trans. Cards. Antiq. Soc.,* viii, 1931.

**940.** WILLIAMS, STEPHEN WILLIAM: The Cistercian abbey of Strata Florida. London, 1889.

### Strata Marcella

**941.** DAVIES, JAMES CONWAY: The records of the abbey of Ystrad Marchell. *Mont. Coll.,* li, 1949–50.

**942.** JONES, EVAN DAVID, DAVIES, NORMA G., and ROBERTS, RHIANNON FRANCIS: Five Strata Marcella charters. *N.L.W. Jnl.,* v, 1947–8.

**943.** JONES, MORRIS CHARLES: The abbey of Ystrad Marchell. *Mont. Coll.,* iv, v, and vi, 1871, 1873, and 1877.

**944.** OWEN, EDWARD: Strata Marcella immediately before and after its dissolution. *Y Cymmr.,* xxix, 1919.

### Talley

BACKMUND, NORBERT: Monasticon Praemonstratense, etc. (No. 863). Tomus ii, pp. 74–6.

**945.** GASQUET, FRANCIS A. (ed.): Collectanea Anglo-Premonstratensia. 3 vols. Camden Soc. 3rd series, vi, x, and xii, 1904–6.

**946.** JONES, SIMON M.: Hanes Talyllychau. Llandilo, 1891.

**947.** O'NEIL, BRYAN HUGH ST. JOHN: Talley abbey, Carmarthenshire. *Arch. Camb.,* 1941.

**948.** OWEN, EDWARD: A contribution to the history of the Praemonstratensian abbey of Talley. *Arch. Camb.,* 1893–4.

For the records of Talley see DANIEL-TYSSEN, JOHN ROBERT: Royal charters and historical documents relating to the town and county of Carmarthen and the abbeys of Talley and Tygwyn-ar-Daf, 1201–1590 (No. 587).

**949.** PRICE, FRED S.: History of Talley and Talley abbey. Swansea, 1934.

### Templars, Order of

**950.** REES, WILLIAM: The templar manor of Llanmadoc. *B.B.C.S.,* xiii, 1950.

### Tintern

**951.** HENDERSON, ARTHUR EDWARD: Tintern abbey, then and now. London, 1935.

### Valle Crucis

**952.** LOVEGROVE, EDWIN WILLIAM: Valle Crucis abbey: its position in monasticism; the men who built it. *Arch. Camb.,* 1936.

**953.** PRICE, GEORGE VERNON: Valle Crucis abbey. Liverpool, 1952.

### Whitland

**954.** RICHARD, ARTHUR JOHN: Castles, boroughs, and religious houses. In A history of Carmarthenshire (No. 605), i.

### Ysbyty Ifan

REES, WILLIAM: A history of the order of St. John of Jerusalem in Wales and on the Welsh border (No. 883).

See also WILLIAMS, WILLIAM OGWEN: A note on the history of Ysbyty Ifan. *Trans. Caerns. Hist. Soc.,* 1954.

## IX. PARISH REGISTERS AND RECORDS

For lists of parish registers see BURKE, ARTHUR MEREDYTH: Key to the ancient parish registers of England and Wales, London, 1908; census returns (1831): abstracts of the answers and returns . . . parish register abstract, vol. iii, 1834; EVANS, GEORGE EYRE: Registers in Wales, *Welsh Outlook,* viii, 1921; X.Y.Z.: List of Carmarthenshire parish registers previous to 1700 in order of their antiquity, *Trans. Carms. Antiq. Soc.,* xxv, 59, 1934. A list of bishops' transcripts formerly at St. Asaph and now in the National Library of Wales will be found in *B.B.C.S.,* i, 2, 1922, pp. 158–66. Registers of the following Shropshire parishes formerly in the diocese of St. Asaph have been published by the Shropshire Parish Register Society: Melverley, 1899; Halston, 1899; Selattyn, 1901; Oswestry, 1904–14; Kinnerley, 1905; Whittington, 1910; Knockin and Llanyblodwel, 1912–13; Llanymynech, 1917; St. Martins, 1920–22.

**955.** Transcripts of parish registers:

(*a*) Brecknock, St. David, 1711–1810. Ed. Edwin Davies. Brecon, 1905.

(*b*) Caerwent, 1568–1812. Ed. Joseph Bradney. London, 1920.

(*c*) Carmarthen, St. Peter's, 1671–1799. *West Wales Hist. Rec.,* vii–xiv.

(*d*) Conway, 1541–1793. Ed. Alice Hadley. London, 1900.

(*e*) Chepstow, 1596–1646 (burials, selections). *Cymru Fu,* ii, 1891.

(*f*) Id.    1597–1737 (excerpts). Ed. Ivor Waters. Chepstow, 1955.

(*g*) Eglwys Cymmin, 1732–1812. *Trans. Carms. Antiq. Soc.,* v, 1909–10.

(*h*) Erbistock, 1679–1778. *Arch. Camb.,* 1888.

(*i*) Glasbury, 1660–1836. Par. Reg. Soc., lii, 1904.

(*j*) Grosmont, 1589–1812. Ed. J. A. Bradney. London, 1921.

(*k*) Kegidog, *alias* St. George, co. Denbigh, 1694–1749. Ed. F. A. Crisp. London, 1890.

(*l*) Kerry, 1602–1707. *Mont. Coll.,* xxxix, 1915–20.

(*m*) Lampeter, 1695–1734. *Welsh Gazette,* 1903–5.

(*n*) Llanbadog, 1582–1709. Ed. J. A. Bradney. London, 1919.

(*o*) Llanddewi Rhydderch, 1670–1783. Ed. J. A. Bradney. 1919.

(*p*) Llanelly, 1685–1837 (marriages). In Arthur Mee: Llanelly parish. church (No. 609).

(*q*) Llanfair Discoed, 1680–1812, in Registra antiqua de Caerwent et Llanfair Discoed. Ed. J. A. Bradney. London, 1920.

(*r*) Llanfihangel Ystern Llewern, 1685–1812. Ed. J. A. Bradney, 1920.

(*s*) Llanllugan, 1602–1790. *Mont. Coll.,* xxxiv–xxxv, 1905–10.

(*t*) Llansannan, 1667–1812 Ed. R. Ellis. Liverpool, 1904.

(*u*) Llantilio Crossenny and Penrhos, 1577–1644. Ed. J. A. Bradney. London, 1916.

(*v*) Llantrithyd, 1571–1810. Ed. H. Seymour Hughes. London, 1888.

(*w*) Mallwyd, 1568–1610. *Mont. Coll.,* xxx–xxxii, 1897–1902.

(*x*) Meliden, 1602–1718. *Northern Flintshire,* i, 1913.

(*y*) Penrhos. See Llantilio Crossenny.

(*z*) Peterston super Ely, 1749–1812. Ed. A. F. C. Langley. 1888.

(*aa*) Rhylofnoyd (Newmarket), 1696–1719. *Northern Flintshire,* i, 1913.

(*bb*) Trefdraeth, 1550–1663. Ed. Hugh Owen. *Trans. Angl. Antiq. Soc.,* 1924.

(*cc*) Trefeglwys, 1625–63. *Mont. Coll.,* xxxii–xxxiii, 1902–4; 1695–6, ed. Sir Thomas Phillips, Middle Hill.

(*dd*) Welshpool, 1634–1758 (extracts). Ibid., xxxvi, 1910–12.

(*ee*) Wrexham, 1618–1823 (extracts), in Palmer, Alfred Neobard: History of the town of Wrexham (No. 644).

For descriptions of parish registers and records, see the following:

**956.** DAVIES, T. A.: The Llanishen register, 1591–1778. *Mons. Review*, i, 1, 1933.

**957.** ELSAS, MADELINE: Parish records. *Jnl. Hist. Soc. Church in Wales*, iv, 1954.

**958.** EVANS, GEORGE EYRE: Cardiganshire: its plate, records, and registers. *Arch. Camb.*, 1906.

**959.** Id.     Carmarthenshire: bishop's transcripts, 1671. *Trans. Carms. Antiq. Soc.*, xiii, 35, 1918–19.

**960.** JAMES, FRANK T.: Notes on the parish register of Merthyr Tydfil from A.D. 1703 to 1763. *Y Cymmr.*, xxxv, 1925.

**961.** JONES, THOMAS IEUAN JEFFREYS: Carmarthenshire parish records. *Carm. Antiq.*, ii, 3 and 4, 1951 and 1957.

**962.** LAWS, EDWARD: The registers of Gumfreston parish, co. Pembroke. *Arch. Camb.*, 1900.

**963.** LEWIS, THOMAS HARRIS: Notes on the Llandebie parish registers, 1695–1812. *Trans. Carms. Antiq. Soc.*, xxvi, 61, 1936.

**964.** MORGAN, JOSEPH (Canon): The old registers of Panteg, Monmouthshire. *Mons. Review*, i, 2, 1933.

**965.** OWEN, THOMAS J.: The records of the parish of Aber. *Trans. Caerns. Hist. Soc.*, 1953.

**966.** PHILLIPS, JAMES: The oldest parish registers in Pembrokeshire. *Arch. Camb.*, 1902, 1903, 1905.

**967.** ROBERTS, ENID PIERCE: Llyfrau festri [Llangadfan, Mont.]. *Yr Haul*, Haf a Hydref, 1953.

**968.** THOMAS, G. BOWEN: Llanaber vestry records, 1726–54. *Jnl. Mer. Hist. and Rec. Soc.*, ii, 4, 1956.

**969.** THOMAS, HENRY: An old vestry book [Towyn, Merioneth, 1723–43]. Ibid., ii, 1, 1953.

**970.** WILLIAMS, O. GAIANYDD: Llyfr festri plwyf Caerhun, 1785–1825. *Y Tyddynwr*, i, 1922–3.

**971.** WILLIAMS, R. R.: The parish registers of Penrhoslligwy, 1578–1837. *Trans. Angl. Antiq. Soc.*, 1957.

**972.** X.Y.Z.: Kidwelly parish registers. *Trans. Carms. Antiq. Soc.*, xviii, 45, 1924–5.

# SECTION C

## ANCIENT WALES TO A.D. 400

Conditions in ancient Wales form part of the general pattern of prehistory, but an attempt has been made to indicate separately material which applies particularly to the present geographical limits of the country.

Especially important are the following:

Royal Commission on ancient monuments in Wales and Monmouthshire, inventories (No. 382); *Arch. Camb.* and *B.B.C.S., passim*; A hundred years of Welsh archaeology, centenary volume of the Cambrian Archaeological Association, Gloucester, 1946; A survey and policy of field research in the archaeology of Great Britain, Council for British Archaeology, London, 1948.

See also Archaeological bulletin for the British Isles, and Archaeological bibliography for Great Britain and Ireland (No. 2).

For a study of the Celtic peoples, works dealing with the Celts of Ireland and the Continent should be consulted. The subject, too, cannot be divorced from the subjects of Celtic religion, law, and language. The following works may be mentioned: ALLEN, JOHN ROMILLY: Celtic art in pagan and Christian times, London, 1906; DE JUBAINVILLE, HENRI D'ARBOIS: Études sur le droit celtique, 2 vols., Paris, 1895; id., Les Celtes depuis les temps les plus anciens jusqu'à l'an 100 avant notre ère, Paris, 1904; id., Les Druides et les dieux celtiques, Paris, 1906; BERTRAND, ALEXANDRE: La religion des Gaulois, les Druides, et le Druidisme, Paris, 1897; DELARGY, JAMES H.: The Gaelic story-teller, Rhŷs Memorial Lecture, *Procs. Brit. Acad.*, xxxi, 1945; DOTTIN, GEORGES: Manuel pour servir à l'étude de l'antiquité celtique, 2nd edn, Paris, 1915; id.: Les anciens peuples de l'Europe, Paris, 1916; id.: La langue Gauloise, Paris, 1920; EVANS, ARTHUR: Origins of Celtic art, *Rhind Lectures*, 1895; Fox, CYRIL FREDERICK : Pattern and purpose, a survey of early Celtic art, Cardiff, 1958; GRENIER, ALBERT: Les Gaules, 2nd edn, Paris, 1945; VAN HAMEL, ANTON GERARD: Aspects of Celtic mythology, Rhŷs Memorial Lecture, *Procs. Brit. Acad.*, xx, 1934; HUBERT, HENRI: The rise of the Celts, London, 1933; id.: The greatness and decline of the Celts, London, 1934; JACOBSTHAL, PAUL: Early Celtic art, Oxford, 1944; KENDRICK, THOMAS DOWNING: The Druids, London, 1927; KRAFT, GEORGE: The origin of the Celts, *Antiquity*, 1929; LAMBRECHTS, PIERRE: Contributions à l'étude des divinités celtiques, Bruges, 1942; MEYER, KUNO: Early relations between Gael and Brython, *Trans. Cymmr.*, 1895–6; NAVARRO, JOSE MARIA: A survey of research on an early phase of Celtic culture, Rhŷs Memorial Lecture, *Procs. Brit. Acad.*, xxii, 1936; DE PAOR, MAIRE and LIAM: Early Christian Ireland, London, 1958; POWELL, THOMAS GEORGE EYRE: The Celtic settlements of Ireland, *Chadwick Memorial Studies,* Cambridge, 1950; id.: The Celts, London, 1958; O'RAHILLY, THOMAS FRANCIS: Early Irish history and mythology, Dublin, 1946; RHŶS, JOHN: Celtic Britain (No. 1194); SJOESTEDT, MARIE-LOUISE: Dieux et heros des Celtes, Paris, 1940; VENDRYES, JOSEPH: La position linguistique du Celtique, Rhŷs Memorial Lecture, *Procs. Brit. Acad.*, xxiii, 1937.

See also the Cambridge Ancient History, vol. i, ch. VII, and vol. ii, ch. xv, with the bibliography appended to each; and EYRE, EDWARD (ed.): European civilisation, Oxford, 1935, vol. ii, ch. 1.

## I. GENERAL PREHISTORY

**973.** ABERCROMBY, LORD JOHN: The bronze age pottery of Great Britain and Ireland. Oxford, 1912.

**974.** ALLCROFT, A. Hadrian: Earthwork of England. London, 1908.

**975.** BRADFORD, JOHN SPENCER PURVIS: Ancient landscapes. London, 1957.

**976.** British Museum Guides: Flint implements, 1950; Antiquities of Roman Britain, 1951; Later prehistoric antiquities of the British Isles, 1953.

> Earlier editions are still useful, viz. Stone age antiquities, 1926; Guide to the antiquities of the bronze age, 1920; Guide to the early iron age antiquities, 1925; and Guide to the antiquities of Roman Britain.

**977.** BRUCE-MITFORD, RUPERT LEO SCOTT: Recent archaeological excavations in Britain. London, 1956.

**978.** BURKITT, MILES CRAWFORD: The old stone age. 3rd edn. Cambridge, 1955.

**979.** BUTLER, JAY, and SMITH, ISOBEL: Razors, urns, and the British middle bronze age. 12th Annual Report of the University of London Institute of Archaeology, 1956.

**980.** CHILDE, VERE GORDON: The bronze age. Cambridge, 1930.

**981.** Id.    Prehistoric communities of the British Isles. 3rd edn. London, 1947.

**982.** Id.    The dawn of European civilisation. 6th edn. London, 1957.

**983.** Id.    The final bronze age in the Near East and temperate Europe. Procs. Prehist. Soc., 1948.

**984.** CLARK, JOHN GRAHAM DOUGLAS: The mesolithic age in Britain. Cambridge, 1932.

**985.** Id.    Prehistoric Europe: the economic basis. Cambridge, 1952.

**986.** Id.    Excavations at Starr Carr. Cambridge, 1954.

**987.** COON, CARLETON STEVENS: The races of Europe. New York, 1939.

**988.** CRAWFORD, OSBERT GUY STANHOPE: The long barrows of the Cotswolds. Gloucester, 1925.

**989.** Id.    The eye goddess. London, 1957.

**990.** DANIEL, GLYN EDMUND: The dual nature of the megalithic colonisation of prehistoric Europe. *Procs. Prehist. Soc.,* 1941.

**991.** Id.       The megalithic monuments of England and Wales. Cambridge, 1950.

**992.** Id.       The long barrow in western Europe. *Chadwick Memorial Studies.* Cambridge, 1950.

**993.** Id.       Who were the Welsh? Rhŷs Memorial Lecture. *Procs. Brit. Acad.,* xl, 1954.

**994.** Id.       The megalith builders of western Europe. London, 1958.

**995.** DAVIES, MARGARET: Types of megalithic monuments of the Irish Sea and North Channel coastlands. *Antiq. Jnl.,* 1945.

**996.** EVANS, JOHN: Ancient bronze implements of Great Britain. London, 1881.

**997.** Id.       Ancient stone implements of Great Britain. 2nd edn. London, 1897.

**998.** FLEURE, HERBERT JOHN: The natural history of man in Britain. London, 1951.

**999.** Id.       and WHITEHOUSE, WALLACE EDWARD: Early distribution and valleyward movement of population. *Arch. Camb.,* 1916.

**1000.** FOX, CYRIL FREDERICK: Burial ritual and customs in the bronze age. *Chadwick Memorial Studies.* Cambridge, 1950.

**1001.** Id.       The personality of Britain. 4th edn, 3rd impression. Cardiff, 1952.

**1002.** GARROD, DOROTHY ELIZABETH: The upper palaeolithic age in Britain. Oxford, 1926.

**1003.** HAWKES, CHARLES FRANCIS CHRISTOPHER: The prehistoric foundations of Europe. London, 1940.

**1004.** Id.       From bronze age to iron age . . . Middle Europe, Italy, the north and west. *Procs. Prehist. Soc.,* 1948.

**1005.** Id.       On some buckets and cauldrons of the bronze and early iron ages. *Antiq. Jnl.,* 1957.

**1006.** HAWKES, JACQUETTA, and CHARLES FRANCIS CHRISTOPHER: Prehistoric Britain. London, 1947. 4th impression, 1953.

**1007.** HODGES, H. W. M.: Studies in the late bronze age in Ireland. *Ulster Arch. Jnl.,* 1954 and 1956.

**1008.** KENDRICK, THOMAS DOWNING, and HAWKES, CHARLES FRANCIS CHRISTOPHER: Archaeology in England and Wales, 1914–31. London, 1932.

**1009.** KENYON, KATHLEEN MARY: A survey of evidence concerning the chronology and origins of iron age 'A' in southern and midland Britain. *8th Annual Report of the University of London Institute of Archaeology*, 1952.

**1010.** LACAILLE, ARMAND DONALD: The stone age in Scotland. Oxford, 1954.

**1011.** LEEDS, EDWARD THURLOW: Celtic ornament in the British Isles down to A.D. 700. Oxford, 1933.

**1012.** MOVIUS, HALLAM L.: The Irish stone age. Cambridge, 1942.

**1013.** PIGGOTT, STUART: The early bronze age in Wessex. *Procs. Prehist. Soc.*, 1938.

**1014.** Id.     British prehistory. Oxford, 1949.

**1015.** Id.     The neolithic cultures of the British Isles. Cambridge, 1954.

**1016.** O'RIORDAIN, SEAN PADRAIG: Antiquities of the Irish countryside. 3rd edn. London, 1953.

**1017.** SANDARS, NANCY: The bronze age cultures of France. Cambridge, 1957.

**1018.** SAVORY, HUBERT NEWMAN: The 'Sword Bearers': A reinterpretation. *Procs. Prehist. Soc.*, 1948.

**1019.** WHEELER, ROBERT ERIC MORTIMER: Maiden castle, Dorset. Oxford, 1943.

**1020.** ZEUNER, FREDERICK EVERARD: Dating the past. An introduction to geochronology. 2nd edn. London, 1950.

## II. ROMAN BRITAIN

**1021.** BIRLEY, ERIC: Roman Britain and the Roman army. Kendal, 1953.

**1022.** BRUCE, JOHN COLLINGWOOD: Handbook to the Roman Wall. 10th edn. Newcastle upon Tyne, 1947.

**1023.** CHARLESWORTH, MARTIN P.: The lost province. Cardiff, 1949.

**1024.** COLLINGWOOD, ROBIN GEORGE: The archaeology of Roman Britain. London, 1930.

**1025.** Id.     Roman Britain. 3rd edn. Oxford, 1934.

**1026.** Id.     Roman Britain, in FRANK, TENNEY: Economic survey of ancient Rome. Vol. iii. Baltimore, 1937.

**1027.** Id.      and MYERS, JOHN LINTON: Roman Britain and the English settlements. Oxford, 1937.

**1028.** DAVIES, OLIVER: Roman mines in Europe. Oxford, 1935.

**1029.** HAVERFIELD, FRANCIS: The Romanization of Roman Britain. 4th edn, revised by G. Macdonald. Oxford, 1923.

**1030.** Id.      The Roman occupation of Britain. Oxford, 1924.

**1031.** MACDONALD, GEORGE: Roman Britain, 1914–28.

**1032.** Id.      The Roman Wall in Scotland. 2nd edn. Oxford, 1934.

Ordnance Survey of Great Britain. Map of Roman Britain (No. 380).

**1033.** RICHMOND, IAN ARCHIBALD: Roman Britain. Harmondsworth, 1955.

**1034.** RIVET, ALBERT LIONEL FREDERICK: Town and country in Roman Britain. London, 1958.

### III. WALES

#### (a) Anthropology and General Prehistory

**1035.** DANIEL, GLYN EDMUND: The cromlechs of Glamorgan. *Morgannwg,* i, 1957.

DAVIES, ELLIS: The prehistoric and Roman remains of Denbighshire (No. 624).

Id.      The prehistoric and Roman remains of Flintshire (No. 657).

**1036.** FLEURE, HERBERT JOHN: Ancient Wales: anthropological evidences. *Trans. Cymmr.,* 1915–16.

**1037.** Id.      Anthropometric tables. *B.B.C.S.,* iv, 2, 1928—vii, 3, 1934.

**1037A.** Id. and DAVIES, ELWYN: Physical character among Welshmen. *Jnl. R. Anthrop. Inst.,* 1958.

**1038.** Id.      and JAMES, THOMAS CAMPBELL: Geographical distribution of anthropological types in Wales. *Jnl. R. Anthrop. Inst.,* 1916.

**1039.** GRIFFITHS, WILLIAM ERIC: Notes on some of the prehistoric pottery of Anglesey. *Trans. Angl. Antiq. Soc.,* 1956.

**1040.** GRIMES, WILLIAM FRANCIS: The prehistoric period. In A hundred years of Welsh archaeology (No. 395).

**1041.** Id.     The prehistory of Wales. 2nd edn. Cardiff, 1951.

**1042.** HEMP, WILFRID JAMES: Bryn yr Hen Bobl chambered cairn, Plas Newydd. *Trans. Angl. Antiq. Soc.*, 1953.

**1043.** PEATE, IORWERTH CYFEILIOG: The Dyfi basin: physical anthropology and dialect distribution. *Jnl. R. Anthrop. Inst.*, 1925.

**1044.** RHŶS, JOHN: Celtic folklore, Welsh and Manx. 2 vols. Oxford, 1901.

**1045.** WHEELER, ROBERT ERIC MORTIMER: Prehistoric and Roman Wales. Oxford, 1925.

### (b) The Stone and Early Bronze Ages

**1046.** CHITTY, LILY FRANCES: Notes on the Irish affinities of three bronze age food vessels of type 1A found in Wales. *B.B.C.S.*, ix, 1937–9.

**1047.** DUNNING, GERALD CLOUGH: A stone circle and cairn on Mynydd Epynt, Brecknockshire. *Arch. Camb.*, 1943.

**1048.** FOX, AILEEN: The dual colonisation of east Glamorgan in the neolithic and bronze ages. *Arch. Camb.*, 1936.

**1049.** FOX, CYRIL FREDERICK: On two beakers of the early bronze age (South Wales); with a record of the distribution of beaker-pottery in England and Wales. Ibid., 1925.

**1050.** Id.     The Ysceifiog circle and barrow, Flintshire. Ibid., 1926.

**1051.** Id.     Corston Beacon: An early bronze age cairn in S. Pembrokeshire. Ibid., 1928.

**1052.** Id.     Two bronze age cairns in South Wales: Simondston and Pond cairns, Coity. *Archaeologia,* lxxxvii.

**1053.** Id.     Stake-circles in turf barrows: a record of excavation in Glamorgan, 1939–40. *Antiq. Jnl.,* 1941.

**1054.** Id.     A bronze age barrow . . . in Llandow parish, Glamorgan. *Archaeologia,* lxxxix.

**1055.** GRIFFITHS, WILLIAM ERIC: The typology and origins of beakers in Wales. *Procs. Prehist. Soc.,* 1957.

**1056.** GRIMES, WILLIAM FRANCIS: The megalithic monuments of Wales. *Procs. Prehist. Soc.,* 1936.

**1057.** Id.     A barrow on Breach farm, Llanbleddian (Glam.). *Procs. Prehist. Soc.,* 1938.

**1058.** Id.      The excavation of Ty-isaf long cairn, Brecknockshire. *Procs. Prehist. Soc.,* 1939.

**1059.** Id.      Pentre-Ifan burial chamber, Pembrokeshire. *Arch. Camb.,* 1948.

**1060.** HEMP, WILFRID JAMES: The Capel Garmon chambered cairn. Ibid., 1927.

**1061.** Id.      The chambered cairn of Bryn Celli Ddu, Anglesey. *Archaeologia,* lxxx.

**1062.** Id.      The chambered cairn known as Bryn yr Hen Bobl near Plas Newydd, Anglesey. *Archaeologia,* lxxxv.

**1063.** LACAILLE, ARMAND DONALD: A hand-axe from Penylan, Cardiff. *Antiq. Jnl.,* 1954.

**1064.** Id.      Excavations on Caldey, Pembrokeshire. *Arch. Camb.,* 1955.

**1065.** Id.      and GRIMES, WILLIAM FRANCIS: The prehistory of Caldey. Ibid., 1956.

**1066.** POWELL, THOMAS GEORGE EYRE: The gold ornament from Mold, Flintshire. *Procs. Prehist. Soc.,* 1953.

**1067.** Id.      and DANIEL, GLYN EDMUND: Barclodiad y Gawres, Anglesey. Liverpool, 1956.

**1068.** SAVORY, HUBERT NEWMAN: Unpublished bronze age pottery from west Wales. *Arch. Camb.,* 1941.

**1069.** Id.      Two middle bronze age palisade barrows at Letterston, Pembrokeshire. Ibid., 1948.

**1070.** Id.      The excavation of the Pipton long cairn, Brecknockshire. Ibid., 1956.

**1071.** Id.      The excavation of 'Twlc-y-filiast' cromlech, Llangynog (Carms.). *B.B.C.S.,* xvi, 4, 1956.

**1072.** Id.      A corpus of Welsh bronze age pottery: 1, beakers; 2, food-vessels, etc.; 3, pygmy cups. Ibid., xvi, 3, 1955; xvii, 3, 1957; and xviii, 1, 1958.

**1073.** SHOTTON, F. W., CHITTY, LILY FRANCES, and SEABY, W. A.: A new centre of stone axe dispersal on the Welsh border. *Procs. Prehist. Soc.,* 1951.

**1074.** SOLLAS, WILLIAM JOHNSON: The Paviland cave—an Aurignacian station in Wales. *Jnl. R. Anthrop. Inst.,* 1913.

**1075.** THOMAS, H. H.: The sources of the stone of the inner circle of Stonehenge. *Antiq. Jnl.,* 1923.

**1076.** THOMAS, R., and DUDLYKE, E. R.: The flint chipping floor at Aberystwyth. *Jnl. R. Anthrop. Inst.*, 1925.

**1077.** WARREN, S. HAZZLEDINE: Excavations at the stone-axe factory, Graig Lwyd, Penmaenmawr. *Jnl. R. Anthrop. Inst.*, 1921.

**1078.** WILLIAMS, AUDREY: Clegyr Boia, St. David's, Pembrokeshire: Excavations in 1943. *Arch. Camb.*, 1952.

### (c) The Late Bronze and Iron Ages

**1079.** BERSU, GERHARD, and GRIFFITHS, WILLIAM ERIC: Concentric circles at Llwyn-du Bach, Penygroes, Caernarvonshire. *Arch. Camb.*, 1949.

**1080.** CRAWFORD, OSBERT GUY STANHOPE, and WHEELER, ROBERT ERIC MORTIMER: The Llynfawr and other hoards of the bronze age. *Archaeologia*, lxxi.

**1081.** FOX, AILEEN: Hill-slope forts and related earthworks in south-west England and South Wales. *Arch. Jnl.*, 1952.

**1082.** FOX, CYRIL FREDERICK: A La Tène I brooch from Wales, with notes on typology and distribution. *Arch. Camb.*, 1927.

**1083.** Id.     A settlement of the early iron age (La Tène I) on Merthyr Mawr warren. Ibid., 1927.

**1084.** Id.     A second cauldron and iron sword from the Llyn Fawr hoard. *Antiq. Jnl.*, 1939.

**1085.** Id.     A shield boss of the early iron age from Anglesey. *Arch. Camb.*, 1945.

**1086.** Id.     A find of the early iron age from Llyn Cerrig Bach, Anglesey. Cardiff, 1947.

**1087.** Id.     Celtic mirror handles in Britain. *Arch. Camb.*, 1948.

**1088.** GRIFFITHS, WILLIAM ERIC: Excavations on Penmaenmawr, 1950. *Arch. Camb.*, 1954.

**1089.** Id.     Excavation of a hut-group near Rhiwlas (Caerns.). Ibid. (Miscellany).

**1090.** Id.     The Pant-y-maen bronze hoard. *B.B.C.S.*, xvii, 1956–8.

**1091.** Id.     and HOGG, ALEXANDER HUBERT ARTHUR: The hill-fort on Conway mountain, Caernarvonshire. *Arch. Camb.*, 1956.

**1092.** HEMP, WILFRID JAMES: A La Tène shield from Moel Hiraddug, Flintshire. *Arch. Camb.*, 1928.

**1093.** HUGHES, IEUAN THOMAS: Earthworks of Montgomeryshire. *Mont. Coll.*, 1924.

**1094.** NASH-WILLIAMS, VICTOR ERLE: An early iron age hill-fort at Llanmelin, near Caerwent, Monmouthshire. *Arch. Camb.*, 1933.

**1095.** Id.     An early iron age coastal camp at Sudbrook, Monmouthshire. Ibid., 1939.

**1096.** SAVORY, HUBERT NEWMAN: List of hill-forts and other earthworks in Wales. *B.B.C.S.*, xiii, 1949–50. In progress.

**1097.** Id.     Discoveries on Merthyr Mawr warren and a burial cave at Llanferres, Denbighshire. Ibid., xiv, 1950–2.

**1098.** Id.     The excavation of an early iron age fortified settlement on Mynydd Bychan, Llysworney, Glamorgan. *Arch. Camb.*, 1954–5 and 1955–6.

**1099.** Id.     The late bronze age in Wales. Ibid., 1958.

**1100.** SHEPHERD, THOMAS: The Parc-y-meirch hoard, St. George, Denbighshire. *Arch. Camb.*, 1941.

VARLEY, WILLIAM JONES: The hill-forts of the Welsh marches (No. 817).

**1101.** WILLIAMS, AUDREY: Excavations at the Knave promontory fort, Rhossili, Glamorgan. *Arch. Camb.*, 1939.

**1102.** Id.     The excavation of the Bishopston valley promontory fort, Glamorgan. Ibid., 1940.

**1103.** Id.     The excavation of High Penard promontory fort, Glamorgan. Ibid., 1941.

**1104.** Id.     A promontory fort at Henllan, Cardiganshire. Ibid., 1945.

### (d) Roman Wales

**1105.** ALCOCK, LESLIE: Castell Collen excavations. *Trans. Rads. Soc.*, 1954–5.

**1106.** BIRLEY, ERIC: Roman garrisons in Wales. *Arch. Camb.*, 1952.

**1107.** CRASTER, O. E.: The east gate and adjoining town wall of the Roman town at Caerwent, Monmouthshire. Ibid., 1954.

DAVIES, ELLIS: Prehistoric and Roman remains in Denbighshire (No. 624).

Id.     Prehistoric and Roman remains in Flintshire (No. 657).

**1108.** DAVIES, OLIVER: Finds at Dolaucothy. *Arch. Camb.*, 1936.

**1109.** FOX, AILEEN: Excavations in Myrtle Cottage orchard, Caerleon, 1939. Ibid., 1940.

**1110.** GRIFFITHS, WILLIAM ERIC: Topographical list of Roman remains found in North Wales. *B.B.C.S.*, xii, 1946–8.

**1111.** Id. Excavations at Caer Gybi, Holyhead. *Arch. Camb.*, 1954 (Miscellany).

**1112.** GRIMES, WILLIAM FRANCIS: Holt, Denbighshire. *Y Cymmr.*, 1930.

**1113.** HALL, JOSEPH PLATT: Caer Llugwy. Manchester, 1923.

**1114.** HAVERFIELD, FRANCIS: Military aspect of Roman Wales. *Trans. Cymmr.*, 1908–9.

**1115.** IRVINE, HUGH COLLEY: The Roman road between Caer Gai and Tomen y Mûr. *B.B.C.S.*, xvii, 1956–8.

**1116.** Id. Note on the Roman station at Pennal, Merionethshire. Ibid.

**1117.** JONES, G. D. BARRI, and THOMSON, R. D.: The Roman fort at Caerau, Brecknockshire. *B.B.C.S.*, xvii, 1956–8.

MARGARY, IVAN DONALD: Roman roads in Britain, II (No. 380).

**1118.** NASH-WILLIAMS, VICTOR ERLE: Topographical list of Roman remains found in South Wales. *B.B.C.S.*, iv, 1927–9.

**1119.** Id. The Roman legionary fortress at Caerleon. Report on the excavation carried out in 1926. *Arch. Camb.*, 1929.

**1120.** Id. Report on the excavations carried out in the Prysg field, Caerleon. Ibid., 1931–3.

**1121.** Id. The Roman legionary fortress at Caerleon, Monmouthshire. 3rd edn. Cardiff, 1952.

**1122.** Id. The Roman villa at Llanfrynach, Brecknockshire. *B.B.C.S.*, xiii, 1948–50.

**1123.** Id. The Roman gold-mines at Dolaucothi. *B.B.C.S.*, xiv, 1950–2.

**1124.** Id. The Roman inscribed and sculptured stones found at Caerwent. Ibid., 1952–4.

**1125.** Id. Caergai and the Roman military occupation of Wales. *Jnl. Mer. Hist. and Rec. Soc.*, ii, 1, 1953.

**1126.** Id.      The forum and basilica and public baths of the Roman town of Venta Silurum at Caerwent in Monmouthshire. Ibid.

**1127.** Id.      The Roman villa at Llantwit Major, Glam. *Arch. Camb.,* 1953.

**1128.** Id.      Excavations at Caerwent and Caerleon. *B.B.C.S.,* xv, 1952–4.

**1129.** Id.      The Roman frontier in Wales. Cardiff, 1954.

**1130.** Id.      Excavations at Caerleon in 1954 and 1955. *Jnl. Rom. Stud.,* 1954–5.

**1131.** Id.      and NASH-WILLIAMS, ALVAH HARRY: Catalogue of the Roman inscribed stones found at Caerleon, Monmouthshire. Cardiff, 1935.

**1132.** PRYCE, FREDERICK NORMAN, and PRYCE, THOMAS DAVIES: Forden Gaer. *Arch. Camb.,* 1927–30.

**1133.** RANDALL, HENRY JOHN: The Roman period. In A hundred years of Welsh archaeology (No. 395).

**1134.** REYNOLDS, PAUL KENNETH BAILLIE: Caerhun. *Arch. Camb.,* 1926–30.

**1135.** THOMAS, HOWARD: Roman discoveries in the vale of Glamorgan. *B.B.C.S.,* xvii, 1956–8, pp. 294–6.

**1136.** WARD, JOHN: The Roman fort of Gellygaer. London, 1903.

**1137.** WEBSTER, GRAHAM: The lead-mining industry in North Wales in Roman times. *Flints. Hist. Soc. Pubns.,* xiii, 1952–3.

**1138.** WHEELER, ROBERT ERIC MORTIMER: Ely Roman villa. *Jnl. Rom. Stud.,* 1921.

**1139.** Id.      Roman coin hoards in Wales. *B.B.C.S.,* i, 1923.

**1140.** Id.      Prehistoric and Roman Wales. Oxford, 1925.

**1141.** Id.      Segontium and the Roman occupation of Wales. *Y Cymmr.,* xxxiii, 1923.

**1142.** Id.      Y Gaer: the Roman fort near Brecon. *Y Cymmr.,* xxxvii, 1926.

**1143.** Id.      The Roman amphitheatre at Caerleon. *Archaeologia,* 1928.

**1144.** Id.      Roman archaeology in Wales: A tribute to V. E. Nash-Williams. B.B.C. annual lecture (Welsh Home Service). London, 1957.
      See review by Lewis, Ceri Williams: Cymru a'r cyfnod Rhufeinig. *Llên Cymru,* iv, 1957.

**1145.** WRIGHT, RICHARD PEARSON, and RICHMOND, IAN ARCHIBALD: The Roman inscribed and sculptured stones in the Grosvenor Museum, Chester. Chester, 1955.

### (e) Native Wales

**1146.** BAYNES, NEIL: Excavations at Din Lligwy. *Arch. Camb.*, 1908 and 1930.

**1147.** GARDNER, WILLOUGHBY: Native hill-forts in North Wales (with bibliographical references to many other papers by Dr. Gardner, notably on Y Gorddyn and Dinorben). Ibid., 1926.

**1148.** GRIFFITHS, WILLIAM ERIC: Early settlements in Caernarvonshire. Ibid., 1950.

**1149.** Id. The development of native homesteads in North Wales. *Antiquity*, 1951.

**1150.** HAWKES, CHARLES FRANCIS CHRISTOPHER: Bronze-workers, cauldrons and bucket-animals in iron age and Roman Britain. In GRIMES, WILLIAM FRANCIS (ed.): Aspects of archaeology in Britain and beyond, being essays presented to O. G. S. Crawford. London, 1951.

**1151.** HEMP, WILFRID JAMES: A hill-fort problem. *Arch. Camb.*, 1942.

**1152.** Id. and GRESHAM, COLIN A.: Hut-circles in north-west Wales. *Antiquity*, 1944.

**1153.** HUGHES, HAROLD: Report on excavations at Tre'r Ceiri, in 1906. *Arch. Camb.*, 1907.

**1154.** Id. Prehistoric remains on Penmaenmawr. Ibid., 1912, 1913, 1915, 1922, 1923.

**1155.** O'NEIL, BRYAN HUGH ST. JOHN: Excavations at Caerau ancient village, Clynnog, Caernarvonshire. *Antiq. Jnl.,* 1936.

**1156.** SAVORY, HUBERT NEWMAN: Some sub-Romano-British brooches from South Wales. In HARDEN, DONALD B. (ed.): Dark age Britain. London, 1956.

**1157.** Id. Excavations at Dinorben hill-fort, Abergele (Denbs.), 1956–7. *B.B.C.S.*, xvii, 1956–8.

**1158.** WHEELER, ROBERT ERIC MORTIMER: Roman and native in Wales: An imperial frontier problem. *Trans. Cymmr.,* 1920–1.

**1159.** WILLIAMS, HOWEL: The Romano-British site at Rhostryfan, Caernarvonshire. *Arch. Camb.*, 1922–3.

# SECTION D

## *A.D.  400—1039*

### I. SOURCES

**1160.** Anglo-Saxon chronicle. Two of the Saxon chronicles parallel. Ed. John Earle and Charles Plummer. 2 vols. Oxford, 1892–9.

> Translations by GARMONSWAY, GEORGE NORMAN: The Anglo-Saxon chronicle, Everyman's Library, 2nd edn, London, 1955; and by WHITELOCK, DOROTHY: English historical documents, i, London, 1955.

**1161.** Annales Cambriae. Ed. John Williams 'Ab Ithel'. *Rolls Series.* London, 1860.

**1162.** ASSER: Life of Alfred. Ed. W. H. Stevenson. Oxford, 1904.

> Translation in Six old English chronicles, Bohn's Antiq. Library, 1900; Welsh translation by J. O. JONES in O lygad y ffynnon, Y Bala, 1899. See also ADAMSON, JOHN WILLIAM: The illiterate Anglo-Saxon, Cambridge, 1946.

**1163.** BEDE: Historical works. Ed. Charles Plummer. 2 vols. i, introduction and text; ii, notes and index. Oxford, 1896.

> Translation by A. M. SELLER, London, 1912.

**1164.** The Bruts:

(i) Brut y tywysogyon. Ed. John Rhŷs and John Gwenogvryn Evans. In The red book of Hergest. Vol. ii. Oxford, 1890.

> Superseded by (vi) below.

(ii) Brenhinedd y Saeson [to 1197; often miscalled 'Brut y Saeson', a title which should properly be reserved for (iii) below], printed in *Myvyrian archaiology of Wales*, vol. ii (No. 117).

(iii) Brut y Saeson. Ed. John Rhŷs and John Gwenogvryn Evans. In No. 1164 (i). Vol. i.

(iv) Brut y tywysogyon. Peniarth MS. 20 version. Ed. Thomas Jones (No. 130 (6)).

(v) Brut y tywysogyon, or the chronicle of the princes. Peniarth MS. 20 version. Translated by Thomas Jones (No. 130 (11)).

(vi) Brut y tywysogyon, or the chronicle of the princes. Red book of Hergest version. Critical text and translation by Thomas Jones (No. 130 (16)).

> On the MSS. and editions of the Brut, see PHILLIMORE, EGERTON: The publications of Welsh historical records, *Y Cymmr.*, xi, 1892; LLOYD, JOHN EDWARD: The Welsh chronicles, Oxford, 1930; JONES, THOMAS: Brut y tywysogion, Caerdydd, 1953.

**1165.** GILDAS: De excidio Britanniae. Ed. with translation and notes by Hugh Williams (No. 109 (3)). Translation in Six old English chronicles (No.

1162); Welsh translation in O lygad y ffynnon (ibid.) and by Wade-Evans, Arthur Wade: Coll Prydain, Liverpool, 1950.

> See also STEVENS, COURTENAY EDWARD: Gildas sapiens, *E.H.R.*, 1941; and HODGKIN, ROBERT HOWARD: A history of the Anglo-Saxons, 2nd edn, 2 vols., Oxford, 1939.

**1166.** Liber Landavensis. The text of the book of Llan Dav. Ed. John Gwenogvryn Evans and John Rhŷs. Oxford, 1893.

> See also REES, WILLIAM JENKIN: Liber Landavensis, Llandovery, 1840; HADDAN, ARTHUR WEST: The original MS. of the Liber Landavensis, *Arch. Camb.*, 1868; WADE-EVANS, ARTHUR WADE: The Llancarfan charter (No. 1252); JONES, EVAN DAVID: The book of Llandaff (No. 835); BROOKE, CHRISTOPHER: The archbishops of St. David's, Llandaff, and Caerleon-on-Usk, in CHADWICK, NORA KERSHAW (ed.): Studies in the early British Church (No. 1175).

**1167.** NENNIUS. Ed. T. Mommsen in Monumenta Germaniae Historia, Berlin, 1894; Welsh translation in O lygad y ffynnon (No. 1162); English translation in Six old English chronicles (ibid.) and by Wade-Evans, Arthur Wade: Nennius's 'History of the Britons', London, 1938; Irish version by Van Hamel, Anton Gerard: Lebor Bretnach, Dublin, [1932].

> See also LIEBERMANN, F.: Nennius, the author of Historia Brittonum, in Essays in medieval history presented to T. F. Tout, Manchester, 1925; LOT, FERDINAND: Nennius et l'histoire Brittonum, Paris, 1934; THURNEYSEN, R.: Zu Nemnius (Nennius), *Zeitschrift f. Celt. phil.*, xx; VAN HAMEL, ANTON GERARD: De Oudste Keltische en Angelsaksische Geschiedbronnen, Middelburg, 1911; WILLIAMS, IVOR: Bellum Cantscaul, *B.B.C.S.*, vi, 1931–3; id.: Notes on Nennius, ibid., vii, 1933–5; id.: The Nennian preface: a possible emendation, ibid., ix, 1937–9; id.: Mommsen and the Vatican Nennius, ibid., xi, 1941–4.

**1168.** PETRIE, HENRY (ed.): Monumenta historica Britannica, or materials for the history of Britain. i. London, 1848.

## II. SECONDARY WORKS

### (a) Political history

**1169.** ANSCOMBE, ALFRED: Indexes to Old-Welsh genealogies. *Arch. f. Celt. lex.*, i, 1898.

**1170.** BANKS, RICHARD W.: Herefordshire and its Welsh border during the Saxon period. *Arch. Camb.*, 1882.

**1171.** BLAIR, PETER HUNTER: An introduction to Anglo-Saxon England. Cambridge, 1956.

**1172.** CHADWICK, NORA KERSHAW: The Celtic background of Anglo-Saxon England. *Yorks. Celtic Studies*, iii, 1940–46.

**1173.** Id.    The Celtic West. In The heritage of early Britain. London, 1952.

**1174.** Id.    (ed.): Studies in early British history. Cambridge, 1954.

**1175.** Id.    (ed.): Studies in the early British Church. Cambridge, 1958.

**1176.** CHAMBERS, EDMUND KERCHEVER: Arthur of Britain. London, 1927.

CHARLES, BERTIE GEORGE. Old Norse relations with Wales (No. 472).

**1177.** CHARLESWORTH, MARTIN PERCIVAL, and CHADWICK, NORA KERSHAW (eds): The heritage of early Britain. London, 1952.

**1178.** CHEVALIER, JACQUES: Essai sur la formation de la nationalité et les reveils religieux au Pays de Galle, des origines à la fin du sixième siècle ... Lyon, Paris, 1923.

COLLINGWOOD, ROBIN GEORGE, and MYERS, JOHN NOWELL LINTON: Roman Britain (No. 1027).

**1179.** CRAWFORD, OSBERT GUY STANHOPE: Arthur and his battles. *Antiquity*, 1935.

**1180.** Id.     Western seaways. In Custom is king. Oxford, 1936.

**1181.** DAVIES, ELLIS W.: The Danes in Anglesey. *Trans. Angl. Antiq. Soc.*, 1932.

**1182.** ELLIS, THOMAS PETER: Hywel Dda, codifier. *Trans. Cymmr.*, 1926–7.
> Eulogistic, but basically uncritical.

**1183.** HOGG, ALEXANDER HUBERT ARTHUR: The date of Cunedda. *Antiquity*, 1948.

**1184.** Id.     The Votadini. In Aspects of archaeology in Britain and beyond. London, 1951.

**1185.** JACKSON, KENNETH HURLSTONE: Once again Arthur's battles. *Modern Philology*, 1945.

**1186.** JONES, GWILYM PEREDUR: Brychan. *Arch. Camb.*, 1926.

**1187.** Id.     Notes on the political history of early Powys. Ibid., 1930.

LLOYD, JOHN EDWARD: History of Wales (No. 144).

**1188.** Id.     Hywel Dda, 928–1928. Bilingual. Cardiff, 1928.

**1189.** Id.     The death of Arthur. *B.B.C.S.*, xi, 1941–4.

**1190.** MONMOUTH, GEOFFREY OF: Historia regum Britanniae. Ed. Acton Griscom. London, 1929. Another edn by FARAL, EDMOND: La légende arthurienne (No. 1265).

Welsh texts:

(i) Ystorya brenhined y Brytanyeit. Ed. John Rhŷs and John Gwenogvryn Evans. In The red book of Hergest. Vol. ii (No. 1164 (i)).

(ii) Brut Tysilio. Printed in Myvyrian archaiology of Wales, vol. ii (No. 117).

(iii) Brut G. ab Arthur. Printed ibid.

(iv) Brut Dingestow. Ed. Henry Lewis. Caerdydd, 1942.

(v) Brut y brenhinedd. Cotton Cleopatra version. Ed. John Jay Parry. Cambridge, Massachusetts, 1937.

> See also revised translation of the Historia by C. W. Dunn (New York, 1958); GRISCOM, ACTON: The 'Book of Basingwerk' and MS. Cotton Cleopatra B.V., *Y Cymmr.*, xxxv and xxxvi, 1925 and 1926; HAMMER, JACOB: Geoffrey of Monmouth, Historia regum Britanniae: a variant version . . . Cambridge, Mass., 1951; JARMAN, A. O. H.: Y ddadl ynghylch Sieffre o Fynwy, *Llên Cymru,* ii, 1952–3; JONES, WILLIAM LEWIS: Geoffrey of Monmouth, *Trans. Cymmr.,* 1898–9; LLOYD, JOHN EDWARD: Geoffrey of Monmouth, *E.H.R.,* 1942; PIGGOTT, STUART: The sources of Geoffrey of Monmouth, *Antiquity,* xv; TATLOCK, JOHN STRONG PERRY: The legendary history of Britain: Geoffrey of Monmouth's Historia regum Britanniae and its early vernacular versions, Berkeley and Los Angeles, 1950 (review by Thomas Jones in *Llên Cymru,* i, 1950–1).

**1191.** MYERS, JOHN NOWELL LINTON: Britain in the dark ages. *Antiquity,* 1935.

**1192.** OMAN, CHARLES WILLIAM CHADWICK: England before the Norman conquest. 9th edn. London, 1949.

O'RAHILLY, CECILE: Ireland and Wales (No. 145).

PALMER, ALFRED NEOBARD: The Welsh settlements east of Offa's dyke (No. 641).

PATERSON, DONALD ROSE: The Scandinavian element in Glamorgan (No. 690).

**1193.** REED, TRELAWNEY DAYRELL: The battle for Britain in the fifth century. London, 1944.

**1194.** RHŶS, JOHN: Celtic Britain. 4th edn. London, 1908.

**1195.** STENTON, FRANK MERRY: Anglo-Saxon England. Oxford, 1943. 2nd edn, 1947.

**1196.** STEVENS, COURTENAY EDWARD: Magnus Maximus in British history. *Études Celtiques,* iii, 1928.

**1197.** WADE-EVANS, ARTHUR WADE: The 'Welsh' in Britain. *Trans. Cymmr.,* 1943 and 1944.

**1198.** Id.    The emergence of England and Wales. Wetteren, Belgium, 1956.

### (b) Archaeology and epigraphy

Reference is made to excavations at single sites or the discussion of individual inscriptions or finds only when the paper concerned contains a *general* discussion valuable to the student of the history of the period.

**1199.** BERSU, GERHARD, and GRIFFITHS, WILLIAM ERIC: Concentric circles at Llwyn-du Bach, Penygroes, Caernarvonshire. *Arch. Camb.*, 1949.

**1200.** BROMWICH, RACHEL: Cantre'r Gwaelod and Ker-is. In Early cultures of N.W. Europe. Cambridge, 1950.

**1201.** CARLYON-BRITTON, PHILIP WILLIAM POOLE: The Saxon, Norman, and Platagenet coinage of Wales. *Trans. Cymmr.*, 1905–6.

**1202.** FOX, AILEEN: The siting of some inscribed stones of the dark ages in Glamorgan and Breconshire. *Arch. Camb.*, 1939.

**1203.** Id.    Early Christian period. In A hundred years of Welsh archaeology (No. 395).

FOX, CYRIL FREDERICK: The boundary line of Cymru (No. 352).

Id.    Offa's dyke (No. 354).

**1204.** HEMP, WILFRID JAMES, and GRESHAM, COLIN A.: Hut circles in north-west Wales. *Antiquity,* 1944.

**1205.** JACKSON, KENNETH HURLESTONE: Notes on the Ogam inscriptions of southern Britain. In Early cultures of N.W. Europe. Cambridge, 1950.

**1206.** JOHNS, C. N.: Long cist graves at Ty'n y felin quarry, Llanddyfnan. *Trans. Angl. Antiq. Soc.*, 1956.

**1207.** MACALISTER, ROBERT ALEXANDER STEWART: Corpus inscriptionum insularum Celticarum. 2 vols. Dublin, 1945–49.

**1208.** NASH-WILLIAMS, VICTOR ERLE: Some dated monuments of the dark ages in Wales. *Arch. Camb.*, 1938.

**1209.** Id.    Some early Welsh crosses and cross-slabs. Ibid., 1939.

Id.    The early Christian monuments of Wales (No. 503).

**1210.** RADFORD, COURTENAY ARTHUR RALEGH: Notes on some Caernarvonshire inscriptions. *Trans. Caerns. Hist. Soc.*, 1955.

**1211.** SAVORY, HUBERT NEWMAN: Dinas Emrys. Ibid., 1956.

**1212.** WILLIAMS, IFOR, and NASH-WILLIAMS, VICTOR ERLE: Some Welsh pre-Norman stones. *Arch. Camb.,* 1937.

### (c) Ecclesiastical history

**1213.** BARING-GOULD, SABINE, and FISHER, JOHN: The lives of the British saints. 4 vols. Cymmrodorion Society. Supplementary vols. London, 1907–13.

**1214.** BARTRUM, P. C.: Some studies in early Welsh history. *Trans. Cymmr.,* 1948.

**1215.** BOWEN, EMRYS GEORGE: The cult of Dewi Sant at Llanddewibrefi. *Ceredigion,* ii, 2, 1953.

**1216.** Id.     The settlements of the Celtic saints in Wales. Cardiff, 1954.

**1217.** Id.     Merioneth in the dark ages. *Jnl. Mer. Hist. and Rec. Soc.,* ii, 3, 1955.

**1218.** BURY, JOHN BAGNELL: Life of St. Patrick. London, 1905.

**1219.** CHADWICK, OWEN: The evidence of dedications in the early history of the Welsh Church. In Studies in early British history (No. 1174).

**1220.** CONYBEARE, FREDERICK CORNWALLIS: The character of the heresy of the early British Church. *Trans. Cymmr.,* 1897–8.

**1221.** CRONIN, JOHN M.: St. Patrick and Wales. *St. Peter's Magazine.* Cardiff, 1927. See also ibid., 1923 and 1926.

**1222.** DOBLE, GILBERT HUNTER: Cornish Saints series, Nos. 1–48, 1923–44.

**1223.** Id.     The Welsh Saints series, Nos. 1–5, 1942–4.

**1224.** Id.     Saint Iltut. Cardiff, 1944.

**1225.** EDWARDS, CYRIL JOHN: St. Teilo at Llandaff. *Jnl. Hist. Soc. Church in Wales,* v, 1955.

**1226.** FAWTIER, ROBERT: La vie de St. Samson. Paris, 1912.

**1227.** FISHER, JOHN: The Welsh calendar. *Trans. Cymmr.,* 1894–5.

**1228.** Id.     Welsh church dedications. Ibid., 1906–7.

**1229.** GOUGAUD, LOUIS: Les Chretientes celtiques. 2nd edn. Paris, 1911. English translation by Maud Joynt: Christianity in Celtic lands. London, 1932.

**1230.** HARRIS, SILAS MORGAN: Saint David in the liturgy. Cardiff, 1940.

**1231.** Id.        Liturgical commemoration of Welsh saints. *Jnl. Hist. Soc. Church in Wales*, v and vi, 1955 and 1956.

**1232.** HOPKIN-JAMES, LEMUEL JOHN: The Celtic gospels. Oxford, 1934. Introduction.

**1233.** JALLAND, TREVOR GERVASE: The church and the papacy. London, 1944.

**1234.** JAMES, JOHN WILLIAMS: The Welsh version of Rhigyfarch's 'Life of David'. *N.L.W. Jnl.*, ix, 1955.

**1235.** Id.        The book of Llan Dâf and bishop Oudoceus. *Jnl. Hist. Soc. Church in Wales*, v, 1955.

**1236.** Id.        The excommunications in the book of Llan Dâf. Ibid., viii, 1958.

**1237.** JONES, GRIFFITH HARTWELL: Celtic Britain and the pilgrim movement. *Y Cymmr.*, xxiii, 1912.

**1238.** LOTH, JOSEPH: Les noms des saints Bretons. Paris, 1910.

**1239.** MEISSNER, JOHN LODWIG GOUGH: The Celtic Church in England. London, 1929.

**1240.** MORRIS, R.: Theology of the early British Church. *Trans. Cymmr.*, 1914–15.

**1241.** PRINGLE, KENNETH DOUGLAS: The home of St. Patrick. Ibid., 1955.

**1242.** REES, RICE: An essay on the Welsh saints. London, 1836.

**1243.** REES, WILLIAM JENKIN: Lives of the Cambro-British saints (Latin and Welsh texts with English translations). Llandovery, 1853.
        See collations by MEYER, KUNO, in *Y Cymmr.*, xiii, 1900.

**1244.** STOKES, GEORGE THOMAS, and LAWLOR, HUGH JACKSON: Ireland and the Celtic Church. London, 1928.

**1245.** TAYLOR, THOMAS: The life of St. Samson of Dol. London, 1925.

**1246.** Id.        Celtic Christianity of Cornwall. London, 1916.

**1247.** THOMAS, RICHARD JAMES: The Brychan dynasty in east Glamorgan. Cardiff, 1936.

**1248.** WADE-EVANS, ARTHUR WADE: The Brychan documents. *Y Cymmr.*, xix, 1906.

**1249.** Id.      The life of St. David (translation and notes). London, 1923 (review by John Lloyd-Jones in *Y Llenor*, ii, 1923). Latin text, translation, and notes by the same author in *Y Cymmr.*, xxiv, 1913.

> See also catalogue of works on St. David published by the Cardiff Public Libraries, 1927.

**1250.** Id.      Beuno Sant (translation and notes). *Arch. Camb.*, 1930.

**1251.** Id.      Bonedd y saint. Ibid., 1931.

**1252.** Id.      The Llancarfan charter. Ibid., 1932.

**1253.** Id.      Welsh Christian origins. Oxford, 1934.

Id.      Vitae sanctorum Britanniae et genealogiae (No. 130 (9)).
> Reviews by Thomas Jones in *Trans. Cymmr.*, 1943–4; E. D. Jones in *Y Llenor*, xxiv, 1945; J. Conway Davies in *Jnl. Hist. Soc. Church in Wales*, i, 1947.

**1254.** WARREN, FREDERICK EDWARD: The liturgy and ritual of the Celtic Church. Oxford, 1881.

**1255.** WILLIAMS, HUGH: Some aspects of the early Christian Church in Wales (5th and 6th centuries). *Trans. Cymmr.*, 1893–4.

**1256.** Id.      Christianity in early Britain. Oxford, 1912.

**1257.** WILLIS-BUND, JOHN WILLIAM: The Celtic Church of Wales. London, 1897.
> To be used with caution.

**1258.** ZIMMER, HEINRICH: The Celtic Church in Britain and Ireland. Translated by A. Meyer. London, 1902.
> Review by Hugh Williams in *Zeitschrift f. Celt. phil.*, iv, 1903.

### (d) Language and literature

**1259.** BRADSHAW, HENRY: Early Welsh, Breton and Cornish MSS. In Collected papers. Cambridge, 1889.

**1260.** BROMWICH, RACHEL: The historical triads: with special reference to Peniarth MS. 16. *B.B.C.S.*, xii, 1946–8.

**1261.** Id.      The character of the early Welsh tradition. In Studies in early British history (No. 1174).

**1262.** CHADWICK, NORA KERSHAW: Intellectual contacts between Britain and Gaul in the fifth century. In Studies in early British history (No. 1174).

**1263.** Id.      Early culture and learning in North Wales. Ibid.

**1264.** DENHOLM-YOUNG, NOEL: Handwriting in England and Wales. Cardiff, 1954.

JACKSON, KENNETH HURLESTONE: Language and history in early Britain (No. 479).

**1265.** FARAL, EDMOND: La légende arthurienne. 3 vols. Paris, 1911–29.

**1266.** JARMAN, ALFRED OWEN HUGHES: Ymddiddan Myrddin a Thaliesin. Caerdydd, 1951.

**1267.** Id.      Lailoken a Llallogan, *B.B.C.S.*, ix, 1937–9.

**1268.** Id.      Peiryan vaban. Ibid., xiv, 1950–2.

**1269.** JONES, THOMAS: Datblygiadau cynnar chwedl Arthur. *B.B.C.S.*, xvii, 1956–8.

**1270.** LINDSAY, WALLACE MARTIN: Early Welsh script. Oxford, 1912.

**1271.** LOOMIS, ROGER SHERMAN: Wales and the Arthurian legend. Cardiff, 1956.

**1272.** MORRIS-JONES, JOHN: Taliesin. *Y Cymmr.*, xxviii, 1918.

**1273.** WILLIAMS, IFOR: Marwnad Cynddylan. *B.B.C.S.*, vi, 1931–3.

**1274.** Id.      The poems of Llywarch Hen. London, 1932.

**1275.** Id.      Hengerdd. *B.B.C.S.*, vii, 1933–5.

**1276.** Id.      Canu Llywarch Hen. Ail argraffiad. Caerdydd, 1953.

**1277.** Id.      Canu Aneirin. Caerdydd, 1938.

**1278.** Id.      When did British become Welsh? *Trans. Angl. Antiq. Soc.*, 1939.

**1279.** Id.      An early Anglesey poem. Ibid., 1941.

**1280.** Id.      Moliant Dinbych Penfro. *Trans. Cymmr.*, 1940.

**1281.** Id.      Lectures on early Welsh poetry. Dublin, 1944.

**1282.** Id.      Hen chwedlau. *Trans. Cymmr.*, 1947.

**1283.** Id.      Wales and the north. *Trans. Cumb. and Westmorland Ant. and Arch. Soc.*, li (new series), 1952.

**1284.** Id.      Armes Prydein. Caerdydd, 1955.

# SECTION E

## *A.D. 1039—1282*

This period is the best-known epoch of medieval Welsh history, the sources available for its study being more abundant than for the earlier periods and more varied than for the two centuries following. It has also a dramatic unity as being the period of the Welsh struggle against the Anglo-Norman power represented by the barons of the marches and the kings of England. The history of Wales during these years—at all events on the sides that can best be known—is, therefore, continuously connected with that of England, and less directly with that of Europe in general, and cannot be studied as a thing apart; at certain critical points there was a close interaction between events in England and Wales, and throughout the period the information available is largely drawn from English sources.

### I. POLITICAL AND CONSTITUTIONAL HISTORY

See ADAMS, GEORGE BURTON: Constitutional history of England, new edn, London, 1935; Cambridge Mediaeval History, vols. i and vi; DAVIES, HENRY WILLIAM CARLESS: England under the Normans and Angevins, 3rd edn, London, 1912; HASKINS, CHARLES HOMER: The Normans in European history, London, 1919; ORPEN, GODDARD HENRY: Ireland under the Normans, 4 vols., Oxford, 1911–20; POOLE, AUSTIN LANE: From Domesday Book to Magna Carta, 1087–1216, 2nd edn, Oxford, 1955; RAMSAY, JAMES HENRY: The foundations of England, or twelve centuries of British history, B.C. 55—A.D. 1154, 2 vols., London, 1898; id.: The Angevin empire, 1154–1216, London, etc., 1903; id.: The dawn of the constitution, 1216–1307, London, etc., 1908; STENTON, FRANK MERRY: Anglo-Saxon England (No. 1195); TOUT, THOMAS FREDERICK: The history of England from the accession of Henry III to the death of Edward III (1216–1377), London, 1905.

#### (a) Sources

These may be conveniently grouped into four main classes: (i) chronicles, (ii) archives, (iii) law books, (iv) collections of sources.

#### (i) The chronicles

The chronicles are mostly monastic, and may be conveniently classified into those of Welsh origin and those from border houses. For other English chronicles see GROSS, CHARLES: Sources and literature of English history (No. 9).

##### (1) Chronicles of Welsh origin

Annales Cambriae (No. 1161).

**1285.** Annales de Margan, 1066–1232. Ed. H. R. Luard. Annales Monastici, i. *Rolls Series*. London, 1864.

Bruts, The (No. 1164).

**1286.** Chronicle of the 13th century, 1066–1298. *Arch. Camb.*, 1862.
Especially useful after 1232 in continuation of Annales de Margan.

**1287.** GIRALDUS CAMBRENSIS: Works, *Rolls Series*, 8 vols., London, 1861–91; and *Y Cymmr.*, xxx, 1920.

> See also The Speculum Dorum, ed. W. S. Davies, in *Arch. Camb.*, 1928. An English translation of the Itinerary and Description of Wales by Richard Colt Hoare is in Everyman's Library; for a Welsh translation see JONES, THOMAS: Gerallt Gymro, Cardiff, 1938.

> The following should also be consulted: BUTLER, HAROLD EDGEWORTH: The autobiography of Giraldus Cambrensis, London, 1937 (translated mainly from the *Rolls Series* text of *De rebus a se gestis* and *De iure et statu Meneuensis ecclesiae*; DAVIES, JAMES CONWAY: Giraldus Cambrensis, 1146–1946, *Arch. Camb.*, 1947; id.: The Kambriae mappa of Giraldus Cambrensis, *Jnl. Hist. Soc. Church in Wales*, ii, 1950; JONES, THOMAS: Gerallt Gymro, bilingual, Cardiff, 1947; id.: Gerald the Welshman's 'Itinerary through Wales' and 'Description of Wales', *N.L.W. Jnl.*, vi, 1949–50; POWICKE, FREDERICK MAURICE: Gerald of Wales, *Bull. of John Rylands Library*, xii, 1928; id.: Gerald of Wales, in The Christian life of the middle ages, Oxford, 1935; ROBERTS, W. RHYS: Gerald of Wales on the survival of Welsh, *Trans. Cymmr.*, 1923–4; WILLIAMS, CHARLES HAROLD: Giraldus Cambrensis and Wales, *Jnl. Hist. Soc. Church in Wales*, i, 1947.

**1288.** History of Gruffydd ap Cynan (1054–1137). Ed. Arthur Jones. Manchester, 1910.

**1289.** JONES, THOMAS: 'Cronica de Wallia' and other documents from Exeter cathedral library MS. 3514. *B.B.C.S.*, xii, 1948; separately published, n.d.

> See also No. 1164 (iv).

**1290.** Register of Aberconway. Ed. Henry Ellis. Camden Soc. *Camden Miscellany*, i. London, 1847.

### (2) Border chronicles

**1291.** Annales Cestrienses, or chronicles of the abbey of S. Werburg at Chester [A.D. 1–1297, with a translation]. Ed. R. C. Christie. Rec. Soc. for Lancs and Cheshire. London, 1887.

**1292.** Annales monasterii de Theokesberia [Tewkesbury], 1066–1263. Ed. H. R. Luard. Annales monastici, ii, 127–411. *Rolls Series*. London, 1865.

**1293.** Annales prioratus de Wigornia [Worcester], A.D. 1–1377. Ed. H. R. Luard. Annales monastici, iv, 353–564. *Rolls Series*. London, 1869.
Translation in *Bohn's Antiquarian Library*.

**1294.** WORCESTER, FLORENCE OF (d. 1118): Chronicon ex chronicis [A.D. 450–1117, with two continuations to 1141 and 1295]. Ed. Benjamin Thorpe. English Hist. Soc. 2 vols. London, 1848–9.
Translation by Thomas Forester in *Bohn's Antiquarian Library*. London, 1854.

### (ii) Archives

For the archives generally see GUISEPPI, MONTAGUE SPENCER: Guide to the MSS. preserved in the Public Record Office (No. 114) and P.R.O.

sectional list No. 24. H.M.S.O. London, 1951. For the administrative routine of the departments which produced them, see TOUT, THOMAS FREDERICK: Chapters in the administrative history of mediaeval England, vols. i–vi, Manchester, 1920–33.

Of the Chancery archives, the most valuable in print are the various series of enrolments which served as 'office copies' of the documents issued by the department. They deal with the widest variety of topics.

Of the Exchequer archives, the most valuable in print are the Pipe Rolls (No. 1317); these contain the yearly accounts of sheriffs and the 'foreign' accounts of other royal officers variously employed in executive and financial administration.

### (1) Chancery archives
#### Charter rolls

**1295.** Rotuli chartarum, 1199–1216. Ed. Thomas Duffus Hardy. *Record Commission.* London, 1837.

**1296.** Calendar of charter rolls, 1226–1516. 6 vols. London, 1903–27.

#### Close rolls

**1297.** Rotuli litterarum clausarum . . . 1204–27. Ed. T. D. Hardy. 2 vols. *Record Commission.* London, 1833–44.

**1298.** Close rolls, 1227–72. 14 vols. London, 1902–38.

**1299.** Calendar of close rolls, 1272–1500. 46 vols. London, 1892–1955.

#### Fine rolls

**1300.** Rotuli de oblatis et finibus . . . temp. regis Iohannis. Ed. T. D. Hardy. *Record Commission.* London, 1835.

**1301.** Excerpta e rotulis finium . . . 1216–72. Ed. C. Roberts. 2 vols. *Record Commission.* London, 1835–6.

**1302.** Calendar of fine rolls, 1272–1471. 20 vols. London, etc., 1911–49.

#### Inquisitions

**1303.** Calendar of inquisitions post mortem and other analogous documents, Henry III–Edward III. 13 vols., London, 1911–52; 2nd series, Henry VII, 2 vols., London, 1898–1915.

**1304.** Calendar of inquisitions, miscellaneous (Chancery), Henry III–Edward III. 3 vols. London, 1916–37.

#### Liberate rolls

**1305.** Rotuli de liberate ac de misis et praestitis, regnante Iohanne. Ed. T. D. Hardy. *Record Commission.* London, 1844.

**1306.** Calendar of liberate rolls, 1226–51. 3 vols. London, 1917–37.

### Patent rolls

**1307.** Rotuli litterarum patentium . . . 1201–16. Ed. T. D. Hardy. *Record Commission*. London, 1833.

**1308.** Patent rolls, 1216–32. 2 vols. London, 1901–3.

**1309.** Calendar of patent rolls, 1232–1509, 52 vols.; 1547–63, 12 vols. London, 1891–1948.

### Treaty rolls

**1310.** Treaty rolls. Vol. i, 1234–1325. London, 1955.

### Warrants

**1311.** Calendar of Chancery warrants. Vol. i, 1244–1326. London, 1927.

### Welsh rolls

**1312.** Calendar of Chancery rolls, various, 1277–1326. London, 1912.

> Includes (pp. 157–362) a calendar of Welsh rolls, 1277–94, which is indispensable for the study of those momentous years in Welsh history. It supersedes the calendar of Welsh rolls in AYLOFFE, JOSEPH: Calendars of the ancient charters and of the Welsh and Scotch rolls, London, 1774.

### (2) Exchequer archives

**1313.** The book of fees (Testa de Nevill), 1198–1293. 3 parts. London, 1921–31.

> Contains much important material for the history of feudal tenures. Supersedes the earlier edition: Testa de Nevill seu liber feodorum, *Record Commission*, London, 1807.

**1314.** Documents illustrative of English history in the 13th and 14th centuries. Ed. Henry Cole. *Record Commission*. London, 1844.

**1315.** Domesday book, seu liber censualis Wilhelmi Primi regis Angliae. 4 vols. *Record Commission*. London, 1783–1816.

> For the extensive literature relating to this document see GROSS, CHARLES: Sources and literature of English history (No. 9). For Cheshire, see The domesday survey of Cheshire, ed. James Tait, Chetham Soc., 1916; and TAIT, JAMES: Flintshire in domesday book, *Flints. Hist. Soc. Pubns*, xi, 1925; for Hereford—PAGE, WILLIAM, and DOUBLEDAY, HERBERT ARTHUR (eds): Herefordshire, vol. i, Victoria County Histories (No. 810); for Shropshire— id.: Shropshire, vol. i, Victoria County Histories (No. 811) (introduction by James Tait). See also LLOYD, JOHN EDWARD: Wales and the coming of the Normans (No. 1364), and EDWARDS, JOHN GORONWY: The Normans and the Welsh march (No. 1357).

**1316.** Issues of the Exchequer. Translated by Frederick Devon. *Record Commission*. London, 1837.

> Covers the period of Henry III to Elizabeth I.

**1317.** Pipe rolls:

> The pipe rolls have been printed in full for the periods 1130–1, 1155–1212, 1229–30, and 1241–3. The rolls of 1130–1, 1155–8, and 1188–9 were edited in four vols. for the Record Commission by J. Hunter, 1833–44. The 1833

edition of the roll of 1130–1 was reproduced in facsimile, Public Record Office, 1929. The rolls of 1158–88, 1189–1212, and 1229–30 have been published in 69 vols. by the Pipe Roll Society, 1884–1957. The roll of 1241–2 has been published by H. L. Cannon, 1918.

**1318.** Roll of expenses of Edward I in Wales, 1281–2. Ed. Samuel Lysons, with translation by John Brand. *Archaeologia*, xvi, 1812.

> The text is inaccurately printed. The roll relates to 1282–3 and not to 1281–2.

### (3) Miscellaneous records

Calendar of ancient correspondence concerning Wales (No. 130 (2)).

**1319.** Flint pleas, 1283–5. Ed. (with translation) J. G. Edwards. *Flints. Hist. Soc. Pubns.*, viii, 1921.

Littere Wallie (No. 130 (5)).

Ministers' accounts for west Wales, 1277–1306 (No. 109 (13)).

**1320.** Registrum epistolarum Johannis Peckham archiepiscopi Cantuariensis. Ed. C. T. Martin. 3 vols. *Rolls Series*. London, 1882–5.

> Cover the period 1279–92. The items of Welsh interest are also printed (with useful notes) by HADDAN and STUBBS (No. 115).

**1321.** RODERICK, ARTHUR JAMES, and REES, WILLIAM (eds): The lordships of Abergavenny, Grosmont, Skenfrith, and White Castle: account of the ministers for the year 1256–1257. *S. Wales and Mon. Rec. Soc. Pubn.*, iii and iv, 1954 and 1957.

### (iii) Law books

**1322.** EDWARDS, JOHN GORONWY: Hywel Dda and the Welsh law books. Bangor, 1929.

> For notes on the main MSS. and editions see LLOYD, JOHN EDWARD: History of Wales (No. 144), i, pp. 354–6, and preface to No. 1325. For further particulars of the MSS. see No. 116, *passim*, and No. 1333.

**1323.** EVANS, JOHN GWENOGVRYN (ed.): Facsimile of the Chirk codex of the Welsh laws. Llanbedrog, 1909.

> The oldest MS. of the laws in Welsh (*c.* A.D. 1200). For a printed edition of the text see No. 1327.

**1324.** JENKINS, DAFYDD: Llawysgrif goll Llanforda o gyfreithiau Hywel Dda. *B.B.C.S.*, xiv, 1950–2.

> Important discussion of the inter-relations of some of the MSS. of the Welsh law books.

**1325.** LEWIS, HUBERT: The ancient laws of Wales. Ed. J. E. Lloyd. London, 1889.

> The editor's introduction is valuable. The theories put forward in the body of the work are largely unsound.

**1326.** LEWIS, TIMOTHY (ed.): The laws of Hywel Dda: a facsimile reprint of Llanstephan MS. 116 in the National Library of Wales. London, 1912.

**1327.** Id. The laws of Hywel Dda: The Black Book of Chirk, Peniarth MS. 29. *Zeitschrift f. Celt. Phil.*, xx, 1936.

An edition of the text reproduced in facsimile in No. 1323.

**1328.** Id. Bibliography of the laws of Hywel Dda. *Aberystwyth Studies*, x, 1928.

**1329.** OWEN, ANEURIN (ed.): Ancient laws and institutes of Wales. 2 vols., 8vo; 1 vol., folio. *Record Commission.* London, 1841.

The only edition covering the texts as a whole, yet in many ways unsatisfactory. The general arrangement is often arbitrary and misleading: thus the distinction made between the so-called 'Codes' in vol. i and the so-called 'Anomalous Laws' in vol. ii is due largely to the editor and is not warranted by the MSS. The Welsh text of the three main recensions of the law books printed in vol. i is a conflation of various versions. The matter contained in vol. ii is rather more satisfactorily treated.

**1330.** RICHARDS, GRAFTON MELVILLE (ed.): Cyfreithiau Hywel Dda o lawysgrif Coleg yr Iesu, Rhydychen, LVII. Caerdydd, 1957.

**1331.** WADE-EVANS, ARTHUR WADE (ed.): Peniarth MS. 37, folios 61A–76B (with translation). *Y Cymmr.*, xvii, 1904.

A portion of the MS. (late thirteenth century) used by Aneurin Owen as a basis of the text of the 'Gwentian Code' in vol. i of his edition (No. 1329).

**1332.** Id. Welsh mediaeval law. Oxford, 1909.

**1333.** WILLIAMS, STEPHEN JOSEPH, a POWELL, J. ENOCH (gol.): Cyfreithiau Hywel Dda yn ôl Llyfr Blegywryd (dull Dyfed): argraffiad beirniadol ac eglurhaol. Caerdydd, 1942.

See also RICHARDS, MELVILLE: The laws of Hywel Dda, Liverpool, 1954 (a translation of Llyfr Blegywryd).

For the language of the laws, see:

**1334.** BINCHY, D. A.: Some Celtic legal terms. *Celtica*, iii, 1956.

**1335.** LEWIS, TIMOTHY: A glossary of mediaeval Welsh law. Manchester, 1913.

**1336.** PARRY-WILLIAMS, THOMAS HERBERT: The language of the laws. *Aberystwyth Studies*, x, 1928.

For modern works relating to the laws, see Nos. 1342, 1348, 1349, 1350 1351, 1358.

### (iv) Collections of sources

The documents collected in DUGDALE's *Monasticon* (No. 111) are valuable for political as well as for ecclesiastical history. For a useful collection of material relating to Powys, see No. 58.

**1337.** Calendar of documents preserved in France, illustrative of the history of Great Britain and Ireland. Ed. J. H. Round. Vol. i. London, 1899.

> Valuable for the Norman conquest and settlement of the Welsh marches.

Calendar of the public records relating to Pembrokeshire (No. 109 (7)).

Catalogue of MSS. relating to Wales in the British Museum (No. 109 (4)).

CLARK, GEORGE THOMAS (ed.): Cartae et alia munimenta quae ad dominium de Glamorgan pertinent (No. 671).

DWNN, LEWYS: Heraldic visitations of Wales (No. 60).

**1338.** LEWIS, EDWARD ARTHUR (ed.): Materials illustrating the history of Dynevor and Newton, from the earliest times to the close of the reign of Henry VIII. *West Wales Hist. Rec.*, i and ii, 1912–13.

**1339.** Id.      (ed.): A collection of historical documents relating to Carmarthen castle from the earliest times to the close of the reign of Henry VIII. Ibid., iii, 1913–14.

**1340.** Parliamentary writs and writs of military summons (Edward I–Edward II). Ed. Francis Palgrave. 2 vols (4 parts). *Record Commission.* London, 1827–34.

Reports on MSS. in the Welsh language (No. 116).

**1341.** Royal and other historical letters illustrative of the reign of Henry III. Ed. W. W. Shirley. 2 vols. *Rolls Series.* London, 1862–6.

> For additional notes on dates, etc., see Calendar of ancient correspondence concerning Wales (No. 130 (2)).

RYMER, THOMAS: Foedera (No. 128).

### (b) Secondary works

**1342.** *Aberystwyth Studies*, vol. x, 1928: The Hywel Dda millenary volume.

**1343.** BARBIER, PAUL: The age of Owain Gwynedd. London, etc., 1908.

BARRACLOUGH, GEOFFREY: The earldom and county palatine of Chester (No. 797).

**1344.** BEMONT, CHARLES: Simon de Montfort. Paris, 1884.

> English translation by E. F. Jacob, Oxford, 1930.

**1345.** BRIDGEMAN, GEORGE THOMAS ORLANDO: Ancient lords of Mechain. *Arch. Camb.*, 1863.

**1346.** Id.     The princes of upper Powys. *Mont. Coll.*, i, 1868.

**1347.** Id.     The Welsh lords of Kerry and Arwystli. Ibid., i, 1868.

      Id.     History of the princes of South Wales (No. 134).

**1348.** BRYNMOR-JONES, DAVID: The study of the Welsh laws. *Cymru Fu,* Dolgellau, 1889.

**1349.** Id.     The criminal law of mediaeval Wales. *Univ. Coll. of South Wales Magazine,* 1890.

**1350.** Id.     The Brehon laws and their relation to the ancient Welsh institutes. *Trans. Cymmr.,* 1904–5.

**1351.** Id.     Foreign elements in Welsh mediaeval law. Ibid., 1916–17.
Only part i was completed and published.

      CLARK, GEORGE THOMAS: The earls, earldom, and castle of Pembroke (No. 777).

      Id.     The land of Morgan (No. 669).

      Id.     Limbus patrum Morganiae et Glamorganiae (No. 15).

      Id.     The signory of Gower (No. 670).

**1352.** DAVIES, JAMES CONWAY: A grant by Llywelyn ap Gruffydd (Sept., 1243). *N.L.W. Jnl.,* iii, 1943.

**1353.** Id.     A grant by David ap Gruffydd (January, 1280). Ibid., iii, 1943.

**1354.** Id.     Lordships of manors. *Mont. Coll.,* xlviii, 1943–4.

      Id.     The Kambriae mappa of Giraldus Cambrensis (No. 1287).

**1355.** DOUIE, DECIMA LANGWORTHY: Archbishop Pecham. Oxford, 1952.
See also WILLIS-BUND, JOHN WILLIAM: Archbishop Peckham, *Trans. Cymmr.,* 1900–1.

**1356.** EDWARDS, JOHN GORONWY: The building of Flint. *Flints. Hist. Soc. Pubns.,* xii, 1951.

**1357.** Id.     The Normans and the Welsh march (British Academy: Raleigh lecture on history). Oxford, 1957.

      Id.     Edward I's castle-building in Wales (No. 387).

      Id.     The early history of the counties of Carmarthen and Cardigan (No. 562).

**1358.** ELLIS, THOMAS PETER: Welsh tribal law and custom in the middle ages. 2 vols. Oxford, 1926.
>An important pioneer work, but of unequal merit.

Id.    Hywel Dda, codifier (No. 1182).

**1359.** FREEMAN, EDWARD AUGUSTUS: History of the Norman conquest. 6 vols, Oxford, 1867–79; 2nd edn of vols. i–iv, 1870–6; 3rd edn of vols. i, ii, 1877.

**1360.** Id.    The reign of William Rufus and the accession of Henry I. 2 vols. Oxford, 1882.

HEMP, WILFRID JAMES: Conway castle (No. 534).

**1361.** HOLDSWORTH, WILLIAM SEARLE: A history of English law. 9 vols, London, 1903–26; 3rd edn of vols. i–iii, 1922–3.

**1362.** LEWIS, FRANK ROBERT: A history of the lordship of Gower from the missing cartulary of Neath abbey. *B.B.C.S.*, ix, 1937–9.
>Twelfth and early thirteenth century.

**1363.** LITTLE, ANDREW GEORGE: Mediaeval Wales, chiefly in the twelfth and thirteenth centuries. London, 1902.

**1364.** LLOYD, JOHN EDWARD: Wales and the coming of the Normans. *Trans. Cymmr.*, 1899–1900.

Id.    History of Wales (No. 144).

**1365.** Id.    Llywelyn ap Gruffydd and the lordship of Glamorgan. *Arch. Camb.*, 1913.

**1366.** Id.    Edward I's commission of enquiry of 1280–1: an examination of its origin and purpose. *Y Cymmr.*, xxv, 1915.
>See also the same author's postscript to this article in ibid., xxvi, 1916.

**1367.** Id.    Who was Gwenllian de Lacy? *Arch. Camb.*, 1919 and 1920.

**1368.** Id.    The death of Llywelyn ap Gruffydd. *B.B.C.S.*, v, 1929–31.
>See also Nos. 1372 and 1384.

**1369.** Id.    Dolforwyn. Ibid., x, 1939–41.

**1370.** Id.    Border notes [on Gorddwr, Buttington, Halcetor, and Tempsiter]. Ibid., xi, 1944.

**1371.** MORRIS, JOHN EDWARD: The Welsh wars of Edward I: a contribution to mediaeval military history. Oxford, 1901.
>For the campaign of 1294–5, see also EDWARDS, JOHN GORONWY: The battle of Maes Madog and the Welsh war of 1294–5; id.: The site of the battle of 'Meismeidoc', 1295 (No. 1441).

**1372.** MORRIS, RUPERT HUGH: The burial of Llywelyn ap Gruffydd. *Arch. Camb.,* 1911.

> See also Nos. 1368 and 1384.

NICHOLL, LEWIS D.: The Normans in Glamorgan, Gower, and Kidweli (No. 689).

**1373.** NORGATE, KATE: John Lackland. London, 1902.

O'NEIL, BRYAN HUGH ST. JOHN: Criccieth castle (No. 541).

**1374.** OWEN, HENRY: The administration of English law in Wales and the marches. London, 1900; repr. with appendices in *Y Cymmr.,* xiv, 1901.

PALMER, ALFRED NEOBARD: Welsh settlements east of Offa's dyke during the 11th century (No. 641).

> See also DODD, ARTHUR HERBERT: Welsh and English in east Denbighshire (No. 625).

**1375.** POWICKE, FREDERICK MAURICE: Henry III and the Lord Edward. 2 vols. Oxford, 1947.

> Vol. ii, ch. xv, contains a valuable discussion of Edward I's relations with Wales.

**1376.** Id.     The thirteenth century. Oxford, 1953.

> Ch. ix contains a valuable account of Anglo-Welsh relations in the thirteenth century.

REES, WILLIAM: Caerphilly castle (No. 697).

Id.     The mediaeval lordship of Brecon (No. 529).

**1377.** RODERICK, ARTHUR JAMES: The dispute between Llywelyn ap Gruffydd and Gruffydd ap Gwenwynwyn (1278–82). *B.B.C.S.,* viii, 1935–7.

> Prints extracts from the assize roll calendared as a whole in No. 130 (7).

**1378.** Id.     The four cantreds: a study in administration (to 1282). Ibid., x, 1939–41.

**1379.** Id.     The feudal relation between the English Crown and the Welsh princes. *History,* xxxvii, 1952.

**1380.** SIMPSON, WILLIAM DOUGLAS: Flint castle. *Arch. Camb.,* 1940.

Id.     Harlech castle and the Edwardian castle plan (No. 397).

**1381.** SMITH, JENKYN BEVERLEY: The lordship of Glamorgan. *Morgannwg,* ii, 1958.

**1382.** STEWARD-BROWN, RONALD: The serjeants of the peace in medieval England and Wales. Manchester, 1936.

**1383.** TAYLOR, ARNOLD JOSEPH: The events of Palm Sunday, 1282. *Flints. Hist. Soc. Pubns.,* xiii, 1952–3.

**1384.** Id.     The death of Llywelyn ap Gruffydd. *B.B.C.S.,* xv, 1952–4.
See also Nos. 1368 and 1372.

Id.     Usk castle and the Pipe Roll of 1185 (No. 398).

Id.     Master James of St. George (No. 401).

**1385.** Id.     The building of Flint—a postscript. *Flints. Hist. Soc. Pubns.,* xvii, 1957.

TOY, SIDNEY: The town and castle of Conway (No. 551).

**1386.** TOUT, THOMAS FREDERICK: Wales and the march during the barons' wars, 1258–67. Collected papers of Thomas Frederick Tout, vol. ii. Manchester, 1934.
Has two illustrative maps. See also JACOB, ERNEST FRASER: The reign of Henry III, *Trans. R.H.S.,* 4th series, x, 1927.

**1387.** TREHARNE, REGINALD F.: The Franco-Welsh treaty of alliance in 1212. *B.B.C.S.,* xviii, 1, 1958.

**1388.** VINOGRADOFF, PAUL: Historical jurisprudence. Vol. i. Oxford, 1923.

**1389.** WAINWRIGHT, FREDERICK THRELFALL: 'Cledemutha'. *E.H.R.,* lxv, 1950.

**1390.** WALTER, FERDINAND: Des alte Wales: ein Beitrag zur Volker-, Rechts- und Kirchen-Geschichte. Bonn, 1859.

WILLIAMS, ALBERT HUGHES: An introduction to the history of Wales (No. 157).

## II. ECCLESIASTICAL HISTORY

### (a) Sources

**1391.** Calendar of entries in the papal registers relating to Great Britain and Ireland. Papal letters, 1198–1484. 13 vols. London, 1893–1955; petitions, 1342–1419. London, 1896.

DAVIES, JAMES CONWAY (ed.): Episcopal Acts and cognate documents relating to Welsh dioceses, 1066–1272 (No. 823).

DUGDALE, WILLIAM: Monasticon Anglicanum (No. 111).
See also the entries relating to religious houses (Nos. 886 to 954).

GIRALDUS CAMBRENSIS: Works (No. 1287).

HADDAN, ARTHUR WEST, and STUBBS, WILLIAM (eds): Councils and ecclesiastical documents (No. 115).

Liber Landavensis (No. 1166).

Register of letters of John Peckham (No. 1320).

**1392.** Taxatio ecclesiastica Angliae et Walliae auctoritate P. Nicolai IV (*c.* A.D. 1291). London, 1802.

> The record of an assessment of clerical incomes completed in 1291–2: diocese of St. David's, pp. 272–7; Llandaff, pp. 278–85; St. Asaph, pp. 285–90; Bangor, pp. 290–4. There are also scattered references to Wales in the sections devoted to the diocese of Hereford, pp. 157–76; Worcester, pp. 216–40; Coventry and Lichfield, pp. 241–65.

> For the interpretation of this evidence see GRAHAM, ROSE: Taxation of pope Nicholas IV, *E.H.R.,* xxiii, 1908, and the introduction to No. 1393 below.

**1393.** Valuation of Norwich. Ed. W. E. Lunt. Oxford, 1926.

> The record of an assessment of clerical incomes made in 1254: diocese of Bangor, pp. 190–6; Llandaff, pp. 314–25; St. Asaph, pp. 467–73; St. David's, pp. 475–7 (a fragment relating to Brecon priory).

For the general history of the Church in England and Wales during the period, see KEMPE, E. W.: Canonization and authority in the western Church, Oxford, 1948; STEPHENS, W. R. W., and HUNT, WILLIAM (eds): History of the English Church, 8 vols., London, 1899–1910 (vols. i–iii). For episcopal succession, see STUBBS, WILLIAM: Registrum sacrum Anglicanum (No. 182), and Handbook of British chronology, ed. F. M. Powicke, London, 1939.

#### (b) Secondary works

**1394.** BULLOCK, J. D.: Early Christian memorial formulae. *Arch. Camb.,* 1956.

DAVIES, EBENEZER THOMAS: An ecclesiastical history of Monmouthshire (No. 734).

DAVIES, J. CONWAY: Black book of St. David's (No. 848).

Id.    The records of the Church in Wales (No. 822).

**1395.** DAVIES, W. S.: Materials for the life of bishop Bernard of St. David's. *Arch. Camb.,* 1919.

DOUIE, DECIMA LANGWORTHY: Archbishop Pecham (No. 1355).

EVANS, DAVID LEWIS: Llyfr Coch Asaph (No. 841).

GRESHAM, COLIN A.: The Aberconway charter (No. 887).

JONES, ARTHUR: Basingwerk abbey (No. 891).

JONES, EVAN DAVID: The book of Llandaff (No. 835).

KNOWLES, DAVID, and HADCOCK, R. NEVILLE: Medieval religious houses: England and Wales (No. 876).

**1396.** LUNT, W. E.: Papal revenues in the middle ages. 2 vols. New York, 1934.

**1397.** Id.        Financial relations of the papacy with England to 1327. Cambridge (Mass.), 1939.

**1398.** PALMER, ALFRED NEOBARD: The portionary churches of mediaeval North Wales, their tribal relations and sinecurism connected therewith. *Arch. Camb.*, 1886; repr. in id.: History of the parish church of Wrexham (No. 642).

**1399.** PIERCE, THOMAS JONES: Einion ap Ynyr (Anian II), bishop of St. Asaph. *Flints. Hist. Soc. Pubns.*, xvii, 1957.

**1400.** PRICE, JOHN ARTHUR: The ecclesiastical constitution of Wales on the eve of the Edwardian conquest. *Y Cymmr.*, xxvi, 1916.

**1401.** TAYLOR, ARNOLD JOSEPH: Rhuddlan cathedral: a 'might have been' of Flintshire history. *Flints. Hist. Soc. Pubns.*, xv, 1954–5.

THOMPSON, ALEXANDER HAMILTON: The Welsh medieval dioceses (No. 824).

WILLIAMS-JONES, KEITH: Llywelyn's charter to Cymer abbey in 1209 (No. 905).

WILLIS-BUND, JOHN WILLIAM: Archbishop Peckham (No. 1355).

## III. SOCIAL AND ECONOMIC HISTORY

### (a) Sources

Original sources for this period are few. In addition to those mentioned below, see also the law books (Nos. 1322–36) and the works of GIRALDUS CAMBRENSIS (No. 1287). For Domesday Book, see No. 1315.

**1402.** BALLARD, ADOLPHUS, and TAIT, JAMES: British borough charters. 2 vols. Cambridge, 1913–23.

**1403.** BATESON, MARY: The laws of Breteuil. *E.H.R.*, xv and xvi, 1900–1.

**1404.** Id.        The creation of the boroughs. Ibid., xvii, 1902.

**1405.** Id.        British borough customs. 2 vols. *Selden Soc.* London, 1904–5.

**1406.** Extent of Merionethshire, *temp.* Edward I. Ed. M. C. J. *Arch. Camb.*, 1867.
    See also THOMAS, DAVID RICHARD: Merionethshire six hundred years ago, ibid., 1884 and 1886.

**1407.** Mabinogion, The:

(i) The text of the Mabinogion and other Welsh tales from the Red Book of Hergest. Ed. John Rhŷs and J. Gwenogvryn Evans. Oxford, 1887.

(ii) Pedair Kainc y Mabinogi. Ed. J. Gwenogvryn Evans. Oxford, 1897. A selection of the Red Book tales.

(iii) The White Book of the Mabinogion: Welsh tales and romances reproduced from the Peniarth MSS. Ed. J. Gwenogvryn Evans. Pwllheli, 1907.

(iv) Pedeir Keinc y Mabinogi. Ed. with notes by Ifor Williams. 2nd edn, Cardiff, 1951.

> The date of these tales is a difficult question, but they may not improbably have assumed their present form about the time of Llywelyn ab Iorwerth (1175–1240). They have been translated into English by Lady Charlotte Guest (available in a variety of editions), by T. P. Ellis and J. Lloyd (Oxford, 1929), and by Gwyn Jones and Thomas Jones (Everyman's Library, London, 1949); and into French by Joseph Loth: Les mabinogion du livre rouge de Hergest avec les variantes du livre blanc de Rhytherch, revised edn, Paris, 1913. The tales are valuable for social history, but their evidence must be treated with great caution, as it is probably an amalgam of materials of different dates. See GRUFFYDD, WILLIAM JOHN: The Mabinogion, *Trans. Cymmr.*, 1912–13; id.: Math vab Mathonwy, Cardiff, 1928; id.: Rhiannon, Cardiff, 1953.

**1408.** MAP, WALTER: De nugis curialium. Ed. M. R. James, Oxford, 1914; older edn by T. Wright for Camden Soc., 1850; translation by M. R. James, with historical notes by J. E. Lloyd, ed. E. S. Hartland, *Cymmr. Rec. Ser.* (No. 109 (9)).

> See also JENKINS, ROBERT THOMAS: Llygad yr esgob. Yn Ymyl y ddalen. Wrecsam, 1958.

#### (b) Secondary works

For the general social and economic history of England during the period, see ASHLEY, W. J.: An introduction to English economic history and theory, 2 vols., London, etc., 1888–93; 3rd edn of vol. i, 1894; BATESON, MARY: Mediaeval England, New York, 1904; CUNNINGHAM, WILLIAM: The growth of English industry and commerce, 2nd edn, 2 vols., Cambridge, 1890–2; 4th edn, 2 vols., 1905–7; LIPSON, EPHRAIM: The economic history of England, vol. i, 7th edn, London, 1937; vols. ii and iii, 4th edn, London, 1947.

**1409.** BANKS, RICHARD W.: On the early charters to towns in South Wales. *Arch. Camb.*, 1878.

> See also *Arch. Camb.* supplement, 1879.

CARLYON-BRITTON, PHILIP WILLIAM POOLE: The Saxon, Norman, and Plantagenet coinage of Wales (No. 1201).

**1410.** GRAY, HOWARD LEVI: English field systems. Cambridge, Mass., 1915.

> Includes a discussion of Welsh arrangements.

**1411.** Gross, Charles: The gild merchant. 2 vols. Oxford, 1890.

**1412.** Hemmeon, Morley de Wolf: Burgage tenure in mediaeval England. Cambridge, Mass., 1914.

**1413.** Knoop, Douglas, and Jones, Gwilym Peredur: A note on the mason in Wales. *Arch. Camb.*, 1941.

**1414.** Maitland, Frederick William: The laws of Wales—the kindred and the blood feud. The collected papers of F. W. Maitland. Ed. H. A. L. Fisher. Vol. i. Cambridge, 1911.

**1415.** Neilson, Nellie: Customary rents. Oxford studies in social and legal history. Ed. Paul Vinogradoff. Vol. ii. Oxford, 1910.

**1416.** Palmer, Alfred Neobard: A history of ancient tenures of land in the marches of North Wales. Wrexham, 1885; 2nd edn (in collaboration with Edward Owen—it does not, however, supersede the first), 1910.

**1417.** Id.     Notes on ancient Welsh measures of land. *Arch. Camb.*, 1897.

> See also Pierce, Thomas Jones: A note on ancient Welsh measurements of land, ibid., 1942–3; and Gresham, Colin A.: A further note on ancient Welsh measurements of land, ibid., 1950–1.

**1418.** Id.     Ancient Welsh measures of capacity. Ibid., 1913.

Id.     The portionary churches of mediaeval North Wales (No. 1398).

Payne, Ffransis George: Yr aradr Gymreig (No. 246).

**1419.** Pierce, Thomas Jones: The growth of commutation in Gwynedd during the thirteenth century. *B.B.C.S.*, x, 1939–41.

**1420.** Id.     Ancient Meirionydd. *Jnl. Mer. Hist. and Rec. Soc.*, i, 1949–51.

**1421.** Id.     The age of the princes. In The historical basis of Welsh nationalism. Cardiff, 1950.

**1422.** Id.     The laws of Wales, the kindred and the blood-feud. *Univ. of Birmingham Hist. Jnl.*, iii, 2, 1952.

Id.     Medieval settlement in Anglesey (No. 516).

**1423.** Rees, William: South Wales and the march, 1284–1415: a social and agrarian study. Oxford, 1924.

Id.     Bibliography of published works on the municipal history of Wales and the border counties (No. 367).

RICHARDS, ROBERT: Cymru'r oesau canol (No. 155).

**1424.** SEEBOHM, FREDERICK: The tribal system in Wales. London, etc., 1895; 2nd edn, 1904.

A classical work on the subject, though its conclusions have met with some criticisms. The author had already discussed the question in his English village community, London, 1883, 4th edn, 1890. He subsequently returned to it in his Tribal custom in Anglo-Saxon law, London, etc., 1902, and in his posthumous Customary acres and their historical importance, London, etc., 1914. The greater part of ch. ix in RHŶS, JOHN, and BRYNMOR-JONES, DAVID, The Welsh people (No. 154), was also written by Seebohm. For criticism of The tribal system in Wales, see MAITLAND, F. W. (No. 1414); also ELLIS, T. P. (No. 1358), PIERCE, THOMAS JONES (No. 1422), and ASHLEY, W. J.: Surveys, historic and economic, London, 1900.

# SECTION F

## A.D. 1282—1500

For the general background of English history in this period the volumes in the standard Oxford History of England published to date are POWICKE, FREDERICK MAURICE: The thirteenth century, 1216–1307 (No. 1376) and McKISACK, MAY: The fourteenth century, 1307–99, Oxford, 1959. A volume on the fifteenth century by E. F. JACOB is in preparation. For a short introduction to the period and a very useful select bibliography, see MYERS, A. R.: England in the late middle ages, vol. iv in the Pelican History of England. For a fuller bibliography, see Cambridge Medieval History, vols. vii and viii.

In addition to works listed under section headings below, official Government publications are, as in the period 1039–1282, the chief original authorities in print (see pp. 93–95). To these may be added: Feudal aids (1284–1431), i–iv, *Rolls Series,* London, 1899–1908; Catalogue of ancient deeds, i–vi, London, 1899–1915; Rotulorum originalium abbreviatio, 2 vols., *Record Commission,* London, 1805–10.

For chronicles covering this period not mentioned below, see GROSS, pp. 326–99 (No. 9), and KINGSFORD, C. L.: English historical literature in the fifteenth century, Oxford, 1913.

Some of the source material and secondary works listed in section E are relevant to this section also.

### I. POLITICAL AND GENERAL HISTORY

For short general surveys of the period, consult the relevant sections under WALES in the Encyclopaedia Britannica, 1955 (J. E. LLOYD), and in the New Chamber's Encyclopaedia (T. JONES PIERCE); and J. E. Lloyd in Cambridge Mediaeval History, vii. BEBB, WILLIAM AMBROSE, Llywodraeth y cestyll, Wrexham, 1934, is an elementary survey, stimulating but often misleading. RICHARDS, ROBERT, Cymru'r oesau canol (No. 155), continues to be useful for this period. Y bywgraffiadur Cymreig (No. 106) and the Dictionary of Welsh biography (No. 107) are also indispensable. REES, WILLIAM, An historical atlas of Wales (No. 379) is useful for this and other periods, while id., Map of South Wales and the border in the fourteenth century (No. 378), is essential for more advanced work.

For material relating to castle-building during this period, see section B III (*b*).

#### (a) Sources

**1425.** ADAM OF USK: Chronicon Adae de Usk. Ed. E. Maunde Thompson. 2nd edn. London, 1904.

Brut y tywysogyon. Peniarth MS. 20 version (No. 130 (6)).

Brut y tywysogyon, or the chronicle of the princes. Peniarth MS. 20 version (No. 130 (11)).
A translation of No. 130 (6).

Brut y tywysogyon, or the chronicle of the princes. Red book of Hergest version (No. 130 (16)).

Calendar of ancient correspondence concerning Wales (No. 130 (2)).

**1426.** Calendar of inquisitions, miscellaneous (Chancery), 1377–88. London, 1957.

**1427.** GRIFFITHS, JOHN: Documents relating to the rebellion of Madoc, 1294–5. *B.B.C.S.*, viii, 1937.

**1428.** Index of wills proved in the prerogative court of Canterbury, 1383–1558, etc. Compiled by J. Challenor C. Smith. 2 vols. British Record Society. Index Library, Nos. 10 and 11, 1893 and 1895.

**1429.** Letters and papers illustrative of the reigns of Richard III and Henry VI. Ed. J. Gairdner. 2 vols. *Rolls Series*. London, 1861–3.

**1430.** Letters and papers on the wards in France (*temp.* Henry VI). Ed. J. Stevenson. *Rolls Series*. London, 1861–4.

Littere Walliae (No. 130 (5)).

See also RYMER, THOMAS: Foedera (No. 128).

**1431.** Narratives of the expulsion of the English from Normandy. Ed. J. Stevenson. *Rolls Series*. London, 1863.

Parliamentary writs and writs of military summons (Edward I–Edward II) (No. 1340).

PARSONS, E. J. S.: The map of Great Britain *c.* 1360, known as the Gough map (No. 377).

**1432.** Royal and historical letters during the reign of Henry IV. Ed. F. C. Hingeston. *Rolls Series*. London, 1860.

### (b) Secondary works

**1433.** BEBB, WILLIAM AMBROSE: Machlud yr oesau canol. Swansea, 1951.

**1434.** BELL, HAROLD IDRIS: A Herefordshire echo of Edward I's Welsh campaigns. *B.B.C.S.*, viii, 1937.

**1435.** BRADLEY, A. G.: Owen Glyndwr and the last struggle for Welsh independence. London, 1901.

**1436.** CHOTZEN, THEODORE MAX: Yvain de Galles. *B.B.C.S.*, iv, 1928.

See also DAVIES, JOHN HUMPHREYS: Owain Lawgoch, *Trans. Cymmr.*, 1899–1900; also printed in *Mont. Coll.*, xxxvii, 1915; MATTHEWS, T.: Owain Lawgoch, *Trans. Carms. Antiq. Soc.*, vi, 1910–11; OWEN, EDWARD: Owen Lawgoch, *Trans. Cymmr.*, 1899–1900 and 1900–1; WILLIAMS, WILLIAM LLEWELYN: Owain Lawgoch, ibid., 1900–1; id.: Owain Lawgoch, *Trans. Carms. Antiq. Soc.*, v, 1909.

**1437.** DAVIES, D. J. Griffith: Owen Glyn Dwr. London, 1934.

**1438.** DAVIES, JAMES CONWAY: The Despenser war in Glamorgan. *Trans. R.H.S.*, 1914.

**1439.** Id.     Some Owen Glyndwr documents. *N.L.W. Jnl.*, iii, 1943.

**1440.** EDWARDS, JOHN GORONWY: Sir Gruffydd Llwyd. *E.H.R.*, xxx, 1915.

**1441.** Id.     The battle of Maes Madog and the Welsh war of 1294–5. Ibid., xxxix, 1924.
> See also id.: The site of the battle of 'Meismeidoc', 1295, ibid., xlvi, 1931.

**1442.** Id.     Madog ap Llewelyn, the Welsh leader in 1294–5. *B.B.C.S.*, xiii, 1950.
> See also ROBERTS, GLYN: Biographical notes . . . Madog ap Llywelyn, *B.B.C.S.*, xvii, 1956.

**1443.** Id.     The treason of Thomas Turberville. In Studies in medieval history presented to F. M. Powicke. Oxford, 1948.

**1444.** EVANS, DAVID LEWIS: Some notes on the history of the principality in the time of the Black Prince. *Trans. Cymmr.*, 1925–6.

**1445.** Id.     The later middle ages. In The history of Carmarthenshire, i (No. 605).
> Useful for the rising of Rhys ap Maredudd and the career of Sir Rhys ap Gruffydd.

**1446.** EVANS, GEORGE EYRE: Seal of Sir Rhys ap Thomas, 1494. *Trans. Carms. Antiq. Soc.*, xxvi, 1936.

**1447.** EVANS, HOWEL T.: William Herbert, earl of Pembroke. *Trans. Cymmr.*, 1909–10.

**1448.** Id.     Wales and the wars of the roses. Cambridge, 1915.

HUGHES, GARFIELD HOPKIN: Y Dwniaid (No. 43).
> See also DUNN, T. W. NEWTON: The Dwn family, ibid., 1946–7, and section A II.

**1449.** GRIFFITHS, JOHN: The revolt of Madog ap Llewelyn, 1294–5. *Trans. Caerns. Hist. Soc.*, 1955.

**1450.** HOLMES, GEORGE ANDREW: The estates of the higher nobility in fourteenth century England. Cambridge, 1957.
> Especially ch. iv.

**1451.** JOHNSTONE, HILDA: Edward of Carnarvon, 1284–1307. Manchester, 1946.
> Review by J. Conway Davies in *Jnl. Hist. Soc. Church in Wales*, i, 1947.

**1452.** JONES, EVAN DAVID: Some fifteenth century Welsh poetry relating to Montgomeryshire. *Mont. Coll.*, liii–liv, 1951–6.
Appendix contains select passages in translation.

**1453.** JONES, FRANCIS: Welsh bonds for keeping the peace, 1283 and 1295. *B.B.C.S.*, xiii, 1950.

Id.    Sir Rhys ap Thomas and the knights of St. John (No. 930).

Id.    An approach to Welsh genealogy (No. 51).

**1454.** JONES, WILLIAM GARMON: Welsh nationalism and Henry Tudor. *Trans. Cymmr.*, 1917–18.

**1455.** KINGSFORD, C. L.: Sir Otho de Grandison, 1238–1328. *Trans. R.H.S.*, 1909.

**1456.** KNIGHT, HENRY: On the insurrection of Llewelyn Bren. *Arch. Camb.*, 1851.

**1457.** L[LOYD], H[OWEL] W[ILLIAM]: Jasper Tudor, earl of Pembroke, at Barmouth. Ibid., 1878.

**1458.** Id.    Sir Rhys ap Thomas and his family. Ibid., 1878.
See also the anonymous life of Sir Rhys ap Thomas in *The Cambrian Register*, i, 1796; should be used with caution.

**1459.** LLOYD, JOHN EDWARD: The Scudamore family. *B.B.C.S.*, iv, 1928.

**1460.** Id.    Owen Glendower. Oxford, 1931.

Id.    The story of Ceredigion (No. 578).

**1461.** MATTHEWS, T.: Welsh records in Paris. Carmarthen, 1910.

MORRIS, JOHN EDWARD: The Welsh wars of Edward I (No. 1371).
In addition to the war of 1294–5, this work deals with the Custom of the March.

**1462.** REES, WILLIAM: The union of England and Wales. *Trans. Cymmr.*, 1937; repr. Cardiff, 1937.

**1463.** ROBERTS, GLYN: Wyrion Eden: The Anglesey descendants of Ednyfed Fychan in the fourteenth century. *Trans. Angl. Antiq. Soc.*, 1951.

**1464.** Id.    The Anglesey submissions of 1406. *B.B.C.S.*, xv, 1954.

**1465.** SANDEFORD, G.: The Mortimers and their fortresses in Powysland and the border. *Mont. Coll.*, xxviii, 1894.

**1466.** SOMERVILLE, R.: History of the duchy of Lancaster. Vol. i, 1265–1603. London, 1953.

**1467.** STEEL, ANTHONY: Richard II. Cambridge, 1941.

**1468.** TENNANT, WINIFRED COOMBE: Croes naid. *N.L.W. Jnl.*, vii, 1951.
See also OWEN, EDWARD: Y croes nawdd, *Y Cymmr.*, xliii, 1932.

**1469.** TOUT, THOMAS FREDERICK: The captivity and death of Edward of Carnarvon. In Collected essays of Thomas Frederick Tout. Vol. iii. Manchester, 1934.

**1470.** WILLIAMS, JOHN: Penmynydd and the Tudors. *Arch. Camb.*, 1869.

**1471.** WILLIAMS, WILLIAM LLEWELYN: Adam of Usk. *Y Cymmr.*, xxxi, 1921.

**1472.** WILLIAMS, W. T.: Henry Richmond's itinerary to Bosworth. *Y Cymmr.*, xxix, 1919.
See also JERMAN, HERBERT NOEL: A map of the routes of Henry Tudor and Rhys ap Thomas through Wales in 1485. *Arch. Camb.*, 1937.

**1473.** WYLIE, J. H.: History of England under Henry IV. 4 vols. London, 1884–98.

**1474.** Id.     The reign of Henry V. 3 vols. Cambridge, 1914–29.

WYNN, SIR JOHN: History of the Gwydir family (No. 79).

YORKE, PHILIP: The royal tribes of Wales (No. 81).

## II. CONSTITUTIONAL AND LEGAL HISTORY

Familiarity with the literature relating to the Welsh laws is essential to an understanding of constitutional and legal history, as well as social and economic developments, in this period. A full bibliography appears in section E (Nos. 1322 to 1336). Much of the material in the second volume of OWEN, ANEURIN, Ancient laws and institutes of Wales (No. 1329), illustrates the decline of native jurisprudence at this time.

The chief study in English administrative history is TOUT, THOMAS FREDERICK: Chapters in the administrative history of mediaeval England, vols. i–v, Manchester, 1920–33; and in legal history, HOLDSWORTH, WILLIAM SEARLE: A history of English law (No. 1361). Both contain references to Wales.

### (a) Sources

BOWEN, IVOR: Statutes of Wales (No. 108).

Calendar of Chancery rolls, various, 1277–1326 (No. 1312).
For the Welsh rolls, 1277–94, see pp. 157–362.

Court rolls of the lordship of Ruthin or Dyffryn Clwyd of the reign of Edward I (No. 109 (2)).

Flint pleas, 1283–5. Ed. J. G. Edwards (No. 1319).

**1475.** John of Gaunt's register, 1371–5. Ed. S. Armitage-Smith. 2 vols. Camden Soc. 3rd series. London, 1911.

> For the administration of the duchy of Lancaster estates, see also Duchy of Lancaster: calendar to pleadings, *Record Commission*, London, 1834; Ducatus Lancastriae calendarium inquisitionum post mortem, Edward I—Charles I, *Record Commission*, London, 1823.

**1476.** JOHNSTONE, HILDA (ed.): Letters of Edward, prince of Wales, 1304–5. *Roxburghe Club*. London, 1931.

**1477.** JONES, GWILYM PEREDUR (ed.): Anglesey court rolls, 1346. *Trans. Angl. Antiq. Soc.,* 1930 and 1933.

Id.     and OWEN, HUGH (eds.): Caernarvon court rolls, 1361–1402 (No. 536).

**1478.** LEWIS, EDWARD ARTHUR (ed.): Proceedings in the small hundred court of Ardudwy, 1325–6. *B.B.C.S.,* iv, 1928.

**1479.** Id.     (ed.): The court rolls of the manor of Broniarth (co. Montgomery), 1429–64. Ibid., xi, 1944.

**1480.** Placita de quo warranto (No. 127).

> Contains the *quo warranto* proceedings for Cardiganshire (18 Edward III). See also The record of Caernarvon (No. 129).

**1481.** Proceedings and ordinances of the Privy Council of England. Ed. H. Nicholas. 7 vols. *Record Commission.* London, 1834–7.

Record of Caernarvon (No. 129).

REES, WILLIAM (ed.): Ministers' accounts . . . west Wales (No. 581).

**1482.** Register of Edward the Black Prince. 4 parts. London, 1930–3.

> In particular parts 1 and 3. The latter deals with the business of the palatinate of Chester. For a calendar of the recognizance rolls of the palatinate, see P.R.O. Deputy Keeper's Reports, xxxvi, app. ii; xxxvii, app. ii.

**1483.** Rotuli parliamentorum, 1278–1503. 6 vols. Published in the late eighteenth century by order of the House of Lords.

**1484.** Scrope and Grosvenor roll, The. Ed. N. H. Nicholas. 2 vols. London, 1832.

**1485.** Statutes of the realm. 11 vols. *Record Commission.* London, 1810–28.

> For the Welsh statutes see BOWEN, IVOR: Statutes of Wales (No. 108).

**1486.** TOUT, THOMAS FREDERICK, and JOHNSTONE, HILDA (eds): State trials of the reign of Edward I, 1289–93. Camden Soc. 3rd series, ix, 1906.

**1487.** WATERS, W. H. (ed.): A North Wales coroner's account. *B.B.C.S.,* iv, 1929.

**1488.** Id. (ed.): Roll of the county court of Anglesey. Ibid.

**1489.** Id.      (ed.): The first draft of the statute of Rhuddlan. Ibid.

**1490.** Id. (ed.): Documents relating to the office of escheator for North Wales for the year 1309–10. Ibid., vi, 1933.

**1491.** Id.      (ed.): Documents relating to the sheriff's turn in North Wales. Ibid.

### (b) Secondary works

BREESE, EDWARD: Kalendars of Gwynedd (No. 83).

**1492.** DAVIES, JAMES CONWAY: Felony in Edwardian Wales. *Trans. Cymmr.,* 1916–17.

**1493.** Id.      The baronial opposition to Edward II. Cambridge, 1916.

EDWARDS, JOHN GORONWY: The building of Flint (No. 1356).
See also TAYLOR, ARNOLD JOSEPH: The building of Flint—a postscript (No. 1385).

Id.      The early history of the counties of Carmarthen and Cardigan (No. 562).

Id.      Edward I's castle-building in Wales (No. 387).

**1494.** GRIFFITHS, WILLIAM ARTHUR: Fifteenth and sixteenth century lords of the manor of Broniarth. *Mont. Coll.,* liv, 1955–6.

**1495.** HEWITT, H. J.: Mediaeval Cheshire: an economic and social history of Cheshire in the reigns of the three Edwards. Manchester, 1929.
See also the Register of Edward the Black Prince (No. 1482).

**1496.** Id.      The Black Prince's expedition of 1355–1357. Manchester, 1958.

**1497.** LEWIS, DAVID: The Court of the president and council of Wales and the marches, 1478–1575. *Y Cymmr.,* xii, 1897.

**1498.** LEWIS, EDWARD ARTHUR: The mediaeval boroughs of Snowdonia. London, 1912.

OWEN, HENRY: The administration of English law in Wales and the marches (No. 1374).

REES, WILLIAM: South Wales and the march, 1284–1415 (No. 1423).
> Part I deals with administration.

**1499.** SKEEL, CAROLINE ANNE JAMES: The council in the marches of Wales: a study in local government during the sixteenth and seventeenth centuries. London, 1903.

**1500.** TOUT, THOMAS FREDERICK: The Welsh shires: a study in constitutional history. *Y Cymmr.*, ix, 1888.

**1501.** WATERS, W. H.: The Edwardian settlement of North Wales in its administrative and legal aspects (1284–1343). Cardiff, 1935.

**1502.** Id.    The making of Caernarvonshire. *Trans. Caerns. Hist. Soc.*, 1942–3.

**1503.** YOUNG, C. G.: An account of the controversy between Reginald, Lord Grey of Ruthyn, and Sir Edward Hastings. London, 1841.
> For the Edwardian castles of North Wales see section B III, Nos. 383–406.

### III. LITERARY HISTORY

An excellent short guide to Welsh literature, with a bibliography, is PARRY, THOMAS: Hanes llenyddiaeth Gymraeg, and the English translation thereof by H. Idris Bell (No. 146). See also *Llên Cymru* (No. 341).

#### (a) Texts

**1504.** BACHELLERY, EDOUARD: L'Oeuvre poetique de Gutun Owain. 2 vols. Paris, 1950–1.

**1505.** BELL, HAROLD IDRIS: Translations from the cywyddwyr. *Trans. Cymmr.*, 1940 and 1942.

**1506.** HARRIES, LESLIE: Gwaith Huw Cae Llwyd ac eraill. Caerdydd, 1953.

**1507.** JONES, EVAN DAVID: Gwaith Lewis Glyn Cothi. Cyf. i. Caerdydd ac Aberystwyth, 1953. In progress.
> See also JONES, JOHN (TEGID), and DAVIES, WALTER: The poetical works of Lewis Glyn Cothi, 2 vols., Oxford, 1837.

**1508.** JONES, THOMAS GWYNN: Gwaith Tudur Aled. 2 gyf. Caerdydd, etc., 1926.

**1509.** LEWIS, HENRY, and ROBERTS, THOMAS, and WILLIAMS, IFOR (eds): Cywyddau Iolo Goch ac eraill. Caerdydd, 1937.

**1510.** LEWIS, SAUNDERS: Iolo Goch. *Y Llenor*, v, 1926.

**1511.** MORRICE, J. C.: Gwaith barddonol Howel Swrdwal a'i fab Ieuan. *Bangor Welsh MSS. Soc.* Bangor, 1908.

**1512.** PARRY, THOMAS: Gwaith Dafydd ap Gwilym. Caerdydd, 1952.

See also No. 1526 below and BELL, HAROLD IDRIS, and BELL, DAVID: Dafydd ap Gwilym: fifty poems, *Y Cymmr.*, xlviii, 1942.

**1513.** ROBERTS, THOMAS: Gwaith Dafydd ab Edmwnd. *Bangor Welsh MSS. Soc.* Bangor, 1914.

**1514.** Id.    The poetical works of Dafydd Nanmor. Cardiff, 1923.

**1515.** Id.    Gwaith Tudur Penllyn ac Ieuan ap Tudur Penllyn. Caerdydd, 1958.

**1516.** WILLIAMS, IFOR: Casgliad o waith Ieuan Deulwyn. *Bangor Welsh MSS. Soc.* Bangor, 1909.

**1517.** Id.    and WILLIAMS, JOHN LLYWELYN: Gwaith Guto'r Glyn. Caerdydd, 1939.

**1518.** WILLIAMS, JOHN ELLIS CAERWYN: Bucheddau'r saint. *B.B.C.S.*, xi, 1941–4.

#### (b) Secondary works

**1519.** CHOTZEN, THEODORE MAX: Recherches sur la poésie de Dafydd ap Gwilym. Amsterdam, 1927.

**1520.** GRUFFYDD, WILLIAM JOHN: Llenyddiaeth Cymru o 1450 hyd 1600. Lerpwl, 1922.

JONES, EVAN DAVID: Some fifteenth century Welsh poetry relating to Montgomery (No. 1452).

**1521.** JONES, THOMAS GWYNN: Bardism and romance: a study of Welsh literary tradition. *Trans. Cymmr.*, 1913–14.

**1522.** LEWIS, HOWELL ELVET: Welsh Catholic poetry in the fifteenth century. Ibid., 1911–12.

**1523.** LEWIS, SAUNDERS: Tudur Aled. *Efryd. Cath.*, i, 1946.

**1524.** MORRIS-JONES, JOHN: Tudur Aled. *Trans. Cymmr.*, 1908–9.

**1525.** RHŶS, JOHN: Welsh cave legends and the story of Owain Lawgoch. Ibid., 1899–1900.

**1526.** WILLIAMS, IFOR, a ROBERTS, THOMAS: Dafydd ap Gwilym a'i gyfoeswyr. Caerdydd, 1935.

See also No. 1512 above.

WILLIAMS, GRIFFITH JOHN: Traddodiad llenyddol Morgannwg (No. 160).

## IV. ECCLESIASTICAL HISTORY

All the diocesan histories noted in section B VI, particularly the S.P.C.K. series (Nos. 825, 836, 843, 847) and BROWNE WILLIS (Nos. 830, 840, 845, 861), as well as many of the studies relating to the religious orders in section B VII, DUGDALE: Monasticon (No. 111) and HADDAN and STUBBS: Councils (No. 115) should also be consulted for the history of this period.

Works dealing with the background of Church history in the thirteenth century, e.g. DAVIES, JAMES CONWAY, Episcopal Acts (No. 823), are important to an understanding of trends in the later middle ages.

For a stimulating introduction, see the lectures by E. W. Williamson, bishop of Swansea and Brecon, and by Professor A. H. Dodd in the Welsh Church Congress handbook (No. 184).

### (a) Sources

Calendar of entries in the papal registers relating to Great Britain and Ireland. Papal letters, 1198–1484 (No. 1391).

See also Petitions to the pope, 1342–1419, *Rolls Series*, London, 1893.

EMMANUEL, HYWEL DAVID: A fragment of the register of Stephen Patryngton, bishop of St. David's (No. 849).

Id.    Early St. David's records (No. 850).

Episcopal registers of the diocese of St. David's (No. 109 (6)).

**1527.** REES, WILLIAM: The possessions of the abbey of Tewkesbury in Glamorgan: accounts of the ministers for the year 1449–50. *S. Wales and Mon. Rec. Soc.*, ii, 1950.

Id.    The templar manor of Llanmadoc (No. 950).

Register of the letters of John Peckham, archbishop of Canterbury (No. 1320).

Taxatio ecclesiastica Angliae et Walliae auctoritate P. Nicolai IV (No. 1392).

This is the most comprehensive ecclesiastical record of this period. It should be studied in conjunction with The valuation of Norwich (No. 1393) and Valor ecclesiasticus (No. 1694).

### (b) Secondary works

BEBB, WILLIAM AMBROSE: Machlud y mynachlogydd (No. 864).

DAVIES, JAMES CONWAY: Dominicans in Wales (No. 868).

Id.    The black book of St. David's (No. 848).

DOUIE, DECIMA LANGWORTHY: Archbishop Pecham (No. 1355).

EVANS, DAVID LEWIS: Llyfr coch Asaph (No. 841).
See also *Arch. Camb.* supplement, 1879.

**1528.** GABRIEL, JACOB REES: Wales and the Avignon papacy. *Arch. Camb.,* 1923.

**1529.** GRAHAM, ROSE: The Cluniac priory of St. Martin des Champs, Paris, and its dependent priories in England and Wales. *Jnl. Brit. Arch. Assoc.,* xi, 1948.

**1530.** JARMAN, ALFRED OWEN HUGHES: Wales and the council of Constance. *B.B.C.S.,* xiv, 1952.

JONES, GRIFFITH HARTWELL: Celtic Britain and the pilgrim movement (No. 1237).

LEWIS, FRANK ROBERT: History of Llanbadarn Fawr, Cardiganshire, in the later middle ages (No. 573).

O'SULLIVAN, JEREMIAH F.: Cistercian settlements in Wales and Monmouthshire (No. 881).

REES, WILLIAM: A history of the order of St. John of Jerusalem in Wales and the border (No. 883).

THOMPSON, ALEXANDER HAMILTON: The Welsh medieval dioceses (No. 824).

WILLIS-BUND, JOHN WILLIAM: Archbishop Peckham (No. 1355).

## V. SOCIAL AND ECONOMIC HISTORY

### (a) Sources

**1531.** EVANS, DAVID LEWIS (ed.): Flintshire ministers' accounts, 1328–53. *Flints. Hist. Soc. Rec. Ser.,* 2, 1929.

**1532.** EVANS, ELWYN (ed.): The manor of Uwchmynydd, Radnorshire, in 1618. *N.L.W. Jnl.,* vi, 1950.

**1533.** GRIFFITHS, JOHN (ed.): Two early ministers' accounts for North Wales. *B.B.C.S.,* ix, 1939.

**1534.** Id. (ed.): Early accounts relating to North Wales, *temp.* Edward I. Ibid., xiv, 1952; xv, 1954; xvi, 1955.

**1535.** JONES, ARTHUR (ed.): Flintshire ministers' accounts, 1301–28. *Flints. Hist. Soc. Pubns.,* iii, 1913.

**1536.** JONES, FRANCIS (ed.): The subsidy of 1292. *B.B.C.S.,* xiii, 1950.

JONES, GWILYM PEREDUR (ed.): The extent of Chirkland (1391–3) (No. 632).

**1537.** LEWIS, EDWARD ARTHUR: The decay of tribalism in North Wales. *Trans. Cymmr.,* 1902–3.

> Contains valuable appendices of original sources. See also the appendices to SEEBOHM, FREDERICK: Tribal system in Wales (No. 1424).

**1538.** Id.     (ed.): Account of the chamberlain of west Wales, 1301–3. *B.B.C.S.,* iv, 1925.

**1539.** Id.     (ed.): Account of the chamberlain of the principality of North Wales, 1304–5. Ibid.

Id.     The mediaeval boroughs of Snowdonia (No. 1498).

Ministers' accounts for west Wales, 1277–1306 (No. 109 (13)).

**1540.** PIERCE, THOMAS JONES (ed.): A Lleyn lay subsidy account. *B.B.C.S.,* v, 1930.

**1541.** Id.     (ed.): Two early Caernarvonshire accounts. i, Nefyn lay subsidy, 1293; ii, Extracts from the sheriff's roll, 1306–7. Ibid.

**1542.** Id.     (ed.): Lleyn ministers' accounts, 1350–1. Ibid., vi, 1933.

Id.     (ed.): An Anglesey crown rental of the sixteenth century (No. 517).
> Throws light on the decay of the tribal structure.

REES, WILLIAM: South Wales and the march, 1284–1415 (No. 1423).

Id.     (ed.): Ministers' accounts . . . west Wales (No. 581).

**1543.** Id.     (ed.): Accounts of the receiver of the mine of coals [in the lordship of Kilvey], Michaelmas, 23 Richard II, to Michaelmas, 1 Henry IV [1399]. *S. Wales and Mon. Rec. Soc.,* i [1949].

**1544.** Id.     (ed.): Records relating to the lordship of Senghenydd with Caerphilly from Edward I to Henry VIII. Part I. Ibid., iv, 1957.

SLACK, WALTER JOHN: The lordship of Oswestry, 1393–1607 (No. 815).

The black book of St. David's (No. 109 (5)).

The first extent of Bromfield and Yale (No. 109 (11)).

VINOGRADOFF, PAUL, and MORGAN, FRANK: Survey of the honour of Denbigh, 1334 (No. 651).
> See also USHER, GWILYM ARTHUR: A survey of the honour of Denbigh in 1334 (No. 651).

**1545.** WATERS, W. H.: Account of the sheriff of Caernarvon for 1303–4. *B.B.C.S.,* vii, 1935.

### (b) Secondary works

A review of the records of the Conway and the Menai ferries
(No. 130 (8)).

**1546.** Ellis, Thomas Peter: The Powys inquisitions, 1293–1311.
*Mont. Coll.*, xli, 1930.

**1547.** Griffiths, Griffith Milwyn: Chirk castle MSS. and documents.
*N.L.W. Jnl.*, viii, 1954.

Hewitt, H. J.: Mediaeval Cheshire (No. 1495).

Holmes, George Andrew: The estates of the higher nobility
in fourteenth century England (No. 1450).
Contains valuable sections on some Welsh lordships.

**1548.** Jones, Emrys: Some aspects of the study of settlements in Britain.
*Advancement of Science*, 29, 1951.

**1549.** Jones, Evan David: Rhannu tir Rhys ap Elise. *N.L.W. Jnl.*,
iii, 1943.

**1550.** Jones, Glanville R.: Some medieval rural settlements in North
Wales. *Trans. Inst. of British Geographers*, 1953.

**1551.** Id.     The distribution of medieval settlement in Anglesey.
*Trans. Angl. Antiq. Soc.*, 1955.

**1552.** Lewis, Edward Arthur: The development of industry and
commerce in Wales during the middle ages. *Trans. R.H.S.*, xvii, 1903.

**1553.** Id.     A contribution to the commercial history of mediaeval
Wales, 1301–1547. *Y Cymmr.*, xxiv, 1913.

Palmer, Alfred Neobard: A history of the ancient tenures
of land in the marches of North Wales (No. 812).

Id.     Notes on ancient Welsh measures of land (No. 1417).

Id.     Ancient Welsh measures of capacity (No. 1418).

**1554.** Pierce, Thomas Jones: Some tendencies in the agrarian history
of Caernarvonshire in the later middle ages. *Trans. Caerns. Hist. Soc.*, 1939.

**1555.** Id.     The gafael in Bangor MS. 1939. *Trans. Cymmr.*, 1944.

Id.     Commutation in Gwynedd during the thirteenth
century (No. 1419).

Id.     A note on ancient Welsh measurements of land
(No. 1417).

Id. (ed.). Clenennau letters and papers (No. 124).
The introduction deals with the rise of an estate in the fifteenth century.

Id.      Medieval settlement in Anglesey (No. 516).

**1556.** REES, WILLIAM: The black death in Wales. *Trans. R.H.S.*, 1920.

**1557.** Id.      The black death in England and Wales. *Procs. Royal Soc. of Medicine*, xvi, 1923.

Id.      South Wales and the march, 1284–1415 (No. 1423).

**1558.** RUSSELL, JOSIAH COX: British mediaeval population. Albuquerque, 1948.

**1559.** USHER, GWILYM ARTHUR: Holyhead as a fourteenth century port. *B.B.C.S.*, xv, 1954.

**1560.** Id.      Welsh students at Oxford in the middle ages. Ibid., xvi, 1955.

## VI. MUNICIPAL HISTORY

### (a) Sources

For a general introduction to this subject, see REES, WILLIAM: Bibliography of published works on the municipal history of Wales and the border counties (No. 367).

**1561.** CHARLES, BERTIE GEORGE (ed.): The records of the borough of Newport in Pembrokeshire. *N.L.W. Jnl.*, vii, 1951–2.

GRANT-FRANCIS, GEORGE (ed.): Charters granted to . . . Swansea . . . 1215–1837 (No. 677).

**1562.** GRIFFITHS, JOHN (ed.): Documents relating to the early history of Conway. *Trans. Caerns. Hist. Soc.*, 1947.

JONES, GWILYM PEREDUR, and OWEN, HUGH (eds): Caernarvon court rolls (No. 536).

**1563.** JONES, WILLIAM GARMON: Ministers' accounts for the borough of Criccieth. *B.B.C.S.*, iii, 1926.
See also id.: Court rolls of the borough of Criccieth, ibid., ii, 1924; Charter of the borough of Criccieth, ibid., iv, 1928.

**1564.** Id.      Documents illustrative of the history of the North Wales boroughs. Ibid., iii, 1926; iv, 1928.

**1565.** PIERCE, THOMAS JONES, and GRIFFITHS, JOHN (eds.): Documents relating to the early history of the borough of Caernarvon. Ibid., ix, 1939.

**1566.** REES, WILLIAM (ed.): The charters of the borough of Newport in Gwynllwg. Newport, 1951.

Id.  (ed.): The charters of the boroughs of Brecon and Llandovery (No. 530).

Id.  (ed.): Records relating to the lordship of Senghenydd with Caerphilly from Edward I to Henry VIII (No. 1544).

**1567.** WYNNE, WILLIAM WATKIN EDWARD (ed.): Documents relating to the town and castle of Harlech, 1284–1650. *Arch. Camb.*, 1846 and 1848.

### (b) Secondary works

**1568.** JENKINS, ROBERT THOMAS: The borough of Bala, *circa* 1350. *B.B.C.S.*, xi, 1944.

**1569.** JONES, GWILYM PEREDUR: Trading in medieval Caernarvon. *Trans. Caerns. Hist. Soc.*, 1949.

JONES, WILLIAM HENRY: History of Swansea and of the lordship of Gower from the earliest times to the fourteenth century (No. 684).

LEWIS, EDWARD ARTHUR: The mediaeval boroughs of Snowdonia (No. 1498).

O'NEIL, BRYAN HUGH ST. JOHN: The castle and borough of Llanidloes (No. 764).

**1570.** PIERCE, THOMAS JONES: A Caernarvonshire manorial borough [Pwllheli]. *Trans. Caerns. Hist. Soc.*, 1941, 1942–3, 1944.

**1571.** Id.  The old borough of Nefyn, 1355–1882. Ibid., 1957.

REES, WILLIAM: History of Cardiff (No. 698).

SANDERS, IVOR JOHN: The boroughs of Aberystwyth and Cardigan in the early fourteenth century (No. 582).

**1572.** USHER, GWILYM ARTHUR: The earliest records of Ruthin. *Trans. Denbs. Hist. Soc.*, 1958.

# SECTION G

## A.D. 1500—1603

The indispensable bibliographical work for all aspects of British history in the sixteenth century is READ, CONYERS: Bibliography of British history: Tudor period, 1485–1603, Oxford, 1933; 2nd edn, 1959. To this may be added the valuable bibliographies to be found in the appropriate volumes of the standard Oxford History of England: MACKIE, JOHN DUNCAN: The earlier Tudors, 1485–1558, Oxford, 1952; BLACK, J. B.: The reign of Elizabeth, Oxford, 1936; 2nd edn, 1959. See also ELTON, GEOFFREY RUDOLPH: England under the Tudors, London, 1955.

The relevant sections in Writings on British history (No. 12) and the Annual bulletin of historical literature (ibid.) provide useful supplementary material.

### I. GENERAL WORKS

#### (a) Sources

The most important repository of unpublished record material for the sixteenth century is the Public Record Office. GIUSEPPI (No. 114) provides a guide to the classes of manuscripts preserved there. MULLINS: Texts and calendars (p. 23) and the current P.R.O. Sectional List No. 24 (H.M.S.O., 1951) should be consulted for a comprehensive list of all published calendars, lists, and indexes of manuscript material at the repository. Some of the more noteworthy of these are mentioned below (Nos. 1573–7). In addition, the publications of the History and Law Committee of the Board of Celtic Studies (No. 130) cover specifically Welsh material, but there are many important collections, manuscript guides to which are to be found only at the Record Office itself.

There are also valuable resources at the British Museum, for which see A catalogue of the manuscripts relating to Wales in the British Museum (No. 109 (4)).

The National Library of Wales has a mass of miscellaneous manuscript material. In addition to the calendars listed below, the Handlist (No. 123), the National Library of Wales Journal (No. 332), and the manuscript catalogues and schedules at the Library itself, should be consulted.

For other general source material, see READ, CONYERS: Bibliography of British history, 8–27.

#### (i) Official and other records

**1573.** Acts of the Privy Council of England. London, 1890 ff.

An inventory of early Chancery proceedings concerning Wales (No. 130 (3)).

BOWEN, IVOR: Statutes of Wales (No. 108).

**1574.** Calendar of letters and papers, foreign and domestic, Henry VIII, 1509–47. London, 1862–1932.
> See also state papers published under the authority of His Majesty's Commission, King Henry VIII. 11 vols. London, 1830–52.

Calendar of the register of the council in the marches of Wales (No. 109 (8)).

**1575.** Calendar of state papers, colonial series, 1574–1712. London, 1856 ff.

**1576.** Calendar of state papers, domestic, 1547–1704. London, 1856 ff.

**1577.** Calendar of state papers, foreign, 1547–89. London, 1863 ff.

Catalogue of Star Chamber proceedings relating to Wales (No. 130 (1)).

**1578.** CHARLES, BERTIE GEORGE (ed.): Haverfordwest accounts, 1563–1620. *N.L.W. Jnl.*, ix, 1955–6.

CLARK, GEORGE THOMAS: Cartae et alia munimenta quae ad dominium de Glamorgan pertinent (No. 671).

**1579.** COLLINS, ARTHUR: Letters and memorials of state . . . written and collected by Sir Henry Sidney . . . Sir Philip Sidney and his brother Sir Robert Sidney . . ., etc. 2 vols. London, 1746.
> Vols. v and vi contain sixteenth century material.

**1580.** Index of inquisitions post mortem, 1509–1660. 4 vols. P.R.O. Lists and indexes Nos. XXIII, XXVI, XXXI, and XXXIII. London, 1907–9.

**1581.** JONES, EMYR GWYNNE (ed.): An Anglesey muster book. *Trans. Angl. Antiq. Soc.*, 1946.

Id. (ed.): Exchequer proceedings (Equity) concerning Wales (No. 130 (4)).

**1582.** MATHEW, DAVID: Some Elizabethan documents. *B.B.C.S.*, vi, 1931–3.

**1583.** Id. Further Elizabethan documents. Ibid.

MATTHEWS, JOHN HOBSON (ed.): Cardiff records (No. 686).

Records of the Court of Augmentations relating to Wales and Monmouthshire (No. 130 (13)).

**1584.** STEELE, ROBERT (ed.): Tudor and Stuart proclamations, 1485–1714. 2 vols. Oxford, 1910.

### (ii) Family papers and correspondence

Calendar of Salusbury correspondence (No. 130 (14)).

Calendar of the Wynn (of Gwydir) papers (No. 122).

Clenennau letters and papers in the Brogyntyn collection (No. 124).

**1585.** Historical Manuscripts Commission reports (see No. 116). Among the more important collections for students of the history of Wales during the Tudor period are the following:

Bagot. 4th r., xiv and app.

Cecil. 3rd–7th r., *passim*; 12th–17th r., *passim*; vols. i–xiv.

De L'Isle and Dudley. 3rd r., xvi and app.

Dovaston. 13th r., app. iv.

Hereford Corporation. 13th r. and app. iv.

Shrewsbury Corporation. 17th r.

Welsh language, MSS. in the (No. 116).

MEYRICK, SAMUEL RUSH (ed.): Heraldic visitations of Wales (by Lewys Dwnn) (No. 60).

Index of wills proved in the prerogative court of Canterbury, 1383–1558 (No. 1428).

**1586.** Index of wills proved in the prerogative court of Canterbury, vol. iii, 1558–1583, compiled by S. A. Smith and edited by L. L. Duncan; vol. iv, 1583–1604, compiled by S. A. Smith and edited by E. A. Fry. Brit. Rec. Soc., Index Library, Nos. 18 and 25, 1898 and 1901.

**1587.** TRAHERNE, JOHN MONTGOMERY: Stradling correspondence: a series of letters written in the reign of Queen Elizabeth. London, 1840.

### (iii) Contemporary chronicles and descriptions

CAMDEN, WILLIAM: Britannia (No. 135).

**1588.** CHURCHYARD, THOMAS: The worthines of Wales. London, 1587; repr. in facsimile. Spenser Soc., 1876.

**1589.** DAVIES, JOHN HUMPHREYS, DAVIES, JOHN GLYN, and BULKELEY-OWEN, FANNY MARY KATHERINE (eds.): Welsh adventurers to the West Indies in the sixteenth century and The ballad of the Welsh buccaneers: two versions of a 'karol' by William Peilyn on Welsh seamen in the West Indian expedition of 1595. *Y Cymmr.*, xxvi, 1916.

**1590.** DRAYTON, MICHAEL: Poly-Olbion, or a chorographical description of Great Britain. 1st part, London (1612); 2nd part, London (1662), by R. Roper. 3 vols., London, 1876; repr. by the Spenser Soc., 1885–95; repr.

in vol. iv (with notes and index in vol. v) of the tercentenary edn of
Drayton's works. Ed. J. William Hebel. 5 vols. Oxford, 1931–41.

> See also GOURVITCH, I: Drayton's debt to Geoffrey of Monmouth. *Rev. of
> English Studies*, iv, 1928.

**1591.** EVANS, EVAN VINCENT (ed.): Andrew Boorde and the Welsh
people. *Y Cymmr.*, xxix, 1919.

**1592.** FISHER, JOHN (ed.): Wales in the time of Queen Elizabeth. *Arch.
Camb.*, 1915.

> Prints anonymous tract: *De presenti statu totius Walliae.*

**1593.** LELAND, JOHN: The itinerary in Wales in or about the years 1536–9.
Ed. Lucy Toulmin Smith. London, 1906.

LEWIS, RICE: A breviat of Glamorgan, 1596–1600 (No. 55).

MERRICK, RICE: A booke of Glamorganshires antiquities
(No. 687).

OWEN, GEORGE: The description of Penbrokeshire (No. 109 (1)).

Id.　　The taylor's cussion (No. 125).

**1594.** PARRY, ROBERT: The diary of Robert Parry (1559–1613). *Arch.
Camb.*, 1915.

WYNN, SIR JOHN: The history of the Gwydir family (No. 79).

#### (iv) Literary sources

See, generally, PARRY, THOMAS: Hanes llenyddiaeth Gymraeg
(No. 146).

DAVIES, WILLIAM LLEWELYN: Welsh books entered in the
Stationers' Company's registers. Part I, 1554–1660. (No. 7).

**1595.** FISHER, JOHN (ed.): The Cefn Coch MSS. Bangor, 1899.

**1596.** FLETCHER, J. Kyrle: The Gwentian poems of Dafydd Benwyn.
Cardiff, 1909.

**1597.** GEORGE, IRENE (ed.): The poems of Syr Dafydd Trefor. *Trans.
Angl. Antiq. Soc.*, 1935.

**1598.** Id.　　A survey of the poems of Syr Dafydd Trefor. Ibid., 1936.

> See also id.: Syr Dafydd Trefor, an Anglesey bard. Ibid., 1934.

**1599.** HOPKIN-JAMES, LEMUEL JOHN ('Hopcyn'), and EVANS, THOMAS
CHRISTOPHER ('Cadrawd'): Hen gwndidau, carolau, a chywyddau. Bangor,
1910.

**1600.** HUGHES, GARFIELD HOPKIN: Rhagymadroddion, 1547–1659. Caerdydd, 1951.

**1601.** JONES, FRANCIS (ed.): Family tales from Dyfed. *Trans. Cymmr.*, 1953.
> Transcripts from B.M. Egerton MS. 2586 with introduction and notes.

**1602.** JONES, JOHN ('Myrddin Fardd'): Cynfeirdd Lleyn. Pwllheli, 1905.

JONES, THOMAS GWYNN: Gwaith Tudur Aled (No. 1508).

**1603.** LEWIS, HENRY: Hen gyflwyniadau. Caerdydd, 1948.

**1604.** LLOYD-JENKINS, DAVID: Cerddi rhydd cynnar. Llandysul [1931].

**1605.** MORRICE, J. C.: Barddoniaeth Wiliam Llŷn. Bangor, 1908.

**1606.** Id.      Detholiad o waith Gruffydd ab Ieuan ap Llewelyn Vychan. Bangor Welsh MSS. Soc. v. Bangor, 1910.
> See also ROBERTS, THOMAS: Dyddiadau Gruffydd ab Ieuan ap Llywelyn Vychan. *B.B.C.S.*, x, 1939.

**1607.** PARRY-WILLIAMS, THOMAS HERBERT: Canu rhydd cynnar. Caerdydd, 1932.

**1608.** Rhyddiaith Gymraeg, cyf. i, detholion o lawysgrifau, 1488–1609 (gol. T. H. Parry-Williams), Caerdydd, 1954; cyf. ii, detholion o lawysgrifau a llyfrau printiedig, 1547–1618 (gol. Thomas Jones), Caerdydd, 1956.

**1609.** ROBERTS, PETER: Y cwtta cyfarwydd. Ed. David Richard Thomas. London, 1883.

### (b) Secondary works

**1610.** BALLINGER, JOHN: Katheryn of Berain. *Y Cymmr.*, xi, 1929.

**1611.** BEBB, WILLIAM AMBROSE: Cyfnod y Tuduriaid. Wrecsam, 1939.

BREESE, EDWARD: Kalendars of Gwynedd (No. 83).

**1612.** CHOTZEN, THEODORE MAX: Some sidelights on Cambro-Dutch relations, 1100–1600. *Trans. Cymmr.*, 1937.

**1612A.** GRUFFYDD, WILLIAM JOHN: Llenyddiaeth Cymru o 1450 hyd 1600. Lerpwl, 1922.

**1613.** Id.      Llenyddiaeth Cymru: rhyddiaith o 1540 hyd 1660. Wrecsam, 1926.

**1614.** HARRIES, FREDERICK JAMES: The Welsh Elizabethans. Pontypridd, 1924.

**1615.** JENKINS, ROBERT THOMAS: Y newid yng Nghymru yng nghyfnod y Tuduriaid. In Yr apêl at hanes. Wrecsam, 1930; cf. *Y Llenor,* 1950.

**1616.** JONES, THOMAS GWYNN: Cultural bases: a study of the Tudor period in Wales. *Y Cymmr.,* xxxi, 1921.

**1617.** LEWIS, THOMAS HARRIS: Carmarthenshire under the Tudors. *Trans. Hist. Soc. of West Wales,* viii, 1919–20.

**1618.** MATHEW, DAVID: The Celtic peoples and Renaissance Europe. London, 1933.

**1619.** NEVINS, J. BIRKBECK: Picture of Wales during the Tudor period. Liverpool, 1893.

**1620.** REES, JAMES FREDERICK: Tudor policy in Wales. Historical Association pamphlet No. 101, 1935.

See also id.: Studies in Welsh history (No. 151).

**1621.** WILLIAMS, DAVID: A note on the population of Wales, 1536–1801. *B.B.C.S.,* viii, 1935–7.

Id. A history of modern Wales (No. 159).

**1622.** WILLIAMS, D. D.: Cymry enwog cyfnod y Tuduriaid. Llangefni, 1914.

**1623.** WILLIAMS, E. ROLAND: Some studies in Elizabethan Wales. Newtown, [? 1924].

WILLIAMS, WILLIAM LLEWELYN: The making of modern Wales: studies in the Tudor settlement of Wales (No. 163).

See also section A II.

## II. POLITICAL AND ADMINISTRATIVE HISTORY

**1624.** BOWEN, IVOR: Grand juries, justices of the peace and quarter sessions in Wales. *Trans. Cymmr.,* 1933–5.

**1625.** BUSHEL, W. D.: The lady Margaret Beaufort and King Henry VII. *Arch. Camb.,* 1916.

See also WILLIAMS, DAVID: The Welsh Tudors. *History Today,* iv, 1954.

**1626.** DAVIES, ARTHUR STANLEY: Aberdovey and the Spanish invasion in 1597. *Arch. Camb.,* 1932.

**1627.** DODD, ARTHUR HERBERT: Wales and the Scottish succession. *Trans. Cymmr.,* 1937.

See also id.: Two Welsh Catholic *emigrés* discuss the accession of James I (No. 1665).

**1628.** Id.      Wales's parliamentary apprenticeship (1536–1625). Ibid., 1942.

**1629.** Id.      North Wales in the Essex revolt of 1601. *E.H.R.*, lix, 1944.
See also *N.L.W. Jnl.*, 1949–50.

DODDRIDGE, JOHN: The history of the ancient and modern estate of the principality of Wales (No. 138).

**1630.** DUCKETT, G. F.: The marches of Wales. *Arch. Camb.*, 1881.

**1631.** EVANS, ELWYN: Some Cyfeiliog manorial customs. *Mont. Coll.*, lii, 1951–2.
With excerpts from sixteenth and seventeenth century court rolls.

GRIFFITHS, WILLIAM ARTHUR: Fifteenth and sixteenth century lords of the manor of Broniarth (No. 1494).

**1632.** HICKS, LEO: The strange case of Dr. William Parry. *Studies,* 1948.

**1633.** JERMAN, H. NOEL: A map showing the territorial divisions of Wales before the Act of Union, 1536. *Arch. Camb.*, 1937.

**1634.** JONES, DAVID: Sir Rhys ap Thomas: a study in family history and Tudor politics. *Arch. Camb.*, 1892.
The Life in *Cambrian Register*, 1795, must be used with caution.

**1635.** JONES, EMYR GWYNNE: County politics and electioneering, 1558–1625. *Trans. Caerns. Hist. Soc.*, 1939.

**1636.** Id.      Anglesey and invasion. *Trans. Angl. Antiq. Soc.,* 1947.

**1637.** JONES, FRANCIS: Sir Rhys ap Thomas. *Trans. Carms. Antiq. Soc.*, xxxix, 1938–9.

Id.      Sir Rhys ap Thomas and the knights of St. John (No. 930).

**1638.** JONES, IFANO: Sir Matthew Cradock and some of his contemporaries. *Arch. Camb.*, 1919.

JONES, WILLIAM GARMON: Welsh nationalism and Henry Tudor (No. 1454).

**1639.** LEWIS, EDWARD ARTHUR (ed.): Three legal tracts concerning the court-leet in Wales after the Act of Union. *B.B.C.S.*, ix, 1937–9.

**1640.** LEWIS, THOMAS HENRY: The justice of the peace in Wales. *Trans. Cymmr.*, 1943–4.

**1641.** Id.      The administration of justice in the Welsh county in its relation to other organs of justice, higher and lower. Ibid., 1945.

**1642.** MATTHEWS, JOHN HOBSON: Welsh materials for English history. *Arch. Camb.,* 1914.

**1643.** NEALE, JOHN ERNEST: Three Elizabethan elections. *E.H.R.,* xlvi, 1931.
> See also id.: The Elizabethan House of Commons. London, 1949. Ch. 5

> OWEN, HENRY: The administration of English law in Wales and the marches (No. 1374).

**1644.** PUGH, T. BRYNMOR: The indenture for the marches between Henry VII and Edward Stafford (1477–1521), duke of Buckingham. *E.H.R.,* lxxi, 1956.

**1645.** Id.,     and ROBINSON, W. R. B.: Sessions in eyre in a marcher lordship: a dispute between the earl of Worcester and his tenants of Gower and Kilvey in 1524. *S. Wales and Mon. Rec. Soc. Pubns.,* iv, 1957.

**1646.** REES, WILLIAM: The union of England and Wales (No. 1462).
> With text of the Act of 1536 and map.

**1647.** ROBERTS, GLYN: The parliamentary representation of the Welsh boroughs. *B.B.C.S.,* iv, 1929.

**1648.** Id.     Political affairs [in Carmarthenshire] from 1536–1900. In A history of Carmarthenshire (No. 605), ii.

**1649.** ROWLANDS, EURYS IONOR: Terwyn a thwrnai. *N.L.W. Jnl.,* ix, 1955–6.

**1650.** ROWSE, ALFRED LESLIE: The expansion of Elizabethan England. London, 1955.
> Ch. I: The borderlands: Wales.

**1651.** SKEEL, CAROLINE ANNE JAMES: Wales under Henry VII. In Tudor studies. Ed. R. W. Seton-Watson. London, 1924.

> Id.     The council in the marches of Wales: a study in local government during the sixteenth and seventeenth centuries (No. 1499).

**1652.** THOMAS, DANIEL LLEUFER: Welsh lawyers of the Tudor and Stuart period. *Trans. Liverpool Welsh Nat. Soc.,* 1899–1900.

> TOUT, THOMAS FREDERICK: The Welsh shires: a study in constitutional history (No. 1500).

**1653.** VAUGHAN, RICE: Practica Walliae. London, 1672.

**1654.** WILLIAMS, PENRY: The Star Chamber and the council in the marches of Wales, 1558–1603. *B.B.C.S.,* xvi, 1956.

**1655.** Id.    The council in the marches of Wales under Elizabeth I. Cardiff, 1958.

**1656.** WILLIAMS, WILLIAM LLEWELYN: A Welsh insurrection. *Y Cymmr.*, xvi, 1902.

**1657.** Id.    The union of England and Wales. *Trans. Cymmr.*, 1907–8.

**1658.** Id.    The king's court of great sessions in Wales. *Y Cymmr.*, xxvi, 1916.

**1659.** WILLIAMS, WILLIAM OGWEN: The county records. *Trans. Caerns. Hist. Soc.*, 1949.

Id.    Calendar of Caernarvonshire quarter sessions (No. 555).

**1660.** WINDER, W. H. D.: Equity in the courts of great sessions. *Law Quarterly Review*, ccxvii, 1939.

### III. ECCLESIASTICAL HISTORY

Much useful material on ecclesiastical history, both original and secondary, will be found in the publications of the Catholic Record Society (1905 ff.), *Efrydiau Catholig* (No. 324), and the *Journal of the Historical Society of the Church in Wales* (No. 322).

#### (a) Sources

Reference should be made to the important collection of Welsh Church records at the National Library of Wales, a preliminary survey of which will be found in No. 822. There are also typewritten schedules of a more detailed character at the National Library. Sixteenth century material is, unfortunately, very scarce among these records.

**1661.** ANON.: A true report of the life and martyrdom of Mr. Richard White, schoolmaster, in LLOYD, JACOB YOUDE WILLIAM: History of . . . Powys Fadog, vol. iii (No. 58).

See also another version in *Cath. Rec. Soc. Pubns.*, v, 1908; and MURPHY, OSWALD J.: Bl. Richard Gwyn, schoolmaster, protomartyr of Wales. Catholic Truth Soc. Cardiff, 1955.

**1662.** BOWEN, DAVID JAMES: Detholiad o englynion o hiraeth am yr hen ffydd. *Efryd. Cath.*, vi, 1954.

**1663.** BRADNEY, JOSEPH ALFRED: The speech of William Blethin and the customs and ordinances of the church of Llandaff. *Y Cymmr.*, xxxi, 1921.

**1664.** CLYNNOG, MORYS: Athravaeth Gristnogawl. Milan, 1568; repr. in facsimile. Cymmrodorion Society, London, 1880.

DAVIES, JAMES CONWAY: The records of the Church in Wales (No. 822).

**1665.** DODD, ARTHUR HERBERT: Two Welsh Catholic *emigrés* discuss the accession of James I. *B.B.C.S.*, viii, 1935–7.

**1666.** Id.　　Correspondence of the Owens of Plas Du, 1573–1604. *Trans. Caerns. Hist. Soc.*, 1939.

DUGDALE, WILLIAM: Monasticon Anglicanum (No. 111).

**1667.** ELY, HUMPHREY: Certaine briefe notes upon a briefe apologie set out under the name of the priestes. Paris [1603].

Episcopal registers of St. David's, 1397–1518 (No. 109 (6)).

See also WILLIAMS, GLANMOR: The second volume of St. David's registers, 1554–64 (No. 859).

**1668.** FOLEY, H.: Records of the English province of the Society of Jesus (1570–*circa* 1800). 7 vols. London, 1877–9.

**1669.** FOXE, JOHN: Actes and monuments, London, 1563; numerous reprints. Standard edn by S. Catley, London, 1837–41; and in Church historians of England, 12 vols., London, 1853–61. (For references to Robert Ferrar and Rawlins White, see vol. vii, pp. 1–28.)

GRIFFITHS, GRIFFITH MILWYN: A St. Asaph 'register' of episcopal acts, 1506–71 (No. 842).

**1670.** GRUFFYDD, GERAINT: Dau lythyr gan Owen Lewis. *Llên Cymru*, ii, 1952–3.

**1671.** Id.　　Bishop Francis Godwin's injunctions for the diocese of Llandaff, 1603. *Jnl. Hist. Soc. Church in Wales*, iv, 1954.

**1671A.** HENSON, E. (ed.): Register of the English college, Valladolid, 1589–1862. *Cath. Rec. Soc. Pubns.*, xxx, 1930.

**1672.** JONES, ARTHUR: The property of the Welsh friaries at the dissolution. *Arch. Camb.*, 1936.

**1673.** JONES, EMYR GWYNNE: A Llandegai pew dispute. *Trans. Caerns. Hist. Soc.*, 1948.

**1674.** JONES, EVAN DAVID: A survey of South Wales chantries. *Arch. Camb.*, 1934.

**1675.** KELLY, W. I. (ed.): The liber ruber of the English College, Rome. Annales Collegii. Pars prima. Nomina alumnorum, i, A.D. 1579–1630. *Cath. Rec. Soc. Pubns.*, xxxvii, 1940; ii, A.D. 1631–1783. Ibid., xl, 1943.

**1675A.** KENNEDY, WILLIAM PAUL McCLURE: Elizabethan episcopal administration. 3 vols. Alcuin Club collections, 1925.

**1676.** KNOX, THOMAS FRANCIS (ed.): Records of the English Catholics under the penal laws. London, 1878.

**1677.** Id.     The first and second diaries of the English College, Douay. London, 1878.

> See also BURTON, EDWIN H., and WILLIAMS, THOMAS L. (eds): The Douay
> college diaries, third, fourth, and fifth, 1598–1654. *Cath. Rec. Soc. Pubns.,*
> x and xi, 1911.

**1678.** KYFFIN, MORYS: Deffynniad ffydd Eglwys Loegr . . . 1595. Gol. W. Prichard Williams. Caerdydd, 1908.

**1679.** LEWYS, HUW: Perl mewn adfyd, 1595. Gol. W. J. Gruffydd. Caerdydd, 1929.

> Llandaff records. Ed. J. A. Bradney and R. Rickards (No. 832).

**1680.** McCANN, J., and CONNOLLY, H. (eds): Memorials of Father Augustine Baker and other documents relating to the English Benedictines. *Cath. Rec. Soc. Pubns.,* xxxiii, 1933.

> OWEN, EDWARD: Documents relating to the dissolved monas-
> tery of Grace Dieu (No. 910).

**1681.** OWEN, LEWIS: Running register. London, 1626.

**1682.** PARRY-WILLIAMS, THOMAS HERBERT: Carolau Richard White. Cardiff, 1931.

**1683.** PEEL, ALBERT: The notebook of John Penry, 1593. *Camden Soc.,* lxvii, 1944.

**1684.** [PENRY, JOHN]: A treatise containing the aequity of an humble supplication which is to be exhibited to her gracious majesty, and the high court of parliament in behalf of the country of Wales . . . Oxford, 1587. Ed. A. J. Grieve. *Cong. Hist. Soc.,* London, 1905.

**1685.** Id.     An exhortation unto the governors and people of . . . Wales to labour earnestly to have the preaching of the gospell planted among them. s.l., 1588.

**1686.** Id.     A viewe of some part of such publicke wants and disorders as are in the service of God within her majestie's countrie of Wales . . . s.l., 1589. Ed. J. O. Halliwell. London, 1861.

**1686A.** Id.     Three treatises concerning Wales. Introduction by David Williams. Cardiff, 1960.

**1687.** PIERCE, WILLIAM (ed.): The Mar-prelate tracts, 1588, 1589. London, 1911.

> PRYCE, ARTHUR IVOR: The diocese of Bangor in the sixteenth
> century (No. 827).

**1688.** PUGH, FRANK HAMER: Glamorgan recusants, 1577–1611. *S. Wales and Mon. Rec. Soc. Pubns.,* iii, 1954.

**1689.** Id.     Monmouthshire recusants in the reigns of Elizabeth and James I. Ibid., iv, 1957.

**1690.** Recusant rolls, 1592–3. *Cath. Rec. Soc. Pubns.,* xviii, 1916.
For Welsh entries, see pp. 357–8.

**1691.** ROBERT, GRUFFYDD: Y drych Cristianogawl. Milan, 1585.

**1692.** SALESBURY, WILLIAM: Ban wedy i dynny air yngair allan o hen gyfreith Howel da. Llundain, 1550.

**1693.** Id.　　The baterie of the Popes botereulx, commonlye called the high altare. London, 1550.
See also article thereon by GLANMOR WILLIAMS in *B.B.C.S.*, xiii, 1949.

**1694.** Valor ecclesiasticus. Ed. John Cayley and Josiah Hunter. 6 vols. London, 1810–34.
For a list of epitomes of the Valor before its publication in full, see
PARGELLIS, STANLEY, and MEDLEY, J.: Bibliography of British history: the eighteenth century. Oxford, 1951, No. 684, p. 96.

**1695.** Visitation articles and injunctions of the period of the Reformation. Ed. Walter Howard Frere and W. P. Kennedy. 3 vols. Alcuin Club collections, xiv and xvi, 1910.

**1696.** WRIGHT, THOMAS: Three chapters of letters relating to the suppression of the monasteries. *Camden Soc.,* 1843.

### (b) Secondary works

For standard histories of the Reformation in England, see CONSTANT, G.: La reforme en Angleterre: I, Le schisme anglican, Henri VIII, Paris, 1930 (English translation, London, 1934); II, Edouard VI, Paris, 1939 (English translation, London, 1941); DIXON, RICHARD W.: History of the Church of England from the abolition of the Roman jurisdiction, 6 vols., Oxford, 1878–1902; HUGHES, PHILIP: The Reformation in England, 3 vols., London, 1950–4 (has extensive bibliographies); POWICKE, FREDERICK MAURICE: The Reformation in England, Oxford, 1941.

See also HILL, CHRISTOPHER: Economic problems of the Church from archbishop Whitgift to the Long Parliament. Oxford, 1956.

Of the general histories of the Church in Wales, the most useful for this period are EDWARDS, ALFRED GEORGE: Landmarks in the history of the Welsh Church (No. 166); HIRSCH-DAVIES, JOHN EDWIN DE: A popular history of the Church in Wales (No. 169); JAMES, JOHN WILLIAMS: A Church history of Wales (No. 173); NEWELL, EBENEZER JOSIAH: History of the Welsh Church to the dissolution of the monasteries (No. 176); JONES, GRIFFITH HARTWELL: Celtic Britain and the pilgrim movement (No. 1237). MATHEW, DAVID : The Celtic peoples and Renaissance Europe (No. 1618) should also be consulted.

### (i) The Protestant Reformation: General

**1697.** ATKINS, IVOR: The authorship of the sixteenth century description of St. David's printed in Browne Willis's survey (1717). *N.L.W. Jnl.,* iv, 1945–6.

**1698.** DODD, ARTHUR HERBERT: The Church in Wales in the age of the Reformation. In Welsh Church Congress handbook, 1953 (No. 184).

**1699.** EDWARDS, THOMAS CHARLES: Wales and the Reformation. *Blackfriars*, xv, 1934.

**1700.** EVANS, ALBERT OWEN: Edmund Prys. *Trans. Cymmr.*, 1922–3.

**1701.** Id.     Nicholas Robinson, 1530?–1585. *Y Cymmr.*, xxxix, 1928.

GREEN, CHARLES ALFRED HOWELL: The chapter of Llandaff cathedral, 1561–1668 (No. 834).

**1702.** JONES, THOMAS GWYNN: Edmwnd Prys. *Y Llenor*, ii and iii, 1923 and 1924.

**1703.** LEWIS, SAUNDERS: Damcaniaeth eglwysig Brotestannaidd. *Efryd. Cath.*, ii, 1947. See also WILLIAMS, GLANMOR: Cipolwg arall ar y ddamcaniaeth Brotestannaidd. *Y Traethodydd*, 1948.

**1704.** LEWIS, THOMAS HARRIS: Carmarthenshire and the Reformation movement. *Trans. Carms. Antiq. Soc.*, xiv, 1919–21.

**1705.** MORRIS-JONES, JOHN: Edmwnd Prys. *Y Geninen*, xli, 1923–4.

NEWCOMBE, RICHARD: Memoir of Dr. Gabriel Goodman, with some account of Ruthin school (No. 211).

**1706.** OWEN, C. E. VAUGHAN: The vicars of Trefeglwys, 1574–1902. *Mont. Coll.*, liv, 1955–6.

**1707.** PIERCE, WILLIAM: An historical introduction to the Marprelate tracts, etc. London, 1909.

**1708.** Id.     John Penry, his life, times, and writings. London, 1923.

**1709.** PRYCE, ARTHUR IVOR: The Reformation in the diocese of Bangor as illustrated in the records. *Trans. Angl. Antiq. Soc.*, 1939.

**1710.** ROBERTS, THOMAS ROWLAND: Edmwnd Prys, archddiacon Meirionydd. Caernarfon, 1899.

**1711.** SEABORNE, M. V. J.: The Reformation in Wales. London, 1952.

THOMAS, LAWRENCE: The Reformation in the old diocese of Llandaff (No. 838).

**1712.** WEBB, W. K. L.: The case of Robert Ferrar, bishop of St. David's. Catholic Truth Soc. (Welsh Province). Cardiff, n.d.

**1713.** WHITE, FRANCIS O.: Lives of the Elizabethan bishops of the Anglican Church. London, 1898.

**1714.** WILLIAMS, DAVID: The enigma of John Penry. *The Welsh Review*, iv, March, 1945.

**1715.** WILLIAMS, GLANMOR: The Elizabethan settlement of religion in Wales and the marches. *Jnl. Hist. Soc. Church in Wales*, ii, 1950.

**1716.** Id.    The Protestant experiment in the diocese of St. David's, 1534–53. *B.B.C.S.*, xv, 1952–3, and xvi, 1954.

**1717.** Id.    Some Protestant views of early British Church history. *History*, xxxviii, 1953.

**1718.** WYNNE, R. O. F.: Y Cymry a'r Diwygiad Protestannaidd. *Efryd. Cath.*, vi, 1954.

### (ii) Monasteries and shrines

See BASKERVILLE, GEOFFREY: English monks and the suppression of the monasteries. London, 1936; also section B VIII above.

ANON.: Pen-rhys, 1179–1538 (No. 926).

BEBB, WILLIAM AMBROSE: Machlud y mynachlogydd (No. 864).

**1719.** BREESE, EDWARD: Dervel Gadarn. *Arch. Camb.*, 1874.

EDWARDS, THOMAS CHARLES, and WILLIAMS, GRIFFITH JOHN: Pen-rhys: y cefndir hanesyddol. Atodiad o gerddi (No. 928).

**1720.** JONES, ARTHUR: The estates of the Welsh abbeys at the dissolution. *Arch. Camb.*, 1937.

Id.    Basingwerk abbey (No. 891).

**1721.** MATHEW, DAVID, AND MATHEW, GERVASE: The survival of the dissolved monasteries in Wales. *Dublin Rev.*, clxxxiv, 1929.

**1722.** OWEN, EDWARD: The spoils of the Welsh religious houses. *Arch. Camb.*, 1897.

**1723.** Id.    The bells of the Welsh dissolved monasteries. Ibid.

Id.    The fate of the structures of Conway abbey and Bangor and Beaumaris friaries (No. 888).

Id.    Strata Marcella immediately before and after its dissolution (No. 944).

**1724.** Id.    The monastery of Basingwerk at the period of its dissolution. *Flints. Hist. Soc. Pubns.*, vii, 1920.

**1725.** RANDOLPH, J. A.: Welsh abbeys, being short accounts of their abbots, lands, buildings, and churches and their values at the dissolution. Carmarthen, 1905.

**1726.** REES, WILLIAM: The suppression of the friaries in Glamorgan and Monmouthshire. *S. Wales and Mon. Rec. Soc. Pubns.*, iii, 1954.
With documentary appendix.

Id.     The houses of the friars at Cardiff and Newport, 1538–9 (No. 898).

ROBERTS, GLYN: The Dominican friary of Bangor (No. 890).

**1727.** THOMAS, DAVID: St. Winifred's well and chapel, Holywell. *Jnl. Hist. Soc. Church in Wales*, viii, 1958.

**1728.** WILLIAMS, D. D.: Hanes mynachdai Gogledd Cymru. Liverpool, 1914.

### (iii) Translation of the Bible and Prayer Book

THOMAS PARRY, Hanes llenyddiaeth Gymraeg (No. 146), and W. J. GRUFFYDD, Llenyddiaeth Cymru (Nos. 1612A–13), give the best guide to the subject from a literary standpoint. Valuable material is also to be found in D. R. THOMAS: The life and work of Davies and Salesbury (No. 1744), and GLANMOR WILLIAMS: Bywyd ac amserau'r Esgob Richard Davies (No. 1745). The principal texts are the following: KYFFIN, EDWARD: Rhann o Psalmae Dafydd Brophwyd, Llundain, 1603, gol. gan John Ballinger, Caerdydd, 1930; Lliver Gweddi Gyffredin a Gweinidogaeth y Sacramentae., ail argraff. Llundain, 1586; trydydd argraff., Llundain, 1599. MIDLETON, WILLIAM: Psalmae y brenhinol brophwyd Dafydd, Llunden, 1603; [MORGAN, WILLIAM]: Y Beibl cyssegr-lan, sef yr Hen Destament a'r Newydd, Llundain, 1588; [id.]: Psalmau Dafydd o'r vn cyfieithiad a'r Beibl cyffredin, Llundain, 1588, gol. gan Thomas Powell, London, 1896; [PRICE, JOHN]: Yny Lhyvyr hwnn, London, 1546, ed. by J. H. Davies, Bangor, 1902; SALESBURY, WILLIAM: Kynniver llith a ban, London, 1551, ed. by John Fisher, Cardiff, 1931; [SALESBURY, WILLIAM, DAVIES, RICHARD, a HUET, THOMAS]: Testament Newydd ein Arglwydd Iesu Grist, Llundain, 1567; adargraff. Caernarfon, 1850.

**1729.** ASHTON, CHARLES: Bywyd ac amserau yr Esgob Morgan. Treherbert, 1891.

**1730.** BALLINGER, JOHN: The Bible in Wales. London, 1906.

**1731.** Id.     The first Welsh prayer book. *Jnl. Welsh Bibl. Soc.*, ii, No. 7, 1922.

**1732.** DAVIES, JOHN HUMPHREYS: Llyfryddiaeth y Bibl Cymraeg. *Trans. Liverpool Welsh Nat. Soc.*, 1897–8.

**1733.** DAVIES, WILLIAM LLEWELYN: Welsh metrical versions of the Psalms. *Jnl. Welsh Bibl. Soc.*, ii, No. 8, 1923.

**1734.** EDWARDS, THOMAS CHARLES: William Salesbury's translation of the New Testament into Welsh. *Trans. Liverpool Welsh Nat. Soc.*, 1885–6.

**1735.** EVANS, ALBERT OWEN: A memorandum on the legality of the Welsh Bible, and the Welsh version of the Book of Common Prayer. Cardiff, 1925.

**1736.** GRUFFYDD, GERAINT: Catecism y Deon Newell yn Gymraeg. *Jnl. Welsh. Bibl. Soc.*, vii, Nos. 2 and 4, 1951–2.

**1737.** JENKINS, ROBERT THOMAS: William Salesbury yn y llannau. *Y Traethodydd*, 1946.

**1738.** JONES, THOMAS: Pre-reformation Welsh versions of the Scriptures. *N.L.W. Jnl.*, iv, 1945–6.
    See also id.: Y Beibl Yngymraec. Cardiff, 1940.

**1739.** LLEWELYN, THOMAS: An historical account of the British or Welsh versions of the Bible. London, 1768, 1793.

**1740.** MATHIAS, WILLIAM ALUN: Gweithiau William Salesbury. *Jnl. Welsh Bibl. Soc.*, vii, Nos. 2 and 4, 1951–2.

**1741.** PARRY-WILLIAMS, THOMAS HERBERT: Coffáu'r Esgob William Morgan. *Trans. Cymmr.*, 1955.

**1742.** ROBERTS, GRIFFITH JOHN: Yr Esgob William Morgan. Dinbych, 1955.

**1743.** THOMAS, DAVID RICHARD: Some early Welsh translations of the Holy Scripture. *Trans. Liverpool Welsh Nat. Soc.*, 1898–9.

**1744.** Id.    The life and work of Davies and Salesbury. Oswestry, 1902.

**1745.** WILLIAMS, GLANMOR: Bywyd ac amserau'r Esgob Richard Davies. Caerdydd, 1953. See also id.: Richard Davies, bishop of St. David's, 1561–81. *Trans. Cymmr.*, 1948.

**1746.** WILLIAMS, GRIFFITH JOHN (gol.): Barddoniaeth neu brydyddiaeth gan William Midleton, yn ôl argraffiad 1593, gyda chasgliad o'i awdlau a'i gywyddau. Caerdydd, 1930.
    The introduction is valuable.

**1747.** WILLIAMS, HUGH: Testament Cymraeg cyntaf y Cymry. *Y Drysorfa*, 1888.

**1748.** WILLIAMS, IFOR: Ar Gymraeg William Salesbury. *Y Traethodydd*, 1946.

### (iv) Catholic exiles and recusants

For original sources relating to this section, see Nos. 1661–1696.

**1749.** ATTWATER, DONALD: The Catholic Church in modern Wales. London, 1935.

**1750.** BOWEN, GERAINT: Gwilym Pue, 'Bardd Mair', a theulu'r Penrhyn. *Efryd. Cath.*, ii, 1947.

**1751.** Id.    Robert Gwyn. *Trans. Caerns. Hist. Soc.*, 1954.

**1752.** CAMM, BEDE: Le venerable Jean Roberts. *La revue bénédictine*, 1895–6.

**1753.** Id.    A Benedictine martyr in England. London, 1897.

**1754.** CHALLONER, RICHARD: Memoirs of missionary priests . . . from the year 1577 to the year 1684. 2 vols. London, 1741–2. Ed. J. H. Pollen. London, 1923.

**1755.** CLEARY, J. MARTIN: Sir Edward Carne. *The Illtydian*, xix, 1947.

**1756.** Id.    The Catholic recusancy of the Barlow family of Slebech. The Cardiff Newman Circle. Paper 1, 1956.

**1757.** Id.    The Catholic resistance in Wales, 1568–1678. *Blackfriars*, March, 1957.

**1758.** Id.    A checklist of Welsh students in the seminaries. Part i, 1568–1603. The Cardiff Newman Circle. Paper 2, 1958.

**1759.** Id.    An episode in the life of John Owen, 'the Epigrammatist'. *B.B.C.S.*, xvii, 1956–8.

**1760.** CREAN, PATRICK J.: Sir William Dai; a life of the venerable William Davies, Catholic martyr executed in North Wales at Beaumaris, 1593. Catholic Truth Soc. of Ireland. Dublin, 1958.

**1761.** CRONIN, JOHN M.: Various papers on Welsh Catholicism in the sixteenth century. *St. Peter's Magazine*, Cardiff.
> The series includes the following: Sir William Guy of Penrhyn (1924); The martyrdom of Mr. Day (or Davis), 1593 (1924); Jane Vaughan (1925); Catholic clergy in South Wales, 1560–80 (1925); The old English college (at Rome) and its Welsh associations (1926); Ven. J. Jones (or Buckley) (1926); Catholicism in Glamorgan (1927); South Wales chantries (1928).

DODD, ARTHUR HERBERT: The correspondence of the Owens of Plas Du (No. 1666).

**1762.** ELLIS, THOMAS PETER: The Catholic martyrs of Wales. London, 1933.
> See also WYNNE, R. O. F.: Welsh martyrs and exile. Catholic Truth Soc. (Welsh province). Cardiff, 1954.

Id.    The Welsh Benedictines of the terror (No. 870).

EVANS, A. LESLIE: The story of Sker House (No. 17).
For the Catholic recusancy of the Turberville family.

**1763.** GASQUET, FRANCIS A.: History of the venerable English college at Rome. London, 1920.

**1764.** GILLOW, J.: A literary and biographical history or bibliographical dictionary of English Catholics, 1534 to the present time. 5 vols. London, 1885–1903.

**1765.** GUILDAY, PETER: The English Catholic exiles on the continent, 1558–1795. London, 1914.

**1766.** JONES, EMYR GWYNNE: The Lleyn recusancy case, 1578–81. *Trans. Cymmr.*, 1936.

**1767.** Id.     Catholic recusancy in the counties of Denbigh, Flint, and Montgomery, 1581–1625. Ibid., 1945.

**1768.** Id.     Robert Pugh of Penrhyn Creuddyn. *Trans. Caerns. Hist. Soc.*, 1946. See also id.: The duality of Robert Pugh of Penrhyn Creuddyn. Ibid., 1957.

**1769.** Id.     Cymru a'r hen ffydd. Caerdydd, 1951.

**1770.** JONES, JOHN HENRY: The will of Hugh Owen of Plas Du. *B.B.C.S.*, ix, 1939.

**1771.** JONES, JOHN JAMES: A Welsh Catholic controversialist (John Gwynedd). *Jnl. Welsh Bibl. Soc.*, v, No. 2, 1938.

**1772.** LAW, T. G.: A historical sketch of the conflicts between Jesuits and seculars in the reign of Queen Elizabeth. London, 1889.

MATHEW, DAVID: The Celtic peoples and renaissance Europe (No. 1618).

**1773.** MATHIAS, WILLIAM ALUN: Rhai sylwadau ar Robert Gwyn. *Llên Cymru*, iii, 1954–5.

**1774.** ROGERS, D. M.: 'Popishe Thackwell' and early Catholic printing in Wales. *Biographical Studies*, 1534–1829, ii, No. 1, 1953.

**1775.** 'TALNANT': John Roberts, priest. *Jnl. Welsh Bibl. Soc.*, i, No. 6, 1914.

**1776.** WILLIAMS, DAVID: The miracle at St. Donat's. *The Welsh Review*, vi, 1947.

**1777.** WILLIAMS, GRIFFITH JOHN: Gramadeg Gruffydd Robert. Caerdydd, 1939.
The introduction is particularly valuable from the historian's point of view.

**1778.** WILLIAMS, WILLIAM LLEWELYN: Welsh Catholics on the continent. *Trans. Cymmr.*, 1901–2.

## IV. SOCIAL AND ECONOMIC HISTORY

### (a) The land and the landed gentry

Important general works on these subjects are: STONE, LAWRENCE: The Elizabethan aristocracy: a restatement, *Econ. Hist. Rev.*, 2nd series, iv, 1952; TAWNEY, RICHARD HENRY: The rise of the gentry, 1540–1640, *Econ. Hist. Rev.*, xi, 1941; id.: The rise of the gentry: a postscript, ibid., 2nd series, vii, 1954; id. and POWER, EILEEN: Tudor economic documents, 3 vols., London, 1924; TREVOR-ROPER, HUGH R.: The Elizabethan aristocracy: an anatomy anatomized, *Econ. Hist. Rev.*, 2nd series, iii, 1951; id., The gentry, 1540–1640, Cambridge, 1953.

#### (i) Sources

An inventory of early Chancery proceedings concerning Wales (No. 130 (3)).

Calendar of Salusbury correspondence, 1553–*circa* 1700 (No. 130 (14)).

Calendar of the Wynn (of Gwydir) papers (No. 122).

Calendar of deeds and documents. National Library of Wales.
    Vol. i, The Coleman deeds (No. 118).
    Vol. ii, The Crosswood deeds (No. 119).
    Vol. iii, The Hawarden deeds (No. 120).

Catalogue of Star Chamber proceedings relating to Wales (No. 130 (1)).

Exchequer proceedings (Equity) concerning Wales, Henry VIII —Elizabeth (No. 130 (4).

CHARLES, BERTIE GEORGE: The records of the borough of Newport, Pembrokeshire (No. 1561).

**1779.** Charters of Henry VII to the bondmen and other inhabitants of North Wales. *Arch. Camb.*, 1847. (Inspeximus of Henry VIII in same vol.). Similar charters were granted to:

(i) Bromfield and Yale (Cal. Pat. Rolls, 1494–1509, p. 471; see *Y Cymmr.*, xix).

(ii) Chirkland (ibid., p. 464); and in MAHLER, MARGARET: Chirk castle and Chirkland (No. 635).

(iii) Denbighland (Cal. Pat. Rolls, 1494–1509, p. 471).

(iv) Ruthin (ibid., p. 586).

**1780.** DODD, ARTHUR HERBERT: An 'electioneering' lease of 1585. *E.H.R.*, lxv, 1950.

**1781.** ELLIS, MEGAN (ed.): Dress and materials for a 'serving maid' *circa* 1600. *N.L.W. Jnl.*, i, 1939–40.

FISHER, JOHN (ed.): Wales in the time of Queen Elizabeth (No. 1592).

**1782.** Flintshire subsidy roll, 1592. *Arch. Camb.*, 1902.

**1783.** GRESHAM, COLIN A.: The township of Dolbenmaen. *Trans. Caerns. Hist. Soc.*, 1956.

**1784.** Id.     The townships of Gest, Treflys, and Ystumllyn. Ibid., 1957.

JONES, EVAN DAVID (ed.): Rhannu tir Rhys ap Elise (No. 1549).

**1785.** JONES, EMYR GWYNNE (ed.): The Caernarvonshire subsidy roll, 1597–8. *B.B.C.S.*, viii, 1935–7.

Id. (ed.): The history of the Bulkeley family (No. 45).

**1786.** Id.     Inventory of the goods and chattels of Edward Jones of Plas Cadwgan. *Trans. Denbs. Hist. Soc.*, 1957.

**1787.** JONES, FRANCIS (ed.): Roll of wards of the lords marcher of Kemes. *B.B.C.S.*, x, 1939–41.

**1788.** Id.     (ed.): Some records of a sixteenth century Pembrokeshire estate. Ibid., xiii, 1948–50.

**1789.** LEWIS, EDWARD ARTHUR (ed.): The court leet of the manor of Llanwddyn. *Mont. Coll.*, xliv, 1936.

**1790.** Id.     and DAVIES, JAMES CONWAY (ed.): Select Montgomeryshire deeds, 1579–98. Ibid., xlix, 1946.

LEWIS, RICE: A breviat of Glamorgan, 1596–1600 (No. 55).

**1791.** MORGAN, F. C.: The will of Sir John Price of Hereford, 1555. *N.L.W. Jnl.*, ix, 1955–6.

**1792.** OWEN, BOB (ed.): A Merioneth subsidy roll. 42 Elizabeth, 1599/1600. *Jnl. Mer. Hist. and Rec. Soc.*, ii, 2, 1954.

OWEN, GEORGE: The description of Penbrokshire (No. 109 (1)).
See also CHARLES, BERTIE GEORGE: The second book of George Owen's Description of Pembrokeshire. *N.L.W. Jnl.*, v, 1947–8.

**1793.** OWEN, HENRY (ed.): A survey of the lordship of Haverford in 1577. *Arch. Camb.*, 1903.

PIERCE, THOMAS JONES (ed.): An Anglesey crown rental of the sixteenth century (No. 517).

Records of the Court of Augmentations relating to Wales and Monmouthshire (No. 130 (13)).

**1794.** SMITH, WILLIAM JAMES: Three Salesbury mansions in 1601. *B.B.C.S.*, xv, 1952–4.

**1795.** STRADLING, JOHN: The story of the lower borowes of Merthyr Mawr. Ed. by H. J. Randall and William Rees. *S. Wales and Mon. Rec. Soc. Pubns.*, i, 1932.

### (ii) Secondary works

**1796.** EMERY, FRANK VIVIAN: West Glamorgan farming *circa* 1580–1620. *N.L.W. Jnl.*, ix and x, 1955–7.

**1797.** EVANS, ELWYN: Arwystli and Cyfeiliog in the sixteenth century. *Mont. Coll.*, li, 1949–50.

**1798.** FOX, CYRIL, and RAGLAN, LORD: Monmouthshire houses: a study of building techniques and smaller house plans in the fifteenth and sixteenth centuries. Part iii. Cardiff, 1954.

**1799.** HOWELLS, BRIAN ELWYN: Pembrokeshire farming. *N.L.W. Jnl.*, ix, 1956.

**1800.** JONES, EMYR GWYNNE: Some notes on the principal county families of Anglesey in the sixteenth and early seventeenth centuries. *Trans. Angl. Antiq. Soc.*, 1939 and 1940.

**1801.** JONES, THOMAS IEUAN JEFFREYS: A study of rents and fines in South Wales in the sixteenth and seventeenth centuries. *Harlech Studies* (ed. Ben Bowen Thomas). Cardiff, 1938.

**1802.** LLOYD, JOHN DAVIES KNATCHBULL: Montgomery castle and the Herberts, with some information on building activities in the sixteenth and seventeenth centuries. *Arch. Camb.*, 1955–6.

**1803.** OWEN, EDWARD: The decline of the Tudors of Penmynydd, Môn. *Trans. Angl. Antiq. Soc.*, 1934–5.

**1804.** PHILLIPS, JAMES: Glimpses of Elizabethan Pembrokeshire. *Arch. Camb.*, 1897, 1899, 1904.

**1805.** PIERCE, THOMAS JONES: Notes on the history of rural Caernarvonshire in the reign of Elizabeth. *Trans. Caerns. Hist. Soc.*, 1940.

**1806.** SMITH, WILLIAM JAMES: The Salusburies as maintainers of murderers. *N.L.W. Jnl.*, vii, 1951–2.

**1807.** WILLIAMS, WILLIAM OGWEN. The Anglesey gentry as business men in Tudor and Stuart times. *Trans. Angl. Antiq. Soc.,* 1948.

### (b) Trade and industry

### (i) Sources

**1808.** Anglia Wallia. *Arch. Camb.,* 1911.

**1809.** HAKLUYT, RICHARD: The principal navigations, voiages and discoveries of the English nation, made by sea or over land. London, 1589; 3 vols., 1599–1600. Best modern edition by Walter Raleigh, 12 vols., Glasgow, 1903–5.

**1810.** JONES, EVAN DAVID: An account book of Sir Thomas Myddelton for the years 1583–1603. *N.L.W. Jnl.,* i, 1940–1.

**1811.** Id.    The register of the corvisers of Ruthin, 1570–1671. Ibid., vii, 1951–2.

LEWIS, EDWARD ARTHUR: The Welsh port books, 1550–1603 (No. 109 (12)).

**1812.** Id.    The port books of the port of Cardigan in Elizabethan and Stuart times. *Trans. Cards. Antiq. Soc.,* vii, 1930.

**1813.** Id.    The toll books of some north Pembrokeshire fairs, 1509–1603. *B.B.C.S.,* vii, 1934.

PARRY, ROBERT: The diary of Robert Parry (1559–1613) (No. 1594).

### (ii) Secondary works

The following works should be consulted for references to Welsh industries of the period in their wider setting: DONALD, M. B.: Elizabethan copper: the history of the mines royal, London, 1955; HAMILTON, HENRY: The English brass and copper industries to 1800 (No. 2401); NEF, JOHN U.: The rise of the British coal industry (No. 2365); SCHUBERT, H. R.: History of the iron industry of Great Britain to 1775, London, 1957; SCOTT, WILLIAM ROBERT: Constitution and finance of English . . . joint stock companies to 1720 (No. 2246) (contains references to Welsh mines *temp.* Elizabeth I).

CHARLES, BERTIE GEORGE (ed.): Haverfordwest accounts, 1563–1620 (No. 1578).

**1814.** CRONIN, JOHN M.: A vanished Irish colony in South Wales (*circa* 1540–1603). *St. Peter's Magazine,* 1925.

**1815.** DAVIES, ARTHUR STANLEY: Salt works in Merioneth. *Arch. Camb.,* 1940.

11

**1816.** GRANT-FRANCIS, GEORGE: The smelting of copper in the Swansea district of South Wales from the time of Elizabeth to the present day. London and Manchester, 1881.

**1817.** JOHN, DAVID GLYN: The organisation of the chartered companies in South Wales in the sixteenth century. *Trans. Neath Antiq. Soc.*, iv, 1934.

KNOOP, DOUGLAS, and JONES, GWILYM PEREDUR: The repair of Beaumaris town wall, 1536–1538 (No. 392).

**1818.** LERRY, GEORGE GEOFFREY: The industries of Denbighshire from Tudor times to the present day. *Trans. Denbs. Hist. Soc.*, 1957 and 1958.

LEWIS, EDWARD ARTHUR: A contribution to the commercial history of mediaeval Wales, 1301 to 1547 (No. 1553).

**1819.** LEWIS, W. J.: A Welsh salt-making venture in the sixteenth century. *N.L.W. Jnl.*, viii, 1954.

**1820.** LLEWELLIN, W.: Sussex iron masters in Glamorganshire. *Arch. Camb.*, 1863.

**1821.** Id.     Some account of the iron and wire works of Tintern. Ibid.

**1822.** MENDENHALL, THOMAS C.: The Shrewsbury drapers and the Welsh wool trade in the XVI and XVII centuries. Oxford, 1953.

See also GRIFFITHS, GRIFFITH MILWYN: The Castle Hill collection. *N.L.W. Jnl.*, viii, 1954, p. 110.

**1823.** Id.     (ed.): A Merioneth wage assessment for 1601. *Jnl. Mer. Hist. and Rec. Soc.*, ii, 3, 1955.

**1824.** OWEN, BOB: Llyfryddiaeth morwyr Cymru. *Jnl. Welsh Bibl. Soc.*, iii, 3 and 4, 1927.

**1825.** ROBERTS, GLYN: Piracy on the Welsh coast. *Trans. Neath Antiq. Soc.*, 2nd series, ii, 1931–2.

**1826.** SKEEL, CAROLINE ANN JAMES: The Welsh woollen industry in the sixteenth and seventeenth centuries. *Arch. Camb.*, 1922.

**1827.** Id.     The cattle trade between England and Wales from the fifteenth to the nineteenth centuries. *Trans. R.H.S.*, 4th series, ix, 1926.

THOMAS, DAVID: Hen longau a llongwyr Cymru (No. 258).

Id.     Hen longau sir Gaernarfon (No. 259).

**1828.** WILLIAMS, DAVID TREVOR: Trade relations between Jersey, Guernsey, and the Welsh ports in Elizabethan times. *Soc. Jersiaise Bull. Ann.*, 1934.

WILLIAMS, JOHN: History of Berw (No. 522).

**1829.** WILLIAMS, M. LUCY: Tide mills . . . between Holy Isle and Anglesey. *Trans. Angl. Antiq. Soc.*, 1939.

## V. LITERATURE AND SCHOLARSHIP

### (a) Texts and sources

An invaluable guide is POLLARD, ALFRED WILLIAM, and REDGRAVE, G. R.: A short-title catalogue of books printed in England, Scotland, and Ireland . . . 1475–1640, Bibliographical Society, London, 1926. DAVIES, WILLIAM LLEWELYN: Welsh books entered in the Stationers' Company's registers, part I, 1554–1660 (No. 7); id.: Short-title list of Welsh books, part I, 1546–1640 (No. 8); and PARRY, THOMAS: Hanes llenyddiaeth Gymraeg (No. 146), should also be consulted.

**1830.** Catalogue of manuscripts . . . illustrating the history of medicine in Wales. British Medical Association. Aberystwyth, 1928.

Cefn Coch MSS. Ed. J. Fisher (No. 1595).

**1831.** DAVIES, JOHN HUMPHREYS: The roll of the Caerwys eisteddfod of 1523. *Trans. Liverpool Welsh Nat. Soc.*, 1904–5 to 1908–9.

**1832.** GRUFFYDD, GERAINT (ed.): Two letters from Richard Parry of Anmer to John Wynn Edward of Bodewryd concerning the translation of certain books into Welsh. *Jnl. Welsh Bibl. Soc.*, viii, 1, 1954.

**1833.** LLWYD, HUMPHREY: Commentarioli descriptionis Britannicae fragmentum. Cologne, 1572; trans. by Twyne, T.: The breviary of Britayne. London, 1573.

**1834.** Id.      The historie of Cambria. Ed. David Powel. London, 1584. Ed. William Wynne (augmented), London, 1697; ed. Richard Llwyd, Shrewsbury, 1832.

**1835.** MIDLETON, WILLIAM: Bardhoniaeth neu brydydhiaeth, y llyfr kyntaf. Llundain, 1593.
See also No. 1746.

**1836.** PERRI, HENRI: Eglvryn phraethineb, sebh dosparth ar retoreg, 1595. Gol. Griffith John Williams, Caerdydd, 1930.

**1837.** PRICE, JOHN: Historiae Brytannicae defensio. London, 1573.

**1838.** RHYS, SION DAFYDD: Cambrobrytannicae Cymraecaeve linguae institutiones et rudimenta. London, 1592.

**1839.** ROBERT, GRUFFYDD: Dosparth byrr ar y rhan gyntaf i ramadeg Cymraeg. Milan, 1567; repr. Carmarthen, 1927 (a reissue of the work as originally published in *Yr Haul*, 1857 and 1860–1); in *Revue Celtique*, Appendix, 1883; and by Griffith John Williams: Gramadeg Gruffydd Robert (No. 1777).

**1840.** SALESBURY, HENRY: Grammatica Britannica in usum linguae studiosorum succincta methodo et perspicuitate facili conscripta. London, 1593.

**1841.** SALESBURY, WILLIAM: Oll synwyr pen Kembero ygyd. (? 1547.) Ed. J. Gwenogvryn Evans. Bangor and London, 1902.

**1842.** Id.      A dictionary in Englyshe and Welshe moche necessary to all suche Welshemen as wil spedly learne the englyshe tongue. 1547. Reprinted in facsimile by the Cymmrodorion Society, London, 1877.

**1843.** Id.      A briefe and a playne introduction teaching how to pronounce the letters in the British tong (now com'enly called Walsh). London, 1550.

**1844.** Id.      Llysieulyfr meddyginiaethol. Gol. E. Stanton Roberts. Caerdydd, 1916.

**1845.** WILLIAMS, GRIFFITH JOHN: Llythyr Sion Dafydd Rhys at y beirdd. *Efryd. Cath.*, ii, 1947.

### (b) Secondary works

**1846.** BOWEN, DAVID JAMES: Gruffudd Hiraethog ac argyfwng cerdd dafod. *Llên Cymru*, ii, 1953.

**1847.** Id.      Ail eisteddfod Caerwys a chais 1594. Ibid., iii, 1955.

**1848.** Id.      Gruffudd Hiraethog a'i oes. Caerdydd, 1958.

**1849.** DAVIES, JOHN HUMPHREYS: Early Welsh bibliography. *Trans. Cymmr.*, 1897–8.

**1850.** EVANS, EVAN LEWIS: William Salesbury. *Y Llenor*, xii, 1933.

**1851.** FLOWER, ROBIN: Richard Davies, William Cecil, and Giraldus Cambrensis. *N.L.W. Jnl.*, iii, 1943–4.

**1852.** Id.      William Salesbury, Richard Davies, and archbishop Parker. Ibid., ii, 1941–2.
> See also GLANMOR WILLIAMS: Bishop Sulien, bishop Richard Davies, and archbishop Parker. Ibid., v, 1948.

**1853.** HARRIES, GERALLT: Ail eisteddfod Caerwys. *Llên Cymru*, iii, 1954.

**1854.** JONES, EVAN DAVID: William Salesbury a'i deulu. *B.B.C.S.*, vii, 1933–5.

**1855.** JONES, JOHN HENRY: John Owen, Cambro-Britannus. *Trans. Cymmr.,* 1940.

**1856.** Id. John Owen, the epigrammatist. *Greece and Rome,* x, 1941.

**1857.** KENDRICK, THOMAS: British antiquity. London, 1950.

**1858.** KER, NEIL R.: Sir John Prise. *The Library,* v, 1955.

LEWIS, SAUNDERS: Tudur Aled (No. 1523).

**1859.** LLOYD, DAVID MYRDDIN: William Salesbury and 'Epistol E. M. at y Cembru'. *N.L.W. Jnl.,* ii, 1941–2.

**1860.** LLOYD, HOWELL WILLIAM: Welsh books printed abroad in the sixteenth and seventeenth centuries, and their authors. *Y Cymmr.,* iv, 1881.

**1861.** LLOYD, JOHN EDWARD: Powel's *Historie* (1584). *Arch. Camb.,* 1943.
See also id., Powel's historie (1584). *N.L.W. Jnl.,* iii, 1943–4.

**1862.** MATHIAS, WILLIAM ALUN: Llyfr rhetoreg William Salesbury. *Llên Cymru,* i a ii, 1951–2.

MORRIS-JONES, JOHN: Tudur Aled (No. 1524).

NORTH, FREDERICK JOHN: Humphrey Lhuyd's maps of England and Wales (No. 376).
See also id.: The map of Wales (No. 375).

**1863.** PARRY, THOMAS: Siôn Dafydd Rhys. *Y Llenor,* ix a x, 1930–1.

**1864.** Id. Tri chyfeiriad at William Salesbury. *B.B.C.S.,* ix, 1937–9.

**1865.** REES, BRINLEY: Dulliau'r canu rhydd. Caerdydd, 1952.

**1866.** ROBERTS, ENID PIERCE: Siôn Tudur. *Llên Cymru,* ii, 1952–3.

**1867.** Id. The renaissance in the vale of Clwyd. *Flints. Hist. Soc. Pubns.,* xv, 1954–5.
See also No. 2222.

**1868.** SCHOLDERER, VICTOR: Powel's *Historie* (1584). *N.L.W. Jnl.,* iii, 1943–4.

WILLIAMS, GLANMOR: Some Protestant views of early British Church history (No. 1717).

**1869.** WILLIAMS, IEUAN MORGAN: Ysgolheictod hanesyddol yn yr unfed ganrif ar bymtheg. *Llên Cymru,* ii, 1952–3.

### (c) Miscellaneous

**1870.** BARTLEY, JAMES ORR: Teague, Shenkin, and Sawney; being an historical study of the earliest Irish, Welsh, and Scottish characters in English drama. Cork University Press, 1954.

EVANS, EVAN VINCENT: Andrew Boorde and the Welsh people (No. 1591).

**1871.** HARRIES, FREDERICK JAMES: Shakespeare and the Welsh. London, 1919.

**1872.** HUGHES, A. E.: Shakespeare and his Welsh characters. *Trans. Cymmr.*, 1917–18.

**1873.** JONES, THOMAS GWYNN: Tudor Welshmen's English. *Y Cymmr.*, xxix, 1919.

**1874.** MILLER, E. J.: Wales and the Tudor drama. *Trans. Cymmr.*, 1948.

**1875.** ROBERTS, R. E.: Welsh music in the Tudor period. Ibid., 1925–6.

**1876.** WILLIAMS, GWYN: Welshmen in Shakespeare's Stratford. Ibid., 1954.

# SECTION H

## A.D. 1603—1714

The standard bibliography of the period is DAVIES, GODFREY: Bibliography of British history, Stuart period, Oxford, 1928. More recent and more selective bibliographies are included in the two relevant volumes of the Oxford History of England—DAVIES, GODFREY: The early Stuarts, Oxford, 1937; and CLARK, GEORGE NORMAN: The later Stuarts, 2nd edn, Oxford, 1955.

See also DAVIES, WILLIAM LLEWELYN: Welsh books entered in the Stationers' Company's registers, part I, 1554–1660; part II, 1660–1708 (No. 7); id.: Short-title list of Welsh books, part I, 1546–1640; part II, 1641–1680; part III, 1681–1700 (No. 8).

### I. GENERAL WORKS

#### (a) Sources

##### (i) Calendars and transcripts of public records

For general sources such as Calendars of state papers, Journals of the Houses of Lords and Commons, Acts of the Privy Council, etc., see the bibliographies cited above.

PARRY, EDWARD: Royal visits and progresses to Wales (No. 126).

WILLIAMS, WILLIAM RETLAW (ed.): Old Wales (No. 131).

##### (ii) Family, estate and manorial records

###### Descriptive accounts

For descriptions of collections relating to the seventeenth century in the National Library of Wales and elsewhere, see:

*Anglesey Antiquarian Society and Field Club Transactions:*

1877. 1935 and 1940. Penrhos (University College of North Wales).

1878. 1940. Baron Hill (U.C.N.W.).

*Bulletin of the Board of Celtic Studies:*

1879. Vol. xvii, 1957. Penrhos (U.C.N.W.).

*Caernarvonshire Historical Society Transactions:*

1880. 1939. Sources of Caernarvonshire history in the National Library of Wales.

149

**1881.** 1940. Baron Hill, Penrhyn, Meillionydd, Ystumcolwyn, Cefn Amwlch, Garthewin (U.C.N.W.).

*Denbighshire Historical Transactions:*

**1882.** 1953 and 1954. Chirk castle, Wynnstay (N.L.W.).

*Montgomeryshire Collections:*

**1883.** Vol. xlii, 1932. Crosswood, Herbert of Cherbury, Wynn (of Gwydir), Cwrt Mawr, Celynog, Willans (N.L.W.).

**1884.** Vol. xlviii, part 1, 1943. Montgomeryshire manorial records in the National Library of Wales from 1536 onwards. (Powis manorial documents, the Wynnstay Collection, Powis Castle Collection.)

*National Library of Wales Journal ·*

**1885.** Vol. ii, 1941–2. Wynnstay, Llanfair and Brynodol, Nanhoron, Dunraven (N.L.W.).

**1886.** Vol. iii, 1943–4. Bronwydd, Glanpaith, Powis (N.L.W.).

**1887.** Vol. v, 1947–8. Badminton, Hanmer, Crosse of Shaw Hill (N.L.W.).

**1888.** Vol. vi, 1949–50. Rûg, Bodfel, Glynllifon, Sweeney Hall (N.L.W.).

**1889.** Vol. vii, 1951–2. Bute, Courtfield, Gwysaney (N.L.W.).

**1890.** Vol. viii, 1953–4. Chirk castle (N.L.W.).

**1891** HUGHES, W. T.: The Gwyn papers: 17th century Monmouthshire. *Mons. Rev.,* i, 1923.

> Account of MSS. in the Newport Public Library.

### Transcripts

**1892.** Bulkeley MSS. (i) Civil war period, *Arch. Camb.,* 1846; (ii) 1681–1706, ibid., 1851.

> Inaccurate transcripts from originals now in U.C.N.W. library, Bangor.

Chirk castle accounts, 1605–66. Ed. W. M. Myddelton (No. 636).

Chirk castle accounts, 1666–1753. Ed. id. (No. 637).

**1892A.** Correspondence during the Great Rebellion. Ed. W. W. E. W[ynne]. *Arch. Camb.,* 1875.

Documents relating to the town and castle of Harlech. Ed. id. (No. 1567).

**1893.** Fonmon MSS. (formerly in the National Library of Wales, now in the Glamorgan Record Office), transcripts from, for the Civil War period. in J. H. MATTHEWS: Cardiff Records, vol. iv, pp. 146–55 (No. 686).

**1894.** Manorial records relating to the manor of Broniarth, 1563–1773. Ed. E. A. Lewis and J. Conway Davies. *Mont. Coll.*, xlix, part II, 1946.

**1895.** Old Herbert papers at Powis castle and in the British Museum. *Mont. Coll.*, xx, 1887.

**1896.** Survey of the lordship of Bromfield and Yale, 1620. By John Norden, sen., and John Norden, jun. Printed in part in *Arch. Camb.*, supplement, 1877 ('Original documents'), and LLOYD, J. Y. W.: Powys Fadog, vols. ii and iii (No. 58); see also PALMER, ALFRED NEOBARD: Town, fields, and folk of Wrexham (No. 640).

**1897.** Surveys of the manors of Radnorshire. Ed. John Lloyd. *Arch. Camb.*, 1900.

**1898.** The lordship of Denbigh, 1649–50. Ed. Edward Owen. *Wales*, iii, 1896.

Two letters . . . concerning the translation of certain books into Welsh. Ed. Geraint Gruffydd (No. 1832).

### Calendars

A survey of the Duchy of Lancaster lordships in Wales, 1609–13 (No. 130 (12)).

On Duchy of Lancaster and other manors in Carmarthenshire, see also indexes and transcripts by Arthur Waight Matthews in *Trans. Carms. Antiq. Soc.*, x–xiii, 1915–17.

Calendar of Salusbury correspondence (No. 130 (14)).

Calendar of the Wynn (of Gwydir) papers (No. 122).

Clenennau letters and papers in the Brogyntyn Collection, part I (No. 124).

Exchequer proceedings concerning Wales *in tempore* James I (No. 130 (15)).

**1899.** Historical Manuscripts Commission reports:

The following reports contain material on seventeenth century Wales:

Beaufort (12th R., ix).
†*Brogyntyn (2nd R.).
*Carreglwyd and Berw (5th R.).

Cecil, xv–xviii.
*Chirk castle (2nd R.).
†Cholmondeley (5th R.).
De L'Isle and Dudley, iii.
Earl of Denbigh (4th R.).
†*Gwysaney (6th R.).
†House of Lords.
Kenyon (14th R., iv).
Portland i. (13th R., i).
Puleston of Emral (2nd R.) and of Worthenbury (15th R., vii).

Collections marked * are now wholly or in part deposited in the National Library of Wales, where more detailed lists may be consulted. For the present location of other collections, consult Migrations of historical MSS. in *Bull. of Inst. of Hist. Research*. Abstracts of Welsh entries in reports marked † are printed in one of the following: *Arch. Camb.*, 1880-3 ; *Bye-Gones*, 1881–2; Old Wales, iii (No. 131). See also UPTON, E. S.: Guide to sources of English history, 1603–1660, in reports of Historical Manuscripts Commission, Washington, 1952.

### (iii) Letters and diaries

**1900.** BRADNEY, JOSEPH ALFRED (ed.): The diary of Walter Powell of Llantilio Crossenny. Bristol, 1907.
> See also FLETCHER, J. KYRLE: Walter Powell and his diary. *The Nationalist*, March, 1906.

**1901.** DODD, ARTHUR HERBERT (ed.): The early days of Edward Lhuyd. *N.L.W. Jnl.*, vi, 1949–50.
> Letters by his father, Edward Lloyd, 1681.

**1902.** HOWELL, JAMES: Epistolae Ho-elianae: Familiar letters, 1685. Ed. Joseph Jacobs. London, 1890–1.
> See also commentaries in *Old Welsh Chips*, 1888; *Trans. Cymmr.*, 1943–4; and those listed in Y Bywgraffiadur Cymreig, p. 346 (No. 106).

**1904.** JENKINS, DAVID (ed.): Llythyr Syr Peter Mutton, 1604. *N.L.W. Jnl.*, v, 1947–8.

**1905.** OWEN, EDWARD, and JONES, GRIFFITH HARTWELL (eds): Correspondence between Dr. John Davies of Mallwyd and Sir Simonds D'Ewes. *Y Cymmr.*, xvii, 1904.

**1906.** OWEN, HUGH (ed.): The diary of Bulkeley of Dronwy, 1630–36. *Trans. Angl. Antiq. Soc.*, 1937. Introduction, transcript, and index.

PARRY, ROBERT: The diary of Robert Parry (1559–1613) (No. 1594).

**1907.** POWELL, EDWARD (ed.): Pryce (Newton Hall) correspondence. *Mont. Coll.*, xxi–xxxii, 1900–01.

> Uncompleted, but covers the period 1555–1698, mainly seventeenth century.

ROBERTS, PETER: Y cwtta cyfarwydd (No. 1609).

> Contains diaries and note books (principally legal) covering the period 1595–1653.

### (iv) Contemporary verse

**1908.** ANON: Caniadau'r gwrthryfel mawr. *Cymru*, xxi, 1901.

> Poems by William Phylip and Edward Dafydd, with several (inaccurate) transcripts of verses from Llanover MSS. (Cardiff), on which see discussion by Thomas Shankland in *Seren Gomer*, 1902; Thomas Richards, Religious developments in Wales, pp. 188 ff. (No. 2112); and Griffith John Williams in *Llên Cymru*, iii, 1954.

See also DAVIES, WILLIAM LLEWELYN: Phylipiaid Ardudwy (No. 712).

**1909.** BETHELL, S. L.: The poetry of Henry Vaughan, Silurist. *Jnl. Hist. Soc. Church in Wales*, i, 1947.

> See also HUTCHINSON, FRANCIS ERNEST: Henry Vaughan, Oxford, 1947, and WILLIAMSON, EDWARD WILLIAM (Bishop): Henry Vaughan, B.B.C. lecture, 1953.

**1910.** BOWEN, GERAINT: Yr halsingod. *Trans. Cymmr.*, 1945.

**1911.** Dau gywydd [gan John Griffith, Llanddyfnan, 1653]. Ed. W. Gilbert Williams. *Trans. Angl. Antiq. Soc.*, 1938.

**1912.** Hen gerddi gwleidyddol. Ed. John Humphreys Davies. *Cymdeithas Llên Cymru*, ii. Caerdydd, 1901.

**1913.** JONES, EVAN DAVID: The Brogyntyn Welsh manuscripts. *N.L.W. Jnl.*, v–vi, viii, 1948–50, 1953.

> Copious extracts, with English translations.

**1914.** Id.     Two political poems. *Jnl. Mer. Hist. Soc.*, ii, 1953–4.

JONES, JOHN ('Myrddin Fardd'): Cynfeirdd Lleyn (No. 1602).

JONES, JOHN HENRY: John Owen, Cambro - Britannus (No. 1855).

Id.     John Owen, the epigrammatist (No. 1856).

> See also id.: John Owen, Plas Du. *Y Llenor*, 1938.

**1915.** MORRIS, EDWARD: Barddoniaeth Edward Morris. Ed. Hugh Hughes. Liverpool, 1902. For a shorter selection, see Gwaith Edward Morus. Ed. Owen Morgan Edwards. *Cyfres y Fil*. Llanuwchllyn, 1904.

**1916.** MORUS, HUW: Eos Ceiriog, sef casgliad o bêr ganiadau Huw Morus. Gol. Walter Davies. Gwrecsam, 1823.

> See also SAMUEL, DAVID: A sketch of the life and writings of Hugh Morris. *Camb. Reg.*, i, 1795 (1796); and bibliographical notes by David Jenkins in *N.L.W. Jnl.*, ii, 1939–40, and vii, 1950–1.

**1917.** OWEN, HUGH: The Llanddyfnan (or Henblas) MSS. *Trans. Angl. Antiq. Soc.*, 1949.

> Seventeenth and eighteenth century verse.

**1918.** PRICHARD, RHYS: Canwyll y Cymru. Ed. Stephen Hughes, London, 1672; 31st edn by Rice Rees, Llanymddyfri, 1841.

> See also BALLINGER, JOHN: Vicar Prichard, *Y Cymmr.*, xiii, 1900, and JONES, DAVID JAMES GWENALLT: Y ficer Prichard a 'Canwyll y Cymry', Caernarfon [1946].

**1919.** VAUGHAN, DAVID: An address to Sir John Price, 1643. *Mont. Coll.*, xxxviii, 1928.

> Welsh, with English translation.

### (v) Travel and topography

**1920.** COTTON, CHARLES: A voyage to Ireland in burlesque. 1670.

**1921.** DEFOE, DANIEL: A tour thro' the whole island of Great Britain. 2 vols. 1724–5. Ed. George Douglas Howard Cole, London, 1927.

> The original tours were undertaken in 1684 and 1688, and supplemented later, but it is doubtful whether Defoe visited Wales. The material included in the Welsh part of letter vi was probably in the main second-hand. Later editions contain up-to-date information contributed by other hands.

**1922.** DINELEY, THOMAS: The account of the official progress of the first duke of Beaufort through Wales, 1684. Ed. R. W. Banks. London, 1888.

> Facsimile with Dineley's original sketches.

**1923.** [FIENNES, CELIA]: Through England on a side saddle in the time of William and Mary, being the diary of Celia Fiennes. Ed. E. W. Griffiths. London, 1888.

LHWYD, EDWARD: Parochialia (*circa* 1696–9) (No. 361).

**1924.** OGILBY, JOHN: Britannia, or an illustration of the kingdom of England and dominion of Wales. London, 1675.

**1925.** SYMONDS, RICHARD: Diary of the marches of the royal army (1644–5). Ed. Charles Edward Long. Camden Soc., 1859.

**1926.** SINGER, SAMUEL WELLER (ed.): Correspondence of Henry Hyde, earl of Clarendon. London, 1828.

> For a description of Clarendon's journey through North Wales to Ireland, see pp. 190–205; it is reprinted in part in PARRY, EDWARD: Railway companion from Chester to Holyhead, pp. 14–16 (No. 3314); and in the *North Wales Chronicle*, November 29 and December 6, 1827.

**1927.** TAYLOR, JOHN: A short relation of a long journey . . . encompassing the principalitie of Wales. 1653. Repr. for the Spenser Society, London, 1876.

**1928.** TOYNBEE, MARGARET R.: A royal journey through Breconshire and Radnorshire in 1645. *Trans. Rads. Soc.*, xx, 1950.

**1929.** Id.    A royal journey through Herefordshire and Radnorshire in 1645. Ibid., xxi, 1951.

> Both articles are illustrated.

### (b) Secondary works

**1930.** DODD, ARTHUR HERBERT: Flintshire politics in the seventeenth century. *Flints. Hist. Soc. Pubns.*, xiv, 1952–3.

**1931.** Id.    The pattern of politics in Stuart Wales. *Trans. Cymmr.*, 1948.

**1932.** Id.    Studies in Stuart Wales. Cardiff, 1952.

**1933.** MATHEW, DAVID (archbishop): Wales and England in the early seventeenth century. *Trans. Cymmr.*, 1955.

## II. LEGAL AND ADMINISTRATIVE HISTORY

### (a) Sources

### (i) Records

**1934.** ANON. (ed.): Pembrokeshire hearths in 1670. *W. Wales Hist. Rec.*, ix–xi, 1920–6.

**1935.** BELL, HAROLD IDRIS: Two Denbighshire MSS. *B.B.C.S.*, v, 1929–31.

> B.M. additional MSS. 40174/5 (court book of manors in the lordship of Chirk and order book of Denbighshire quarter sessions, 1675–8, 1679–81). Description and extracts.

CHARLES, BERTIE GEORGE (ed.): The records of the borough of Newport, Pembs. (No. 1561).

Id. (ed.). Haverfordwest accounts, 1563–1620 (No. 1578).

**1937.** First report of the the Royal Commission on public records, 1800.

> Appendices H and I, pp. 246–52, 295–303. Much of the information given here is now out of date, and the subsequent reports of the Commissioners (1800–1819, 1837) are superseded by First report of the Royal Commission on public records, vol. i, 1912 (reprinted 1914); vol. ii, 1914; vol. iii, 1917. These contain much useful information on Welsh records.

**1938.** FISHER, JOHN (ed.): Ruthin corporation records, 1642–92. *Arch. Camb.*, 1921.

> See also JONES, EVAN DAVID: Register of the corvisors of Ruthin, 1570–1671 (No. 1811).

**1939.** HANCOCK, THOMAS W. (ed.): The court of the marches: Montgomeryshire cases, 1617. *Mont. Coll.*, xix, 1886.

**1940.** JONES, EVAN DAVID: Gleanings from the Radnorshire file of great sessions papers, 1691–9. *Trans. Rads. Soc.*, xiii, 1943.
> Abstracts of documents.

**1941.** LEWIS, EDWARD ARTHUR (ed.): Proceedings of the leet courts of north Radnorshire, 1688. Ibid., iv–v, 1934–5.
> Transcript with introduction.

**1942.** Id.     Schedule of the quarter sessions records of the county of Montgomery at the National Library of Wales (1614–1737). *Mont. Coll.*, xlvi and xlvii, 1939–42.
> Full summary of contents.

**1943.** Id. and DAVIES, JAMES CONWAY: Leet proceedings of the borough of Newtown, 1665–83. Ibid., xlviii, 1943–4.

**1944.** LEWIS, THOMAS HENRY: Documents illustrating the county gaol and house of correction in Wales. *Trans. Cymmr.*, 1946–7.

**1945.** LLOYD, JOHN DAVIES KNATCHBULL: The borough records of Montgomery, 1633–1879. *Mont. Coll.*, xlv, 1937–8.
> Full catalogue of records at the National Library of Wales.

**1946.** LLOYD, WILLIAM VALENTINE (ed.): Lay subsidy rolls for the hundred of Chirbury, 1621 and 1624 (etc.). Ibid., xxii, 1888.
> Annotated transcripts.

**1947.** MATTHEWS, ARTHUR WAIGHT (ed.): Transcripts of documents on local taxation in Carmarthenshire, mainly post-Restoration. *Trans. Carms. Antiq. Soc.*, viii–x, 1914–15; xiii, 1918–19.

**1948.** OWEN, HUGH (ed.): Corporation of Beaumaris minute book, 1694–1723. *Trans. Angl. Antiq. Soc.*, 1932.
> Excerpts.

**1950.** PALMER, ALFRED NEOBARD (ed.): Rolls of pleas of the great sessions of Denbighshire, 1625–6. *Arch. Camb.*, 1897.

**1951.** Id.     John Lloyd's notebook, 1637–51. Ibid., 1888.
> Notes of a Great Sessions attorney.

**1952.** PARKINS, WILLIAM TREVOR: The lords of Mold. *Cheshire Sheaf,* ii, 1880–2. Repr. (ed. Henry Taylor) in *Flints. Hist. Soc. Pubns.,* vi, 1916–17.
> The principal documents are printed *in extenso,* especially for the seventeenth century.

REES, WILLIAM (ed.): The charters of the borough of Newport in Gwynllwg (No. 1566).

**1953.** SKEEL, CAROLINE ANNE JAMES: The instructions to the earl of Bridgewater, 1633. *Arch. Camb.,* 1917.

**1954.** THOMAS, GRIFFITH THOMAS (ed.): Carmarthenshire magistrates (and Carmarthen borough officials) in 1662. *Trans. Carms. Antiq. Soc.,* xxix, 1939.
> From the Egerton MSS. and Corporation order book; fully annotated.

**1955.** WILLIAMS, RICHARD (ed.): Apportionment of taxes, Denbighshire, 1675. *Arch. Camb.,* 1881 (pp. 329–30).

### (ii) Contemporary legal treatises

DODDRIDGE, JOHN: The history of the ancient and modern estate of the Principality of Wales (No. 138).

LEWIS, EDWARD ARTHUR (ed.): Three legal tracts concerning the court-leet in Wales (No. 1639).
> Tracts II and III cover the periods *circa* 1623–6 and 1665 respectively.

VAUGHAN, RICE: Practica Walliae (No. 1653).

**1956.** VAUGHAN, WILLIAM: The golden-grove. 1st edn, 1600; 2nd edn, 1608.
> A Welsh writer's views on government.

### (b) Secondary works

BOWEN, IVOR: Grand juries, justices of the peace, and quarter sessions in Wales (No. 1624).

EVANS, ELWYN: Some Cyfeiliog manorial customs (No. 1631).

**1957.** GRIFFITHS, WILLIAM ARTHUR: Some account of John Reynolds (d. 1626) and Lewis Reynolds (d. 1624). *Mont. Coll.,* li, 1949–50.
> Two bailiffs of Welshpool.

**1958.** HENDERSON, B. L. K.: The commonwealth charters. *Trans. R.H.S.,* 1912.

LEWIS, THOMAS HENRY: The justice of the peace in Wales (No. 1640).

**1959.** LLOYD, REES L.: Welsh masters of the bench of the Inner Temple. *Trans. Cymmr.,* 1937 and 1939.
> Biographies of some important figures in seventeenth century history.

**1960.** MATHEW, DAVID: The Welsh influence among the legal advisers of James II. Ibid., 1938.
Synopsis of Cymmrodorion lecture.

SKEEL, CAROLINE ANNE JAMES: The council in the marches of Wales (No. 1499), ch. v ff.

**1961.** Id.     The council of the marches in the seventeenth century. *E.H.R.*, xxx, 1915.

WILLIAMS, WILLIAM RETLAW: The history of the Great Sessions in Wales, 1542–1830, together with the lives of the Welsh judges (No. 104).

### III. FAMILY HISTORY AND GENEALOGY

Articles, etc., on county families of importance in the seventeenth century will be found in section A II.

**1962.** BERRY, G. C.: Sir Hugh Myddelton and the New River. *Trans. Cymmr.*, 1956.

**1963.** GRIFFITHS, WILLIAM ARTHUR: An account of Arthur Vaughan of Trederwen Hall, Arddleen, sheriff of Montgomeryshire, 1691. *Mont. Coll.*, lii, 1951–2.

**1964.** Id.     Some notes on various Kyffin families residing around Llanfyllin in the 17th century. Ibid., liv, 1955–6.

**1965.** HEMP, WILFRID JAMES: The pedigree roll of Sir William Meredith of Stansty. *Arch. Camb.*, 1932.

**1966.** IRVINE, W. F.: Watkin Owen of Llangar, 1631–79. *N.L.W. Jnl.*, viii, 1953–4.

JONES, EMYR GWYNNE: Some notes on the principal county families of Anglesey in the sixteenth and early seventeenth centuries (No. 1800).

Id.     (ed.): History of the Bulkeley family (No. 45).

**1967.** JONES, EVAN DAVID, Robert Vaughan of Hengwrt. *Jnl. Mer. Hist. and Rec. Soc.*, i, 1949–52.
See also GLENN, THOMAS ARTHUR: Robert Vaughan of Hengwrt and Robert Vaughan the London engraver. *Arch. Camb.*, 1934.

**1968.** LONDON, HUGH STAMFORD: George Owen, York Herald. *Trans. Cymmr.*, 1943–4.

**1969.** MACKENZIE, NORMAN: Sir Thomas Herbert of Tintern. *Bull. Inst. of Hist. Res.*, xxix, 1956.

**1970.** MERCHANT, WILLIAM MOELWYN: Lord Herbert of Cherbury and seventeenth-century historical writing. *Trans. Cymmr.,* 1956.

**1971.** MORRICE, J. C.: Wales in the seventeenth century: its literature and men of letters and action. Bangor, 1918.

> A compendium. Largely superseded, but containing some information not easily available elsewhere.

> OWEN, EDWARD: The decline of the Tudors of Penmynydd (No. 1803).

**1972.** RANSOM, MARY: The parliamentary activity of Sir H. Mackworth. *Univ. of Birmingham Hist. Jnl.,* i, 1947.

**1973.** ROBERTS, BETTY DEW: Cheadles against Bulkeleys. *Trans. Angl. Antiq. Soc.,* 1945.

**1974.** Id.     Bulkeleys in exile. Ibid., 1950.

> WILLIAMS, JOHN GWYNN: Sir John Vaughan of Trawscoed, 1603–74 (No. 77).

### IV. POLITICAL HISTORY

#### (a) 1603-42

#### (i) Sources

**1975.** DODD, ARTHUR HERBERT: A spy's report, 1604, and 'A spy's report'—addenda. *B.B.C.S.,* ix, 1937–9.

**1976.** GORDON, M. N.: The collection of shipmoney in the reign of Charles I. *Trans. R.H.S.,* 1910.

> Statistical abstracts.
> For Welsh material see *Mont. Coll.,* ii, 1869 (full texts); *Trans. Carms. Antiq. Soc.,* xii, 1917–18 (calendar).

**1977.** JONES, EMYR GWYNNE (ed.): The county election of 1620: two unpublished letters. *Trans. Caerns. Hist. Soc.,* 1940.

**1978.** MATTHEWS, JOHN HOBSON (ed.): Civil war memoranda. Memorandum on the payment of subsidies in Wales, *temp.* James I. In Cardiff records (No. 686), iv.

**1979.** VAUGHAN, WILLIAM: The spirit of detraction. London, 1611.

> Pp 321 ff. give his views on contemporary Welsh politics.

#### (ii) Secondary works

**1980.** DODD, ARTHUR HERBERT: The Spanish Treason, the Gunpowder Plot, and the Catholic refugees. *E.H.R.,* liii, 1938.

> Id.     Wales and the Scottish succession (No. 1627).

12

Id.   Wales's parliamentary apprenticeship (1536 – 1625) (No. 1628).

**1981.** Id.   Wales in the parliaments of Charles I. *Trans. Cymmr.*, 1945 and 1946–7.

**1982.** Id.   Caernarvonshire elections to the Long Parliament. *B.B.C.S.,* xii, 1946.

**1983.** Id.   Wales and the second Bishops' War (1640). *Ibid.*, xii, 1948.

**1984.** Id.   Welsh opposition lawyers in the Short Parliament. *Ibid.*, xii, 1948.

**1985.** Id.   The Caernarvonshire election dispute of 1640–1 and its sequel. *Trans. Caerns. Hist. Soc.*, 1950.

JONES, EMYR GWYNNE: County politics and electioneering (No. 1635).

**1986.** JONES, FRANCIS: Disaffection and dissent in Pembrokeshire. *Trans. Cymmr.*, 1946–7.
Seventeenth and eighteenth centuries.

**1987.** ROBERTS, GLYN: The parliamentary history of Beaumaris, 1555–1832. *Trans. Angl. Antiq. Soc.*, 1933.

Id.   Political affairs [in Carmarthenshire] from 1536 to 1900 (No. 1648).

**1988.** TIBBOTT, GILDAS: Welshmen with Prince Charles in Spain. *N.L.W. Jnl.*, i, 1939–40.

### (b) 1642-60

### (i) Sources

**1989.** ADDAMS-WILLIAMS, ALBERT: Address to the Welsh Bibliographical Society. *Jnl. Welsh Bibl. Soc.*, ii, 1925–31.
On some local pamphlets of the Civil War period.

**1990.** ANON.: A true character of the deportment . . . of the principal gentry within the counties of Carmarthen, Cardigan, and Pembroke (*circa* 1661). *Cambrian Register*, i, 1795.

**1991.** ANON. (ed.): Inedited letters of . . . [John] Jones [&c.]. *Trans. Hist. Soc. Lancs. and Chesh.* New series, i, 1861.
Extensive transcripts from the letter book of John Jones the regicide, 1651–60 (Plas Yolyn MSS., now in the National Library of Wales). Some are reprinted in DAVIES, DAVID: Ardudwy a'i gwron (No. 711), and in PALMER, ALFRED NEOBARD: Older Nonconformity of Wrexham (No. 643).

**1992.** ANON. (ed.): Thomas Bowen of Trefloyn. *W. Wales Hist. Rec.*, vi, 1916.
Pembrokeshire petition of 1646.

**1993.** ATKINSON, J. A. (ed.): Tracts relating to the Civil War in Cheshire. Chetham Soc., 1909.

**1994.** British Museum: Catalogue of the pamphlets, books, newspapers, and manuscripts relating to the Civil War, the Commonwealth, and the Restoration, collected by George Thomason, 1640–1661. 2 vols. London, 1908.

**1995.** Calendar of . . . the committee for compounding. 5 vols. London, 1889–92.

> There is an incomplete summary of the Welsh entries in *Arch. Camb.*, 1887; those for the North Wales counties are more completely listed in *Bye-Gones*, 1903–4 and 1905–6; those for South Wales in *Old Wales* (No. 131), i and ii; and in *Cymru Fu*, 1889; the documents for Montgomeryshire are fully calendared in *Mont. Coll.*, xviii and xix, 1885–6; one of those for Pembrokeshire is transcribed in *W. Wales Hist. Rec.*, xiv, 1929.

**1996.** Calendar of . . . the committee for the advance of money. 3 vols. London, 1888.

**1997.** CARTE, THOMAS: Life of James duke of Ormond. Oxford, 1851.

> Vols. v and vi of this edition contain the correspondence between Ormond and archbishop Williams; these may be supplemented by letters in the same author's Original letters, 1739, i, and in *Arch. Camb.*, 1869 and 1870.

**1998.** ELLIS, MEGAN: Cyflwyniad Rowland Vaughan, Caergai, i'w gyfieithiad o Eikon Basilike. *N.L.W. Jnl.*, i, 1939–40.

**1999.** HALL, JAMES (ed.): Memorials of the Civil War in Cheshire. *Rec. Soc. Lancs. and Chesh.*, xix, 1889.

> Contains two Cheshire diaries: Edward Burghall: Providence improved (1638–42 and 1649–63), and Thomas Malbon: Memorials of the Civil War (1642–56).

**2000.** HEMP, WILFRID JAMES (ed.): Commonwealth marriages. *Trans. Caerns. Hist. Soc.*, 1950.

> For a Flintshire example see EVANS, JOHN: North Wales (xvii, i, The beauties of England and Wales, Ed. E. W. Brayley and J. Britton, 1801–14, p. 726).

**2001.** LEIGHTON, STANLEY (ed.): Mytton manuscripts. Letters and papers of Thomas Mytton of Halston. *Mont. Coll.*, vii and viii, 1874–5.

> Valuable for civil war campaigns. For further correspondence and documents relative to the Civil War, see ibid., xii–xiii, 1879–80; xvi, 1883; xxi–xxiii 1887–9; xxix, 1896; *Arch. Camb.*, 1846–8, 1853, 1869, 1875, 1915; and *Flints. Hist. Soc. Pubns.*, vi, 1916–17.

**2002.** LEWIS, JOHN: The parliament explained to Wales, 1646. Reprinted by Cymdeithas Llên Cymru. Cardiff, 1907.

**2003.** [MAURICE, WILLIAM]: An account of the Civil War in North Wales. Ed. Robert Williams. *Arch. Camb.*, 1846.

**2004.** MORRIS, RUPERT HUGH: The siege of Chester, 1643–6. Ed. P. H. Lawson. Chester, 1924.

**2005.** National Library of Wales: Catalogue of tracts of the Civil War and Commonwealth period. Aberystwyth, 1911.

> Some of these are reprinted in No. 2006, others in *Cymru Fu*, ii, 1889–91. Many additional pamphlets have been acquired since this catalogue was issued; most will be found listed in B.M. catalogue of Thomason tracts (No. 1994). See also collections of Welsh items from civil war news-sheets reprinted in *Bye-Gones*, 1889–94, 1913–15; *Mont. Coll.*, xiii, 1880; xxii, 1888.

**2006.** PHILLIPS, JOHN ROLAND: Memoirs of the Civil War in Wales and the marches. 2 vols. London, 1874; 2nd edn, London, 1878.

> The second volume of the 1874 edn consists of documents.

**2007.** POWELL, ANTHONY DYMOKE (ed.): Radnorshire and the Commonwealth and Protectorate. *Trans. Rad. Soc.*, xii, 1942.

> Gleanings from State Papers and Harleian MSS., with useful lists of names.

**2008.** STEARNS, RAYMOND PHINEAS (ed.): Letters and documents relating to Hugh Peter. *Essex Institute Historical Collections* (Mass., U.S.A.), lxii–lxxiii, 1935–6.

> Valuable for excerpts from contemporary news-letters on South Wales affairs, 1650. See also YONGE, WILLIAM: England's shame . . . 1663, and on Yonge, *Jnl. Welsh Bibl. Soc.*, iii, 1925–31, pp. 89–91.

SYMONDS, RICHARD: Diary of the marches of the royal army (1644–5) (No. 1925).

[WILLIAMS, JOHN]: Historia Bellomarisei (No. 521).

> Contains contemporary account of the second Civil War in Anglesey; also printed (with some variations) as appendix to LLWYD, RICHARD: Poetical works. Chester, 1837.

### (ii) Secondary works

**2009.** BERRY, JAMES, and LEE, STEPHEN G.: A Cromwellian major-general: the career of Colonel James Berry. Oxford, 1938.

**2010.** CLARK, ARTHUR: Raglan castle and the Civil War in Monmouthshire. Chepstow, Newport and Monmouthshire branch of the Historical Association, and the Chepstow Society, 1953.

**2011.** DAVID, W.: The antiquities of St. Fagans, with specific reference to the battle of 1648. *Trans. Cardiff Nat. Soc.*, ix, 1877.

**2012.** DODD, ARTHUR HERBERT: The tragedy of Colonel John Bodvel. *Trans. Caerns. Hist. Soc.*, 1945.

**2013.** Id.      Colonel Thomas Trafford. *B.B.C.S.*, xiv, 1950–2.

**2014.** Id.      Anglesey in the Civil War. *Trans. Angl. Antiq. Soc.*, 1952.

**2015.** Id.    Caernarvonshire in the Civil War. *Trans. Caerns. Hist. Soc.*, 1953.

**2016.** Id.    The Civil War in east Denbighshire. *Trans. Denbs. Hist. Soc.*, 1954.

**2017.** Id.    A remonstrance from Wales, 1655. *B.B.C.S.*, xvii, 1958.

**2018.** EAMES, ALED: Sea power and Caernarvonshire, 1642–60. *Trans. Caerns. Hist. Soc.*, 1955.

**2019.** FARROW, W. J.: The great Civil War in Shropshire. Shrewsbury, 1926.

**2020.** GARDINER, SAMUEL RAWSON: Charles I and the earl of Glamorgan. *E.H.R.*, ii, 1887.

> See also id.: History of the great civil war, ii, 1889 (repr. 1901); reply in ROUND, JOHN HORACE: Studies in peerage and family history, 1901, ch. ix; and discussion in DODD, ARTHUR HERBERT: Studies in Stuart Wales (No. 1932).

**2021.** HACKET, JOHN: Scrinia reserata. A memorial offered to . . . John Williams, D.D. London, 1693.

> For other lives of Archbishop Williams, see PHILLIPS, AMBROSE: Life of John Williams, London, 1700; ROBERTS, BETTY DEW: Mitre and musket, London, 1938; and BOWEN, IVOR: John Williams of Gloddaeth, *Trans. Cymmr.*, 1927–8.

**2022.** JOHNSTONE, HILDA: Two governors of Shrewsbury during the great Civil War and the Interregnum. *E.H.R.*, xxvi, 1911.

**2023.** LEACH, ARTHUR LEONARD: The history of the Civil War (1642–1649) in Pembrokeshire. London, 1937.

**2024.** LLOYD, JOHN: Colonel John Jones of Maesygarnedd. *Jnl. Mer. Hist. and Rec. Soc.*, ii, 1953–4.

PHILLIPS, JOHN ROLAND: Memoirs of the ancient family of Owen of Orielton (No. 65).
> Period of the Civil War and after, pp. 33–60.

REES, JAMES FREDERICK: Studies in Welsh history (No. 151).
> Ch. iv–viii are on this period.

**2025.** SIMPKINSON, C. H.: Thomas Harrison. Temple Biographies. London, 1905.

> Valuable appendices. See also FIRTH, C. H., in *Amer. Antiq. Soc.*, 1893; and ASHLEY, MAURICE: Cromwell's generals, London, 1954, ch. v.

**2026.** STEARNS, RAYMOND PHINEAS: The strenuous puritan. Hugh Peter (1598–1660). Urbana (Ill., U.S.A.), 1954.

> Important for his South Wales connection. See also No. 2008 above.

**2027.** TERRY, W. H.: Judge Jenkins. London, 1929.
See also RICHARDS, THOMAS: The indiscretion of Anthony Wood. *Y Cymmr.*, xxxvi, 1926.

TOYNBEE, MARGARET R.: A royal journey through Breconshire and Radnorshire in 1645 (No. 1928).

Id.     A royal journey through Herefordshire and Radnorshire in 1645 (No. 1929).

**2028.** TUCKER, NORMAN: Civil War colonel: Sir John Carter. *Trans. Caerns. Hist. Soc.,* 1952.

**2029.** Id.     Captain Morgan's lonely grave. *Procs. Llandudno . . . Field Club.,* xxvi, 1953.

**2030.** Id.     John Robinson. Civil War colonel. *Trans. Denbs. Hist. Soc.* 1955.

**2031.** Id.     Denbigh's loyal governor. Ibid., 1956.

**2032.** Id.     Colonel Sir Roger Mostyn. First baronet, 1624–1690. *Flints. Hist. Soc. Pubns.,* xvii, 1957.

**2033.** Id.     North Wales in the Civil War. Denbigh, 1958.

**2034.** VAUGHAN, HERBERT MILLINGCHAMP: Oliver Cromwell in South Wales, 1648–9. *Trans. Cymmr.,* 1936.

**2035.** WEBB, JOHN: Memorials of the Civil War . . . as it affected, Herefordshire and the adjacent counties. 2 vols. London, 1879.

**2036.** WILLIAMS, WILLIAM GILBERT: Arfon y dyddiau gynt. Caernarfon, [1915].
Articles on Caernarvonshire in the Civil War period reproduced from *Cymru*, xlvi–xlvii, 1914–15; other articles in the series, not reprinted, are in ibid., xliii, xlv, xlviii, 1912–13, 1915.

### (c) 1660-1714
#### (i) Sources

**2037.** ANON. (ed.): Montgomery election petition, 1685. *Mont. Coll.,* xxi, 1887.

**2038.** BRADNEY, JOSEPH ALFRED (ed.): A puzzle or two. *Jnl. Welsh Bibl. Soc.,* iii, 1925–31.
Note on 'An address to the English Protestant officers in the present army', attributed to 'a Welsh gent. of £100 per annum' (p. 91).

**2039.** DODD, ARTHUR HERBERT (ed.): Caernarvonshire and the Restoration: four letters. *Trans. Caerns. Hist. Soc.,* 1950.
See also WILLIAMS, W. GILBERT, in *Y Genedl Gymreig*, Mai–Mehefin, 1923; and RICHARDS, THOMAS: Richard Edwards of Nanhoron: a Restoration study, *Trans. Caerns. Hist. Soc.,* 1947.

2040. EVANS, GEORGE EYRE (ed.): Merionethshire election agreement, 1671. *Arch. Camb.*, 1919, pp. 220–1.

2041. J[ONES], M[ORRIS] C[HARLES]: Montgomeryshire magistracy, 1687. *Mont. Coll.*, xiii, 1880.

> For the background of the incident, see RICHARDS, THOMAS: Declarasiwn 1687: tipyn o hanes a barn Cymru amdano (No. 2144).

2042. [PRICE, ROBERT]: Gloria Cambriae: or the speech of a bold Briton, 1702. Somers Tracts, 1814, xi.

2043. RICHARDS, THOMAS: The Glamorgan loyalists of 1696. *B.B.C.S.*, iii, 1926.

2044. TAYLOR, HENRY (ed.): Flint borough election, 1697. *Flints. Hist. Soc. Pubns.*, xi, 1925.

### (ii) Secondary works

2045. DE BEER, E. S.: The court party in the House of Commons, 1670–8. *Bull. Inst. of Hist. Res.*, xi, 1933–4.

> Details of many Welsh M.P.s. See also GEORGE, Mrs. ERIC: Elections and electioneering, 1679–81, *E.H.R.*, xlv, 1930.

2046. C[URLL], E[DMUND]: Life of . . . Robert Price . . . one of the justices of His Majesty's court of common pleas. London, 1734.

> See No. 2042.

2047. DODD, ARTHUR HERBERT: 'Tuning' the Welsh bench, 1680. *N.L.W. Jnl.*, vi, 1950.

2048. EVANS, A. M.: North Wales (with particular reference to Anglesey) in the seventeenth century. Gleanings from State Papers. *Trans. Angl. Antiq. Soc.*, 1924.

RICHARDS, THOMAS: Declarasiwn 1687: tipyn o hanes a barn Cymru amdano (No. 2144).

Id.	Richard Edwards of Nanhoron: a Restoration study (No. 2039).

2049. Id.	Piwritaniaeth a pholitics, 1689–1719. Wrecsam, 1927.

2050. WYNNE, WILLIAM: Life of Sir Leoline Jenkins. London, 1724.

### V. ECCLESIASTICAL HISTORY

For the output of Welsh religious works during the period, see PARRY, THOMAS: Hanes llenyddiaeth Gymraeg (No. 146), pennod ix; and for rarer titles: *Jnl. Welsh Bibl. Soc.*, ii, 1916–23 (pp. 189, 276); iii, 1925–31 (p. 219); vii, 1950–3 (p. 158).

## A. The (Anglican) Church in Wales

### (a) Before 1660

#### (i) Sources

**2051.** ANON. (ed.): Statistics of the Church of England, 1603. *Trans. Cong. Hist. Soc.*, vi, 1913–15.
From Harleian and Stowe MSS.

**2052.** ANON. (ed.): Llanllyfni papers. *Arch. Camb.*, 1863.
See pp. 283–5: 'A Breviat of all the Presentments against the Clergie of the Dioces of Bangor . . . 1623'.

GRUFFYDD, GERAINT (ed.): Bishop Francis Godwin's injunctions for the diocese of Llandaff, 1603 (No. 1671).

**2053.** JONES, FRANCIS (ed.): The personalty of a Welsh cleric, 1634. *Jnl. Hist. Soc. Church in Wales*, i, 1947.
Inventory and introduction.

**2054.** KENNEDY, WILLIAM PAUL MCCLURE: List of visitation articles and injunctions, 1604–1715. *E.H.R.*, xl, 1925.

**2055.** MORRIS, EDWARD ROWLEY (ed.): Documents relating to the tithes and other property belonging to the dean and chapter of St. Asaph. *Arch. Camb.*, 1887.

PRYCE, ARTHUR IVOR: The diocese of Bangor in the sixteenth century (No. 827).

Id.    The diocese of Bangor during three centuries (No. 828).

**2056.** VAUGHAN, WILLIAM: The Church militant. London, 1640.
Versified Church history applied to current controversies.

**2057.** WALKER, JOHN: Sufferings of the clergy of the Church of England. London, 1714.
See also MATTHEWS, ARNOLD GWYNNE: Walker revised, Oxford, 1948; TATHAM, G. B.: Dr. Walker and the sufferings of the clergy, Cambridge, 1911 (with calendar of Walker MSS. at the Bodleian).

**2058.** WILLIAMS, ANEURIN (ed.): A Welsh parish in the Interregnum. *E.H.R.*, ix, 1894.
Merthyr Tydfil (Nathaniel Jones's MS.); see also: WILKINS, CHARLES: History of Merthyr Tydfil (No. 707); JAMES, FRANK T.: Notes on the parish register of Merthyr Tydfil from A.D. 1703 to 1763, Appendix (No. 960).

[WRIGHT, THOMAS (ed.)]: Anglesea (No. 524).
Pp. 75–9: 'Of the clergy'.

#### (ii) Secondary works

**2059.** ANON.: Jeremy Taylor in Carmarthenshire, 1644–53. *Trans. Carms. Antiq. Soc.*, xix, 1925–6.

**2060.** BOSHER, ROBERT S.: The making of the Restoration settlement. The influence of the Laudians, 1649–1662. London, 1950.

DODD, ARTHUR HERBERT: The Church in Wales in the age of the Reformation (No. 1698).
For the seventeenth century, see pp. 34–41.

**2061.** HOWSE, WILLIAM HENRY: Contest for a Radnorshire rectory in the seventeenth century. *Jnl. Hist. Soc. Church in Wales*, vii, 1957.

**2062.** JAMES, JOHN WILLIAMS: Dr. John Davies of Mallwyd, 1578–1644. *Jnl. Hist. Soc. Church in Wales*, i, 1947.

See also OWEN, EDWARD, and JONES, GRIFFITH HARTWELL (eds): Correspondence of Dr. John Davies with Sir Simonds D'Ewes (No. 1905).

OWEN, C. E. VAUGHAN: The vicars of Trefeglwys, 1574–1902 (No. 1706).

**2063.** RICHARDS, THOMAS: Cymru a'r Uchel Gomisiwn, 1633–40. Liverpool, 1930.

**2064.** WAKEMAN, HENRY OFFLEY: The Laudian movement in Wales. *Cymru Fydd*, iii, 1890.

### (b) After 1660

### (i) Sources

**2065.** ANON.: Ecclesiastical appointments, Patent Rolls, Charles II. *Arch. Camb.*, 1886.

**2066.** [BEAW, WILLIAM]: Dr. William Beaw, bishop of Llandaff. Ed. C. Waldron. *Red Dragon*, ix, 1886.
Autobiographical letter to Archbishop Tennison, 1699, *inex tenso*, with introduction.

BRADNEY, JOSEPH ALFRED, and RICKARDS, R.: Llandaff records (No. 832).
Vols. i–iii, 1660–1708, contain declarations, oaths, subscriptions, etc.

**2067.** ECTON, JOHN: A state of the proceedings of the corporation of the governours of the bounty of Queen Anne. London, 1719; 2nd edn, 1721.
The section on Wales will be found on pp. 233–47.

**2068.** EVANS, GEORGE EYRE: Churchwardens' presentments [Carmarthenshire], 1671–2, 1678–9. *Trans. Carms. Antiq. Soc.*, xiv, 1919–21; 1684, ibid., x–xi, 1914–17; 1705, ibid., xi–xii, 1916–18.

Id.     Carmarthenshire: bishops' transcripts, 1671 (No. 959).

**2069.** Id.     Eleven Pembrokeshire parishes' presentments, 1678, 1684, 1688, 1708. *Arch. Camb.*, 1935 (pp. 298–304).

**2070.** GORDON, ALEXANDER: An anonymous MS. *Jnl. Welsh Bibl. Soc.*, iii, 1925–31.
> Sermon notes of a Flintshire parson, 1657–1702.

**2071.** HUMPHREYS, HUMPHREY (Bishop): Ymoddion i'w hateb gan brocatorion, wardeinied, a swyddogion eraill . . . 1690. In EVANS, ALBERT OWEN: A few episcopal visitation returns. Bangor, 1937.

**2072.** KENNET, WHITE (Bishop): The case of impropriations and of the augmentation of vicarages. London, 1704.

**2073.** [KETTLEWELL, JOHN]: A compleat collection of the works of . . . John Kettlewell . . . to which is prefix'd the life of the author. Ed. George Hickes and Robert Nelson. 2 vols. London, 1719.
> For references to the Welsh non-jurors, see vol. ii, appendix vi, v–xiii.
> See also BOWLES, WILLIAM LISLE: Life of bishop Ken, London, 1830.

**2074.** PRING, JOSEPH: Papers, documents, law proceedings, etc., respecting the maintenance of the choir of the cathedral of Bangor, as provided for by an Act of Parliament passed . . . 1685. Bangor, 1819.

**2075.** TURNER, GEORGE LYON: The clerical subsidy of 1661. *Trans. Cong. Hist. Soc.*, vii, 1916–18.

**2076.** WYNNE, ROBERT: A short narrative of the proceedings against the bishop of St. Asaph. London, 1702.

### (ii) Secondary works

BOSHER, ROBERT S.: The making of the Restoration settlement. The influence of the Laudians, 1649–1662 (No. 2060).

**2077.** HART, ARTHUR TINDAL: William Lloyd, 1627–1717. Bishop, politician, author and prophet. London, 1952.

OWEN, C. E. VAUGHAN: The vicars of Trefeglwys, 1574–1902 (No. 1706).

**2078.** RICHARDS, THOMAS: The Whitford leases. A battle of wits. *Trans. Cymmr.*, 1924–5.

**2079.** Id.     Two studies in the history of the diocese of Bangor. *Arch. Camb.*, 1925.

**2080.** Id.     The troubles of Dr. William Lucy. *Y Cymmr.*, xxxviii, 1927.

**2081.** SODEN, GEOFFREY INGLE: Godfrey Goodman, bishop of Gloucester, 1583–1656. London, 1953.

**2082.** WRIGHT, EVAN GILBERT: Humphrey Humphreys, 1648–1712.
*Trans. Angl. Antiq. Soc.*, 1949.

**2083.** Id.　　Humphrey Humphreys, bishop of Bangor and Hereford.
*Jnl. Hist. Soc. Church in Wales*, ii, 1950.
　　　　See also OWEN, BOB: Esgob Humphreys. *Cymru*, lx, 1921.

**2084.** Id.　　Dean John Jones, 1650–1727. *Trans. Angl. Antiq. Soc.*,
1952.

### B. Protestant Dissenters

#### (a) Before 1660

#### (i) Sources

**2085.** An Act for the propagation of the Gospel in Wales, 1650–1.
Cymdeithas Llên Cymru reprint, 1908.
　　　　Includes also the minutes of the commissioners for North Wales, 1650–1,
　　　　and a letter of Vavasour Powell on the work of the commission, reprinted
　　　　from a contemporary diurnal.

**2085A.** A word for God. Or a testimony on truth's behalf, 1655.
　　　　See also No. 2017.

**2086.** CHARLES, THOMAS, and OLIVER, PHILIP (eds): The works of
the late Rev. Walter Cradock, with a short account of his life. Chester, 1800.

**2087.** ERBERY, WILLIAM: The testimony. London, 1658.

**2088.** GRIFFITH, ALEXANDER: Strena Vavasoriensis, 1654. Cymdeithas
Llên Cymru reprint, 1915.

**2089.** JONES, EVAN DAVID: Llyfr eglwys Mynydd-bach. *Y Cofiadur*, 1947.
　　　　The first entry relates to the foundation of the Church in 1650; subsequent
　　　　entries are all eighteenth century.

**2090.** Id.　　(ed.): Ten Merioneth ministers' petition to Oliver
Cromwell. *Jnl. Mer. Hist. and Rec. Soc.*, ii, 1953–4.

　　　　KENRICK, W. BYNG: Chronicles of a Nonconformist family:
the Kenricks of Wynne Hall, Exeter and Birmingham (No. 54).

**2091.** LEE, MATHEW HENRY (ed.): Diaries and letters of Philip Henry.
London, 1882.

**2092.** LLWYD, MORGAN: Gweithiau. Vol. i, ed. Thomas Edward Ellis,
Bangor 1899; vol. ii, ed. John Humphreys Davies, Bangor, 1908.
　　　　See also BEVAN, HUGH: Morgan Llwyd y llenor, Caerdydd, 1954; EVANS,
　　　　EVAN LEWIS: Morgan Llwyd, Lerpwl, 1930; id.: Morgan Llwyd y llenor,
　　　　*Llên Cymru*, iv, 1955; GRUFFYDD, WILLIAM JOHN: Morgan Llwyd a llyfr y
　　　　tri aderyn, *Y Cofiadur*, iii, 1925; JONES, JOHN WILLIAM (gol.): Coffa Morgan
　　　　Llwyd, Llandysul, 1952; LEWIS, SAUNDERS: Morgan Llwyd, *Efryd. Cath.*, vii,
　　　　1955.

**2093.** MITCHELL, ALEXANDER F., and STRUTHERS, JOHN: Minutes of
the sessions of the Westminster Assembly of divines, 1644–9. Edinburgh,
1874.

2094. SHANKLAND, THOMAS: Notes on MSS. at Lambeth. *B.B.C.S.*, i, 1921.

STEARNS, RAYMOND PHINEAS (ed.): Letters and documents relating to Hugh Peter (No. 2008).

2095. UNDERHILL, EDWARD BEAN (ed.): The records of a church of Christ meeting at Broadmead, Bristol. *Hanserd Knollys Soc.*, 1847; another edn, ed. Nathaniel Haycroft, 1865.
>An indispensable source for the beginnings of Welsh separatism.

### (ii) Secondary works

2096. DAVIES, J. D. GRIFFITH: Protestant Nonconformity in Monmouthshire before 1715. *Mons. Rev.*, i, 1923.
>With tabular appendices.

2097. DAVIES, PENNAR: Episodes in the history of Brecknockshire dissent. *Brycheiniog*, iii, 1957.

2098. DAVIES, T. IDRIS: Dyddiau cynnar Annibyniaeth ym Mrycheiniog a Maesyfed. *Y Cofiadur*, xvi, 1946.

2099. Id.    Plaid y Bumed Frenhiniaeth yng Nghymru. *Y Traethodydd*, 1940.

2100. DODD, ARTHUR HERBERT: New England influences in early Welsh puritanism. *B.B.C.S.*, xvi, 1954.

Id.    A remonstrance from Wales (No. 2017).

2101. Id.    The background of the Welsh Quaker migration to Pennsylvania. *Jnl. Mer. Hist. and Rec. Soc.*, iii, 2, 1958.

2102. GLASCODINE, C. H.: Marmaduke Mathews of Swansea. *Trans. Cong. Hist. Soc.*, v, 1911–12.
>See also *N.L.W. Jnl.*, i, 1939–40 (p. 166).

2103. GRIEVE, ALEXANDER JAMES: Puritanism in 'Little England beyond Wales'. Ibid., vi, 1913–15.

2104. Id.    Independency in 'Little England beyond Wales'. Ibid., vii, 1916–18.

2105. HUGH, RICHARD LEONARD: Annibyniaeth yng ngorllewin Morgannwg. *Y Cofiadur*, xviii, 1948.
>See also: REES, THOMAS MARDY: Dechreuad Annibyniaeth yng nghylchoedd Abertawe. *Y Dysgedydd*, 1939.

2106. JONES, JOHN MORGAN: Walter Cradoc a'i gyfoeswyr. *Y Cofiadur*, xv, 1938.

**2107.** JONES, ROBERT TUDUR: Vavasor Powell and the Protectorate. *Trans. Cong. Hist. Soc.*, xvii, 1953.

> See also id.: Vavasor Powell a'r Bedyddwyr, *Traf. Cymd. Hanes Bed.* 1948-9. For the background of Powell's ideas, see BROWN, LOUISE FARGO: Political and religious ideas of the Baptists and Fifth Monarchy men, London, 1912.

**2108.** NUTTALL, GEOFFREY F.: The Welsh saints, 1640–1660. Walter Cradock, Vavasor Powell, Morgan Llwyd. Cardiff, 1957.

**2109.** OWEN, BOB: Rhai agweddau ar hanes Annibynwyr sir Gaernarfon. *Y Cofiadur*, xx, 1950.

> See also WILLIAMS, WILLIAM GILBERT: Hanes Annibyniaeth tref Caernarfon, *Y Dysgedydd*, 1939.

**2110.** PHILLIPS, D. RHYS: Eglwys Ilston. *Traf. Cymd. Hanes Bed.*, 1928.

**2111.** RICHARDS, THOMAS: The puritan movement in Wales, 1639–53. London, 1920.

**2112.** Id.    Religious developments in Wales, 1654–62. London, 1923.

**2113.** Id.    The puritan visitation of Jesus College, Oxford, and the principalship of Dr. Michael Roberts (1648–1657). *Trans. Cymmr.*, 1923.

> See also HALL, MARJORIE FOLJAMBE, in *Jnl. Welsh Bibl. Soc.*, 1923.

Id.    Cymru a'r Uchel Gomisiwn (No. 2063).

**2114.** Id.    Nonconformity [in Carmarthenshire] from 1620 to 1715. In The history of Carmarthenshire (No. 605), ii.

**2115.** Id.    Eglwys Llanfaches. *Trans. Cymmr.*, 1941.

**2116.** Id.    Flintshire and the puritan movement. *Jnl. Flints. Hist. Soc.*, 1952-3.

**2117.** Id.    The puritan movement in Anglesey. A re-assessment. *Trans. Angl. Antiq. Soc.*, 1954.

**2118.** Id.    Meirionnydd: Piwritaniaeth gynnar. *Jnl. Mer. Hist. and Rec. Soc.*, ii, 2, 1954.

> See also JONES, EVAN DAVID (ed.): Ten Merioneth ministers' petition to Oliver Cromwell (No. 2090).
> See also JENKINS, ROBERT THOMAS: Hanes cynulleidfa Hen Gapel Llanuwchllyn, Bala, 1937 (ch. ii); and OWEN, BOB: Bodwenni, plwyf Llandderfel, Meirionydd; preswyl Annibynwyr Penllyn o tua 1650 hyd tua 1750, *Y Cofiadur*, xvii, 1947.

**2119.** SHANKLAND, THOMAS: John Myles. *Traf. Cymd. Hanes Bed.*, 1910-22.

> See also No. 2250.

**2120.** Id.    Stephen Hughes. *Y Beirniad*, ii, 1912.

**2121.** Id.    Anghydffurfwyr ac Ymneilltuwyr cyntaf Cymru. *Y Cofiadur*, i, 1923.

STEARNS, RAYMOND PHINEAS: The strenuous puritan. Hugh Peter (1598–1660) (No. 2026).

**2122.** WHITLEY, WILLIAM THOMAS: Radnorshire Baptists, 1646–76. *Trans. Rads. Hist. Soc.*, v, 1935.

**2123.** WILLIAMS, JANE: An account of Henry Williams of Ysgafell. *Mont. Coll.*, iv, 1871.

### (b) After 1660

#### (i) Sources

**2124.** BATE, FRANK: The Declaration of Indulgence, 1672. London, 1908.

For Welsh licences, see appendices. See also: EVANS, GEORGE EYRE: The licences of Daniel Higgs and Stephen Hughes, *Trans. Carms. Antiq. Soc.*, xvii, 1924.

**2125.** CALAMY, EDWARD: An account of the ministers . . . ejected after the Restoration in 1660. London, 1713.

An amplification of ch. ix of his abridgement of the life of Baxter, 1702, with additional Welsh names supplied by James Owen of Oswestry. For further amplifications and corrections, see id.: Continuation of the account, 2 vols., London, 1727; PALMER, SAMUEL: Nonconformists memorial, 3 vols., London, 1802–3 (and other editions); MATTHEWS, ARNOLD GWYNNE: Calamy revised, Oxford, 1934.

**2126.** EDWARDS, CHARLES: Autobiography. An afflicted man's testimony . . . 1691. *Cymru Fydd*, ii, 1889.

See also JAMES, IVOR: Charles Edwards a'i amserau, *Y Traethodydd*, xli, 1886; and the introduction by Griffith John Williams to the reprint of the third edition of Hanes y ffydd ddiffuant (No. 2154).

**2127.** EVANS, GEORGE EYRE: Llangyfelach (Tirdoncyn) Nonconformists. Annals and registers, 1666 *et seq. Trans. Carms. Antiq. Soc.*, xv and xvi, 1921–2.

Id.    Eleven    Pembrokeshire    parishes'    presentments (No. 2069).

**2128.** JONES, EVAN DAVID: Llyfr eglwys Pant-teg, sir Gaerfyrddin. *Y Cofiadur*, xxiii, 1953.

**2129.** Id.    Nonconformity in Merioneth, 1675. *N.L.W. Jnl.*, viii, 1953–4.

**2130.** OWEN, BOB: Some details about the Independents in Caernarvonshire. *Trans. Caerns. Hist. Soc.*, 1945.

**2131.** OWEN, CHARLES: Some account of . . . Mr. James Owen. London, 1809.

**2132.** RICHARDS, THOMAS: The religious census of 1676. *Trans. Cymmr.* supplement, 1925–6.

**2133.** TURNER, GEORGE LYON: Original records of Nonconformity under persecution and indulgence. Vol. i, text, London, 1911; vol. ii, summaries and indexes, London, 1911; vol. iii, historical and expository, London, 1914.

**2134.** Id.    Welsh Nonconformity in 1672. *Trans. Cong. Hist. Soc.,* ii, 1905–6.

**2135.** WILLIAMS, RICHARD: Montgomeryshire Nonconformity; extracts from gaol files, 1662–1705. *Mont. Coll.,* xxiv–xxviii, 1890–4.

### (ii) Secondary works

**2136.** BOWEN, EMRYS GEORGE: Bedyddwyr Cymru tua 1714. *Traf. Cymd. Hanes Bed.,* 1957.

**2137.** DAVIES, JOHN HUMPHREYS: Trwyddedau Anghydffurfwyr Cymru yn 1672. *Y Traethodydd,* 1901.

DAVIES, PENNAR: Episodes in the history of Brecknockshire dissent (No. 2097).

**2138.** DAVIES, T. EIRUG: Philip Pugh a'i ragflaenwyr yng nghanolbarth sir Aberteifi. *Y Cofiadur,* xiv, 1937.

**2139.** DAVIES, WILLIAM: John Owen, Bronyclydwr [1669–1700]. *Y Dysgedydd,* 1941.

**2140.** GORDON, ALEXANDER: Freedom after ejection, a review of Presbyterian and Congregational Nonconformity in England and Wales, 1691–2. Manchester, 1917.
Contains a valuable index.

**2141.** LEWIS, D. MORGAN: Eglwysi Henllan a Rhydyceisiaid. *Y Cofiadur,* 1925.
With a reprint of a tract by Mathias Maurice (1727) on controversies in the latter church, 1707–9, on which see OWEN, JEREMY: Golwg ar y beiau, Caerfyrddin, 1732–3; ed. R. T. Jenkins, Caerdydd, 1950.

**2142.** OWEN, JOHN DYFNALLT: Camre cyntaf Anghydffurfiaeth ac Annibyniaeth yn sir Gaerfyrddin, 1660–1710. *Y Cofiadur,* 1936.

REES, THOMAS: History of Protestant Nonconformity (No. 178).
Pp. 259–65: lists of Nonconformist causes, etc., compiled by John Evans, 1715, but reflecting conditions since 1687.

**2143.** REES, THOMAS MARDY: Robert Thomas, Baglan (bu farw 1692). *Y Cofiadur,* 1948.

**2144.** RICHARDS, THOMAS: Declarasiwn 1687: tipyn o hanes a barn Cymru amdano. *Traf. Cymd. Hanes Bed.,* 1924.

**2145.** Id.     Wales under the penal code, 1662–87. London, 1925.

     Id.      Piwritaniaeth a pholitics, 1689–1719 (No. 2049).

**2146.** Id.     Wales under the Indulgence, 1672–5. London, 1928.

**2147.** Id.     Henry Maurice, Piwritan ac Annibynnwr. *Y Cofiadur*, 1928.

**2148.** Id.     Eglwys Rhydwilym. *Traf. Cymd. Hanes Bed.*, 1938.

     Id.      Nonconformity [in Carmarthenshire] from 1620 to 1715 (No. 2114).

**2149.** Id.     Y dechreuadau: golwg newydd. *Traf. Cymd. Hanes Bed.*, 1948–9.

     A study in the working of the Carmarthen and Brecon consistory courts, 1661–1670.

**2150.** TURNER, GEORGE LYON: Congregationalists and the 'Great Ejectment'. *Trans. Cong. Hist. Soc.*, vi, 1913–15.

**2151.** WATKIN, WILLIAM RHYS: Bedyddwyr Llangyfelach. *Traf. Cymd. Hanes Bed.*, 1916–19.

**2152.** WHITING, CHARLES EDWIN: Studies in English Puritanism, 1660–88. London, 1931.

**2153.** WILLIAMS, GRIFFITH JOHN: Stephen Hughes a'i gyfnod. *Y Cofiadur*, 1926.

     See also EVANS, WALTER J.: Vicar Stephen Hughes of Mydrim, *Trans. Carms. Antiq. Soc.*, xvi, 1922 (a note on his forbears); and SHANKLAND, THOMAS: Stephen Hughes (No. 2120).

**2154.** Id.     Introduction to the reprint of Charles Edwards's Hanes y ffydd ddi-ffuant. Caerdydd, 1936.

### C. The Society of Friends

#### (a) Sources

**2155.** BESSE, JOSEPH: A collection of the sufferings. London, 1753.

     See especially vol. i, pp. 735–62.

**2156.** DAVIES, JOHN HUMPHREYS: Bibliography of Quaker literature relating to Wales. *Jnl. Welsh Bibl. Soc.*, i, 1912–15.

     See also OWEN, BOB: Llyfryddiaeth Crynwyr Meirionydd, ibid., vii, 1950–3.

**2157.** DAVIES, RICHARD: An account of the convincement . . . London, 1710 (and many subsequent edns, including Welsh translation, 1840).

**2158.** [I. H. E.] (ed.): Documents relating to Friends' burial grounds in Merioneth. *Mont. Coll.*, xv, 1882 (pp. 415–20).

**2159.** Lowe, Rachel J.: Farm and its inhabitants, with an account of the Lloyds of Dolobran. Privately printed. London, 1883.

See also Evans, George Eyre: Friends in Montgomeryshire, *Jnl. Friends Hist. Soc.*, xi, 1914; Lloyd, Samuel: The Lloyds of Birmingham, London, 1907 (ch. i–iii); Williams, Richard: Quakerism in Montgomeryshire, *Wales*, iii, 1896 (pp. 7–12); id.: Montgomeryshire worthies (No. 773).

**2160.** Myles, John: An antidote against the infection of the times, 1656. Ed. Thomas Shankland. *Traf. Cymd. Hanes Bed.*, 1904.

**2661.** Penney, Norman (ed.): Extracts from state papers relating to Friends, 1654–72. London, 1913. *Jnl. Friends Hist. Soc.* supplements, 8–11.

See especially pp. 115, 263, 346, 354.

**2162.** Id.    (ed.): John ap John, and early records of Friends in Wales. Ibid., supplement, 6, 1906.

**2163.** Roberts, Hugh: Brief journal of . . . travels from Pennsylvania to England and Wales (1697–8). *Pennsylvania Mag. of History and Biography*, 1894. Reprinted with modernised spelling in *Wales*, ed. O. M. Edwards, iii, 1896 (pp. 335, 370).

### (b) Secondary works

**2164.** Bebb, William Ambrose: John ap John, apostol y Crynwyr. *Cymru*, lxi–lxiii, 1921–2.

**2165.** Braithwaite, W. C.: The beginnings of Quakerism. London, 1912.

**2166.** Id.    The second period of Quakerism. London, 1919.

Dodd, Arthur Herbert: The background of the Welsh Quaker migration to Pennsylvania (No. 2101).

**2167.** Evans, George Eyre: Carmarthenshire 'People called Quakers'. *Trans. Carms. Antiq. Soc.*, iii, 1907–8.

See also Thomas, Charles: The Trewern Quakers, ibid., xv, 1921.

**2168.** Id.    Friends in Denbighshire. *Jnl. Friends Hist. Soc.*, xii, 1915.

**2169.** Id.    Friends in Carmarthenshire. Ibid., xiv, 1917.

**2170.** Gibbins, F. J.: Historical survey of the yearly meetings for Wales. *The Friend*, n.s., x, 1870.

**2171.** Griffith, Edward: Crynwyr Cymreig ardal Dolgellau. *Y Geninen*, vii–viii, 1889–90.

**2172.** Hanbury, Ferdinand Pakington John: Coldbrook Park. The Hanbury and Herbert families. Privately printed. Newport, 1925.

See also 'The Hanbury family, *Jnl. Friends Hist. Soc.*, xiv, 1917.

**2173.** JONES, RICHARD: Crynwyr bore Cymru, 1653–99. Abermaw, 1931.

**2174.** OWEN, BOB: Hen Grynwyr Llŷn. *Trans. Caerns. Hist. Soc.*, 1940.

**2175.** PHILLIPS, HERCULES D.: The beginnings of Quakerism in Radnorshire. *Trans. Rads. Soc.*, xi, 1941.

> See also EVANS, GEORGE EYRE: Friends in Radnorshire. *Jnl. Friends Hist. Soc.*, xi, 1914.

**2176.** REES, THOMAS MARDY: A history of the Quakers in Wales. Carmarthen, 1925.

**2177.** SALMON, DAVID: The Quakers of Pembrokeshire. *W. Wales Hist. Rec.*, ix, 1923.

**2178.** Id.        The Pembrokeshire Quakers' monthly meeting. Ibid., xii, 1927.

> See also GREEN, FRANCIS: The Musgraves of Llanina (No. 22) and WHITING, EVELYN SOUTHALL, MORRIS, E. RONALD, and HUGHES, JOHN R.: The background of Quakerism in Wales and the border, Malvern [1952].

### D.  Catholic recusants

### (a) Sources

**2179.** BELL, HAROLD IDRIS: Our Lady of Loretto. *N.L.W. Jnl.*, iii, 1943–4.

> A Welsh broadside of 1635 (facsimile and commentary). See also ibid., iv, 1945–6 (pp. 90 and 204).

**2180.** BIRRELL, T. A. (ed.): Warner's history of the English persecution of Catholics and the Presbyterian plot. *Cath. Rec. Soc. Pubns.*, xlvii, 1953, and xlviii, 1955.

BURTON, EDWIN H., and WILLIAMS, THOMAS L.: The Douay College diaries, 1598–1654 (No. 1677).
> For the first and second diaries, see No. 1677.

**2181.** CANNING, JOSEPH HERBERT. The Titus Oates plot in South Wales and the marches. *St. Peter's Mag.*, 1923–4.

> See also DAVIES, LEONARD TWISTON: William Bedloe, 1650–80, *Mon. Rev.*, i, 1923; POOLE, EDWIN (ed.): Wales and the Popish plot, *Cymru Fu*, i, 1889; REES, WILLIAM (ed.): The names of people, priests and Jesuits in the county of Munmouth, 1678 (No. 2191).

DODD, ARTHUR HERBERT (ed.): Correspondence of the Owens of Plas Du (No. 1666).

Id.        (ed.): A spy's report, 1604 (No. 1975).

Id.        (ed.): Two Welsh Catholic *émigrés* discuss the accession of James I (No. 1665).

**2182.** 'DODD, CHARLES' (TOOTEL, HUGH): Church history of England. Ed. Mark Aloysius Tierney. Vols. iv–vi. London, 1834.

The narrative is unreliable, but the long excerpts from original sources in footnotes and appendices are of great value. See especially vol. iv, app. i.

**2183.** EVANS, JOHN R.: The Popish plot. *N.L.W. Jnl.,* vi, 1940–50.

List of tracts in the National Library of Wales, with addenda (p. 183). The only items of specifically Welsh interest are 34–6, 60a, and 64, but see also ANON.: Short memorandums upon the deaths of Mr. Philip Evans and Mr. John Lloyd, n.d. (Roman Catholic account of the martyrdoms, with scurrilous Protestant comments, the former reprinted in CHALLONER, RICHARD: Memoirs of missionary priests, 1577–1684 (No. 1754), the latter in MATTHEWS, JOHN HOBSON (ed.): Cardiff records, vol. iv, p. 155 (No. 686)); ANON.: The Popes down-fall at Abergavenny, 1679; ANON.: Y gwir er gwaethed yw . . . 1684 ( see *Jnl. Welsh Bibl. Soc.,* iv, 1932–6); LLOYD, WILLIAM (dean of Bangor): A sermon at the funeral of Sir Edmund Berry Godfrey, October, 1678; id.: A sermon preached before the king at White-hall, November, 1678, 1679.

FOLEY, H.: Records of the English province of the Society of Jesus (No. 1668).

See especially vol. iv (South and North Wales missions) and vol. v (Popish plot).

**2184.** GLENN, THOMAS ARTHUR (ed.): Presentments of churchwardens at Whitford, 1682. *Northern Flintshire,* i, 1913.

For Pembrokeshire presentments see EVANS, GEORGE EYRE : Eleven Pembrokeshire parishes' presentments (No. 2069).

**2185.** GUINEY, LOUISE (ed.): A chapter necrology. *Cath. Rec. Soc. Pubns.,* iii, 1906.

HENSON, E. (ed.): Register of the English college, Valladolid, 1589–1862 (No. 1671A).

**2186.** H[UGHES], J[OHN]: Allwydd neu agoriad paradwys i'r Cymry, 1670. Ed. John Fisher. Cardiff, 1929.

KELLY, W. I. (ed.): The liber ruber of the English college, Rome. Annales collegii. Pars prima. Nomina alumnorum. i, A.D. 1579–1630; ii, A.D. 1631–1783 (No. 1675).

McCANN, J., and CONNOLLY, H. (eds.): Memorials of Father Augustine Baker and other documents relating to the English Benedictines (No. 1680).

**2187.** MATTHEWS, JOHN HOBSON (ed.): Records relating to Catholicism in the South Wales marches. *Cath. Rec. Soc. Pubns.,* ii, 1906.

**2188.** MORGAN, GWENLLIAN ELIZABETH FANNY: Welsh papists in 1680. *Old Wales,* iii, 1907.

OWEN, LEWIS: Running register (No. 1681).

**2189.** Id.      Jesuites looking-glass. London, 1629.

**2190. PRICE, EVAN:** Eye-salve for England. 1667.
Protestant attack on popish practices at Abergavenny, etc.

PUGH, FRANK HAMER: Glamorgan recusants, 1577–1611 (No. 1688).

Id.     Monmouthshire recusants in the reigns of Elizabeth and James I (No. 1689).

**2191. REES, WILLIAM** (ed.): The names of people, priests, and Jesuits that live publickly, the persons names that keep them and the names of places where publick chapels are . . . in the county of Munmouth [March 7, 1678]. *S. Wales and Mon. Rec. Soc. Pubns.,* i [1949].

**2192. STANFIELD, R.** (ed.): Secular priests in North Wales, 1692. *Cath. Rec. Soc. Pubns.,* ix, 1911.

**2193. THOMAS, GRIFFITH THOMAS** (ed.): Recusants in Carmarthenshire, 1637. *Trans. Carms. Antiq. Soc.,* xi, 1917.

**2194. TRAPPES-LOMAX, R.** (ed.): Necrology of the English province of friars minor of the order of St. Francis, 1618–1761. *Cath. Rec. Soc. Pubns.,* xxiv, 1923.

### (b) Secondary works

ATTWATER, DONALD: The Catholic church in modern Wales (No. 1749).

BOWEN, GERAINT: Gwilym Pue, 'Bardd Mair' a theulu'r Penrhyn (No. 1750).

**2195. Id.**     John Salisbury. *N.L.W. Jnl.,* viii, 1953–4.

**2196. Id.**     Gweithiau defosiynol Gwilym Pue. Ibid., ix, 1955–6.

**2197. CAMM, DOM. BEDE:** Nine martyr monks. London, 1932.

CHALLONER, RICHARD (bishop): Memoirs of missionary priests . . . 1577–1684 (No. 1754).

CLEARY, J. MARTIN: The Catholic resistance in Wales, 1568–1678 (No. 1757).

**2198. CRONIN, JOHN M.:** Various papers on seventeenth century Welsh Catholics in *St. Peter's Mag.,* Cardiff, 1921–9.
The series includes the following: Ven. Charles Mahoney, o.s.f. (1679), 1924, 1929 (incomplete); Thomas Vaughan, priest (*circa* 1644), 1924; 'Massing Stuff', 1924; Legend of the Darren Brook (*circa* 1604), 1924; Welsh Franciscans in exile, 1926; St. Winifred's well (1606), 1927.

**2199. DAVIES, J. D. GRIFFITH:** The Catholic Nonconformists of Monmouthshire. *Mons. Rev.,* ii, 1924.

ELLIS, T. P.: The Catholic martyrs of Wales (No. 1762).

Id.     Welsh Benedictines of the terror (No. 870).

GUILDAY, PETER: The English Catholic exiles on the Continent, 1558–1795 (No. 1765).

EVANS, A. LESLIE: The story of Sker House (No. 17).

**2200.** HEMPHILL, DOM. BASIL: The early vicars apostolic of England, 1685–1750. London, 1954.

**2201.** HODGES, ROSE: A Carmelite Welsh nun (Mother Margaret Mostyn, 1625–9). *St. Peter's Mag.*, Cardiff, 1925 and 1926.

**2202.** JONES, EMYR GWYNNE: Hugh Owen of Gwenynog. *Trans. Angl. Antiq. Soc.*, 1938.

> See also LEWIS, SAUNDERS: Thomas à Kempis yn Gymraeg. *Efrydiau Catholig*, iv, 1949.

Id.     Catholic recusancy in the counties of Denbigh, Flint, and Montgomery, 1581–1625 (No. 1767).

Id.     Cymru a'r hen ffydd (No. 1769).

**2203.** JONES, F. E. LLEWELLYN: Blessed Philip Powell: a Catholic martyr of Breconshire. Brecon, 1946.

**2204.** LLOYD, DAVID TECWYN: Rome and Wales. *Dock Leaves*, Winter, 1952.

> A report on recusant material in Italian archives.

**2205.** MATTHEWS, JOHN HOBSON: The Vaughans of Courtfield. London, 1912.

**2206.** VAUGHAN, JOHN: John Vaughan of Courtfield, 1603–80, a Welsh recusant poet. *Dublin Review*, 1923 and 1924.

## VI. SOCIAL AND ECONOMIC HISTORY

### (a) General

The general works listed on pp. 149–55 have relevance to this section also.

### (i) Sources

**2207.** JONES, EMYR GWYNNE (ed.): The perils of Traeth Lavan. *B.B.C.S.*, ix, 1937–9.

> A seventeenth-century petition.

**2208.** JONES, EVAN DAVID (ed.): An inventory of a Pembrokeshire squire's chattels, 1629. *N.L.W. Jnl.*, vii, 1953–4 (p. 222).

**2209.** JONES, FRANCIS (ed.): Wynnstay in 1683–6. *Arch. Camb.*, 1940.
Inventory of furniture.

**2210.** PARRY, OWEN (ed.): The hearth tax of 1662 in Merioneth. *Jnl. Mer. Hist. and Rec. Soc.*, ii, 1, 1953.

**2211.** SUMMERS, H. H. C. (ed.): The poor, 1685–1734. *Mont. Coll.*, xxxviii, 1918.
Transcripts of indentures of apprenticeship, Oswestry.

**2212.** VAUGHAN, WILLIAM: The golden fleece. 1626.
Part II, ch. vi, contains criticisms of social and economic life in contemporary Wales.

[WRIGHT, THOMAS (ed.)]: Anglesea (No. 524).

### (ii) Secondary works

**2213.** AXON, W. E. A.: Welsh folk-lore of the seventeenth century. *Y Cymmr.*, xxi, 1908.

GRESHAM, COLIN A.: The township of Dolbenmaen (No. 1783).

Id. The townships of Gest, Treflys, and Ystumllyn (No. 1784).

HEMP, WILFRID JAMES, and GRESHAM, COLIN A.: Park, Llanfrothen, and the unit system (No. 450).
Domestic architecture of the seventeenth century.

**2214.** JONES, R. OSBORNE: Ty dawns. *Trans. Cards. Antiq. Soc.*, iv, 1926.
The Book of Sports in Cardiganshire.

LLOYD, JOHN DAVIES KNATCHBULL: Montgomery castle and the Herberts, with some information on building activities in the sixteenth and seventeenth centuries (No. 1802).

**2215.** SKEEL, CAROLINE ANNE JAMES: Social and economic conditions in Wales in the early seventeenth century. *Trans. Cymmr.*, 1916–17.

### (b) Education

### (i) Sources

ANON. (ed.): Llanllyfni papers (No. 2052).
Letter from archbishop William Laud on Ruthin school, p. 286.

**2216.** BURROWS, MONTAGU (ed.): Register of the visitors of the university of Oxford, 1647–8. London, 1881.
See also RICHARDS, THOMAS: The Puritan visitation of Jesus College (No. 2113).

**2217.** DAVIES, WILLIAM LLEWELYN: The first Welsh 'Copy-book' (1683). *Jnl. Welsh. Bibl. Soc.*, iv, 1932–6.

With facsimiles.

**2218.** FISHER, JOHN (ed.): Licences to schoolmasters, etc. *Arch. Camb.*, 1923, pp. 167–70.

GRUFFYDD, GERAINT (ed.): Two letters from Richard Parry . . . to John Wynn Edwards (No. 1832).

**2219.** JONES, M. G. (ed.): Two accounts of the Welsh Trust, 1675 and 1678. *B.B.C.S.*, ix, 1937–9.

See also STOW, JOHN: Survey of London, 1598 and 1603, ed. John Strype, London, 1720, v (p. 43 reprinted in *Trans. Cymmr.*, 1904–5, pp. 82–3); WYNNE, WILLIAM: History of Wales, 1697, ed. Richard Llwyd, 1832 (No. 165) (p. 288).

**2220.** NUTTALL, GEOFFREY F. (ed.): The correspondence of John Lewis, Glasgrug, with Richard Baxter and Dr. John Ellis, Dolgelley. *Jnl. Mer. Hist. and Rec. Soc.*, ii, 1953–4.

On the project of a national college for Wales. See also BAXTER, RICHARD: Certainty of the world of spirits, London, 1691; LEWIS, JOHN: ΕΥΑΓΓΕΛΙΟΡΑΘΑ, London, 1656 (p. 30); PETER, HUGH: A good work for magistrates, 1651.

**2221.** OWEN, JAMES: Moderation still a virtue. London, 1704.

See also PALMER, SAMUEL: A defence of the Dissenters' education in their private academies. London, 1703–5.

(ii) **Secondary works**

**Endowed grammar schools and diocesan education**

CAMPBELL, M. COLNEY: Some records of the free grammar school of Deythyr in the county of Montgomery, 1690–1900 (No. 200).

**2222.** GRIFFITHS, GRIFFITH MILWYN: Educational activity in the diocese of St. Asaph, 1500–1650. *Jnl. Hist. Soc. Church in Wales*, iii, 1953.

See also RICHARDS, THOMAS: Wales under the penal code (No. 2145) (pp. 161–8).

**2223.** HARLECH, WILLIAM GEORGE ARTHUR, LORD: The Brogyntyn library of printed books. *N.L.W. Jnl.*, v, 1947–8.

JONES, E. MADOC: The free grammar school of Beaumaris (No. 206).

JONES, WILLIAM BELL: Hawarden grammar school (No. 207).

MORGAN, J.: Coffadwriaeth am Henry Rowlands . . . sylfaenydd ysgol Bottwnog (No. 210).

Id.    David Hughes, founder of Beaumaris free school (No. 209).

NEWCOMBE, RICHARD: Memoir of Dr. Gabriel Goodman, with some account of Ruthin school (No. 211).

**2224.** WARLOW, WILLIAM MEYLER: A history of the charities of William Jones at Monmouth (etc.). Bristol, 1899.

> Ch. i–xi. See also JONES, GRIFFITH HARTWELL: Rhamant mab o Fynwy (William Jones, 1545–1615), *Y Ford Gron*, Gorffennaf, 1931.

WATSON, FOSTER: The English grammar schools to 1660 (No. 195).

WILLIAMS, ALBERT HUGHES: Origins of the old endowed grammar schools of Denbighshire (No. 220).

WILLIAMS, WILLIAM OGWEN: Friars School [Bangor] from its foundation to the year 1789, in *The Dominican*, 1957 (No. 216).

### Puritan schools and Dissenting academies

**2225.** CRIPPEN, T. G.: Early Nonconformist academies. *Trans. Cong. Hist. Soc.*, iii–vi, 1907–15.

**2226.** JAMES, JAMES SPINTHER: Ymchwiliad i hanes Thomas Gouge a'i ysgolion. *Y Geninen*, 1899.

> See also CORNISH, JOSEPH: Life of Mr. Thomas Firmin. London, 1780 (ch. ii).

**2227.** JONES, M. G.: The charity school movement: a study of eighteenth century Puritanism in action. Cambridge, 1938.

**2228.** JEREMY, WALTER D.: The Presbyterian fund and Dr. Williams's trust. London, 1885.

> See also [CRIPPEN, T. G.] (ed.): Origin of the Congregational fund board, *Trans. Cong. Hist. Soc.*, v, 1911–12.

**2229.** OWEN, GERAINT DYFNALLT: James Owen a'i academi. *Y Cofiadur*, 1952.

> See also OWEN, JAMES: Moderation still a virtue (No. 2221) and *Jnl. Welsh Bibl. Soc.*, iii, 1925–31 (two of Owen's letters, pp. 91–5; and note on Samuel Jones of Llangynwyd, pp. 89–91).

**2230.** PARKER, IRENE: History of the dissenting academies. Cambridge, 1914.

**2231.** ROBERTS, H. P.: Nonconformist academies in Wales. *Trans. Cymmr.*, 1928–9.

**2232.** SHANKLAND, THOMAS: 'Diwygwyr Cymru' Beriah Gwynfa Evans. *Seren Gomer*, 1900–4.

**2233.** VINCENT, W. A. A.: The state and education, 1640–60, in England and Wales. London, 1950.

> See also RICHARDS, THOMAS: Religious developments in Wales (No. 2112), part I, ch. iv.

Id.     Wales under the penal code (No. 2145), ch. xiv.
Id.     Wales under the Indulgence (No. 2146), ch. xvii.

**2234.** WATSON, FOSTER: The state and education under the Commonwealth. *E.H.R.*, xv, 1900.

### (c) Agriculture, industry, and commerce

### (i) Sources

**2235.** ANON. (ed.): The manor of Castellan (1627). *W. Wales Hist. Rec.*, v, 1915.

Transcript of MS. in the Cardiff Free Library.

**2236.** DAVIES, D. STEDMAN: The parliamentary surveys of the manors of Radnorshire in 1649. *Trans. Rads. Soc.*, xi, 1941.

A summary of No. 1897.

**2237.** EVANS, ELWYN (ed.): Two Machynlleth toll books (1632). *N.L.W. Jnl.*, vi, 1949–50.

From Powis castle MSS.

Id.     (ed.): The manor of Uwchmynydd (Radnorshire) in 1618 (No. 1532).

From Hereford cathedral MS.

**2238.** EVANS, GEORGE EYRE (ed.): Llanarth cum Llanina, Cardiganshire, 1695–1721. *Old Wales*, ii, 1906.

Transcripts from MS. notebook relating to tithes, etc.

**2239.** JONES, EVAN DAVID (ed.): A rental of crown lands in the commote of Estimanner, 1633. *Jnl. Mer. Hist. and Rec. Soc.*, ii, 4, 1956.

**2240.** OWEN, HUGH (ed.): A list of Anglesey wills, 1691–9. *Trans. Angl. Antiq. Soc.*, 1932.

**2241.** Record Commission: Reports from . . . commissioners respecting the public records, i, 1800–1819, 1819.

Appendix on Welsh port books. See also ANON.: A Carmarthen port-searcher of 1630, *Trans. Carms. Antiq. Soc.*, xx, 1927; LEWIS, EDWARD ARTHUR: Maritime trade in Stuart Wales, *The Times* trade supplement, December 6, 1924; id.: The port books of Cardigan in Elizabethan and Stuart times, *Trans. Cards. Antiq. Soc.*, vii and ix, 1930–1 (full tabular appendix, 1603–99); MATTHEWS, ARTHUR WAIGHT: A shipping dispute at Carmarthen, *Trans. Carms. Antiq. Soc.*, x, 1914–15; REES, WILLIAM: The port of Cardiff and its member ports, 1606–10 [a tabular analysis]. *S. Wales and Mon. Rec. Soc. Pubns.*, iii, 1954.

**2242.** WALLER, WILLIAM: An essay on the value of the mines, late of Sir Carberry Pryce. London, 1698.

### (ii) Secondary works

DAVIES, DAVID J.: The economic history of South Wales prior to 1800 (No. 137).

**2243.** GOUGH, J. W.: The superlative prodigall. A life of Thomas Bushell. Bristol, 1932.

See also EVANS, GEORGE EYRE: King Charles and the Cardiganshire mines, *Old Wales*, i, 1905–6 (letters of Charles I, 1638–43).

GRANT-FRANCIS, GEORGE: The smelting of copper in the Swansea district (No. 1816).

MEYRICK, SAMUEL RUSH: History and antiquities of the county of Cardigan (No. 579).

Introduction.

**2244.** HUNT, ROBERT: British mining. London, 1884; 2nd edn, 1887.

Cardiganshire mines in the seventeenth century, pp. 151–60.

JENKINS, DAVID: The Pryse family of Gogerddan (No. 44).

The third instalment refers to seventeenth-century mining in Cardiganshire.

**2245.** JENKINS, RHYS: Copper smelting in England: revival at the end of the seventeenth century. *Trans. Newcomen Soc.*, xxiv.

JONES, EVAN DAVID: The register of the corvisors of Ruthin, 1570–1671 (No. 1811).

JONES, THOMAS IEUAN JEFFREYS: Rents and fines in South Wales (No. 1801).

KNOOP, DOUGLAS, and JONES, GWILYM PEREDUR (eds): The Carreglwyd building account, 1636 (No. 457).

MENDENHALL, THOMAS C.: The Shrewsbury drapers and the Welsh wool trade in the XVI and XVII centuries (No. 1822).

See also EVANS, D. J.: A note on Dr. John Ellis and the drapers of Shrewsbury. *Jnl. Mer. Hist. and Rec. Soc.*, ii, 1, 1953.

PALMER, ALFRED NEOBARD: Town, fields, and folk of Wrexham in the reign of James I (No. 640).

**2246.** SCOTT, WILLIAM ROBERT: Constitution and finance of . . . joint-stock companies to 1720. 3 vols. Cambridge, 1911.

For Cardiganshire mines, sixteenth and seventeenth centuries.

SKEEL, CAROLINE ANNE JAMES: The Welsh woollen industry in the sixteenth and seventeenth centuries (No. 1826).

Id.    The cattle trade between England and Wales from the fifteenth to the nineteenth centuries (No. 1827).

**2247.** WILKINS, CHARLES: The history of the iron, steel, tinplate, and other trades of Wales. Merthyr Tydfil, 1903.

**2248.** Id.    The South Wales coal trade and its allied industries from the earliest days to the present time. Cardiff, 1888.
Early chapters of both deal with the seventeenth century.

WILLIAMS, M. LUCY: Tide mills . . . between Holy Isle and Anglesey (No. 1829).

**2249.** WILLIAMS, MOELWYN I.: A contribution to the commercial history of Glamorgan, 1666–1735. *N.L.W. Jnl.,* ix, 1955–6.

WILLIAMS, WILLIAM OGWEN: The Anglesey gentry as business men in Tudor and Stuart times (No. 1807).

## VII. WELSHMEN ABROAD

**2250.** BICKNELL, T. W.: John Myles. Religious toleration in Massachusetts. *Mag. of New England Hist.* Boston, Mass., 1892.

**2251.** BROWNING, C. H.: The Welsh settlement of Pennsylvania. Philadelphia, Pa., 1912.

**2252.** BURR, NELSON R.: The Welsh episcopalians of colonial Pennsylvania and Delaware. *Hist. Mag. of Prot. Episc. Church.* New Brunswick, N.J., viii, 1939.

**2253.** CLEMENT, JOHN: Griffith Hughes, S.P.G. missionary to Pennsylvania (etc.). Ibid., xvii, 1948.
See also DALLETT, FRANCIS JAMES: Griffith Hughes dissected. *Jnl. Barbados Museum and Hist. Soc.,* xxiii, 1955.

**2254.** DODD, ARTHUR HERBERT: The character of early Welsh emigration to the United States. Cardiff, 1953; 2nd edn, Cardiff, 1957.

Id.    New England influences in early Welsh Puritanism (No. 2100).

Id.    The background of the Welsh Quaker migration to Pennsylvania (No. 2101).

**2255.** FOTHERGILL, GERALD: List of emigrant ministers to America. London, 1904.
See also CLEMENT, JOHN: List of . . . clergymen licensed by the bishop of London for overseas service, 1696–1710 and 1715–16. *Hist. Mag. of Prot. Episc. Church,* New Brunswick, N.J., xvi, 1947.

**2256.** GLENN, THOMAS ALLEN: Merion in the Welsh tract. Morriston, Pa., 1896.

**2257.** Id.    Welsh founders of Pennsylvania. Oxford, 1913.

**2258.** HOTTEN, JOHN CAMDEN: Original lists of . . . emigrants . . . from Great Britain to the American plantations, 1600–1700. London, 1874; New York, 1931.
See also BOWMAN, W. D., and HARDING, N. D.: Bristol and America, a record of the first settlers in the colonies of North America, 1654–85, Bristol,

n.d.; [SHERWOOD, GEORGE (ed.)]: American colonists in English records. A guide to . . . passenger lists not in Hotton, etc., 2 vols., 1932–3.

**2259.** JENKINS, HOWARD M.: Historical collections relating to Gwynedd [Pa.]. Philadelphia, 1884.

**2260.** LEVICK, J.: John ap Thomas and his friends. Philadelphia, Pa., 1886.

**2261.** Id.    The early Welsh Quakers and the emigration to Pennsylvania. Philadelphia, 1893.

> See also THOMAS, HUGH EVAN: Hen Gymry Philadelphia, Pennsylvania, *Y Geninen*, 1883; id.: Hen Grynwyr Cymreig America, ibid.; id.: Ymchwil eto i hanes hen Gymry dwyreinbarth Pennsylvania, ibid., 1886; id.: De a Gogledd Cymru yn cydsylfaenu Pennsylvania, ibid., 1895.

**2262.** OWEN, BOB: Yr ymfudo o sir Gaernarfon i'r Unol Daleithiau. *Trans. Caerns. Hist. Soc.*, xiii, 1952.

> Pp. 42–4 on seventeenth-century emigrants.

**2263.** PALMER, ALFRED NEOBARD: The adventures of a Denbighshire gentleman in the seventeenth century in the West Indies. [Roger Myddleton.] *Arch. Camb.*, 1902.

**2264.** VAUGHAN, WILLIAM: Cambrensium Caroleia. 1625.

**2265.** Id.    Directions for health. 1st edn, 1600; 7th edn, 1633.

**2266.** Id.    The Newlanders' cure. 1630.

> See also WILLIAMS, E. ROLAND: Some studies in Elizabethan Wales. (No. 1623), ch. xiv (Cambriol: a forgotten colony).

**2267.** WILLIAMS, WILLIAM LLEWELYN: Sir Thomas Morgan. *Hist. Sketches of Glamorgan*, i, 1907.

**2268.** Id.    Sir Henry Morgan. *Trans. Cymmr.*, 1903–4.

# SECTION J

## *A.D. 1714–89*

For the general bibliographical background see PARGELLIS, STANLEY, and MOTLEY, D. J. (eds): A bibliography of British history, The eighteenth century, Oxford, 1951. See also WILLIAMS, BASIL: The Whig supremacy, 1714–1760, Oxford History of England, vol. xi, and WATSON, JOHN STEVEN: The reign of George III, 1760–1815. Ibid., vol. xii.

An introductory sketch of the history of the century in Wales, with some notes on books, is JENKINS, ROBERT THOMAS: Hanes Cymru yn y ddeunawfed ganrif, Caerdydd, 1928.

### I. POLITICS AND LOCAL GOVERNMENT

**2269.** ARBERRY, A. J.: Asiatic Jones: the life and influence of Sir William Jones, 1746–94. London, 1946.

**2270.** BRADNEY, JOSEPH ALFRED: Poll of the burgesses of Monmouth, Newport, and Usk, 1715. Usk, 1906.

**2271.** CONE, CARL B.: Torchbearer of freedom: the influence of Richard Price on eighteenth century thought. Lexington (Kentucky), 1952.

**2272.** CRONIN, JOHN M.: Local Jacobites (Glamorgan), 1715–43. *St. Peter's Magazine.* Cardiff, 1925.

**2273.** EVANS, KENRICK: Eighteenth century Caernarvon. *Trans. Caerns. Hist. Soc.*, 1946–8, 1950.

**2274.** HOWSE, WILLIAM HENRY: Records of the Radnorshire general sessions at the shirehall, Presteign. *Trans. Rads. Soc.*, xiii and xiv.

**2275.** Id.    Court rolls of the manor of Norton. Ibid., xiv.

**2276.** HUGHES, EDWARD: The letters of Chief Justice Spencer Cowper from the North Wales circuit, 1717–19. *Trans. Cymmr.*, 1955.

JENKINS, DAVID: The Pryse family of Gogerddan (No. 44), part II.

**2277.** JENKINS, ROBERT THOMAS: Political propaganda in West Wales in 1793. *B.B.C.S.*, vi, 1931–3.

**2278.** JONES, EVAN DAVID: Cardiganshire quarter sessions order books, 1739–1800. *Trans. Cards. Antiq. Soc.*, xii, 1937.

**2279.** JONES, THOMAS IEUAN JEFFREYS: The court leet presentments of the town, borough and liberty of St. Clears, 1719–1889. *B.B.C.S.*, xiii, 1948.

Lewis, Edward Arthur: A schedule of the quarter sessions records of the county of Montgomery at the National Library of Wales (No. 1942).

**2280.** Id.    Leet proceedings of the manor of Arwystli Uwchcoed at the National Library of Wales: 1784–1800. *Mont. Coll.,* xlvii and xlviii.

**2281.** Llewellin, William: David Morgan, the Welsh Jacobite. *Cambrian Journal,* 1861. Reprinted in *Trans. Liverpool Welsh Nat. Soc.,* 1894–5.

**2282.** Lloyd, Robert John Herbert: Henry Leach (1770–1848), collector of taxes at Milford. *Trans. Cymmr.,* 1956.

**2283.** Morgan, Walter Thomas: County elections in Monmouthshire, 1705–1847. *N.L.W. Jnl.,* x, 1957–8.

**2284.** Nicholas, David: The Welsh Jacobites. *Trans. Cymmr.,* 1948.

**2285.** Oldfield, T. H. B.: The representative history of Great Britain and Ireland. 6 vols. (vol. vi, Wales). London, 1816.

**2286.** Owen, Hugh John: Merionethshire quarter sessions court rolls and nomina ministrorum. *Jnl. Mer. Hist. and Rec. Soc.,* i, 3, 1951.

**2287.** Id.    Merionethshire quarter sessions: session roll, Easter, 1733 Ibid., ii, 1, 1953.

**2288.** Id.    The common gaols of Merioneth during the eighteenth and nineteenth centuries. Ibid., iii, 1, 1957.

**2289.** Owen, R. H.: Jacobitism and the church in Wales. *Jnl. Hist. Soc. Church in Wales,* iii, 1953.

**2290.** Pennant, Thomas: The literary life of the late Thomas Pennant, Esq., by himself. London, 1793.
      A letter from a Welsh freeholder to his representative. Appendix No. 3.

**2291.** Porritt, Edward, and Porritt, Annie G.: The unreformed House of Commons. 2 vols. (vol. i, ch. vi: The representation of Wales). Cambridge, 1903.

**2292.** Price, John Arthur: Wales and the White Rose. *Wales.* Ed. O. M. Edwards, i and ii, 1894–5.

**2293.** Id.    Sidelights on Welsh Jacobitism. *Y Cymmr.,* xiv, 1901.

**2294.** Raphael, D. Daiches (ed.): A review of the principal questions on morals by Richard Price. Oxford, 1948.

**2295.** Richards, Thomas: The Anglesey election of 1708. *Trans. Angl. Antiq. Soc.,* 1943.

**2296.** ROBERTS, GLYN: The county representation of Anglesey in the eighteenth century. Ibid., 1930.

Id.    The parliamentary history of Beaumaris, 1555–1832 (No. 1987).

**2297.** Id.    Anglesey and Newcastle correspondence. *Trans. Angl. Antiq. Soc.*, 1935.

Id.    Caernarvon borough records (No. 547).
See also id.: Borough records at Caernarvon (No. 546).

Id.    Political affairs [in Carmarthenshire] from 1536 to 1900 (No. 1648).

Id.    The Glynnes and Wynns of Glynllifon (No. 69).

**2298.** STUART-JONES, EDWYN HENRY: The last invasion of Britain. Cardiff, 1950.

**2299.** TEIGNMOUTH, LORD: Memoir of Sir William Jones. London, 1807.
See also *Bull. of the School of Oriental and African Studies.* Univ. of London. Vol. xi, part 4, 1946 (Sir William Jones memorial volume).

THOMAS, HENRY: An old vestry book [Towyn, Merioneth]. (No. 969).

**2300.** THOMAS, PETER DAVID GARNER: The parliamentary representation of Merioneth in the eighteenth century. *Jnl. Mer. Hist. and Rec. Soc.*, iii, 2, 1958.

**2301.** THOMAS, ROLAND: Richard Price. Oxford, 1924.

**2302.** 'T.P.D.': Extracts from the records of some Radnorshire manorial courts. *Trans. Rads. Soc.*, xviii and xix, 1948 and 1949.

**2303.** VAUGHAN, HERBERT MILLINGCHAMP: Welsh Jacobitism. *Trans. Cymmr.*, 1920–1.

**2304.** WEBB, SIDNEY, and WEBB, BEATRICE: English local government from the Revolution to the Municipal Reform Act: the manor and the borough. 2 parts (part I, ch. v: The boroughs of Wales). London, 1924.

WILLIAMS, WILLIAM RETLAW: The parliamentary history of the principality of Wales (No. 103).

## II. SOCIAL LIFE AND LETTERS

Popular and other Welsh literature of the eighteenth century throws considerable light on the contemporary manners and modes of life and thought. For a general treatment see PARRY, THOMAS: Hanes llenyddiaeth

Gymraeg (No. 146), and particularly the chapter bibliographies. For a translation, see A history of Welsh literature by Thomas Parry, translated by H. Idris Bell (No. 146).

There is a great mass of topographical and other material in the works of the many tourists whose accounts of their journeys in Wales in the eighteenth and early nineteenth centuries have been published. For a bibliography of these works see HUGHES, WILLIAM JOHN: Wales and the Welsh in English literature (No. 10).

**2305.** CHARLES, BERTIE GEORGE: Letters of Hester Lynch Piozzi. *N.L.W. Jnl.*, ii, 1941.

CUST, ALBINIA LUCY: Chronicles of Erthig on the dyke (No. 16).

**2306.** DAVIES, ARTHUR STANLEY: The ballads of Montgomeryshire; life in the eighteenth century. Welshpool, 1938.

**2307.** DAVIES, JOHN: Bywyd a gwaith Moses Williams (1685–1742). Caerdydd, 1937.

**2308.** DAVIES, JOHN HUMPHREYS: Bibliography of Welsh ballads. *Trans. Cymmr.*, 1906–7, 1909–10.

**2309.** DAVIES, LEONARD TWISTON, and EDWARDS, AVERIL: Welsh life in the eighteenth century. London, 1939.

**2310.** DODD, ARTHUR HERBERT: The rise of the North Wales coastal resorts. N.U.T. souvenir handbook. Llandudno, 1939.

**2311.** EDWARDS, THOMAS ('Twm o'r Nant'): Works. First edns, various years (see Cardiff Library catalogue (No. 4)); collected edns, Merthyr, 1849; Liverpool, 1874; selection, ed. O. M. Edwards, 2 vols., Llanuwchllyn, 1909–10.

See also ASHTON, GLYN MILLS: Hunangofiant a llythyrau Twm o'r Nant, Caerdydd, 1948, and GRIFFITH, WYN: Twm o'r Nant (Thomas Edwards), bilingual, Cardiff, 1953.

EVANS, GWENLLIAN NESTA: Social life in mid-eighteenth century Anglesey (No. 506).

Id.: Religion and politics in mid-eighteenth century Anglesey (No. 507).

**2312.** GRIFFITHS, GRIFFITH MILWYN: Eight letters from Edmund Gibson to Bishop Humphreys, 1707–9. *N.L.W. Jnl.*, x, 1957–8.

**2313.** GRIFFITHS, WILLIAM ARTHUR: Notes on the descendants of Henry Kyffin, bailiff of Llanfyllin, 1708. *Mont. Coll.*, lii, 1951–2.

**2314.** GUNTHER, ROBERT THEODORE: Life and letters of Edward Lhuyd. Oxford, 1945.

Review by D. A. Quinn in *Irish Hist. Studies,* March, 1946 (valuable for omitted letters).

For additional letters see JONES, EMYR GWYNNE: The family papers of the Owens and Stanleys of Penrhos, Holyhead, *B.B.C.S.*, xxvii, 1957, and GRIFFITHS, GRIFFITH MILWYN: An Edward Lhuyd letter, *N.L.W. Jnl.*, x, 1957–8. See also DODD, ARTHUR HERBERT (ed.): The early days of Edward Lhuyd (No. 1901).

**2315.** Historical Manuscripts Commission. Kenyon MSS. XIVth report, app. iv.

**2316.** INGLIS-JONES, ELISABETH: Peacocks in paradise. London, 1950.
> A biography of Thomas Johnes of Havod, Cardiganshire. See also id.: Sir Herbert Lloyd of Peterwell. *Wales*, ed. Keidrych Rhys. Vol. v, Nos. 8 and 9, 1945. See also No. 2351.

**2317.** JENKINS, ROBERT THOMAS: Bardd a'i gefndir [Edward Evan, Aberdâr]. *Trans. Cymmr.*, 1947.

**2318.** Id.    and RAMAGE, HELEN MYFANWY: A history of the Honourable Society of Cymmrodorion and of the Gwyneddigion and Cymreigyddion Societies (1751–1951). *Y Cymmr.*, i, 1951.

**2319.** JONES, E. ALFRED: The Welsh correspondents of John Wilkes. Ibid., xxix, 1919.

**2320.** Id.    The society or garrison of Fort Williamsburg: the old Glynllifon volunteers. Ibid., xliv, 1935.

**2321.** JONES, EMYR GWYNNE: Correspondence of the Owens of Penrhos, 1712–1742. *Trans. Angl. Antiq. Soc.*, 1954.

**2322.** JONES, HUGH (Llangwm): Diddanwch teuluaidd. London, 1763, and later edns.

**2323.** JONES, ROBERT (Rhos-lan): Gwaith Robert Jones, Rhos Lan. *Y Llenor* (ed. O. M. Edwards), xv and xvi, 1898.
> See also ASHTON, GLYN MILLS (ed.): Drych yr amseroedd. Cardiff, 1958; ROBERTS, GRIFFITH THOMAS: Robert Jones, Rhos-lan, 1745–1829. *Cylch. Cymd. Hanes M.C.*, xli, 1, 1956.

**2324.** JONES, R. W.: Bywyd cymdeithasol Cymru yn y ddeunawfed ganrif. Llundain, 1931.

**2325.** LLOYD, JOHN: Ellis Wynne o Las Ynys. *Jnl. Mer. Hist. and Rec. Soc.*, i, 1, 1949.

**2326.** LLOYD-JOHNS, HERBERT JOHNES: Account book of Thomas Morgan of Carmarthen. *N.L.W. Jnl.*, ix, 1955–6.

**2327.** MORRIS, LEWIS (and his brothers RICHARD, WILLIAM, and JOHN): Letters (1728–65). Ed. J. H. Davies. 2 vols. Oxford, 1906–9. For index, see *Trans. Angl. Antiq. Soc.*, 1942, 1944.

**2328.** Id.    Additional letters (1735–86). Ed. Hugh Owen. *Y Cymmr.*, xlix, part I, 1947; part II, 1949.
> See also *Y Llenor*, 1948, and *Trans. Angl. Antiq. Soc.*, 1950, for reviews; GRUFFYDD, WILLIAM JOHN: Y Morysiaid, bilingual, Cardiff, 1939; and HUMPHREYS, EDWARD MORGAN: Morysiaid Môn, *Trans. Cymmr.*, 1953.

14

**2329.** OWEN, HUGH: The diary of William Bulkeley of Brynddu, Anglesey. *Trans. Angl. Antiq. Soc.,* 1931.

**2330.** Id.    The life and works of Lewis Morris, 1701–65. Angl. Antiq. Soc. supplement vol., 1951.

**2331.** PARRY, THOMAS: Baledi'r ddeunawfed ganrif. Caerdydd, 1935.

**2332.** PRICE, CECIL JOHN LAYTON: The English theatre in Wales in the eighteenth and nineteenth centuries. Cardiff, 1948.

**2333.** Id.    Polite life in eighteenth century Wales. *Welsh Anvil,* v, 1953.

**2334.** Id.    The unpublished letters of Evan Lloyd. *N.L.W. Jnl.,* viii, 1954.

**2335.** ROBERTS, BETTY DEW: Mr. Bulkeley and the pirate. London, 1936.

**2336.** Id.    Maria Stella (Lady Newborough). *Trans. Caerns. Hist. Soc.,* 1954.

**2337.** ROBERTS, GRACE: Mrs. Hester Thrale's connexions with the vale of Clwyd. *Trans. Cymmr.,* 1953.

**2338.** THOMAS, BEN BOWEN: The old order, based on the diary of Elizabeth Baker (Dolgelley, 1778–1786). Cardiff, 1945.
    See also id.: Elizabeth Baker and her diary. *N.L.W. Jnl.,* iii, 1944.

**2339.** WILLIAMS, GRIFFITH JOHN: Bywyd Cymreig Llundain yng nghyfnod Owain Myfyr. *Y Llenor,* 1939.

**2340.** Id.    Llythyrau at Ddafydd Jones o Drefriw. *N.L.W. Jnl.* Suppt. Series III, no. 2, 1943.

    Id.    Traddodiad llenyddol Morgannwg (No. 160).

    Id.    Iolo Morganwg: y gyfrol gyntaf (No. 710).

**2341.** Id.    Dyddiadur William Thomas o Lanfihangel-ar-Eláì. *Morgannwg,* i, 1957.
    A Glamorgan schoolmaster's diary, 1750–95.

### III. ECONOMIC HISTORY

For works on the British economy generally, see ASHTON, THOMAS SOUTHCLIFFE: An economic history of England. The eighteenth century. London, 1955; CLARK, GEORGE NORMAN: The wealth of England, 1496–1760, London, 1946; COURT, WILLIAM HENRY BASSANO: A concise economic history of Britain from 1750, London, 1954; HABAKKUK, HROTHGAR JAMES: English population in the eighteenth century, *Econ. Hist. Rev.,* vi, 2,

1953; MANTOUX, PAUL: The industrial revolution in the eighteenth century, London, 1928.

Many of the principal works on the industrial revolution in Wales are listed in section K III. For emigration see section K III *(b)* (ii).

### (a) General works

DAVIES, DAVID J.: The economic history of South Wales prior to 1800 (No. 137).

**2342.** DODD, ARTHUR HERBERT: The industrial revolution in North Wales. Cardiff, 1933; 2nd edn, 1951.
> Contains a very full bibliography.

**2343.** GRIFFITHS, WILLIAM ARTHUR: Notes on an early eighteenth century account book of the family of Davies of Trewylan, Llansantffraid. *Mont. Coll.*, lii, 1951–2.

**2344.** JOHN, ARTHUR HENRY: The industrial development of South Wales. Cardiff, 1950.

**2345.** JONES, E. H.: The romance of Welsh inventors. *Wales and Monmouthshire*, ii, 1, 1938.

WILLIAMS, DAVID: A note on the population of Wales, 1536–1801 (No. 1621). 1937.

Id.    A history of modern Wales (No. 159).

WILLIAMS, DAVID TREVOR: The economic development of Swansea and of the Swansea district to 1921 (No. 709).

### (b) Agriculture

**2346.** BOWEN, IFOR: The great enclosures of common lands in Wales. London, 1914.
> See also amplification for North Wales by A. H. Dodd in *B.B.C.S.*, iii, 1926. Detailed analyses of local enclosure awards are given in many Welsh historical journals; for a list of these see id.: The industrial revolution in North Wales, 2nd edn (No. 2342), pp. xxv, xxxvi, xxxviii.

**2347.** DAVIES, JOHN HUMPHREYS: Cardiganshire freeholders in 1760. *W. Wales Hist. Rec.*, iii, 1912–13.

**2348.** EDMUNDS, HENRY: History of the Brecknockshire agricultural society, 1755–1955. *Brycheiniog,* ii and iii, 1956 and 1957.

**2349.** FUSSELL, GEORGE EDWIN: Glamorgan farming: an outline of its modern history. *Morgannwg*, i, 1957.

**2350.** HOWSE, WILLIAM HENRY: Encroachments of the king's wastes in Cantref Maelienydd as recorded in 1734. *Trans. Rads. Soc.*, xxv, 1955.

**2351.** JENKINS, DAFYDD: Thomas Johnes o'r Hafod, 1784–1816. Cardiff, 1948.

See also INGLIS-JONES, ELISABETH: Peacocks in paradise (No. 2316), and VAUGHAN, HERBERT MILLINGCHAMP (ed.): Some letters of Thomas Johnes of Hafod (1749–1907). *Y Cymmr.*, xxxv, 1925.

**2352.** JENKINS, ROBERT THOMAS: Hywel Harris y ffarmwr. *Lleufer*, viii, 1952.

JONES, ANNA MARIA: The rural industries of England and Wales (No. 235).

**2353.** JONES, FRANCIS: A squire of Anglesey (Edward Wynne, Bodewryd). *Trans. Angl. Antiq. Soc.*, 1940.

**2354.** OLIVER, J.: The weather and farming in the mid-eighteenth century in Anglesey. *N.L.W. Jnl.*, x, 1958.

**2355.** OWEN, GERAINT DYFNALLT: Agriculture [in Carmarthenshire]. In A history of Carmarthenshire (No. 605), ii.

**2356.** PARRY, OWEN: The financing of the Welsh cattle trade in the eighteenth century. *B.B.C.S.*, viii, 1935.

**2357.** RAWSON, R. REES: The open field in Flintshire, Devonshire and Cornwall. *Econ. Hist. Rev.*, vi, 1, 1953.

**2358.** THOMAS, DAVID: Cau'r tiroedd comin. Lerpwl, 1953.

See review by R. O. Roberts in *Y Traethodydd*, 1954.

**2359.** VAUGHAN, HERBERT MILLINGCHAMP: The South Wales squires. London, 1926.

**2360.** YOUNG, ARTHUR: A six weeks' tour through the southern counties of England and Wales. London, 1768, and later edns.

**2361.** Id.      (ed.): Annals of agriculture. 46 vols., 1784–1815.

References to Wales are in vols. viii, 31–51; ix, 647–50; xii, 151–2; xiii, 13; xiv, 407–10; xxii, 623–8; xxiii, 70; xxiv, 260, 262–6; xxvi, 11–12, 539–47; xxviii, 157; xxix, 278–305; xxx, 10–14; xxxi, 307–33; xxxiii, 164, 199–203, 481–7; xxxiv, 162, 164; xxxv, 5–8; xlii, 124–36; xliii, 577–83; xlv, 516–17, 556–8. For detailed references see the earlier edition of this BIBLIOGRAPHY, pp. 112–13.

(c) **Industry**

(i) **Coal**

**2362.** ASHTON, THOMAS SOUTHCLIFFE, and SYKES, JOSEPH: The coal industry of the eighteenth century. Manchester, 1929.

**2363.** GALLOWAY, R. L.: Annals of coal mining and the coal trade. 2 vols. London, 1898–1900.

**2364.** HARE, ANTHONY EDWARD CHRISTIAN: The anthracite coal industry of the Swansea district. Social and economic survey of Swansea and district. Pamphlet No. 5. Cardiff, 1940.

**2365.** NEF, JOHN U.: The rise of the British coal industry. 2 vols. London, 1932.

**2366.** PHILLIPS, ELIZABETH: A history of the pioneers of the Welsh coalfield. Cardiff, 1925.

**2367.** PHILLIPS, MARTIN: Early mining records of the [Neath] district. *Trans. Aberafan and District Hist. Soc.,* 1931–2.

**2368.** RAWSON, R. REES: The coal-mining industry of the Hawarden district on the eve of the industrial revolution. *Arch. Camb.,* 1941.

WILKINS, CHARLES: The South Wales coal trade and its allied industries from the earliest days to the present time (No. 2248).

### (ii) Iron

**2369.** ADDIS, JOHN PHILIP : The Crawshay dynasty : a study in industrial organisation and development, 1765–1867. Cardiff, 1957.

**2370.** ASHTON, THOMAS SOUTHCLIFFE: Iron and steel in the industrial revolution. London, 1924; 2nd edn, Manchester, 1951.

**2371.** CHALONER, WILLIAM H.: John Wilkinson, ironmaster. *History To-day,* i, 1951.
See also PALMER, ALFRED NEOBARD: John Wilkinson and the old Bersham iron works. *Trans. Cymmr.,* 1897–8.

**2372.** Id. Isaac Wilkinson, potfounder, *circa* 1704–1784. In Studies in the Industrial Revolution presented to T. S. Ashton. Ed. L. S. Prezznell. London, 1960.

**2373.** CHAPPELL, EDGAR LEYSHON: Historic Melingriffith: an account of Pentyrch iron works and Melingriffith tinplate works. Cardiff, 1940.

**2374.** DAVIES, ARTHUR STANLEY: Early iron industry in North Wales. *Newcomen Soc. Trans.,* xxv, 1947–8.

**2375.** Id. The charcoal iron industry of Powys land. *Mont. Coll.,* xlvi, 1946.

**2376.** EVANS, LESLIE WYNNE: The early iron and coal industries [in Carmarthenshire]. In A history of Carmarthenshire (No. 605), ii.

**2377.** Id. Robert Morgan of Kidwelly, ironmaster. *Trans. Carms. Antiq. Soc.,* xxviii, 1938.

**2378.** HULME, E. WYNDHAM: Statistical history of the iron trade of England and Wales, 1717–1750. *Trans. Newcomen Soc.,* ix, 1928–9.

**2379.** JOHN, ARTHUR HENRY: Iron and coal on a Glamorgan estate, 1700–40. *Econ. Hist. Rev.*, xiii, 1943.

**2380.** JONES, HARRI GWYNN: The charcoal iron industry. *Jnl. Royal Soc. Arts*, lxxxviii, 1939.

**2381.** LLOYD, JOHN: The early history of the old South Wales iron works, 1760–1840. London, 1906.

**2382.** NAMIER, LEWIS BERNSTEIN: Anthony Bacon, an eighteenth century merchant. *Jnl. Economic and Business History*, 1929.

**2383.** PRICE, WATKIN WILLIAM: The legend of Anthony Bacon. *B.B.C.S.*, xi, 1943.

**2384.** SCRIVENOR, HARRY: History of the iron trade from the earliest records to the present period. London 1841; new edn, 1854.

WILKINS, CHARLES: The history of the iron, steel, tinplate, and other trades of Wales (No. 2247).

### (iii) Tinplate

**2385.** BROOKE, EDWARD HENRY: Monograph on the tinplate works of Great Britain. Swansea, 1932.

**2386.** Id.     Chronology of the tinplate works of Great Britain. Cardiff, 1944.

**2387.** Id.     Appendix to the chronology of the tinplate works of Great Britain, 1665–1949. Cardiff, 1949.

CHAPPELL, EDGAR LEYSHON: Historic Melingriffith: an account of Pentyrch iron works and Melingriffith tinplate works (No. 2373).

**2388.** EVANS, F.: Tinplate through the ages. *The British Steelmaker*, November, 1952.

**2389.** GIBBS, F. W.: The rise of the tinplate industry. *Annals of Science*, 1950, 1951.

**2390.** GREEN, FRANCIS: Carmarthen tinworks and its founder. *W. Wales Hist. Rec.*, vi, 1915.

**2391.** JOHN, WILLIAM DAVID: Pontypool and Usk japanned wares with the early history of the iron and tinplate industries at Pontypool. Newport, 1953.

**2392.** JONES, JOHN HENRY: The tinplate industry. London, 1914.

**2393.** MINCHINTON, WALTER EDWARD: The British tinplate industry: a history. Oxford, 1957.

**2394.** National Museum of Wales: Guide to the collections of Pontypool and Usk japan. Cardiff, 1926.

### (iv) Non-ferrous metals

**2395.** ALEXANDER, W. O.: A brief review of the development of the copper, zinc, and brass industries of Great Britain from A.D. 1500 to 1900. *Murex Limited Review*, i, 1955.

**2396.** BARKER, THEODORE CARDWELL, and HARRIS, JOHN RAYMOND: A Merseyside town in the industrial revolution: St. Helens, 1750–1900. Liverpool, 1953.

**2397.** CARPENTER, K.: Notes on the history of Cardiganshire lead mines. *Aberystwyth Studies*, v, 1923.

> See also THOMAS, DANIEL LLEUFER: Lewis Morris in Cardiganshire. *Y Cymmr.*, xv, 1902.

**2398.** CHALLONER, WILLIAM H.: Charles Roe of Macclesfield (1715–81): an eighteenth century industrialist. *Trans. Lancs. and Chesh. Antiq. Soc.,* lxii and lxiii, 1950–1 and 1952–3.

**2399.** EVANS, DAVID OWEN: The non-ferrous metallurgical industries of South Wales and Welshmen's share in their development. *Trans. Cymmr.,* 1929–30.

**2400.** GIBBS, DAVID ELWYN, and ROBERTS, ROBERT OWEN: Early copper smelting in West Glamorgan: an edition of an Exchequer Court case of 1724. *S. Wales and Mon. Rec. Soc.,* iv, 1955.

> GRANT-FRANCIS, GEORGE: The smelting of copper in the Swansea district from the time of Elizabeth to the present day (No. 1816).

**2401.** HAMILTON, HENRY: The English brass and copper industries to 1800. London, 1926.

**2402.** HARRIS, JOHN RAYMOND: Michael Hughes of Sutton: the influence of Welsh copper on Lancashire business, 1780–1815. *Trans. Hist. Soc. Lancs. and Chesh.,* ci, 1949.

**2403.** HUNT, ROBERT: Notices of the history of the lead mines of Cardiganshire. *Geological Survey*, ii, 1848.

**2404.** JONES, HARRI GWYNN: The Llandudno copper mines in the eighteenth century. *B.B.C.S.,* x, 1939.

**2405.** LEWIS, W. J.: The Cwmsymlog lead mine. *Ceredigion*, ii, 1952.

**2406.** PHILLIPS, MARTIN: The copper industry in the Port Talbot district. Neath, 1935.

**2407.** ROBERTS, ROBERT OWEN: The development and decline of the copper and other non-ferrous industries in South Wales. *Trans. Cymmr.,* 1956.

**2408.** Id.     Copper and economic growth in Britain, 1729–1784. *N.L.W. Jnl.,* x, 1957–8.

### (v) Wool

**2409.** DAVIES, BRYAN LLOYD, and JONES, ALAN BEYNON: The woollen industry [in Carmarthenshire]. In A history of Carmarthenshire (No. 605), ii.

**2410.** JONES, MOSES J.: The Merioneth woollen industry from 1750 to 1820. *Trans. Cymmr.,* 1939.

**2410A.** SKEEL, CAROLINE ANNE JAMES: The Welsh woollen industry in the eighteenth and nineteenth centuries. *Arch. Camb.,* 1924.

> See discussion in ibid., 1924.

### (d) Trade and transport

A review of the records of the Conway and the Menai ferries (No. 130 (8)).

**2411.** BALLEN, DOROTHY: Bibliography of road-making and roads in the United Kingdom. London, 1914.

**2412.** BARFOOT, PETER, and WILKES, JOHN: The universal British directory of trade and commerce. 5 vols. London, 1790.

**2413.** DAVIES, ARTHUR STANLEY: The river trade and craft of Montgomeryshire and its borders. *Mont. Coll.,* xliii and xliv, 1935 and 1936.

**2414.** EVANS, LESLIE WYNNE, and OWEN, GERAINT DYFNALLT: The development of communications [in Carmarthenshire]. In A history of Carmarthenshire (No. 605), ii.

**2415.** FORDHAM, HERBERT GEORGE: Road books and itineraries of Great Britain, 1570–1850: a catalogue. Cambridge, 1924.

**2416.** Id.     The road books of Wales. *Arch. Camb.,* 1927.

**2417.** HOWSE, WILLIAM HENRY: The old fairs of Radnorshire and its borders. *Trans. Rads. Soc.,* xvii, 1947.

**2418.** HUGHES, P. G.: Wales and the drovers. London, *circa* 1944.

> See also GRIFFITHS, GRIFFITH MILWYN: Letters from two Welsh drovers. *N.L.W. Jnl.,* vi, 1951.

**2419.** Id.    Porthmona ym Morgannwg. *Trans. Cymmr.,* 1946–7.

**2420.** JENKINS, ROBERT THOMAS: Y ffordd yng Nghymru. Wrecsam, 1933.

**2421.** LLOYD, WYNNE LL.: Trade and transport: an account of the trade of the Port of Swansea and the transport facilities and industry in the district. Social and economic survey of Swansea and district. Pamphlet No. 6. Cardiff, 1940.

**2422.** MORRIS, LEWIS: Plans of harbours, bars, bays, and roads in St. George's Channel. London, 1748; 2nd edn, 1801.

> SKEEL, CAROLINE ANNE JAMES: The cattle trade between England and Wales from the fifteenth to the nineteenth centuries (No. 1827).

> THOMAS, DAVID: Hen longau a llongwyr Cymru. Bilingual. (No. 258).

> Id.    Hen longau sir Gaernarfon (No. 259).

**2423.** WILLIAMS, DAVID TREVOR: The port books of Swansea and Neath, 1709–19. *Arch. Camb.,* 1940.

> WILLIAMS, MOELWYN I.: A contribution to the commercial history of Glamorgan, 1666–1735 (No. 2249).

## IV. RELIGION AND EDUCATION

### (a) The (Anglican) Church in Wales

#### (i) General

> WYNNE, ROBERT: A short narrative of the proceedings against the bishop of St. Asaph (No. 2076).

**2424.** CLEMENT, MARY: A calendar of Welsh letters to the S.P.C.K., 1743–1783. *N.L.W. Jnl.,* x, 1957–8.

> DAVIES, J. CONWAY: The records of the Church in Wales (No. 822).

**2425.** EVANS, ALBERT OWEN: Ellis Wynne's contribution to the literature of the church. *Jnl. Welsh Bibl. Soc.,* iv, 5, 1934.

**2426.** EVANS, GEORGE EYRE: Llanedi: a non-parochial register, 1745–1837. *Trans. Carms. Antiq. Soc.,* xxvi, 1936.

**2427.** Id.    Adam Ottley, bishop of St. David's, 1713–1723. Ibid., xxviii, 1938.

See also 'X.Y.Z.': Will of Adam Otley, bishop of St. David's. Ibid., xxvi, 1936.

**2428.** HAVARD, WILLIAM THOMAS (bishop of St. David's): The eighteenth century background of church life in Wales. *Jnl. Hist. Soc. Church in Wales,* v, 1955.

**2429.** JONES, EVAN DAVID: Some aspects of the history of the church in north Cardiganshire in the eighteenth century. *Jnl. Hist. Soc. Church in Wales,* iii, 1953.

**2430.** JONES, T. LLECHID: Llenor eglwysig angofiedig [Richard Jones, rheithor Llanychan, sir Ddinbych]. *Yr Haul,* 1939.

**2431.** LEWIS, EWART: The Cowbridge diocesan library, 1711–1848, its establishment, constitution, and contents. *Jnl. Hist. Soc. Church in Wales,* iv and vii, 1954 and 1957.

**2432.** LEWIS, SAUNDERS: Y bardd cwsc. *Y Llenor,* ii, 1923.

**2433.** MERCHANT, WILLIAM MOELWYN: Richard Watson, bishop of Llandaff. *Jnl. Hist. Soc. Church in Wales,* i, 1947.

**2434.** MORGAN, WALTER THOMAS: Two cases concerning dilapidations to episcopal property in the diocese of St. David's. *N.L.W. Jnl.,* vii, 1951–2.

OWEN, C. E. VAUGHAN: The vicars of Trefeglwys, 1574–1902 (No. 1706).

OWEN, R. H.: Jacobitism and the church in Wales (No. 2289).

**2435.** RICHARDS, GWYNFRYN: Royal briefs for the restoration of churches in Wales. *Jnl. Hist. Soc. Church in Wales,* vi, vii, and viii, 1956, 1957, and 1958.
See also JONES, EVAN DAVID: Welsh briefs published in Winterbourne Steepleton, 1714–65. *N.L.W. Jnl.,* x, 1957–8.

RICHARDS, THOMAS: Piwritaniaeth a pholitics (No. 2049).
Particularly valuable for ecclesiastical politics (e.g. non-jurors) at the turn of the century.

**2436.** ROBERTS, GOMER MORGAN: Gleanings from the St. David's episcopal registers. *Cylch. Cymd. Hanes M.C.,* xxvi, 1, 1951.

**2437.** SAUNDERS, ERASMUS: A view of the state of religion in the diocese of St. David's. London, 1721. Univ. of Wales reprint. Cardiff, 1949.

**2438.** THOMAS, JOHN ALUN: A Welsh churchman in colonial Pennsylvania. *Jnl. Hist. Soc. Church in Wales,* iv, 1954; v, 1955.

**2439.** THOMAS, R. GEORGE: The complete reading-list of a Carmarthenshire student, 1763–7. *N.L.W. Jnl.,* ix, 1955–6.

**2440.** WILLIAMS, WILLIAM GILBERT: Y parchedig Richard Farrington, M.A. *Y Llenor,* xx, 1941.

WILLIAMS, WILLIAM MOSES, and JONES, IDWAL: An inventory of records at the palace of Abergwili (No. 860).

WILLIS, BROWNE: A survey of the cathedral church of Bangor (No. 830).

Id.     A survey of the cathedral church of Llandaff (No. 840).

Id.     A survey of the cathedral church of St. Asaph (No. 845).

Id.     A survey of the cathedral church of St. David's (No. 861).

**2441.** Id.     Parochiale Wallicanum. Ed. A. W. Wade-Evans. *Y Cymmr.*, xxii.

WRIGHT, EVAN GILBERT: Dean John Jones (1650–1727) (No. 2084).

YARDLEY, EDWARD: Menevia sacra (No. 862).

#### (ii) The Anglican revival and Griffith Jones

**2442.** ANON.: A present for a Welsh clergyman. London, 1779.
Includes papers on Bishop Beveridge and Griffith Jones.

**2443.** CAVENAGH, F. A.: Griffith Jones. Cardiff, 1930.

**2444.** CLEMENT, MARY: Ciwradiaeth gyntaf Griffith Jones, Llanddowror. *Cylch. Cymd. Hanes M.C.*, xxix, 2, 1944.

**2445.** Id.     The S.P.C.K. and Wales, 1699–1740: the history of the S.P.C.K. in Wales from its foundation to the early years of the Welsh Methodist movement. London, 1954.

Id.     Correspondence and minutes of the S.P.C.K. relating to Wales, 1699–1740 (No. 130 (10)).

DAVIES, JOHN: Bywyd a gwaith Moses Williams (No. 2307).

**2446.** EVANS, JOHN: Some account of the Welsh charity schools. London, 1752.
See also SALMON, DAVID: J. Evans and the Welsh Bible. *Jnl. Welsh Bibl. Soc.*, ii, 1916–23.

**2447.** JENKINS, ROBERT THOMAS: Gruffydd Jones, Llanddowror. Bilingual. Cardiff, 1930.

**2448.** Id.     A conspectus of Griffith Jones' schools in North Wales, 1738–61. *B.B.C.S.*, v, 1929–31.

**2449.** JONES, D.: Life and times of Griffith Jones. London and Bangor, 1902.

**2450.** JONES, DAVID AMBROSE: Griffith Jones, Llanddowror. Wrecsam, 1923.

**2451.** JONES, EVAN JOHN: A letter concerning Griffith Jones. *B.B.C.S.*, x, 1940.

**2452.** JONES, GRIFFITH: An address to the charitable and well-disposed. London, 1741.

**2453.** Id.        A letter to a clergyman. London, 1745.

**2454.** Id.        Rheolau yr ysgolion Cymraeg, a llythyr, etc. London, 1744–5.

> Reprinted in No. 2443.

**2455.** Id.        Letters. Ed. E. Morgan (Syston). London, 1832.

**2456.** Id.        Letters. Supplement. Ed. M. H. Jones. *Trans. Carms. Antiq. Soc.*, xiv and xv, 1909.

**2457.** Id.        Holl ysgrifeniadau Cymraeg. Ed. E. Morgan. Caernarfon, 1838.

> See also a bibliography of Griffith Jones's works, mainly in his relation to Methodism, in *Cylch. Cymd. Hanes M.C.,* vi, 2, 1921; vii, 1, 1922; ix, 1 and 3, 1924; for the remainder of his works, mostly theological, see Cardiff Welsh Library catalogue (No. 4), pp. 263–5. For his will see *Trans. Carms. Antiq. Soc.*, xxii, 1930.

**2458.** Id.        and BEVAN, MADAM: Welch piety. London [from 1737–1776].

> See also appendix i to No. 2443 and No. 2469.

JONES, M. G.: The charity school movement: a study of eighteenth century Puritanism in action (No. 2227).

> See also JENKINS, ROBERT THOMAS: Yr ysgolion elusennol. *Y Llenor*, 1938.

**2459.** KELLY, THOMAS: Griffith Jones, pioneer in adult education. Cardiff, 1950.

LEWIS, EWART: Cowbridge diocesan library, 1711–1848 (No. 2431).

**2460.** NELSON, ROBERT: Companion for the festivals and fasts of the Church of England, etc. London, 1704. Translated by Thomas William of Denbigh: Cydymaith i ddyddiau gwylion . . . Eglwys Loegr. London, 1712.

**2461.** Id.        On the advantage of clerical seminaries, etc. Carmarthen, 1813.

**2462.** OWEN, HUGH: Gruffydd Jones's circulating schools in Anglesey. *Trans. Angl. Antiq. Soc.,* 1936.

**2463.** ROBERTS, GOMER MORGAN: Griffith Jones's opinion of the Methodists. *Cylch. Cymd. Hanes M.C.,* xxxv, 3, 1950.

**2464.** SALMON, DAVID: A Russian report on Griffith Jones' schools. *Trans. Carms. Antiq. Soc.,* xix, 1926.

SHANKLAND, THOMAS: 'Diwygwyr Cymru' Beriah Gwynfe Evans (No. 2232).

**2465.** Id.     Sir John Philipps and the charity schools movement. *Trans. Cymmr.,* 1904–5.

**2466.** THOMAS, G. TUCKER: A short study in Welsh genealogy: the lineage of the Rev. Griffith Jones, vicar of Llanddowror. *Arch. Camb.,* 1923.

**2467.** Id.     Archdeacon Tenison *v.* Griffith Jones. *Trans. Carms. Antiq. Soc.,* xvii, 1924, p. 57.

**2468.** THOMAS, JOHN (of Rhaeadr): Rhad ras. Abertawe, 1810.
On this see OWEN, JOHN DYFNALLT, in *Y Cyfarwyddwr,* Mai, 1930.

**2469.** WILLIAMS, WILLIAM MOSES: Selections from Welch piety. Cardiff, 1938.

**2470.** Id.     The friends of Griffith Jones. *Y Cymmr.,* xlvi, 1939.

### (b) The older dissent

### (i) General

**2471.** ANON.: The diocese of Bangor in 1776. *Wales.* Ed. O. M. Edwards, i and ii, 1894 and 1895.

**2472.** EMMANUEL, HYWEL DAVID: Dissent in the counties of Glamorgan and Monmouth. *N.L.W. Jnl.,* viii, 1953–4; ix, 1955–6.
Licences of Nonconformist meeting-houses, eighteenth and nineteenth centuries. See also GRIFFITHS, GRIFFITH MILWYN: A Monmouth conventicle, 1709. Ibid., x, 1957–8.

**2473.** JONES, EDMUND: State of religion in Wales in 1742. *Wales.* Ed. O. M. Edwards, i, 1894.
On Edmund Jones, see No. 2490.

**2474.** PETER, DAVID: Hanes crefydd yng Nghymru. 2nd edn. Colwyn, 1851.

REES, THOMAS: History of Protestant Nonconformity in Wales (No. 178).

**2475.** RICHARDS, THOMAS: Y Diwygiad Methodistaidd a'r Hen Ymneilltuwyr. *Traf. Cymd. Hanes Bed.,* 1928.

Id.      Piwritaniaeth a pholitics (No. 2049).

**2476.** RICHARDS, WILLIAM (of Lynn): The Welsh Nonconformist memorial, or Cambro-British biography. London, 1820.

### (ii) The academies

For academies in general, see JEREMY, WALTER D.: The Presbyterian fund and Dr. Williams's trust (No. 2228); McLACHLAN, H.: English education under the Test Acts. The history of the Nonconformist academies, 1662–1820, Manchester, 1931; PARKER, IRENE: History of the dissenting academies (No. 2230).

CONE, CARL B.: Torchbearer of freedom: the influence of Richard Price on eighteenth century thought (No. 2271).

**2477.** DAVIES, J.: Ogof Craig y Wyddon. In Dylanwad Ymneilltuaeth ar fywyd y genedl. Llanelli, 1913.

On Ystrad Wallter.

**2478.** EVANS, W. J.: Carmarthen College. *Yr Ymofynydd,* 1900 and 1901.

JAMES, JAMES SPINTHER: Hanes y Bedyddwyr yng Nghymru (No. 172).

See especially vol. iii.

**2479.** JONES, E. PAN: Oriel Coleg Caerfyrddin. Merthyr, 1909.

**2480.** OWEN, D. EDMONDES: Who was Williams Pantycelyn's tutor at Llwynllwyd ? *Cylch. Cymd. Hanes M.C.,* iv, 4, 1918.

See also SHANKLAND, THOMAS: Pwy oedd athro Williams Pantycelyn yn Llwynllwyd? *Y Beirniad,* viii, 1919.

**2481.** OWEN, GERAINT DYFNALLT: Ysgolion a cholegau yr Annibynwyr. Abertawe, 1939.

See also JENKINS, ROBERT THOMAS: Academïau yr Annibynwyr yng Nghymru. *Y Llenor,* 1939.

Id.      James Owen a'i academi (No. 2229).

PETER, DAVID: Hanes crefydd yng Nghymru (No. 2474).

REES, THOMAS, and THOMAS, JOHN: Hanes eglwysi Annibynnol Cymru (No. 179).

See especially vol. iv.

ROBERTS, H. P.: Nonconformist academies in Wales (No. 2231).

THOMAS, ROLAND: Richard Price (No. 2301).

**2482.** WILLIAMS, J. Rufus: Hanes athrofeydd y Bedyddwyr yn sir Fynwy, Hwlffordd a Llangollen. Aberdâr, 1863.

### (iii) The Independents

See *Y Cofiadur* (No. 323).

On the general history of the Independents, see DALE, R. W.: History of Congregationalism. London, 1908.

In this and the following subsection books or articles on local congregations have been included only when those congregations were of marked significance in the history of their denominations during the eighteenth century.

DAVIES, PENNAR: Episodes in the history of Brecknockshire dissent (No. 2097).

DAVIES, T. EIRUG: Philip Pugh a'i ragflaenwyr yng nghanolbarth sir Aberteifi (No. 2138).

**2483.** DAVIES, WILLIAM LLEWELYN: Defnyddiau hanes yr Annibynwyr yng Nghymru. Aberystwyth, 1936.

**2484.** EVANS, EVAN LEWIS: Hanes Capel Isaac. Llandysul, 1950.

**2485.** Id. (gol.): Trwyddedau tai cyrddau a gweinidogion ym Morgannwg. *Y Cofiadur*, xix a xx, 1949 a 1950.

**2486.** EVANS, WILLIAM ABRAHAM: Thomas Baddy ac ymddiriedolwyr cronfa Dr. Daniel Williams. Ibid., xxvii, 1957.

**2487.** HUGHES, GARFIELD HOPKIN: Emynyddiaeth yr hen Ymneilltuwyr. *Jnl. Welsh Bibl. Soc.*, viii, 1955.

**2488.** JENKINS, ROBERT THOMAS: Yr Annibynwyr Cymreig a Hywel Harris. *Y Cofiadur*, xii, 1935.

Id. Hanes cynulleidfa Hen Gapel Llanuwchllyn (No. 2118).

**2489.** JONES, D. R., a JONES, GRIFFITH (goln): Cipdrem ar hanes eglwys Annibynnol Pendref, Caernarfon. Llawlyfr Undeb yr Annibynwyr Cymraeg. Caernarfon, 1930.

**2490.** JONES, EVAN (Ieuan Gwynedd): Edmund Jones a'i amserau. In Gweithiau Ieuan Gwynedd. Dolgellau, 1876.

**2491.** JONES, EVAN DAVID: Eglwysi Annibynnol gogledd Ceredigion. Llawlyfr Undeb gogledd Ceredigion. Aberystwyth, 1955.

Id. Llyfr eglwys Mynydd-bach (No. 2089).

**2492.** Jones, H. Ivor: Hanes Annibyniaeth sir Gaernarfon hyd ddiwedd y ddeunawfed ganrif. Caernarfon, 1897.

**2493.** Jones, John Morgan (gol.): Ysgrifau Thomas Morgan, Henllan. *Y Cofiadur*, i, 1923.

**2494.** Id.    (gol.): Llyfr eglwys y Cilgwyn. Ibid., i, 1923.

**2495.** Id.    (gol.): Cyfamodau eglwys Llanbrynmair. Ibid., ii, 1924.

**2496.** Jones, Robert Tudur: Trefniadaeth ryngeglwysig yr Annibynwyr. Ibid., xxi, 1951.

**2497.** Lewis D. Morgan: Morgan Rhys a'i gyfnod. *Y Cofiadur*, x a xi, 1934.

Id.    Eglwysi Henllan a Rhydyceisiaid (No. 2141).

**2498.** Lewis, T.: George Lewis, 1763–1822. Ibid., x a xi, 1934.

Owen, Bob: Some details about the Independents in Caernarvonshire (No. 2130).

Id.    Rhai agweddau ar hanes Annibynwyr sir Gaernarfon (No. 2109).

**2499.** Owen, John Dyfnallt: Hanes eglwys Heol Awst [Carmarthen, 1926].

Id.    Camre cyntaf Anghydffurfiaeth ac Annibyniaeth yn sir Gaerfyrddin (No. 2142).

**2500.** Id.    Jones, J. D., a Davies, Ben: Hanes eglwys Cwmllynfell. Caerfyrddin, 1935.

**2501.** Peate, Iorwerth Cyfeiliog (ed.): Hen gapel Llanbrynmair, 1739–1939. Llandysul, 1939.

Rees, Thomas: History of Protestant Nonconformity in Wales (No. 178).

Rees, Thomas, and Thomas, John: Hanes eglwysi Annibynnol Cymru (No. 179).

Richards, Thomas: Nonconformity from 1620–1715 [in Carmarthenshire] (No. 2114).

**2502.** Roberts, Gomer Morgan: Henry Thomas, Gelli Dochlaethe. *Y Cofiadur*, xvii, 1947.

**2503.** Id.    Dafydd Jones o Gaeo. Aberystwyth, 1948.

**2504.** Id.　　Annibynwyr a llythyrau Trefeca. *Y Cofiadur*, xxvii, 1957.

**2505.** Roberts, John (of Llanbryn-mair): Cofiant Lewis Rees. Abertawe, 1852.

**2506.** Thomas, Isaac: Y gronfa gynulleidfaol ac Annibynwyr Cymru. *Y Cofiadur*, xxviii, 1958.

**2507.** Walters, D. Eurof: Y Parchedig Edward Williams (1750–1813). *Y Cofiadur*, viii a ix, 1932.

**2508.** Williams, Griffith John: Sabeliaid Aberthin. Ibid., xxv, 1955.

### (iv) The Baptists

See *Trafodion Cymdeithas Hanes Bedyddwyr Cymru* (No. 321).

**2509.** Bassett, Thomas: Dafydd Hughes y cenhadwr i'r gogledd. *Traf. Cymd. Hanes Bed.*, 1931.

　　Bowen, Emrys George: Bedyddwyr Cymru tua 1714 (No. 2136).

**2510.** Davies, J. D.: Y Bedyddwyr Albanaidd a'r Bedyddwyr Campbel-aidd yng Nghymru. *Traf. Cymd. Hanes Bed.*, 1940.

**2511.** Evans, J.: Memoir of the life and writings of William Richards (of Lynn). London, 1819.

> See also Jenkins, Robert Thomas: William Richards of Lynn (with appendix on the history of the General Baptists in Wales). *Traf. Cymd. Hanes Bed.*, 1930 and 1931.

**2512.** Evans, John James: Morgan John Rhys a'i amserau. Caerdydd, 1935.

> See also Griffith, John T.: The Welsh Baptist hero of civil and religious liberty of the eighteenth century. Lansford (Pa.), 1899, and Carmarthen, 1910.

**2513.** Francis, Enoch: Gwaith a gwobr ffyddlon weinidogion yr Efengyl, neu bregeth a bregethwyd mewn cymmanfa o weinidogion a gynhaeliwyd yn Llangloffan yn sir Bem'ro yn wythnos y Sulgwyn 1729, etc. Reprinted and edited by Thomas Shankland in *Traf. Cymd. Hanes Bed.*, 1911–12.

**2514.** Humphreys, B.: Timothy Thomas o Aberduar. Ibid., 1909–10.

**2515.** Id.　　Hanes Bedyddwyr Felinfoel. Llanelli, 1909.

　　James, James Spinther: Hanes y Bedyddwyr yng Nghymru (No. 172).

**2516.** Jenkins, Robert Thomas: Rhai o gymdogion Joshua Thomas. *Traf. Cymd. Hanes Bed.*, 1935.

15

**2517.** Id.　　Cwrdd chwarter Bedyddwyr glannau Teifi. Ibid., 1942.

**2518.** John, James Mansel: John Reynolds y Felinganol (1759–1824). Ibid., 1951.

**2519.** Jones, E. K.: Llythyr y Gymanfa. Ibid., 1922.

**2520.** Id.　　The circular letters of the Baptist Association of Wales. *Jnl. Welsh Bibl. Soc.*, i, 5, 1910–15.

**2521.** Jones, E. T.: Pennod o hanes Titus Lewis. *Traf. Cymd. Hanes Bed.*, 1908–9.

**2522.** Id.　　Rhai o weinidogion cyntaf Cilfowyr a'i changhennau. Ibid., 1913–14.

**2523.** Jones, R.: Miles Harri. Ibid., 1926.

**2524.** Jones, W.: Hanes cymanfa[oedd] y Bedyddwyr Neillduol yng Ngymru. Cardiff, 1831; 2nd edn, Llangollen, 1889.

**2525.** Morris, Silas: Thomas Llewelyn, 1720–83. *Traf. Cymd. Hanes Bed.*, 1907–8.

**2526.** Owens, Benjamin George: Joshua Thomas, hanesydd y Bedyddwyr. *Y Llenor*, 1948.

**2527.** Id.　　Rhai o lawysgrifau Coleg y Bedyddwyr, Bangor. *Seren Gomer*, xli, 1949.

**2528.** Price, George Vernon: The 'Old Meeting'. The history of the Chester Street Baptist Church, Wrexham. Wrexham, n.d.

**2529.** Richards, Thomas: Bedyddwyr y dwyrain. *Traf. Cymd. Hanes Bed.*, 1950.

**2530.** Shankland, Thomas (ed.): Llythyrau oddi wrth y gymanfa at yr eglwysi, 1760–1790. Rhan i, hyd 1765 (all published). Caerdydd, n.d. [1910].

**2531.** Thomas, Joshua: History of the Welsh Association. London, 1795.

**2532.** Id.　　Hanes y Bedyddwyr, etc. Pontypridd, 1885.

> A translation by B. Davies from Joshua Thomas's MS. of a projected English edition of No. 183. It has corrections of the 1st edn, and also deals with the period to 1794. Valuable.

Id.　　Hanes y Bedyddwyr yng Nghymru (No. 183).

Whitley, William Thomas: Radnorshire Baptists (No. 2122).

### (v) The Society of Friends

**2533.** KELSALL, JOHN: Diary. *Wales.* Ed. O. M. Edwards, ii, 1895.
See also JENKINS, ROBERT THOMAS: John Kelsall yn sir Gaernarfon ac ym Môn. *Trans. Caerns. Hist. Soc.*, 1940.

OWEN, BOB: Llyfryddiaeth Crynwyr Meirionydd (No. 2156).

REES, THOMAS MARDY: A history of the Quakers in Wales (No. 2176).

WILLIAMS, RICHARD: Quakerism in Montgomeryshire (No. 2159).

### (vi) Arians and Unitarians

**2534.** DAVIES, D. JACOB: Hen dy cwrdd Aberdâr (1751–1951). Llandysul [1915].

**2535.** DAVIS, DAVID (of Castell Hywel): Telyn Dewi. Reprint. Aberystwyth, 1927.

**2536.** EVANS, GEORGE EYRE: Vestiges of Protestant dissent. Liverpool, 1897.
Contains a list of Unitarian churches, with dates, etc.

**2537.** Id.   (ed.): Lloyd letters (1754–95). Aberystwyth, 1908.

**2538.** GRIFFITHS, T.: Cofiant D. Davies. Caerfyrddin, 1828.

**2539.** JONES, R. J.: Dechreuad a chynnydd Undodiaeth yng Nghymru. *Y Geninen*, 1905.

**2540.** LEWIS, TOM: Hen dy cwrdd Cefn Coed y Cymmer. Llandysul, n.d.

**2541.** LLOYD, C.: Particulars of the life of a dissenting minister. London, 1813, and Gloucester, 1911.

**2542.** LLOYD (LLWYD), DAVID (of Brynllefrith): Gwaith prydyddawl. Caerfyrddin, 1785.

**2543.** LLOYD-THEAKSTON, L., and DAVIES, J.: Some family records and pedigrees of the Lloyds of Allt yr Odyn, Castell Hywel . . . and Waun Ifor. Privately printed. Oxford, 1913.

Royal Commission on the Church . . . in Wales (No. 2937). Minutes of evidence. Book I, pp. 168–73, and 238–48.

**2544.** WILLIAMS, THOMAS OSWALD: Hanes capeli'r enwad [Undodaidd]. *Yr Ymofynnydd*, 1929 a 1930.
A series of articles. Those on the meeting-houses of Cardiganshire have been reprinted under the title: Hanes Cynulleidfaol Undodaidd sir Aberteifi. Llandysul, 1930.

**2545.** Id.    Cae'ronnen (Cellan, Ceredigion): tri chan mlwyddiant, 1654–1747 – 1846–1954. Lampeter, 1954.

### (c) Methodism (Calvinistic)

See *Cylchgrawn Cymdeithas Hanes Methodistiaid Calfinaidd Cymru* (No. 325).

### (i) General

**2546.** BENNETT, RICHARD: Blynyddoedd cyntaf Methodistiaeth. Caernarfon, 1909.

**2547.** Id.    Methodistiaeth Trefaldwyn Uchaf, 1738–52. Y Bala, 1929.

**2548.** Id.    Yr hen gymdeithasfaoedd. *Cylch. Cymd. Hanes M.C.*, xvi, 1, 1931.

**2549.** Id.    Methodistiaeth foreol dwyrain Dinbych. Ibid., xxv, 4, 1940.

**2550.** BEYNON, TOM: Morgan Rhys a chylch Cilycwm hyd at Ystrad Ffin. Ibid., xx, 4, 1935.

**2551.** Id.    Cylch a chefndir sasiwn Dugoedydd, 1742. Ibid., xxvii, 3, 1942.

**2552.** CENNICK, JOHN (1718–1755): Letters (copied by Gomer Morgan Roberts). Ibid., xl, 3, 1955.

**2553.** CHARLES, THOMAS: Ymddiddanion rhwng 'Scrutator' a 'Senex'. *Trysorfa Ysprydol,* 1813; reprint, Machynlleth, 1885.

**2554.** DAVIES, JOHN HUMPHREYS (and DAVIES, DANIEL): Local histories of Welsh Methodism. *Cylch. Cymd. Hanes M.C.*, ii, 1, 1916 (pp. 26–9); ii, 3, 1917 (pp. 87–90); iii, 1, 1918 (pp. 21–3).

**2555.** EVANS, BERIAH GWYNFE: Diwygwyr Cymru. Caernarfon, 1900.
> Highly controversial; called forth a number of replies and rejoinders of which No. 2232 is the most important.

**2556.** GRIFFITH, WILLIAM: Methodistiaeth Môn, 1740–1751. Caernarfon, 1955.

**2557.** Id.    John Griffith Ellis (1723–1805), Llŷn. 'Cynghorwr pennaf Llŷn'. Pennod yn hanes Methodistiaeth fore Llŷn. Caernarfon, 1957.

**2558.** HUGHES, GARFIELD HOPKIN: Herbert Jenkins. *Cylch. Cymd. Hanes M.C.*, xxxii, 1, 1947.

**2559.** Id.    Thomas Dafydd, un o emynwyr sir Gaerfyrddin. *Jnl. Welsh Bibl. Soc.*, vii, 2, 1951.

HUGHES, JOHN: Methodistiaeth Cymru (No. 171).

**2560.** JENKINS, DAVID ERWYD: Calvinistic Methodist Holy Orders. Caernarvon, 1911.

**2561.** JENKINS, ROBERT THOMAS: Methodistiaeth ym mhapurau Thomas Morgan, Henllan. *Cylch. Cymd. Hanes M.C.*, xvii, 3, 1932.

**2562.** JONES, ELIAS PERCIVAL: Methodistiaeth Calfinaidd Dinbych, 1735–1909. Dinbych, 1936.

**2563.** JONES, JOHN MORGAN, and MORGAN, W.: Y Tadau Methodistaidd. 2 vols. Abertawe, 1895.

**2564.** JONES, MORGAN HUGH, DAVIES, JOHN HUMPHREYS, and BENNETT. RICHARD (eds): A bibliography of Welsh Calvinistic Methodism. *Cylch, Cymd. Hanes M.C.*, ii, 1, 1916, and iii, 1, 1918.
    Mainly concerned with Howell Harris.

**2565.** JONES, MORGAN HUGH: Bibliographies of early Welsh Methodism. Ibid., v, 1 and 3, 1920; x, 2, 1925.

**2566.** Id.    The Trevecka letters. Caernarvon, 1932.

JONES, ROBERT (Rhos-lan): Gwaith Robert Jones, Rhos Lan. (No. 2323).

**2567.** JONES, THOMAS (of Creaton): Drws yr eglwys weledig. Caerlleon, 1799.

**2568.** Id.    The Welsh looking-glass. London, 1812.
    See also OWEN, JOHN: The renown of the Rev. Thomas Jones of Creaton. London, 1851.

**2569.** LLOYD, DAVID MYRDDIN: Nathaniel Rowland and the Tabernacle, Haverfordwest. *Cylch. Cymd. Hanes M.C.*, xxxvi, 2, 1951.

**2570.** MORGAN, JAMES HUBERT: Edward Charles (Siamas Wynedd). *Y Llenor*, x, 1931.

**2571.** OWEN, ALUN WYN: Thomas Roberts (1753–1804). *Cylch. Cymd. Hanes M.C.*, xli, 1, 1956.

**2572.** OWEN, BOB: Y Methodistiaid Calfinaidd yn esgobaeth Llanelwy yn ôl atebion ymweliadau yr esgob am 1745, 1749, a 1753 (copïwyd gan Bob Owen). Ibid., xxxi, 1, 1946.

**2573.** OWEN, J.: Golygiad ar adfywiad crefydd yn yr Eglwys Sefydledig, etc. Aberystwyth, 1818.

**2574.** PRICE, WATKIN WILLIAM: The diary of William Thomas (1762– 1795). *Cylch. Cymd. Hanes M.C.*, xxxiv, 2, 1949.
    See also ROBERTS, GOMER MORGAN: Extracts from William Thomas's diaries, 1762–94. Ibid., xxxv, 3, 1950.

**2575.** RICHARDS, THOMAS (ed.): Er clod: saith bennod ar hanes Methodistiaeth yng Nghymru. Wrecsam, 1934.

**2576.** ROBERTS, GOMER MORGAN: Methodistiaeth fy mro, sef ymchwil i ddechreuad Methodistiaeth yn nwyrain Myrddin. Treforus, 1938.

**2577.** Id.     Y tair sasiwn gyntaf, 1742—Dugoedydd, Llwynyberllan, a Glanyrafonddu Ganol. *Cylch. Cymd. Hanes M.C.*, xxvi, 4, 1941.

**2578.** Id.     John Richard, Llansamlet. Ibid., xxvii, 4, 1942.

**2579.** Id.     Pennod yn hanes Richard Tibbott. Ibid., xxxiv, 3, 1949.

**2580.** Id.     Llyfrau o waith awduron Methodistaidd, 1739–53. Ibid., xxxviii, 1, 1953.

**2581.** Id.     (ed.): Visitation returns: Glamorgan, 1774–1788, ibid., xl, 2 and 3, 1955; xli, 3, 1956; Monmouth, 1763–1788, ibid., xli, 3, 1956; xlii, 3, 1957; St. David's, 1755–1799, ibid., xliii, 1, 2, and 3, 1958.

**2582.** Id.     Methodism in Gower. *Gower*, x, 1957.

**2583.** Id.     Nodiadau ar David Jones, Llan-gan. *Cylch. Cymd. Hanes M.C.*, xliii, 1, 1958.

**2584.** ROBERTS, GRIFFITH THOMAS: Nodiadau ar Fethodistiaeth Llŷn. Ibid., xxxiv, 1, 1949.

ROBERTS, JOHN: Methodistiaeth Galfinaidd Cymru (No. 181).

**2585.** ROWLAND, NATHANAEL: Journal of the Welsh Association. *Cylch. Cymd. Hanes M.C.*, xi, 2, 1926.

**2586.** WILLIAMS, D. D.: Llawlyfr hanes Cyfundeb y Methodistiaid Calfinaidd. Caernarfon [1927].

**2587.** WILLIAMS, W. GILBERT: Dechreuad a chynnydd Methodistiaeth yn sir Gaernarfon. *Cylch. Cymd. Hanes M.C.*, xxxvii, 3, 1952.

**2588.** WYNNE, ERNEST E.: Methodistiaeth gynnar y goror. Ibid., xlii, 3, 1957; xliii, 1, 2, 1958.

### (ii) Leading personalities

**Thomas Charles**

**2589.** GRIFFITH, DOROTHI MARY: Nationality in the Sunday school movement. Bangor, 1925.

**2590.** JENKINS, DAVID ERWYD: Life of the Rev. Thomas Charles of Bala. 3 vols. Denbigh, 1908.

The work is so full as to make reference to earlier biographies unnecessary. For a list of these, and of Charles's own writings, consult the bibliography at the end of vol. iii, or the Cardiff Welsh Library catalogue (No. 4), pp. 107–8.

For the Separation of 1811, the 'Methodist controversy' during the French revolution, and the Sunday schools, see section K below.

**2591.** JONES, E. G.: Un o ysgolfeistri Thomas Charles [Lewis Wiliams]. *Y Traethodydd*, 1936.

**2592.** ROBERTS, GOMER MORGAN: Thomas Charles of Bala: two new letters. *Cylch. Cymd. Hanes M.C.*, xxxiv, 2, 1949.

**Howell Davies**

**2593.** BENNETT, RICHARD: Howell Davies. *Cylch. Cymd. Hanes M.C.*, iii, 4, 1918.

>   Extracts from Howell Harris's diaries relating to Howell Davies.

**2594.** EVANS, EIFION: Letter from Howell Davies to Howell Harris. *Ibid.*, xlii, 2, 1957.

**2595.** MORGAN, WALTER THOMAS: A note on Howell Davies. *Ibid.*, xxxii, 4, 1947.

**2596.** ROBERTS, GOMER MORGAN: Nodyn am Howell Davies. *Ibid.*, xxxii, 1, 1947.

**2597.** WATSON, W. T.: Rev. Howell Davies, Woodstock. *Ibid.*, xx, 2, 1935.

**Howell Harris**

The literature on Howell Harris is voluminous. Much of the basic material has been published in *Cylchgrawn Cymdeithas Hanes Methodistiaid Calfinaidd Cymru* (No. 325). The following is a classified description of this and other material relating to him.

Bibliography:

**2598.** BENNETT, RICHARD: Harrisiana—a bibliography. *Cylch. Cymd. Hanes M.C.*, i, 1 and 2, 1916; ii, 1 and 2, 1917; iii, 1 and 4, 1918; collected and revised in xiii, 2, 1928.

Biographies, family, etc.:

**2599.** HUGHES, H. J.: The life of Howell Harris. Newport, 1892.

**2600.** JONES, MORGAN HUGH: Descendants of Joseph Thomas and Howell Harris, of Trevecka. *Cylch. Cymd. Hanes M.C.*, x, 2, 1925.

**2601.** Id.       Joseph Harris, Trevecka. *Ibid.*, xiii, 3, 1928.

**2602.** MORGAN, E.: Life and times of Howell Harris. Holywell, 1852.

>   For the earliest 'Lives' consult the bibliography (No. 2598 above) or the Cardiff Welsh Library catalogue (No. 4).

**2603.** OWEN, ALUN WYN: Howell Harris's children. *Cylch. Cymd. Hanes M.C.*, xli, 1, 1956.

**2604.** ROBERTS, GOMER MORGAN: Howell Harris's will. Ibid.

**2605.** ROBERTS, GRIFFITH THOMAS: Howell Harris. London, 1951.

Diaries:
**2606.** DAVIES, KATHERINE MONICA: A list of diaries and manuscripts of Howell Harris. *Cylch. Cymd. Hanes M.C.,* xxvii, 2, 1942.

**2607.** JENKINS, DAVID ERWYD, and JONES, MORGAN HUGH (eds): The Latin diaries of Howell Harris. Ibid., ii, 4, 1917.

Itineraries:
**2608.** JONES, MORGAN HUGH: The itinerary of Howell Harris. Ibid., viii, 3, 1923; x, 3, 1925; xii, 4, 1927.
> See also ibid., xxix, 1, 1944 (Birmingham); *Bathafarn,* ix, 1954 (Bristol); *Cylch. Cymd. Hanes M.C.,* xxxiv, 2 and 3, 1949; xxxvi, 1 and 2, 1951; xxxvii, 2, 1952; xxxviii, 1 and 3, 1953; xxxix, 1, 2, and 3, 1954; xli, 2 and 3, 1956 (Builth); ibid., xxix, 3 and 4, 1944; xxx, 2 and 4, 1945; xxxi, 1, 2, 3, and 4, 1946; xxxii, 1, 2, 3, and 4, 1947 (Cardiganshire); ibid., xxvi, 1, 2, 3, and 4, 1941; xxvii, 1 and 3, 1942; xxviii, 4, 1943 (Carmarthenshire); ibid., xxiv, 3 and 4, 1939; xxv, 1 and 4, 1940 (Kidwelly and district); ibid., xxvii, 4, 1942 (Llansamlet and district); ibid., xxxiii, 1, 1948; *Bathafarn,* iv, 1949, and x, 1955 (London); *Cylch. Cymd. Hanes M.C.,* xxv, 2, 1940; xxvi, 2, 1941; xxx, 3, 1945; xxxi, 1, 2, 3, and 4, 1946; xxxii, 1, 2, and 3, 1947; xxxiii, 2 and 3, 1948; xxxiv, 2, 1949; xxxv, 1, 1950 (North Wales).

**2609.** THICKENS, JOHN: Howel Harris yn Llundain: neu gyfraniad Cymru i'r mudiad Methodistaidd yn y brifddinas. Cyf. i, 1739–40. Caernarfon, 1938.

Letters:
**2610.** DAVIES, JOHN HUMPHREYS, BENNETT, RICHARD, JENKINS, DAVID ERWYD, and JONES, MORGAN HUGH (eds): The Trevecka letters. *Cylch. Cymd. Hanes M.C.,* ii, 4, 1917; iii, 3, 1918; v, 2, 1920; vi, 1, 1921; ix, 2, 1924; xi, 3, 1926.
> See also (by various editors): ibid., xv, 3, 1930; xix, 1 and 3, 1934; xx, 3, 1935; xxi, 3, 1936; xxii, 2, 1937; xxiii, 2, 1938; xxiv, 2, 1939; xxix, 1, 2, and 4, 1944; xxx, 1, 1945; 2 and 4, 1946; xxxii, 1, 2, and 3, 1947; xxxv, 2, 1950; xxxvii, 1, 1952; xxxviii, 2, 1953; xl, 1, 1955; xlii, 1 and 3, 1957.

**2611.** ROBERTS, GOMER MORGAN (ed.): Selected Trevecka letters (1742–1747). Caernarvon. 1956.
> Review by R. T. Jenkins in *Cylch. Cymd. Hanes M.C.,* xlii, 2, 1957.

**2612.** Id.    Gleanings from the Trevecka letters. *Brycheiniog,* ii and iii, 1956 and 1957.

Id.    Annibynwyr a llythyrau Trefeca (No. 2504).

The Trevecka community and allied matters:
**2613.** BEYNON, TOM: Howell Harris, Trefecca, ac eglwys Talgarth. *Cylch. Cymd. Hanes M.C.,* xx, 1, 1935.

**2614.** DAVIES, KATHERINE MONICA: Lady Huntingdon a Threfecca. *Cylch. Cymd. Hanes M.C.*, xxvii, 2, 1942.

**2615.** Id.      Yr Arglwyddes Huntingdon. *Y Traethodydd*, xii, 1943.

**2616.** JENKINS, ROBERT THOMAS: Bryste a Threfecca. *Y Llenor*, xiv, 1935.

**2617.** JONES, MORGAN HUGH: Howell Harris, citizen and patriot. *Trans. Cymmr.*, 1908–9.

**2618.** Id.      Talgarth parish registers and the Trevecka family. *Cylch. Cymd. Hanes M.C.*, ix, 3, 1924.

**2619.** Id.      Sir Ddinbych a theulu Trefecca. Ibid., x, 1, 1925.

**2620.** Id.      Hen deulu Trefecca. Ibid., x, 2, 1925.

**2621.** OWEN, JOHN: Howell Harris fel trefnydd. Ibid., xx, 1, 1935.

**2622.** ROBERTS, H. P.: Prif gymeriadau Trefecca. *Y Traethodydd*, xxiii, 1935.

**2623.** THICKENS, JOHN: An association of Harris' people at Trevecka, October 2–4, 1751. *Cylch. Cymd. Hanes M.C.*, xxv, 3, 1940.

Miscellaneous:

JENKINS, ROBERT THOMAS: Yr Annibynwyr Cymreig a Hywel Harris (No. 2488).

**2624.** Sail, dibenion, a rheolau'r societies, etc. Bristol, 1742; reprinted in No. 2629.

### Griffith Jones

**2625.** JONES, MORGAN HUGH: Griffith Jones, Llanddowror, a'r Methodistiaid. *Cylch. Cymd. Hanes M.C.*, vi, 2, 1921, and ix, 3, 1924.

See also Nos. 2442–570.

### Daniel Rowland

**2626.** DAVIES, JOHN HUMPHREYS: A side-light on the history of Daniel Rowland. Ibid., i, 1, 1916.

**2627.** Id.      Daniel Rowland: contemporary descriptions (1746 and 1835); ibid., i, 2, 1916.

**2628.** Id.      Pregeth Daniel Rowland yn Llangeitho. Ibid., ii, 1, 1916.

**2629.** DAVIES, MORRIS: Cofiant a gweithiau Daniel Rowland. Bangor, 1876.

Includes the rules of the societies and the pamphlet against Howell Harris's theological views.

**2630.** HUGHES, D. R.: Pa le yr ordeiniwyd Daniel Rowland? *Cylch. Cymd. Hanes M.C.*, xxxv, 4, 1950.

**2631.** JONES, DAVID JOHN ODWYN: Daniel Rowland, Llangeitho. Llandysul, 1938.

**2632.** JONES, MORGAN HUGH: Daniel Rowland of Llangeitho: the sources and literature for the study of his life and work. *Cylch. Cymd. Hanes M.C.*, xii, 2, 1927.

> See also id.: Supplement to the Daniel Rowland bibliography. Ibid., xii, 3, 1927.

**2633.** OWEN, BOB: Daniel Rowland yn Llŷn. Ibid., xli, 3, 1956.

**2634.** OWEN, J.: Coffhad am Daniel Rowlands, etc. Chester, 1839; revised edn, 1844 [and in English: Memoir of Daniel Rowlands, etc., London, 1840; revised edn, 1848].

**2635.** ROBERTS, GOMER MORGAN: Daniel Rowland's ordination, etc. *Cylch. Cymd. Hanes M.C.*, xx, 4, 1935.

**2636.** Id.    Daniel Rowland and the living of Trefdraeth. Ibid., xxix, 1, 1944.

**2637.** WORTHINGTON, D.: Cofiant . . . Daniel Rowland. Caerfyrddin, 1905.

> See also footnote on Llangeitho by A. W. Wade-Evans in his edition of Browne Willis's Parochiale Wallicanum (No. 2441).

**George Whitefield**

**2638.** JONES, MORGAN HUGH: George Whitefield yn ei berthynas â Methodistiaeth Cymru. Ibid., v, 1, 1920.

**2639.** Id.    Y flwyddyn 1751 fel trobwynt yn hanes Methodistiaeth. Ibid., x, 1, 1925.

**Peter Williams**

For bibliography see the Cardiff Welsh Library catalogue (No. 4), pp. 523–4.

**2640.** DAVIES, JOHN HUMPHREYS: Peter Williams of Carmarthen. *Cylch. Cymd. Hanes M.C.*, vi, 3, 1921.

**2641.** JENKINS, JOHN (GWILI) (gol.): 'Dialogous [*sic*] neu ymddiddan rhwng Philalethes ac Eusebes, etc.' 1791. *Traf. Cymd. Hanes Bed.*, 1920–1.

> A reprint with introductory note. Ascribed by some (wrongly) to William Williams, by others to Morgan John Rhys or Nathaniel Williams.

**2642.** Id.    Heresi Peter Williams. *Y Geninen*, 1922 a 1923.

**2643.** JENKINS, ROBERT THOMAS: Diarddeliad Peter Williams. *Y Traethodydd*, 1944.

**2644.** ROBERTS, GOMER MORGAN: Bywyd a gwaith Peter Williams. Caerdydd, 1943.

**2645.** Id.    Llythyr oddi wrth Peter Williams at wasg Trefecca. *Cylch. Cymd. Hanes M.C.*, xxx, 4, 1945.

**2646.** WILLIAMS, PETER: Life. Written by himself. Printed in Eliezer Williams's English works. London, 1840.

**2647.** Id.    Cofiant . . . allan o'i ysgrifenlaw ef ei hun, wedi ei gasglu a'i gyfieithu gan Owen Williams. Caernarfon, 1817.

**William Williams, Pantycelyn**

**2648.** DAVIES, JOHN HUMPHREYS: The printed works of Williams, Pantycelyn. *Cylch. Cymd. Hanes M.C.*, iii, 2, 1917.

**2649.** Id.    Rhestr o lyfrau . . . William Williams. *Jnl. Welsh Bibl. Soc.*, 1918.

**2650.** JONES, J. T. ALUN: Llawysgrifau Williams Pantycelyn yn athrofa'r Bala. *Cylch. Cymd. Hanes M.C.*, iii, 2, 1917.

**2651.** JONES, LLEWELYN (gol.): Aleluia gan y Parch. William Williams, Pant y Celyn: argraffiad diplomatig o'r rhannau I–VI. Lerpwl, 1926.

**2652.** JONES, MORGAN HUGH: William Williams, Pantycelyn: y prif ffeithiau a dyddiadau yn hanes ei fywyd. *Cylch. Cymd. Hanes M.C.*, iii, 2, 1917.
> An outline of his life with valuable bibliography and extracts from original sources.

**2653.** JONES, THOMAS GWYNN: Williams Pantycelyn. *Y Traethodydd*, 1929 a 1930.

**2654.** ROBERTS, GOMER MORGAN: Gwerth hanesyddol rhai o farwnadau Williams Pantycelyn. *Cylch. Cymd. Hanes M.C.*, xix, 2, 1934.

**2655.** Id.    Y pêr ganiedydd (Pantycelyn). Cyf. i. Aberystwyth, 1949; cyf. ii, Aberystwyth, 1958.

**2656.** WILLIAMS, JOHN (ed.): Gwaith prydyddawl William Williams. Caerfyrddin, 1811.
> On John Williams (W.W.'s son) see DAVIES, MAURICE: Coffadwriaeth . . . John Williams o Bantycelyn. Pontypwl, 1830.

**2657.** WILLIAMS, WILLIAM: Gweithiau. Standard edn, ed. Cynhafal Jones. 2 vols. Vol. i, Holywell, 1887; vol. ii, Newport, 1891. (Older edn, ed. J. R. Kilsby Jones. Glasgow, 1867.)
> The Cardiff Welsh Library catalogue (No. 4), pp. 531 *seq.*, contains a fairly complete list of the *Gweithiau*.

### (iii) Miscellaneous

**Methodist meeting-houses: early registrations**

**2658.** Aberthin (Glamorgan). *Cylch. Cymd. Hanes M.C.*, v, 3, 1920, pp. 34–6.

**2659.** Melin y Coed (near Llanrwst). Ibid., iv, 1, 1918, pp. 26–7.

**2660.** Tŷ Round, Rock, Mon. Ibid., iv, 3, 1919.
    See also JENKINS, DAVID ERWYD: Life of the Rev. Thomas Charles of Bala
    (No. 2590) and id.: Calvinistic Methodist Holy Orders (No. 2560).

### Welsh Methodists and the Moravians
**2661.** DAVIES, IDRIS: William Seward, confessor. *Cylch. Cymd. Hanes M.C.,* xxv, 3, 1940.

**2662.** GRIFFITH, ELNITH R.: Moravians and Methodists. A sidelight on their early relations. Ibid., xvi, 3, 1931.

**2663.** Id.     A Moravian diary. Ibid., xvi, 4, 1931.

**2664.** Id.     William Holland's journey through South Wales in 1746. Ibid., xvii, 1, 1932.

**2665.** JENKINS, ROBERT THOMAS: La Trobe yn neheudir Cymru (1775). In Er Clod (No. 2575).

**2666.** Id.     Dyddiau Methodistaidd Francis Pugh. *Y Traethodydd,* 1936.

**2667.** Id.     The Moravian brethren in Carmarthenshire. *Cylch. Cymd. Hanes M.C.,* xxi, 2, 1936.

**2668.** Id.     The Moravian brethren in North Wales. *Y Cymmr.,* xlv, 1938.

**2669.** JONES, DAVID JOHN ODWYN: References to Methodism in the Moravian diaries, Haverfordwest. *Cylch. Cymd. Hanes M.C.,* xxxix, 2, 1954; xl, 2, 1955.

**2670.** JONES, MORGAN HUGH: The Moravians and the Methodists. Ibid., iv, 1 and 2, 1918–19; v, 1, 1920.

**2671.** ROBERTS, GRIFFITH THOMAS: Morafiaeth ym Môn. *Cylch. Cymd. Hanes M.C.,* xxxii, 2, 1947.

**2672.** ROBERTS, GOMER MORGAN: Gleanings from the Moravian records, Haverfordwest. Ibid., xxxvii, 3, 1952.

**2673.** Id.     The Moravians and John Relly and his people. Ibid., xxxviii, 1, 1953.

### The Welsh Sandemanians
**2674.** DAVIES, THOMAS WITTON: The McLeanite (Scotch) and Cambellite Baptists in Wales. *Trans. Bapt. Hist. Soc.* (of England), 1921.

    JONES, ROBERT (Rhos-lan): Gwaith Robert Jones, Rhos Lan
    (No. 2323).

**2675.** LEWIS, TITUS: Hanes Prydain Fawr. Caerfyrddin, 1810.

**2676.** ROBERTS, GOMER MORGAN: Nodiadau ar John Popkin. *Cylch. Cymd. Hanes M.C.*, xxxix, 2 and 3, 1954.

**2677.** WILLIAMS, DAVID: Cofiant J. R. Jones o Ramoth. Caerfyrddin, 1913.

### Early Anti-Methodist Literature

**2678.** ANON.: Llenyddiaeth wrth-Fethodistaidd a dadleuol. *Cylch. Cymd. Hanes M.C.*, v, 3, 1920.

> A short (unfinished) bibliography. See also DAVIES, JOHN HUMPHREYS: Bibliography of Welsh ballads (No. 2308), introduction, p. xv.

**2679.** EVANS, THEOPHILUS: Llythyr addysg esgob Llundain . . . yn erbyn clairwch . . . a sel danbaid, etc. Gloucester, 1740.

**2680.** Id.     A history of modern enthusiasm. London, 1752.

> On this see JENKINS, ROBERT THOMAS, in Yr apêl at hanes (No. 141).

**2681.** HUMPHREY, R.: Cân ynghylch y Methodistiaid. No imprint. 1747.

**2682.** JONES, RHYS (o'r Blaenau): Fflangell ysgorpionog i'r Methodistiaid.

> [In JONES, HUGH: Dewisol ganiadau. Shrewsbury, 1759, and later edns]; reprint in *Cymru*, 1906.

**2683.** ROBERTS, W. (Llannor): Ffrewyll y Methodistiaid. Shrewsbury, 1745.

> See also extracts by Bob Owen in *Y Genedl Gymreig*, October 6, 1930.

**2684.** 'SOPHRONIKOS': A shock to enthusiasm. London, 1775.

### (d) Methodism (Wesleyan)

**2685.** BEYNON, TOM (ed.): Howell Harris meets Charles Wesley, November, 1740. *Bathafarn*, iv, 1949.

> Extracts from the diaries of Howell Harris.

**2686.** Id.     (ed.): Howell Harris meets John Wesley at Cardiff. Ibid., vi, 1951.

> Extracts from the diaries.

**2687.** BRYAN, JOHN: The journal of the Revd. Mr. Bryan. Ed. A. H. Williams. Ibid., ix, 1954.

**2688.** HUMPHREYS, T. J.: Hanes Methodistiaeth Wesleyaidd yng Nghymru. Treffynnon, 1900.

**2689.** JENKINS, ROBERT THOMAS: John Wesley in North Wales. *Bathafarn*, ii, 1947.

2690. Id.      John Hughes o Aberhonddu. Ibid., 5, 1950.

JONES, HUGH: Hanes Wesleyaeth yng Nghymru (No. 175).

2691. MEYLER, L. J.: Wesley in Pembrokeshire. *Procs. Wesley Hist. Soc.*, xxi, 8, 1939.

2692. MORGAN, E. ATHAN: The Wesleys and Fonmon castle, Glamorgan. *Bathafarn*, ix, 1954.

2693. RICHARDS, THOMAS: Llawysgrifau Coleg y Gogledd. 2727–2852, 4193–4209: Papurau W. H. Evans (Gwyllt y Mynydd). Ibid., i, 1946.
>    Sources of Welsh Wesleyan Methodist history in the library of the University College of North Wales, Bangor.

2694. ROBERTS, GRIFFITH THOMAS: Wesley a Harris. *Cylch. Cymd. Hanes M.C.*, xxx, 3 and 4, 1945.
>    See also WILLIAMS, ALBERT HUGHES: Wesley a Harris. In Er Clod (No. 2575).

2695. Id.      The Wesleys and Anglesey Methodism. *Procs. Wesley Hist. Soc.*, xxiv, 8, 1944; xxv, 1 and 2, 1945.

2696. Id.      Seiadau cynnar John Wesley yng Nghymru. *Bathafarn*, i, 1946.

2697. Id.      The Wesleys and Sir John Philipps of Picton castle. Ibid.

2698. Id.      Wesley's first society in Wales. *Procs. Wesley Hist. Soc.*, xxvii, 5 and 6, 1950.

2699. THICKENS, JOHN: Henry Lloyd, Rudri. *Cylch. Cymd. Hanes M.C.*, xxix, 3, 1944.

2700. WILLIAMS, ALBERT HUGHES: Dr. Coke and the beginnings of Welsh Wesleyan Methodism. *Procs. Wesley Hist. Soc.*, xviii, 3, 4, and 5, 1931–2.

2701. Id.      Welsh Wesleyan Methodism, 1800–1858. Bangor, 1935.

2702. Id.      Defnyddiau crai yr Eglwys Fethodistaidd yng Nghymru. *Bathafarn*, i, 1946.

2703. Id.      Glimpses of early Methodism in and around Cardiff. Ibid., ix, 1954.

2704. WILLIAMS, DANIEL: Thomas Foulks, 1731–1802. Ibid., iv, 1949.

2705. YOUNG, DAVID: Origin and history of Methodism in Wales, etc. London, 1893.

#### (e) The (Roman) Catholic Church

**2706.** BURTON, EDWIN H.: Life of bishop Challoner. 2 vols. Catholic Truth Society. London, 1909.

**2707.** Id.    and NOLAN, EDMOND (ed.): The Douay College diaries. The seventh diary, 1715–1778. *Cath. Rec. Soc. Pubns.*, 1928.

**2708.** CRONIN, JOHN M.: Various articles on eighteenth-century Welsh Catholicism. *St. Peter's Mag.*, Cardiff.

> The series includes the following: A Glamorgan lady recusant [1726], 1922 (April–May); Fr. John Butler [1760–88], 1923 (p. 229); The last resident missionaries in Glamorgan [down to *circa* 1745], 1924 (p. 194); The itinerant missionaries in Glamorgan [1745–1800], 1924 (p. 228); Return of the Papists in the diocese of St. Davids in 1767, 1924 (p. 338); New light on Catholicism in South Wales in the 18th century, 1925 (p. 170); A forgotten chapter in South Wales Catholic history: (1) secular clergy, 1927 (p. 170), (2) regular clergy (incomplete)—(*a*) Jesuits, 1927 (p. 170) (incomplete), (*b*) Franciscan recollects, 1927 (pp. 227, 258, 290, 322, 354); Catholic Caerleon in the eighteenth century, 1928 (p. 106).

**2709.** 'D.P.': A Welsh prayer book printed 1776. *Y Cennad Catholig*, i, 1911, p. 446.

FOLEY, H.: Records of the English province of the Society of Jesus (No. 1668).

GILLOW, J.: Literary and biographical history . . . of English Catholics (No. 1764).

**2710.** HOOK, PAUL (ed.): Catholic registers of Holywell, Flintshire, 1698–1829. *Cath. Rec. Soc. Pubns.*, iii, 1906.

**2711.** KIRK, J., and GILLOW, J.: Historical account of Lisbon College. Barnet, 1902.

**2712.** KIRK, J., POLLEN, J. H., and BURTON, EDWIN H.: Biographies of English (and Welsh) Catholics in the xviii century. London, 1909.

**2713.** MATTHEWS, JOHN HOBSON (ed.): Catholic mission register of Perthir, 1758–1818. *Cath. Rec. Soc. Pubns.*, 1905.
> See also corrections, ibid., ix, 1911, pp. 161–2.

**2714.** Id.    (ed.): Catholic registers of Llanarth, Monmouthshire, 1773–1832. Ibid., iii, 1906.

Id.    Records relating to Catholicism in the South Wales marches (No. 2187).

**2715.** Id. (ed.): Some records of the Monmouth mission. *Cath. Rec. Soc. Pubns.*, ix, 1911.

**2716.** O'BRIEN, J.: Old Afan and Margam. Aberavon, 1926.

**2717.** OLIVER, G.: Collections illustrating the biography of the Society of Jesus. Exeter, 1838.

See also BRUSHFIELD, T. N.: Bibliography of G. Oliver. Devon Assoc., 1885.

**2718.** THADDEUS, FATHER: Franciscans in England, 1600–1850. London, 1898.

# SECTION K

## A.D. 1789–1914

The background to the history of Wales in the nineteenth century may be studied in the two relevant volumes in the Oxford History of England— WOODWARD, ERNEST LLEWELLYN: The age of reform, Oxford, 1938; and ENSOR, ROBERT CHARLES KIRKWOOD: England, 1870–1914, Oxford, 1936. Both volumes include extensive bibliographies. The appendices to the report of the Royal Commission on land in Wales and Monmouthshire, 1896 (No. 2723) are indispensable for the history of the period.

### I. PERIODICALS AND THE PRESS

The periodicals are an essential source of nineteenth century history in Wales. The Welsh press tends to reflect the opinions of its readers rather than those of its proprietors.

#### (a) Lists of periodicals

**2719.** ASHTON, CHARLES: Hanes llenyddiaeth Gymreig o 1651 hyd 1850. Liverpool [1893].

BALLINGER, JOHN, and JONES, JAMES IFANO (eds): Catalogue of printed literature in the Welsh department of the Cardiff Free Library (No. 4).

**2720.** Cardiff National Eisteddfod, 1883. Transactions.
Lists periodicals down to 1883.

**2721.** EVANS, THOMAS: The background of modern Welsh politics, 1789–1846. Cardiff, 1936.

**2722.** JONES, THOMAS MORRIS: Llenyddiaeth fy ngwlad. Treffynnon, 1893.
See also JENKINS, GWYNETH ELIZABETH: Mynegai i Llenyddiaeth fy ngwlad, 1893. *Jnl. Welsh Bibl. Soc.*, vi, 2, 1944.

**2723.** Royal Commission on land in Wales and Monmouthshire: bibliographical, statistical, and other miscellaneous memoranda, being appendices to the report. London, 1896.
Appendix C (compiled by D. Lleufer Thomas) brings the list down to 1895, has useful extracts from the earlier periodicals, and includes English newspapers printed in Wales and the border counties.

**2724.** *Times, The*: Tercentenary handlist of English and Welsh newspapers, magazines, and reviews. London, 1920.

#### (b) The growth of the press

ASHTON, CHARLES: Hanes llenyddiaeth Gymreig o 1651 hyd 1850 (No. 2719).

**2725.** DAVIES, JOHN ('Gwyneddon'): Llenyddiaeth newyddiadurol Cymru. *Y Traethodydd,* 1884.

**2726.** FOULKES, ISAAC: Llenyddiaeth gyfnodol Gymreig. *Trans. Liverpool Welsh Nat. Soc.,* 1887–8.

**2727.** HUMPHREYS, EDWARD MORGAN: Y wasg Gymreig. Cyfres Pobun, iii. Liverpool, 1945.

JONES, JAMES IFANO: A history of printing and printers in Wales and Monmouthshire (No. 11).

**2728.** JONES, THOMAS GWYNN: Llenyddiaeth Gymraeg yn y xix ganrif. Caernarfon, 1920.

**2729.** RICHARDS, THOMAS: Dinbych a'r wasg Gymraeg. *Trans. Cymmr.,* 1939.

**2730.** Id.    Hen bapurau newydd. *Jnl. Welsh Bibl. Soc.,* v, 1940.

### (c) Individual editors and journalists

**Thomas Gee**
**2731.** JONES, THOMAS GWYNN: Cofiant Thomas Gee. Dinbych, 1913.

**John Griffiths ('Y Gohebydd')**
**2732.** GRIFFITHS, RICHARD: 'Y Gohebydd': cofiant. Dinbych, 1905.

**Joseph Harris ('Gomer')**
**2733.** HARRIS, JOSEPH: Gweithiau. Llanelli, 1839.

**2734.** JENKINS, ROBERT THOMAS: Y papur newydd Cymraeg cyntaf. *Yr Efrydydd,* 1934.

**2735.** *Seren Gomer.* Centenary number. September, 1925.

**2736.** SHANKLAND, THOMAS: Joseph Harris a chychwyniad llenyddiaeth gyfnodol yng Nghymru. *Traf. Cymd. Hanes Bed.,* 1912–13.

**Evan Jones ('Ieuan Gwynedd')**
**2737.** JONES, EVAN: Gweithiau Ieuan Gwynedd. Dolgellau, 1876.

**2738.** REES, BRINLEY (gol.): Ieuan Gwynedd. Detholiad o'i ryddiaith. Caerdydd, 1957.

**2739.** THOMAS, CADWALADR TAWELFRYN: Cofiant Ieuan Gwynedd. Dolgellau, n.d.

**Michael D. Jones**
**2740.** JONES, EVAN PAN: Oes a gwaith Michael Daniel Jones. Y Bala, 1903.

**2741.** JONES, DAVID JAMES GWENALLT: Michael D. Jones. Yn PIERCE, GWYNEDD OWEN (gol.): Triwyr Penllyn. Caerdydd, 1956.

**2742.** PHILLIPS, T. TALWYN: Y Prifathro Michael D. Jones. Y Geninen, xvii, 1899.

### Robert Ambrose Jones ('Emrys ap Iwan')

**2743.** JONES, ROBERT AMBROSE: Detholiad o erthyglau a llythyrau Emrys ap Iwan. Gol. David Myrddin Lloyd. 3 cyf. Aberystwyth, 1937, 1939, 1940.

**2744.** JONES, THOMAS GWYNN: Emrys ap Iwan. Cofiant. Caernarfon, 1912.

### David Owen ('Brutus')

**2745.** 'GLASWYN': Brutus. Red Dragon, iii, 1883.

**2746.** JONES, JAMES RHYS ('Kilsby'): Brutus. Y Traethodydd, 1867.
See also Cymru (ed. Owen Jones), ii. London, 1875.

**2747.** JONES, THOMAS (gol.): Wil Brydydd y Coed. Caerdydd, 1949.

**2748.** Id.      (gol.): Bugeiliaid Epynt. Caerdydd, 1950.

### John Peter ('Ioan Pedr')

**2749.** JENKINS, ROBERT THOMAS: John Peter ('Ioan Pedr'). Jnl. Welsh Bibl. Soc., iv, 4, 1933.

### Thomas Price

**2750.** EVANS, BENJAMIN ('Telynfab'): Bywgraffiad y diweddar T. Price, M.A., PH.D., Aberdâr. Aberdâr, 1891.

### David Rees

**2751.** DAVIES, THOMAS: Bywyd ac ysgrifeniadau D. Rees, Llanelli, 1871.

**2752.** WILLIAMS, GLANMOR (gol.): David Rees, Llanelli; detholion o'i weithiau. Caerdydd, 1950.

### William Rees ('Gwilym Hiraethog')

**2753.** GRIFFITH, DAVID: Y diweddar Barch. William Rees, D.D. Y Traethodydd, 1884.

**2754.** REES, WILLIAM: Rhydd-weithiau. Liverpool, n.d.

**2755.** Id.      Llythyrau 'rhen ffarmwr. Gol. Edward Morgan Humphreys. Caerdydd, 1939.

**2756.** ROBERTS, THOMAS ('Scorpion'), a ROBERTS, DAVID ('Dewi Ogwen'): Cofiant y Parch. W. Rees, D.D. (Gwilym Hiraethog). Dolgellau, n.d.

**2757.** THOMAS, JOHN: Atgofion am y Parch. William Rees. *Y Geninen*, ii, 1884.

#### Henry Richard

**2758.** APPLETON, LEWIS: Memoirs of Henry Richard. London, 1889.

**2759.** MIALL, CHARLES S.: Life of Henry Richard. London, 1889.

**2760.** ROBERTS, ELEAZER: Bywyd Henry Richard. Wrexham, n.d.

#### Samuel Roberts ('S.R.')

**2761.** CHALMERS, LEAH: A forgotten pioneer [Rev. Samuel Roberts, 1800–85]. *Bull. of the Postal History Soc.*, March, 1948.

**2762.** EDWARDS, OWEN MORGAN (gol.): Gwaith Samuel Roberts. *Cyfres y Fil*. Llanuwchllyn, 1906.

**2763.** JONES, EVAN: S.R. *Y Geninen*, ix, 1891, a xv, 1897.

**2764.** JONES, EVAN PAN: Cofiant y tri brawd. Y Bala, 1892.

**2765.** PEATE, IORWERTH CYFEILIOG (gol.): Cilhaul ac ysgrifau eraill. Caerdydd, 1951.

**2766.** ROBERTS, SAMUEL: Gweithiau Samuel Roberts. Dolgellau, 1856.

**2767.** Id.      Helyntion bywyd S.R. . . . ganddo ei hun. Y Bala, 1875.

**2768.** WILLIAMS, GLANMOR: Samuel Roberts, Llanbrynmair. Bilingual. Cardiff, 1950.

#### John Thomas

**2769.** EDWARDS, OWEN MORGAN (gol.): Gwaith John Thomas. *Cyfres y Fil*. Llanuwchllyn, 1905.

**2770.** THOMAS, OWEN, a REES, JOHN MACHRETH: Cofiant John Thomas. London, 1898.

### II. POLITICAL HISTORY

Some of the more important parliamentary papers are listed in FORD, GRACE, and FORD, PERCY: Select list of British parliamentary papers, 1833–1899. Oxford, 1953.

#### (a) General

**2771.** DAVIES, JOHN (Ystradgynlais): Holwyddoreg y caethwas; hefyd twyll arglwydd Tori. Llandilo, 1840.

**2772.** DAVIES, WILLIAM WATKIN: Lloyd George, 1863–1914. London, 1939.

**2773.** ELLIS, THOMAS IORWERTH: Thomas Edward Ellis: cofiant. 2 gyf. Lerpwl, 1944 a 1948.

**2774.** EVANS, HENRY TOBIT: Y berw Gwyddelig. Aberaeron, 1889.

**2775.** EVANS, JOHN: Yr etholiad cyffredinol (1880). *Y Traethodydd*, 1880.

EVANS, THOMAS: The background of modern Welsh politics, 1789–1846 (No. 2721).

**2776.** EVANS, WILLIAM: Trem ar wleidyddiaeth 1868. *Y Traethodydd*, 1869.

**2777.** GEE, THOMAS: Rhyddfrydiaeth a Thoriaeth. Dinbych, 1896.

**2778.** GEORGE, WILLIAM: My brother and I. London, 1958.

**2779.** GRIFFITH, ELLIS JONES: Cymru a'r Iwerddon. *Y Traethodydd*, 1887.

**2780.** GRUFFYDD, WILLIAM JOHN: Owen Morgan Edwards. Cofiant. Cyf. i, 1858–1883. Aberystwyth, 1937.

**2781.** HAMER, FREDERICK EDWARD (ed.): The personal papers of Lord Rendel. London, 1931.

**2782.** HAVARD, GRIFFITH: Yr Iwerddon, sef hanes gwladlywiaeth y Seison yn yr Iwerddon. Rhymney, 1888.

**2783.** HUMPHREYS, EDWARD MORGAN: David Lloyd George. Llyfrau'r Dryw. Llandybie, 1943.

**2784.** JENKINS, ROBERT THOMAS: Hanes Cymru yn y bedwaredd ganrif ar bymtheg. Y gyfrol gyntaf (1789–1843). Caerdydd, 1933.

**2785.** JONES, D. LLOYD (Llandinam): Goleuni ar gyflwr yr Iwerddon. London (1888).

**2786.** JONES, EMYR GWYNNE: Borough politics and electioneering, 1826–1852. *Trans. Caerns. Hist. Soc.*, 1956.

**2787.** JONES, EVAN PAN: Oes gofion. Y Bala, n.d.

**2788.** Id.      Articles in *Cwrs y Byd*. Llandysul and Ystalyfera, 1894–1903.

**2789.** JONES, IEUAN GWYNEDD: Franchise reform and Glamorgan politics, 1832–1868. *Morgannwg*, ii, 1958.

**2790.** JONES, J. (Brymbo): Llawlyfr etholiadaeth Cymru. Llangollen, 1867.

**2791.** JONES, JAMES RHYS ('Kilsby'): Diwygiad seneddol a chyllidol. *Y Traethodydd*, vi, 1850.

**2792.** JONES, THOMAS: Lloyd George. London, 1951.

JONES, THOMAS GWYNN: Cofiant Thomas Gee (No. 2731).

**2793.** LEWIS, THOMAS HARRIS: Y mudiad heddwch yng Nghymru. *Trans. Cymmr.,* 1958.

**2794.** MAINWARING, THOMAS: Glimpses of Welsh politics. Llanelly, 1881.

**2795.** MORGAN, GEORGE OSBORNE: Dwy flynedd ar hugain yn Nhy'r Cyffredin. *Y Traethodydd,* 1891.

**2796.** MORGAN, JOHN VYRNWY: Welsh political and educational leaders of the Victorian era. London, 1908.

**2797.** OWEN, BOB: Cymru a mudiad heddwch 1814–1824. *Y Geninen,* xliii, 1925.

**2798.** PARRY, ROBERT IFOR: Yr Annibynwyr Cymraeg a threth yr ŷd, 1828–45. *Y Cofiadur,* xix, 1949.

**2799.** REES, JAMES FREDERICK: The problem of Wales. *Nineteenth Century and After,* April, 1949.

REES, WILLIAM ('Gwilym Hiraethog'): Rhydd-weithiau (No. 2754).

**2800.** RHONDDA, MARGARET, VISCOUNTESS (ed.): D. A. Thomas, Viscount Rhondda. London, 1921. Ch. vi and vii: Political life, contributed by Llewelyn Williams.

**2801.** RICHARD, EDWARD W.: Deddfau yr ŷd, a'r cynghrair i'w diddymu. *Y Traethodydd,* 1847.

**2802.** RICHARDS, ROBERT J.: Y Ceidwadwyr a'r Rhyddfrydwyr. Ibid., 1865.

ROBERTS, GLYN: Political affairs [in Carmarthenshire] from 1536 to 1900 (No. 1648).

**2803.** ROWLANDS, WILLIAM: Yr eglwys sefydledig yn Iwerddon. *Y Traethodydd,* 1851.

**2804.** SEYMOUR, CHARLES: Electoral reform in England and Wales, 1832–97. London, 1928.

**2805.** THOMAS, BEN BOWEN: Agwedd ar wleidyddiaeth Cymru. *Y Llenor,* xxii, 1943.

### (b) Local government

For the general background, see KEITH LUCAS, BRYAN: The English local government franchise, Oxford, 1952; REDLICH, JOSEPH, and HURST, F.:

Local government in England, 2 vols., London, 1903; WEBB, SIDNEY, and
WEBB, BEATRICE: English local government: the parish and the county,
London, 1907; id.: The manor and the borough. 2 vols., London, 1908.

**2806.** CHAPPELL, EDGAR LEYSHON: Llywodraeth leol: ei dyfodol yng
Nghymru. Lerpwl, 1945.
> Ch. ii is historical.

**2807.** County Councils, Jubilee of, 1889–1939. Fifty years of local
government: Anglesey, Caernarvonshire, Flintshire, Glamorgan, Merioneth,
Montgomeryshire, Pembrokeshire. 7 vols. County Councils Association.
London, 1939.

**2808.** DAVIES, CHRIS: The chartered borough. In A history of Wrexham
(No. 626).

**2809.** HOGG, THOMAS JEFFERSON: Reports upon certain boroughs
. . . London, 1837–8.

**2810.** HUMPHREYS-OWEN, ARTHUR CHARLES: Y cynghorau sirol.
*Y Traethodydd*, 1889.

**2811.** JONES, R. W.: History of the Pembrokeshire police force.
Caernarvon, 1957.

JONES, THOMAS IEUAN JEFFREYS: The court leet presentments
of . . . St. Clears, 1719–1889 (No. 2279).

**2812.** Id.     Parochial     administration     in     Carmarthenshire.     *Trans.
Cymmr.*, 1952.

**2813.** LERRY, GEORGE GEOFFREY: The policemen of Denbighshire.
*Trans. Denbs. Hist. Soc.*, ii, 1953.

MORGAN, WALTER THOMAS: County elections in Monmouthshire, 1705–1847 (No. 2283).

**2814.** OWEN, HUGH: The history of the Anglesey constabulary. Bangor,
1952.

OWEN, HUGH JOHN: The common gaols of Merioneth during
the eighteenth and nineteenth centuries (No. 2288).

RANDALL, HENRY JOHN: Bridgend: the story of a market town
(No. 695).

**2815.** Reports of the Royal Commission on the proposed division of
counties and the boundaries of boroughs. London, 1832.

**2816.** Reports of the Royal Commission on municipal corporations in
England and Wales. London, 1835.

**2817.** Reports of the Royal Commission on municipal corporations boundaries. London, 1837.

**2818.** Report of the Royal Commission on the establishment of a constabulary force in the counties of England and Wales. London, 1839.

**2819.** Report of the Royal Commission into municipal corporations not subject to the Municipal Corporations Act. London, 1880.

ROBERTS, GLYN: The municipal development of the borough of Swansea (No. 701).

**2820.** THOMAS, JOHN GARETH: Local government areas in Wales. *Geography*, xxxvii, 1952.

**2821.** WILLIAMS, MRS. A. BAILEY: Local government in Llanymynech in the nineteenth century. *Mont. Coll.*, liii, 1953.

**2822.** WILLIAMS, DAVID: The borough of Kidwelly in the nineteenth century. *B.B.C.S.*, xvi, 1954–6.

### (c) The French revolution and Wales

For bibliographies of contemporary texts, see Nos. 2824 and 2826 below. The following have been reissued since these works were published: ROBERTS, THOMAS (Llwynrhudol): Cwyn yn erbyn gorthrymder, Caerdydd, 1928; JONES, JOHN ('Jac Glan-y-gors'): Seren tan gwmwl, Lerpwl, 1923; JONES, THOMAS (Dinbych): Gair yn ei amser. *Trans. Denbs. Hist. Soc.*, vi, 1956.

**2823.** DAVIES, ALUN: La révolution Française et le pays de Galles. *Annales Historiques de la Révolution Française*, xxvii, July–Sept., 1955.

**2824.** DAVIES, DAVID: The influence of the French revolution on Welsh life and literature. Carmarthen, 1926.

**2825.** DAVIES, WILLIAM LLEWELYN: David Samwell. *Trans. Cymmr.*, 1926–7.

EVANS, BENJAMIN ('Telynfab'): Bywgraffiad y diweddar T. Price (No. 2750).

**2826.** EVANS, JOHN JAMES: Dylanwad y chwyldro Ffrengig ar lenyddiaeth Cymru. Lerpwl, 1928.

JENKINS, ROBERT THOMAS: Political propaganda in West Wales in 1793 (No. 2277).

**2827.** SALMON, DAVID: The descent of the French on Pembrokeshire. Carmarthen, 1930.

THOMAS, ROLAND: Richard Price (No. 2301).

See also CONE, CARL B.: Torchbearer of freedom: the influence of Richard
Price on eighteenth century thought (No. 2271).

STUART-JONES, EDWYN HENRY: The last invasion of Britain
(No. 2298).

**2828.** WILLIAMS, DAVID: The David Williams manuscripts. *N.L.W.
Jnl.*, vii, 1951–2.

**2829.** Id.    A bibliography of the printed works of David Williams
(1738–1816). Ibid., x, 1957–8.

See also id.: The mission of David Williams and James Tilly Matthews to
England, 1793. *E.H.R.*, liii, 1938.

### (d) Religion and politics

### (i) The theological background

**2830.** EDWARDS, THOMAS CHARLES: Bywyd a llythyrau Lewis Edwards.
Liverpool, 1901.

Editor and founder of *Y Traethodydd*, of which the earlier volumes are
important.

JENKINS, DAVID ERWYD: Life of the Rev. Thomas Charles
of Bala (No. 2590).

**2831.** Id.    John Elias a gwleidyddiaeth y cyfundeb. *Y Traethodydd,*
1937.

**2832.** JONES, IDWAL (ed.): Hunangofiant y Parch. Thomas Jones . . .
o dref Dinbych. Aberystwyth, 1937.

See also HUMPHREYS, JOHN, and HUMPHREYS, ROBERT: Cofiant Thomas
Jones, Dinbigh, Denbigh, 1820; JONES, FRANK PRICE: Thomas Jones o
Ddinbych, 1756–1820, Dinbych, 1956; JONES, KITTY IDWAL: Thomas Jones
of Denbigh, 1756–1820, *Flints. Hist. Soc. Pubns.*, xvii, 1957.

**2833.** JONES, JONATHAN: Cofiant Thomas Jones, Dinbych. Dinbych,
1897.

**2834.** PARRY, ROBERT IFOR: Cefndir gwleidyddol yr Annibynwyr
Cymraeg. *Y Cofiadur*, xix, 1949.

Id.    Yr Annibynwyr Cymraeg a threth yr ŷd, 1828–45
(No. 2798).

**2835.** PRITCHARD, WILLIAM: John Elias a'i oes. Caernarfon, 1911.

**2836.** ROBERTS, ROBERT: Life and opinions of Robert Roberts, a wandering scholar. Ed. J. H. Davies. Cardiff, 1923.

**2837.** THOMAS, OWEN: Cofiant John Jones, Talsarn. Wrexham, 1874.

**2838.** WILLIAMS, ALBERT HUGHES: Wesleaeth Gymreig a pholitics, 1800–1900. *Bathafarn*, vi, 1951.

WILLIAMS, DAVID: Cofiant J. R. Jones o Ramoth (No. 2677). The important section, pp. 742–98, is by Thomas Shankland.

### (ii) The Methodist controversy

**2839.** 'ARVONIUS' (Thomas Roberts, Llwynrhudol): Defence of the Methodists. Carmarthen, 1806.

**2840.** CHARLES, EDWARD: Epistolau Cymraeg at y Cymry. London, 1797.

**2841.** CHARLES, THOMAS, and JONES, THOMAS: The Welsh Methodists vindicated. Chester, 1802 (Welsh trans. H. Hughes. Caernarfon, 1894.)

**2842.** DAVIES, HUGH: Cyngor difrif periglor i'w blwyfolion. Caernarfon, 1801; reprinted, ed. David Erwyd Jenkins. Conway, 1906.

**2843.** DAVIES, JOHN: Awduriaeth cyngor difrif periglor. *Y Traethodydd*, 1901.

JONES, THOMAS (of Creaton): The Welsh looking-glass (No. 2568).

MORGAN, JAMES HUBERT: Edward Charles (Siamas Wynedd) (No. 2570).

**2844.** OWEN, THOMAS ELLIS: Methodism unmasked. London, 1802.

**2845.** Id. Hints to heads of families. London, 1802; reprinted, ed. David Erwyd Jenkins. Conway, 1905.

**2846.** Rules and designs of the religious societies among the Welsh Methodists read and agreed upon at the quarterly association at Bala, June 16 and 17, 1801. Chester, 1802; Welsh version, Chester, 1801.

**2847.** WILLIAMS, PETER BAILEY: Short vindication of the Established Church. Oxford, 1803.

### (e) The Court of Great Sessions

**2848.** First report of the commissioners on the courts of common law, 1829.

**2849.** JONES, JOHN (Glan-y-gors): Y sessiwn yng Nghymru. Gwaith Glanygors. Ed. Owen Morgan Edwards. *Cyfres y Fil*. Llanuwchllyn, 1905.

**2850.** THOMAS, DANIEL LLEUFER: 'Y sessiwn yng Nghymru'. *Y Geninen*, x, 1892.

WILLIAMS, WILLIAM LLEWELYN: The king's court of great sessions in Wales (No. 1658); see also id.: The making of modern Wales (No. 163), ch. iv.

### (f) Parliamentary reform

**2851.** ABADAM, EDWARD: Y tugel. Carmarthen, 1835.

**2852.** DAVIES, EDWARD: Etholiad '59. *Cymru.* Ed. O. M. Edwards, 1909.

GRIFFITHS, RICHARD: 'Y Gohebydd': cofiant (No. 2732).

**2853.** HANSARD, 3rd ser., vol. 43 (pp. 670–83).
Debate on interference with voters during Carmarthen election; 3rd ser., vol. 197 (pp. 1294-1329), Resolution moved by Henry Richard after the 1868 election.

JONES, THOMAS GWYNN: Cofiant Thomas Gee (No. 2731).

**2854.** JONES, JAMES RHYS ('Kilsby'): Etholiadau Ceredigion a Meirion-ydd. *Traethodydd,* xx, 1865.

**2855.** PARRY, OWEN: Lecsiwn 1852—bwrdeisdrefi Arfon. In Er clod, saith bennod ar hanes Methodistiaeth yng Nghymru (No. 2575).

**2856.** Report of the select committee on the Pembrokeshire county election petition. 1831.

**2857.** Report of the select committee on parliamentary and municipal elections, 1868. (See evidence of Michael D. Jones and others.)

ROBERTS, SAMUEL: Gweithiau Samuel Roberts (No. 2766).

**2858.** SPANKIE, R.: Llythyr at ei etholwyr (a translation). Llandovery, 1834.

### (g) Chartism

**2859.** ANON. [DOWLING, EDWARD]: The rise and fall of Chartism in Monmouthshire. London, 1840.

**2860.** ANON. [THOMAS, GEORGE]: History of the Chartists and the bloodless wars of Montgomeryshire. Welshpool, 1840.

**2861.** COLE, GEORGE DOUGLAS HOWARD: Chartist portraits. London, 1941.
Ch. v, John Frost.

**2862.** DAVIES, JAMES: The Chartist movement in Monmouthshire. Newport, 1939.

DODD, ARTHUR HERBERT: The industrial revolution in North Wales (No. 2342).

**2863.** GUNN, WILLIAM ALEXANDER, and WARNER, JOHN: John Frost and the Chartist movement in Monmouthshire; a catalogue of Chartist literature, prints, and relics. Newport, 1939.

**2864.** GWALCHMAI, HUMPHREY: Y Chartists yn Llanidloes. *Yr Athraw,* Llanidloes, 1839.

**2865.** HAMER, EDWARD: Brief account of the Chartist outbreak at Llanidloes, 1867; reprinted 1939.

**2866.** MORGAN, WALTER THOMAS: Chartism and industrial unrest in South Wales in 1842. *N.L.W. Jnl.,* x, 1957–8.

**2867.** NICHOLAS, THOMAS ISLWYN: One hundred years ago; the story of the Montgomeryshire Chartists. Aberystwyth, 1939.

**2868.** ROBERTS, W. G.: Y Siartiaid yng Nghymru. *Cymru.* Ed. O. M. Edwards, xxxvi, 1909; xxxvii, 1910.

**2869.** SAMUEL, J. E.: The Montgomeryshire Chartist riots. *Cymru Fu,* ii, 1889.

**2870.** SPENCER, JOHN DENLEY: The Chartist movement in Wales [Llanidloes and Newtown]. *Wales* (ed. O. M. Edwards), ii, 1895.

**2871.** WILLIAMS, DAVID: John Frost: a study in Chartism. Cardiff, 1939.

This contains a full bibliography.

### (h) The Rebecca riots

**2872.** ANON.: Hanes Becca a'i phlant. *Tarian y Gweithiwr,* Awst 19— Tachwedd 4, 1886.

A series of twelve articles, the reminiscences of a participant.

**2873.** *Carmarthen Antiquary,* i, 3 and 4, 1943–4.

These parts are devoted entirely to this subject. For a bibliography see JONES, THOMAS GWYNN: Rebeccaism, a bibliography. Ibid., pp. 64–70.

**2874.** DAVIES, WILLIAM LLOYD: Notes on Hugh Williams and the Rebecca riots. *B.B.C.S.,* xi, 1944.

**2875.** EVANS, GEORGE EYRE (ed.): Rebecca riots; unpublished letters. *Trans. Carms. Antiq. Soc.,* lvi, 1932.

**2876.** EVANS, HENRY TOBIT: Rebecca and her daughters. Cardiff, 1910.

**2877.** Report of the commissioners of inquiry for South Wales, 1844.

**2878.** WILLIAMS, DAVID: The Rebecca riots; a study in agrarian discontent. Cardiff, 1955.

### (j) Education and politics

See also section IV below.

### (i) The voluntaryist issue

DAVIES, THOMAS: Bywyd ac ysgrifeniadau David Rees (No. 2751).

**2879.** EVANS, DANIEL: The life and work of William Williams, M.P. for Coventry, 1835–1847, M.P. for Lambeth, 1850–1865. Llandysul, n.d. [1940].

**2880.** JONES, IDWAL: The voluntary system at work: a chapter in Welsh education, based on unpublished correspondence. *Trans. Cymmr.*, 1931–32.

JONES, THOMAS GWYNN: Cofiant Thomas Gee (No. 2731).

REES, WILLIAM ('Gwilym Hiraethog'): Llythyrau 'rhen ffarmwr (No. 2755).

ROBERTS, SAMUEL: Gweithiau Samuel Roberts (No. 2766).

### (ii) 'Brad y Llyfrau Gleision'

**2881.** BAINES, EDWARD: Letter to Lord John Russell on . . . the report . . . with articles from the *Leeds Mercury* in reply to Mr. J. C. Symons, etc. Leeds, 1848.

**2882.** Cyfarchiad y cyfeisteddfod cyffredinol . . . i wynebu cynllun addysg y llywodraeth. London, 1847.

**2883.** DERFEL, ROBERT JONES: Brad y llyfrau gleision. Ruthin, 1854.

**2884.** EDWARDS, ALFRED GEORGE (Archbishop of Wales): Memories. London, 1927.

**2885.** EDWARDS, JOHN GORONWY: Flintshire one hundred years ago. *Flints. Hist. Soc. Pubns.*, xvii, 1957.

**2886.** EDWARDS, LEWIS: Traethodau llenyddol. Wrexham, n.d.

EVANS, DANIEL: The life and work of William Williams, M.P. (No. 2879).

**2887.** HUGHES, WILLIAM (ed.): The life and speeches of the Very Rev. J. H. Cotton. Bangor, 1874.

**2888.** JONES, EVAN ('Ieuan Gwynedd'): The dissent and morality of Wales. London, 1847.

**2889.** Id.    A vindication of the educational and moral conditions of Wales. Llandovery, 1848.

**2890.** Id.     Facts, figures, and statements in illustration of the dissent and morality of Wales. London, 1849.

JONES, THOMAS GWYNN: Cofiant Thomas Gee (No. 2731).

**2891.** LEWIS, THOMAS HARRIS: Addysg grefyddol yng Nghymru yn ôl y llyfrau gleision. *Y Cofiadur*, 1954.
    This issue of *Y Cofiadur* is devoted entirely to this article, and contains a full bibliography.

**2892.** LLOYD, JOHN EDWARD: Addysg yng Nghymru hyd 1870. Adroddiad cyfarfodydd yr Undeb [Annibynwyr] yn Llanbedr Pont Stephan. Dolgellau, 1910, pp. 1249–54.

**2893.** PHILLIPS, SIR THOMAS: Wales: the language, social condition, moral character, and religious opinions of the people, considered in their relation to education. London, 1849.

**2894.** Reports of the commissioners of enquiry into the state of education in Wales. 3 vols. London, 1847.
    A single volume containing the three reports, but without the appendices, appeared in 1848.

**2895.** RICHARD, HENRY: Letters on Wales. London, 1867; 2nd edn, 1884.

**2896.** ROBERTS, OWEN OWEN: Addysg yng ngogledd Cymru. Caernarfon, 1847.

**2897.** SALISBURY, ENOCH ROBERT GIBBON: Letters to William Williams, Esq., and to the Marquis of Lansdowne. London, 1848 and 1849.

**2898.** SALMON, DAVID: The story of a Welsh education commission. *Y Cymmr.*, xxiv, 1913.

**2899.** SMITH, FRANK: A new document bearing on the . . . commission of 1846–7. *Aberystwyth Studies*, iv, 1922.

**2900.** Id.     The life of Sir James Kay-Shuttleworth. London, 1923.

**2901.** SYMONS, JELINGER COOKSON: A letter to the Lord President. London, 1848.

THOMAS, CADWALADR TAWELFRYN: Cofiant Ieuan Gwynedd (No. 2739).

**2902.** *Traethodydd, Y.* See index in the vol. for 1880 for articles by Hugh Owen, 1847, Kilsby Jones, 1849, Ieuan Gwynedd, 1850, etc., showing various attitudes towards the state's educational policy.

**2903.** WILLIAMS, EDWARD IVOR: Thomas Stephens and Carnhuanawc on the blue books of 1847. *B.B.C.S.*, ix, 1938.

**2904.** WILLIAMS, JANE (Ysgafell): Artegall, or remarks on the reports. London, 1848.

**2905.** WILLIAMS, WILLIAM: Letter to Lord John Russell on the report. London, 1848.
> See also EVANS, DANIEL: The life and work of William Williams, M.P. for Coventry, 1835–1847, M.P. for Lambeth, 1850–1865 (No. 2879).

**2906.** Id.     A second letter to Lord John Russell on the present defective state of education in Wales. London, 1848.
> See also EVANS, DANIEL, op. cit.

### (k) Church and Nonconformity

### (i) Disestablishment

See pamphlet literature published by the Society for the Liberation of Religion from State-patronage and control, in Dr. Williams's Library, London.

**2907.** BEVAN, WILLIAM LATHAM: The case of the Church in Wales. London, 1886.

**2908.** BRADLEY, JOHN JAMES FOVARGUE: The case against Welsh disendowment. London, 1911.

**2909.** Id.     The case against Welsh disestablishment. London, 1911.

**2910.** Id.     Nonconformists and the Welsh Church Bill. London, 1912.

**2911.** BRYNMOR-JONES, SIR DAVID (ed.): The disestablishment and disendowment of the Church of England and Wales. London, 1912.

**2912.** Census of Great Britain, 1851: reports and tables, religious worship. England and Wales. London, 1853.

**2913.** CLARKE, HENRY WILLIAM: History of the Church in Wales. London, 1896.

**2914.** CLASS, T.: True history of the Church of England in Wales. London, 1890.

**2915.** DAVIES, HYWEL ISLWYN: The Church in Wales in the nineteenth and twentieth centuries. In Welsh Church Congress handbook, 1953 (No. 184).

> EDWARDS, ALFRED GEORGE (Archbishop of Wales): Landmarks in the history of the Welsh Church (No. 166).

> Id. Memories (No. 2884).

**2916.** EDWARDS, HENRY THOMAS (dean of Bangor): Church of the Cymry. London, 1870.

**2917.** Id.    National religion and the Church in Wales. Bangor, 1882.

**2918.** Id.    Wales and the Welsh Church. London, 1889.

**2919.** EDWARDS, WILLIAM: Four centuries of Nonconformist disabilities, 1509–1912. London, 1912.

**2920.** EVANS, EVAN ('Ieuan Glan Geirionydd'): Claims of the Church in North Wales. Chester and London, 1843.

**2921.** EVANS, HOWARD: The case for disestablishment in Wales. London, 1907.

**2922.** FOWELL, RICHARD WARREN, and DIBDIN, L.: The Welsh Disestablishment Bill, with explanatory notes. London, 1909.

**2923.** HUGHES, THOMAS: Yr esgobion, neu gwymp Dagon o flaen yr arch. Rhuthyn, 1833.

**2924.** HUMPHREYS-OWEN, ARTHUR CHARLES: Dadsefydliad yng Nghymru. Y Traethodydd, 1891.

**2925.** JOHNES, ARTHUR JAMES: An essay on the causes which have produced dissent from the Established Church in the principality of Wales. London, 1832. Reprint with additional preface, 1870.
   See also JONES, MARIAN HENRY: The letters of Arthur James Johnes. N.L.W. Jnl., x, 1957–8.

   JONES, DAVID AMBROSE: History of the Church in Wales (No. 174).

**2926.** JONES, EVAN: Dadgysylltiad a dadwaddoliad. Y Traethodydd, 1878.

**2927.** Id.    Edward Miall. Ibid., 1882.

**2928.** JONES, GRIFFITH: The Welsh Church Bill controversy. London, 1913.

**2929.** JONES, JAMES EIDDON, HUGHES, EDWARD, and ROBERTS, JOHN: Dadgysylltiad a dadwaddoliad yng Nghymru. Y Traethodydd, 1885.

**2930.** JONES, RICHARD (Llanfair), and EDWARDS, LEWIS: Yr Eglwys sefydledig a'r Ymneillduwyr. Ibid., 1845.

   JONES, THOMAS (Creaton): The Welsh looking-glass (No. 2568).

**2931.** MORRIS, THOMAS (Dowlais): Amcan bodolaeth Eglwys Crist yn y byd. Merthyr, 1889.

**2932.** ORMSBY-GORE, WILLIAM GEORGE ARTHUR (LORD HARLECH): Welsh disestablishment and disendowment. London, 1912.

PHILLIPPS, SIR THOMAS: Wales, the language, social condition, etc. (No. 2893).

**2933.** PUGH, HUGH (Mostyn): Nodwedd, ymgais a bwriad Ymneill-duwyr. Llanrwst, 1838.

RICHARD, HENRY: Letters on Wales (No. 2895).

**2934.** Id.    and WILLIAMS, J. CARVELL: Disestablishment. London, 1885.

**2935.** ROBERTS, OWEN OWEN: Y Parchedig gecryn penchwiban, neu ddrych y bugail drwg, rhwng Sion Bryn Teg a Dafydd Dweyd y Gwir. Caernarfon, 1833.

**2936.** Id.    Y bugail, neu flaidd yn rhith dafad. Caernarfon, 1834.

ROBERTS, SAMUEL: Gweithiau Samuel Roberts (No. 2766).
See especially 'Traethawd ar . . . sefydliadau eglwysig'.

**2937.** Royal commission on the Church of England and other religious bodies in Wales and Monmouthshire. Report, minutes of evidence, appendices. 7 vols. 1910.

**2938.** SELBORNE, ROUNDELL, EARL OF: A defence of the Church of England against disestablishment. London, 1906.

**2939.** 'VINDEX': Amddiffyniad yr eglwys sefydledig. Y Traethodydd, 1850.

**2940.** WADE-EVANS, ARTHUR WADE: Papers for thinking Welshmen. London, 1909.

**2941.** Welsh Nonconformity and the Welsh representation. Papers and speeches (by various authors). London, 1866.

### (ii) The tithe agitation

**2942.** ANON.: Caneuon y degwm. Dinbych, 1887.

**2943.** ANON. [VINCENT, JAMES EDMUND]: Letters from Wales: a republication of a series of letters in *The Times* dealing with the state of Wales in especial relation to the land, the Church, and the tithes. By a special correspondent. London, 1889.

**2944.** COX, HOMERSHAM: Y degymau. Y Traethodydd, xlv, 1890.

EDWARDS, ALFRED GEORGE (Archbishop of Wales): Memories (No. 2884).

**2945.** EVANS, ELWYN (ed.): Tithe schedule for the parish of Garn Dolbenmaen. Trans. Caerns. Hist. Soc., 1952.

17

**2946.** Id.     (ed.): Tithe schedule for Boduan. Ibid., 1956.

**2947.** EVERETT, ROBERT LACY: Y degwm, etc. Dolgellau, 1887.

**2948.** JONES, EVAN: Degymau. *Y Traethodydd*, 1890.

**2949.** JONES, FRANK PRICE: Rhyfel y degwm. *Trans. Denbs. Hist. Soc.*, ii, 1953.

JONES, THOMAS GWYNN: Cofiant Thomas Gee (No. 2731).

**2950.** LLOYD, JOHN: Glebe lands and tithes in South Wales. London, 1888.

**2951.** OWEN, JOHN (bishop): Morality of the anti-tithe agitation in Wales. St. Asaph, 1890.

**2952.** PARRY, JOHN: Helynt y degwm. *Y Traethodydd*, 1887.

**2953.** PRICE, DAVID: Dyddiau y dreth. Dinbych, 1855.

**2954.** PRICE, THOMAS: The case of the tithes simply stated. Rhyl, 1887.

**2955.** PROTHERO, ROWLAND EDMUND (LORD ERNLE): The anti-tithe agitation in Wales. London, 1889.

**2956.** Report of the enquiry into the tithe agitation in Wales. London, 1887.

**2957.** Royal commission on tithe rent charge, 1934–5. Minutes of evidence and appendices. London, 1934–6.

**2958.** WATKINS, ROBERT FOULKES: Y gwir am y degwm. Wrexham, 1933.

#### (l) The land question

**2959.** ASHBY, ARTHUR WILFRED, and EVANS, IFOR LESLIE: The agriculture of Wales and Monmouthshire. Cardiff, 1944.

**2960.** DERFEL, ROBERT JONES: Ail drefniad cymdeithas. Manchester, 1888.

EDWARDS, OWEN MORGAN (gol.): Gwaith Samuel Roberts (No. 2762).

**2961.** ELLIS, THOMAS EDWARD: Addresses and speeches. Wrexham, 1912.

**2962.** Id.     Deddfau'r tir yng Nghymru. *Y Geninen*, x, 1892.

ELLIS, THOMAS IORWERTH: Thomas Edward Ellis: cofiant (No. 2773).

**2963.** HOWELLS, JOHN: The land question from the tenant's point of view. *Red Dragon*, ii, 1882.

**2964.** HUGHES, T. J.: Landlordiaeth yng Nghymru. *Y Traethodydd*, 1887.

**2965.** Id.     Neglected Wales. London, 1888.

**2966.** JONES, JOHN OWEN: Y tir i'r genedl. *Y Geninen*, x, 1892.

**2967.** JONES, R. A.: The land question, and a land bill with special reference to Wales. Wrexham, 1887; Welsh translation, 1888.

JONES, THOMAS GWYNN: Cofiant Thomas Gee (No. 2731).

**2968.** MORGAN-RICHARDSON, CHARLES: Does Wales require a land bill? Cardiff, 1893; Welsh translation, Carmarthen, 1893.

**2969.** OWEN, DANIEL: Tenant right in Breconshire. *Red Dragon*, viii, 1885.

**2970.** OWEN, GEORGE H. M.: The land agitation in Wales. London, 1893.

REES, WILLIAM (Gwilym Hiraethog): Llythyrau 'rhen ffarmwr (No. 2755).

**2971.** Report of the royal commission on land in Wales and Monmouth-shire. Minutes of evidence. 4 vols. Appendices to the report. London, 1896.

These are fundamental to the study of the land question. A digest of the report is given in THOMAS, DANIEL LLEUFER: The Welsh land commission: a digest of its report. London, 1896. See also The Welsh land commission: leading articles and correspondence from *The Times* (reprinted). London, 1896.

**2972.** Return of owners of land in England and Wales, 1873. 2 vols. London, 1875. Vol. ii: Wales.

VAUGHAN, HERBERT MILLINGCHAMP: The South Wales squires (No. 2359), part 1.

**2973.** VINCENT, JAMES EDMUND: The land question in North Wales. London, 1896; Welsh translation, Caernarvon, 1896.

**2974.** Id.     The land question in South Wales. London, 1897.

**2975.** WILLIAMS, WILLIAM LLEWELYN: Pwnc y tir. *Y Geninen*, xxxii, 1914.

### (m) Industrial relations
### (i) Robert Owen

**2976.** Bibliography on Robert Owen. National Library of Wales. 1925.

**2977.** COLE, GEORGE DOUGLAS HOWARD: The life of Robert Owen. London, 1930.

**2978.** ROBERTS, ROBERT OWEN: Robert Owen o'r Dre Newydd. Llandysul, 1948.

(ii) Trade Unionism

**2979.** BEVAN-EVANS, M.: The Mold riot of 1831—a note. *Flints. Hist. Soc. Pubns.,* xiii, 1952–3.

**2980.** DALZIEL, ALEXANDER: The colliers' strike in South Wales: its cause, progress, and settlement. Cardiff, 1872.

**2981.** DALZIEL, WILLIAM GASCOYNE: Records of the several coal owners' associations in Monmouthshire and South Wales, 1864–95. London, 1895.

**2982.** EDWARDS, NESS: A history of the South Wales Miners' Federation. Vol. i. London, 1938.

**2983.** GRIFFITHS, B. A., and B.: Safle y gweithiwr. Caernarfon, 1854.

**2984.** 'IGNOTUS': The last thirty years in a mining district: or scotching and the candle versus lamp and trades unions. London, 1867.

**2985.** JONES, EVAN JOHN: Scotch cattle. *Economic Jnl.* supplement, 1928.

**2986.** JONES, W. HUGH: A strike at Talargoch lead mine one hundred years ago. *Flint. Hist. Soc. Pubns.,* xvi, 1956.

**2987.** 'LOOKER ON': The oaths taken in the Union Club, etc. Newport, 1831.

**2988.** MORRIS, JOHN HENRY, and WILLIAMS, LAURENCE JOHN: The discharge note in the South Wales coal industry. *Econ. Hist. Rev.,* x, 1957.

**2989.** NICHOLAS, ISLWYN AP (Thomas Islwyn): Dic Penderyn, Welsh rebel and martyr. London, 1945.
      See also WEBB, HARRI: Dic Penderyn and the Merthyr rising of 1831. Swansea, 1956.

**2990.** PARRY, OWEN: Undeb y chwarelwyr, 1908–1929. Caernarfon, 1929.

**2991.** Rheolau Cymdeithas Mwynglawdd Môn yn Amlwch, 1819. Llanerchymedd, 1823.

**2992.** Rheolau cymdeithas o grefftwyr . . . [yn] . . . Nantyglo. Abergavenny, 1844.

**2993.** ROGERS, EMLYN: Helyntion glowyr Dinbych a Fflint yn 1830–1. *Lleufer,* ii, 1946; iii, 1947.

**2994.** Id.    Labour struggles in Flintshire, 1830–1850. *Flints. Hist. Soc. Pubns.,* xiv, 1953–4; xv, 1954–5.

**2995.** THOMAS, BEN BOWEN: Mabon. *Y Traethodydd,* 1948.

**2996.** THOMAS, DANIEL LLEUFER: Labour unions in Wales. Privately printed. Swansea, 1901.

**2997.** THOMAS, PHILIP SYDNEY: Industrial relations: a short study of the relations between employers and employed in Swansea and neighbourhood, from about 1800 to recent times. Social and economic survey of Swansea and district. Pamphlet No. 3. Cardiff, 1940.

### (iii) The Penrhyn disputes

**2998.** ANON.: Chwareli y Penrhyn. Yr ohebiaeth. Bethesda, 1885.

**2999.** ANON.: The Penrhyn quarries dispute. 1903.

**3000.** JONES, C. SHERIDAN: What I saw at Bethesda. London, 1900.

**3001.** NORTH WALES QUARRYMEN'S UNION: The struggle for the right of combination. Caernarvon, 1897.

**3002.** PARRY, WILLIAM JOHN: Caebraichycafn, yr ymdrafodaeth. Bangor, 1875.

**3003.** Id.      Undeb Chwarelwyr Gogledd Cymru a pherchenogion y chwarelau. Caernarfon, 1884.

**3004.** Id.      The Penrhyn lock-out. London, 1901.

**3005.** Report of the royal commission on labour. The North Wales quarrying industry. Caernarvon, 1892.

**3006.** Report on the Penrhyn dispute by the General Federation of Trade Unions. Caernarvon, 1901.

**3007.** WILLIAMS, WILLIAM JOHN: The royal commission on labour. Caernarvon, 1893.

### (iv) Socialism

See the articles on this subject in *Y Geninen,* 1898; and the articles by D. Rhys Jones in *Tarian y Gweithiwr* and *Cymru Fydd,* and consult appendices to the report of the land commission in Wales and Monmouthshire (No. 2723).

DERFEL, ROBERT JONES: Ail drefniad cymdeithas (No. 2960).

**3008.** Id.      Social songs. Manchester, 1889.

**3009.** Id.      Common misconceptions about socialism. Manchester, 1891.

**3010.** Id.     Detholiad o ryddiaith Gymraeg R. J. Derfel. Gol. David
James Gwenallt Jones. 2 gyf. Dinbych, 1945.
Contains bibliography.

**3011.** HUGHES, EMRYS: Keir Hardie. London, 1956.

**3012.** HUMPHREYS, EDWARD MORGAN: Socialism and Welsh nationality.
*Socialist Rev.*, Oct., 1909.

**3013.** NICHOLAS, THOMAS EVAN: R. J. Derfel. *Y Geninen*, xxx, 1912;
xxxii, 1914; xxxiii, 1915.

**3014.** STEWART, WILLIAM: James Keir Hardie: a biography. London,
1925.

(n) **Nationalism and home rule**

**3015.** ANON.: Home rule for Wales; what does it mean? Cymru Fydd
Soc. London, 1888.

**3016.** BONSALL, HENRY: Tynged Cymru. Aberystwyth, 1891.

**3017.** Id.     Undeb. Aberystwyth, 1893.

**3018.** BREESE, CHARLES EDWARD: Welsh nationality. Caernarvon, 1895.

**3019.** COUPLAND, REGINALD: Welsh and Scottish nationalism. A study.
London, 1954.

**3020.** DARLINGTON, THOMAS: Welsh nationality and its critics. Wrexham,
1895.

**3021.** DAVID, EVAN: Ymreolaeth i Gymru. Ystalyfera, 1890.

DAVIES, WILLIAM WATKIN: Lloyd George, 1863–1914
(No. 2772).

**3022.** ELLIS, THOMAS EDWARD: Gwleidyddiaeth genedlaethol. *Y Geninen*,
1886.

Id.     Addresses and speeches (No. 2961).

**3023.** GEORGE, WILLIAM: Cymru Fydd: hanes y mudiad cenedlaethol
cyntaf. Lerpwl, 1945.

HAMER, FREDERICK EDWARD (ed.): The personal papers of
Lord Rendel (No. 2781).

**3024.** JENKINS, ROBERT THOMAS: The development of nationalism in
Wales. *Sociological Review*, xxvii, 1935.

**3025.** JOHN, EDWARD THOMAS: Senedd Gymreig, ei neges a'i gwaith. Caernarfon, 1911.

**3026.** Id.    Home rule for Wales. Bangor, 1912.

**3027.** Id.    Wales, its politics and economics. Cardiff, 1919.

**3028.** JONES, DAVID JAMES GWENALLT: Hanes mudiadau Cymraeg a chenedlaethol y bedwaredd-ganrif-ar-bymtheg. Yn LLOYD, DAVID MYRDDIN (ed.): Seiliau hanesyddol cenedlaetholdeb Cymru. Caerdydd, 1950; English translation, Cardiff, 1950.

**3029.** JONES, EVAN (Machynlleth): Plaid Gymreig a deddfwriaeth i Gymru. Machynlleth, 1886.

JONES, ROBERT AMBROSE ('Emrys ap Iwan'): Detholiad o erthyglau a llythyrau Emrys ap Iwan. Vol. i, Gwlatgar, cymdeith-asol, hanesiol (No. 2743).

JONES, THOMAS GWYNN: Cofiant Emrys ap Iwan (No. 2744).

Id.    Cofiant Thomas Gee (No. 2731).

**3030.** PHILLIPS, WILLIAM FRANCIS: Y ddraig goch ynte'r faner goch. Cardiff, 1912.

**3031.** PRICE, JOHN ARTHUR: Thomas E. Ellis. In MORGAN, JOHN VYRNWY: Welsh political and educational leaders of the Victorian era (No. 2796).

**3032.** Id.    and RICHARDS, DAVID: Ymreolaeth i Gymru. *Y Geninen*, ix, 1891.

**3033.** RANDALL, DAVID, GEORGE, DAVID LLOYD, and PARRY, WILLIAM JOHN: Home rule bill for Wales. Caernarfon, 1890.

REES, WILLIAM ('Gwilym Hiraethog'): Llythyrau 'rhen ffarmwr (No. 2755).

RHONDDA, MARGARET VISCOUNTESS (ed.): D. A. Thomas, Viscount Rhondda (No. 2800).

**3034.** WILLIAMS, GLANMOR: The idea of nationality in Wales. *Cambridge Jnl.*, vii, 1953.

**3035.** WILLIAMS, THOMAS MARCHANT: Home rule for Wales. Aberdare, 1888.

**3036.** WILLIAMS, WILLIAM LLYWELYN: The Young Wales movement. *Cymru Fydd*. Cardiff, 1894.

## III. SOCIAL AND ECONOMIC HISTORY

The background to the social and economic history of Wales in the nineteenth century may be studied in CLAPHAM, SIR JOHN HAROLD: An economic history of modern Britain: the early railway age, 1820–1850, 2nd edn, Cambridge, 1950; Free trade and steel, 1850–1886, reprinted Cambridge, 1952; Machines and national rivalries, 1887–1914, with an epilogue, 1914–1929, reprinted Cambridge, 1951. For a brief discussion, see COURT, WILLIAM HENRY BASSANO: A concise economic history of Great Britain from 1750 to recent times. Cambridge, 1954.

Since industrial disputes were intimately connected with the awakening of political consciousness in Wales during this period, references to them are included in section K II (*m*). See also section J III.

### (a) Geographical background

BOWEN, EMRYS GEORGE: Wales: a study in geography and history (No. 132). Cardiff, 1947.

Id.     (ed.): Wales: a physical, historical, and regional geography (No. 133).

CARLISLE, NICHOLAS: A topographical dictionary of the dominion of Wales (No. 348).

**3037.** CUNDALL, LEONARD B., and LANDMAN, THOMAS: Wales: an economic geography. London, 1925.

FULLARTON, ANDREW: Parliamentary gazeteer of England and Wales (No. 355).

GEORGE, THOMAS NEVILLE: The geology, physical features, and natural resources of the Swansea district (No. 676).

**3038.** LAND UTILISATION SURVEY. The land of Britain. London.
Part 31. Glamorgan (A. N. Thomas). 1938.
Part 32. Pembrokeshire (Margaret F. Davies). 1939.
Part 33. Merioneth (L. A. Holliday). 1940.
Part 34. Anglesey (Aubrey and Lewis). 1940.
Part 35. Radnor (L. K. Redford). 1940.
Part 36. Montgomeryshire (J. May and S. F. Wells). 1942.
Part 37. Brecon (Rosalind M. Whyte). 1943.
Part 38. Monmouth (A. Rhys Clarke). 1943.
Part 39. Carmarthenshire (B. L. Danes and H. Miller). 1944.
Part 40. Cardiganshire (Emrys J. Howells). 1946.
Parts 41–3. North Wales: Caernarvon, Denbigh, and Flint (Emrys J. Howell). 1946.

LEWIS, SAMUEL: Topographical dictionary of Wales (No. 360).

PEATE, IORWERTH CYFEILIOG: Cymru a'i phobl (No. 147).

WILLIAMS, DAVID TREVOR: Gower: a study in linguistic movements and historical geography (No. 708).

### (b) Population changes

### (i) Migration and growth of towns

**3039.** BALLINGER, JOHN (ed.): Cardiff: an illustrated handbook. Cardiff, 1896.

**3040.** BRITISH ASSOCIATION: Handbook to Cardiff and the neighbourhood. Cardiff, 1920.

**3041.** CARTER, HAROLD: Urban grades and spheres of influence in south-west Wales: an historical consideration. *Scottish Geographical Mag.*, lxxi, 1955.

CHAPPELL, EDGAR LEYSHON: Old Whitchurch: the story of a Glamorgan parish (No. 667).

DAVIS, HENRY JOHN: The rise and progress of Newport (Monmouthshire) (No. 736).

**3042.** DAVIES, V. CHALLINOR: Some geographical aspects of the decline in the rural population of Wales with special reference to Merioneth. *Jnl. Mer. Hist. and Rec. Soc.*, ii, 1, 1953.

EDWARDS, JOHN GORONWY: Flintshire since 1801 (No. 658).

**3043.** HODGES, THOMAS MANSEL: The peopling of the hinterland and the port of Cardiff, etc. *Econ. Hist. Rev.*, xvii, 1947.

**3044.** HOWELL, EMRYS JONES: Movement of miners in the South Wales coalfield. *Geographical Jnl.*, xciv, 1939.

**3045.** JONES, JOHN RICHARD: The Welsh builder on Merseyside. Liverpool, 1946.

**3046.** LITTLE, E. L.: Loudon Square; a community study. *Sociological Review*, xxxiv, 1942.

**3047.** MARSHALL, T. H.: The population of England and Wales from the industrial revolution to the world war. *Econ. Hist. Rev.*, v, 1934–5.

**3048.** THOMAS, BRINLEY: The migration of labour into the Glamorganshire coalfields, 1861–1911. *Economica*, x, 1930.

THOMPSON, HERBERT METFORD: Cardiff (No. 706).

**3049.** TRUEMAN, ARTHUR ELIJAH: Population changes in the South Wales coalfield. *Geographical Jnl.*, liii, 1919.

WILLIAMS, DAVID: A note on the population of Wales, 1536–1801 (No. 1621).

3050. WILLIAMS, J. ROLAND: The influence of foreign nationalities on the life of the people of Merthyr Tydfil. *Sociological Review*, xviii, 1926.

3051. WILLIAMS, MOELWYN I.: Seasonal migration of Cardiganshire harvest-gangs to the vale of Glamorgan in the nineteenth century. *Ceredigion*, iii, 2, 1957.

### (ii) Emigration

3052. BAUR, J. B.: The Welsh in Patagonia. *Hispanic American Historical Review*, xxxiv, 1954.

3053. BEBB, HERBERT: Bebb genealogy: the descendants of William Bebb and Martha Hughes of Llanbrynmair, Wales. Chicago, 1944.

3054. BERTHOFF, ROWLAND TAPPAN: British immigrants in industrial America. Cambridge, Mass., 1953.

3055. CHIDLAW, BENJAMIN W.: Yr American, yn cynwys nodau ar daith o Ddyffryn Ohio i Gymru, golwg ar dalaeth Ohio, hanes sefydliadau Cymreig yn America. 2nd edn, Llanrwst, 1840; English translation in publications of the Historical and Philosophical Society of Ohio, vi, 1911.

3056. Id.      The story of my life. Philadelphia, 1890.

3057. CONWAY, ALAN: A Welshman in Russia (Evan Williams). *N.L.W. Jnl.*, ix, 1955–6.

3058. Id.      Welsh gold miners in British Columbia during the 1860s. Ibid., x, 1957–8.

3059. Id.      Welshmen in the Union armies. *Civil War History*. Univ. of Iowa publications, iv, 1958.

3060. DAVIES, DAVID (gol.): Hanes y Cymry yn swyddau Winnebago a Fond du Lac, Wisconsin, 1847–1897. Oshkosh, Wis., 1898.

3061. DAVIES, DAVID, and DAVIES, HOWELL D.: History of the Oshkosh Welsh settlement, 1847–1947. Amarillo, Texas, 1947.
        A translation and extension of No. 3060 above.

3062. DAVIES, JOHN GLYN: Cambria, Wisconsin, in 1898. *Trans. Cymmr.*, 1958.

3063. DODD, ARTHUR HERBERT: Letters from Welsh settlers in New York state, 1816–1844. *N.L.W. Jnl.*, ix, 1955.

3064. Id.      Letters from Cambria county, 1800–23. *Pennsylvania History*, xxii, 1955.

**3065.** Id.    A Merioneth pioneer of the American mid-west: John Rice Jones. *Jnl. Mer. Hist. and Rec. Soc.*, ii, 4, 1956.

Id.    The character of early Welsh emigration to the United States (No. 2254).

**3066.** 'ELLIS O'R NANT': Yr ymfudwr Cymreig. Blaenau Ffestiniog, 1883.

EVANS, JOHN JAMES: Morgan John Rhys a'i amserau (No. 2512).

**3067.** EVANS, WILLIAM R.: Hanes sefydliadau Cymreig siroedd Jackson a Gallia, Ohio. Utica, 1896.

GRIFFITH, JOHN T.: The Welsh Baptist hero of civil and religious liberty of the eighteenth century [Morgan John Rhys] (No. 2512).

**3068.** HARRIES, FREDERICK JAMES: Welshmen in the United States. Pontypridd, 1927.

**3069.** HUGHES, T. E., ac EDWARDS, DAVID (goln.): Hanes Cymry Minnesota. Foreston, Iowa, 1895.

**3070.** JAMES, THOMAS LEMUEL: The Welshman's contribution to the development of the United States. *The Royal Blue Book*. Pittsburgh, 1913.

**3071.** JONES, ALEXANDER: The Cymry of '76, or Welshmen and their descendants of the American revolution. 2nd edn. New York, 1855.

**3072.** JONES, CHESTER LLOYD: Youngest son. Madison, Wisconsin, 1938.

**3073.** JONES, DAVID: Welsh Congregationalists in Pennsylvania, 1797–1931: a memorial volume. Utica, 1934.

**3074.** JONES, EMYR GWYNNE: Annibynwyr Cymraeg Awstralia. *Y Cofiadur*, xxvi, 1956.

**3075.** JONES, ERASMUS W.: The Welsh in America. *Atlantic Monthly*, xxxvii, 1876.

**3076.** JONES, W. HARVEY: Welsh settlements in Ohio. *Ohio Archaeological and Historical Pubns.*, xvi, 1907.

**3077.** LEWIS, THOMAS HARRIS: Y Mormoniaid yng Nghymru. Caerdydd, 1956.

**3078.** *National Library of Wales Journal:* Wales and the United States of America. Vol. ii, 3 and 4, 1942.

**3079.** OWEN, BOB: Yr ymfudo o sir Gaernarfon i'r Unol Daleithiau. *Trans. Caerns. Hist. Soc.*, 1952–3–4.

**3080.** Id.      Ymfudo o sir Aberteifi i Unol Daleithiau America o 1654 hyd 1860. *Ceredigion*, ii, 1954.

**3081.** Id.      Bedyddwyr Cymraeg yr Unol Daleithiau, 1795–1894. *Traf. Cymd. Hanes Bed.*, 1954.

**3082.** PEATE, IORWERTH CYFEILIOG (ed.): Hunangofiant George Roberts. *Y Cofiadur*, xxii, 1952.

     The autobiography is in English.

**3083.** PHILLIPS, HARRY: Phillips family history. Lebanon, Tennessee, 1935.

**3084.** PHILLIPS, WILLIAM: Rhagolygon ymfudiaeth o Gymru tuag 1850. *Y Traethodydd*, 1939.

**3085.** ROSSER, FREDERICK THOMAS: The Welsh settlement in Upper Canada. London, Ontario, 1954.

**3086.** THOMAS, ROBERT DAVID: ('Iorthryn Gwynedd') yr ymfudwr, yn cynnwys hanes America ac Awstralia, ynghyd a phob hyfforddiadau i ymfudwyr. Drefnewydd, 1854.

**3087.** Id.      Hanes Cymry America, a'u sefydliadau, etc. Utica, 1872.

**3088.** WILLIAMS, DANIEL JENKINS: The Welsh of Columbus, Ohio: a study in adaptation and assimilation. Oshkosh, Wisconsin, 1913.

**3089.** Id.      One hundred years of Welsh Calvinistic Methodism in America. Philadelphia, 1937.

**3090.** WILLIAMS, DAVID: Some figures relating to emigration from Wales. *B.B.C.S.*, vii, 1935; viii, 1936.

**3091.** Id.      Cymru ac America. Bilingual, Cardiff, 1946.

**3092.** Id.      John Evans's strange journey. *Amer. Hist. Rev.*, liv; also in *Trans. Cymmr.*, 1948.

**3093.** Id.      An Anglesey emigration project. *Trans. Angl. Antiq. Soc.*, 1956.

**3094.** WILLIAMS, R. BRYN: Cymry Patagonia. Aberystwyth, 1942.

**3095.** WILLIAMS, STEPHEN RIGGS: The saga of Paddy's Run. Oxford, Ohio, 1945.

## (c) Rural Wales

## (i) Agriculture

**3096.** BOARD OF AGRICULTURE: General view of the agriculture of North Wales and of each of the counties of South Wales. 8 reports. 1794–96.
> The reports are by John Clark, John Fox, Charles Hassall, George Kay, Thomas Lloyd, and the Rev. D. Turnor.

ASHBY, ARTHUR WILFRED, and EVANS, IFOR LESLIE: The agriculture of Wales and Monmouthshire (No. 2959).

**3097.** DAVIES, DAVID: The case of labourers in husbandry. 1795.

**3098.** DAVIES, JAMES LLEFELYS: The livestock trade in west Wales in the nineteenth century. *Aberystwyth Studies*, xiii, 1934.

**3099.** DAVIES, WALTER: A general view of the agriculture and domestic economy of North Wales. London, 1810; reprinted 1813.

**3100.** Id.　　A general view of the agriculture and domestic economy of South Wales. 2 vols. London, 1814.

**3101.** DAVIES, WILLIAM LLOYD: The Henllan (Denbighshire) enclosure award [1814]. *B.B.C.S.*, ix, 1937–9.

**3102.** EDEN, FREDERICK: The state of the poor. London, 1797.

EDMUNDS, HENRY: The history of the Brecknockshire Agricultural Society, 1755–1955 (No. 2348).

**3103.** EVANS, DAVID: Y wlad, ei bywyd, ei haddysg, a'i chrefydd. Liverpool, 1933.

EVANS, ELWYN (ed.): Tithe schedule for the parish of Garn Dolbenmaen (No. 2945).

Id.　　(ed.): Tithe schedule for Boduan (No. 2946).

EVANS, HUGH: Cwm Eithin (No. 627).

**3104.** FUSSELL, GEORGE EDWIN: Welsh farming in 1879. *Trans. Cymmr.*, 1938.

Id.　　Glamorgan farming: an outline of its modern history (No. 2349).

**3105.** GIBSON, J.: Agriculture in Wales. London, 1879.

HALL, EDMUND HYDE: A description of Caernarvonshire, 1809–1811 (No. 533).
> See also WILLIAMS, DEINIOL: An eye witness account of agrarian conditions in Caernarvonshire during the Napoleonic era. *Trans. Caerns. Hist. Soc.*, 1941.

**3106.** HASSALL, CHARLES: General view of the agriculture of the county of Monmouth. London, 1812.

**3107.** HUGHES, JOHN: Amaethyddiaeth iseldir Cymru. *Y Traethodydd,* 1854; reprinted Dinbych, 1854.

HOWELLS, JOHN MARTIN: The Crosswood estate, 1547–1947 (No. 77).

JENKINS, DAFYDD: Thomas Johnes o'r Hafod, 1748–1816 (No. 2351).

**3108.** JOHNES, THOMAS: A Cardiganshire landlord's advice to his tenants. Bristol, 1800. Welsh translation by William Owen [Pughe]: Cynghorion priodor o Geredigion i ddeiliaid ei dyddynod. Llundain, 1800.

JONES, CADWALADR BRYNER (ed.): Atgofion amaethwr, gan Gomer Roberts (No. 725).

**3109.** JONES, FRANCIS: Some farmers of bygone Pembrokeshire. *Trans. Cymmr.,* 1943–4.

**3110.** JONES, THOMAS IEUAN JEFFREYS: The pumrhydau and corsydd of the parish of Llandanwg. *Jnl. Mer. Hist. and Rec. Soc.,* ii, 2, 1954.

LERRY, GEORGE GEOFFREY: The industries of Denbighshire from Tudor times to the present day. Part I. Agriculture (No. 1818).

**3111.** LEWIS, HENRY (ed.): Llanwynno, gan Glanffrwd. Cardiff, 1949.

**3112.** OTTER, MURIELLE E.: The land utilisation of Llanrug parish. *Trans. Caerns. Hist. Soc.,* vii, 1946.

OWEN, GERAINT DYFNALLT: Agriculture [in Carmarthenshire]; the eighteenth and early nineteenth centuries (No. 2355).

PEATE, IORWERTH CYFEILIOG: Diwylliant gwerin Cymru (No. 241).

**3113.** RANKIN, HUGH RHYS: Cattle droving from Wales to England. *Agriculture,* lxii, 1955.

**3114.** READ, CLARE SEWELL: On the farming of South Wales. *Jnl. of the Royal Agricultural Society,* x, 1849.

**3115.** ROBERTS, ROBERT ALUN: Welsh home-spun: studies in rural Wales. Newtown, 1930.

**3116.** ROWLANDSON, T.: The agriculture of North Wales. *Jnl. of the Royal Agricultural Society,* vii, 1846.

**3117.** WILLIAMS, DAVID: The acreage returns of 1801 for Wales. *B.B.C.S.*, xiv, 1950–1.

> See also THOMAS, DAVID: The acreage returns of 1801 for Wales: an addendum. Ibid., xvii, 1956–8.

**3118.** Id.     Rural Wales in the nineteenth century. *Jnl. of the Royal Agricultural Society*, xxxiv, 1953.

**3119.** Report of the royal commission on agriculture, Wales, 1882.

> YOUNG, ARTHUR: A six weeks' tour through the southern counties of England and Wales (No. 2360).

> Id.     (ed.): Annals of agriculture (No. 2361).

### (ii) Enclosures

> BOWEN, IFOR: The great enclosures of common land in Wales (No. 2346 and appended note).

**3120.** DAVIES, MARGARET: The open fields of Laugharne. *Geography*, xl, 1955.

**3121.** Id.     Field patterns in the vale of Glamorgan. *Trans. Cardiff Nat. Soc.*, 1954–5.

**3121A.** Id.     Common lands in south-east Monmouthshire. *Ibid.*, 1955–6.

**3122.** Id.     Rhosili open fields and related South Wales field patterns. *Agric. Hist. Rev.*, iv, 2, 1956.

> DAVIES, WILLIAM LLOYD: The Henllan (Denbighshire) enclosure award (1814) (No. 3101).

**3123.** JONES, EVAN JOHN: The enclosure movement in Anglesey. *Trans. Angl. Antiq. Soc.*, 1925–6.

**3124.** LLOYD, JOHN: The great forest of Brecknock. London, 1905.

**3125.** Report of the royal commission on common land. London, 1958.

**3126.** Report of the select committee on commons inclosure. London, 1844.

**3127.** SYLVESTER, DOROTHY: Settlement patterns in rural Flintshire (excluding Maelor Saesneg). *Flints. Hist. Soc. Pubns.*, xv, 1954–5.

> Id.     The rural landscape of eastern Montgomeryshire (No. 772).

**3128.** Id.    The common fields of the coastland of Gwent. *Agric. Hist. Rev.*, iv, 1958.

THOMAS, DAVID: Cau'r tiroedd comin (No. 2358).

**3129.** THOMAS, JOHN GARETH: The distribution of the commons in part of Arwystli at the time of enclosure. *Mont. Coll.*, liv, 1955.

**3130.** THOMAS, SPENCER: Land occupation, ownership, and utilisation in the parish of Llansantffraid. *Ceredigion*, iii, 2, 1957.

**3131.** WILLIAMS, DAVID: Rhyfel y Sais Bach. *Ceredigion*, ii, 1952.

### (iii) Rural industries

**3132.** BEACHAM, ARTHUR: Industries in Welsh country towns. London, 1951.

CRANKSHAW, WILLIAM P.: Report on a survey of the Welsh textile industry (No. 280).

**3133.** HUGHES, MAIRWEN: The marram grass industry of Newborough, Anglesey. *Trans. Angl. Antiq. Soc.*, 1956.
See also OWEN, HUGH: The mat-weaving industry in Newborough. Ibid., 1923.

**3134.** JONES, ALAN BEYNON, and DAVIES, BRYAN LLOYD: The woollen industry [in Carmarthenshire]. In A history of Carmarthenshire (No. 605), ii.

JONES, ANNA MARIA: The rural industries of England and Wales: a survey (No. 235).
Vol. iv, Wales.

JONES, MOSES J.: The Merioneth woollen industry, 1750–1820 (No. 2410).

PEATE, IORWERTH CYFEILIOG: A north Cardiganshire woollen yarn factory (No. 282).

**3135.** Report of the Royal Commission on hand-loom weavers. London, 1840.

**3136.** THOMAS, DANIEL LLEUFER: Memorandum on the woollen industries of Wales. Privately printed, c. 1900.

### (iv) Social conditions: rural

See also sections K II (*g*), (*h*), and (*l*).

ANON. [VINCENT, JAMES EDMUND]: Letters from Wales (No. 2943).

**3137.** ASHBY, ARTHUR WILFRED, and JONES, JOHN MORGAN: The social origins of farmers in Wales. *The Sociological Review*, xviii, 1926.

**3138.** DAVIES, JAMES LLEFELYS: The diary of a Cardiganshire farmer, 1870–1900. *Welsh Jnl. of Agriculture*, x, 1934.

EDWARDS, JOHN GORONWY: Flintshire one hundred years ago (No. 2885).

**3139.** FLYNN-HUGHES, CLEDWYN: The Bangor workhouse. Ibid., 1944.

**3140.** Id.      The workhouses of Caernarvonshire, 1760–1914. Ibid., 1946.

**3141.** Id.      Aspects of the old poor law administration and policy in Amlwch parish, 1770–1837. *Trans. Angl. Antiq. Soc.*, 1945.

**3142.** Id.      Aspects of poor law administration and policy in Anglesey. Ibid., 1950.

**3143.** FRANKENBERG, RONALD: Village on the border: a social study of religion, politics, and football in a North Wales community. London, 1957.

**3144.** HOWSE, WILLIAM HENRY: The early friendly societies of Radnorshire. *Trans. Rads. Soc.*, xviii, 1948.

**3145.** Id.      The True Ivorites in Radnorshire. Ibid., xx, 1950.

HUGHES, WILLIAM JOHN: Wales and the Welsh in English literature (No. 10).

**3146.** INGMAN, JOHN: The early days of the Caernarvonshire and Anglesey Hospital, with notes on some of Bangor's medical practitioners, 1772–1856. *Trans. Caerns. Hist. Soc.*, 1950.

**3147.** JENKINS, DAVID, JONES, EMRYS, HUGHES, THOMAS JONES, and OWEN, TREFOR MEREDITH: Welsh rural communities. Cardiff, 1960.

**3148.** JONES, THOMAS IEUAN JEFFREYS: The parish vestries and the problem of poverty. *B.B.C.S.*, xiv, 1951.

**3149.** OWEN, DANIEL: Gwen Tomos. Wrecsam, 1937.

**3150.** Id.      Profedigaethau Enoc Huws. Wrecsam, 1939.

**3151.** Id.      Hunangofiant Rhys Lewis. Caerdydd, 1948.

OWEN, DAVID ('Brutus'): Wil Brydydd y Coed (No. 2747).

Id.      Bugeiliaid Epynt (No. 2748).

18

**3152.** OWEN, GERAINT DYFNALLT: The poor law system in Carmarthenshire during the eighteenth and early nineteenth centuries. *Trans. Cymmr.,* 1941.

OWEN, HUGH JOHN: Echoes of old Merioneth (No. 722).

**3153.** OWEN, RICHARD GRIFFITH: A Caernarvonshire scrap book, 1818–1823. *Trans. Caerns. Hist. Soc.,* 1942–3.

**3154.** OWENS, BENJAMIN GEORGE: Gwir Iforiaid 'Castell Gwallter'. *Ceredigion,* iii, 1956.

PARRY-JONES, DANIEL: Welsh country upbringing (No. 237).

PEATE, IORWERTH CYFEILIOG: The Welsh house: a study in folk culture (No. 463).

REES, ALWYN DAVID: Life in a Welsh countryside (No. 769).

**3155.** REES, WILLIAM ('Gwilym Hiraethog'): Helyntion bywyd hen deiliwr. Aberystwyth, 1940.

Id.      Llythyrau 'rhen ffarmwr (No. 2755).

**3156.** RICHARDS, HAMISH, and LEWIS, J. PARRY: House building in the South Wales coalfield, 1851–1913. *Econ. and Social Studies, Manchester School,* September, 1956.

**3157.** Reports of the royal commission for enquiring into the administration of the poor laws. 1834. See subsequent annual reports.

Reports of the commissioners of enquiry into the state of education in Wales (No. 2894).

**3158.** Reports of the royal commission on the employment of children and women in agriculture. 1867–70.

**3159.** Report of the royal commission on labour. The agricultural labourer; Wales. 1893–4.

**3160.** Reports of commissioners on wages and conditions of employment in agriculture: reports on the individual Welsh shires. 1919.

ROBERTS, ROBERT: The life and opinions of Robert Roberts, a wandering scholar (No. 2836).

**3161.** ROBERTS, SAMUEL: Farmer Careful of Cilhaul Uchaf. (Welsh and English), 1850; 2nd edn, Conway, 1881.

**3162.** Id.      Letters on improvements, addressed to the landlords and road commissioners, by a Llanbrynmair farmer. Newtown, 1852.

**3163.** Id.    Diosg farm: a sketch of its history. Newtown, 1854.

**3164.** SPALDING, KEITH: A German account of life in Wales in 1856. *Gwerin*, ii, 1, 1958.

**3165.** THOMAS, BEN BOWEN: The old poor law in Ardudwy Uwch-Artro. *B.B.C.S.*, vii, 1934.

**3166.** Id.    Rhestr o faledi rhai o brif faledwyr Cymru yn y bedwaredd ganrif ar bymtheg. *Jnl. Welsh Bibl. Soc.*, vii, 2, 1951.
> See also LEWIS, IDWAL: Ychwanegiadau at . . . (as above). Ibid., 3, 1952; and viii, 2, 1955.

**3167.** Id.    Drych y baledwr. Aberystwyth, 1958.

**3168.** THOMAS, DANIEL LLEUFER, *et al.*: Social problems in Wales. London, 1913.

**3169.** THOMAS, ROBERT (AP FYCHAN): Hunangofiant ac ysgrifau. Caerdydd, 1948.

> TWISTON-DAVIES, LEONARD, and LLOYD-JOHNES, HERBERT JOHNES: Welsh furniture (No. 290).

**3170.** WILLIAMS, MRS. A. BAILEY: Customs and traditions connected with sickness, death, and burial in Montgomeryshire in the late nineteenth century. *Mont. Coll.*, lii, 1951–2.

**3171.** Id.    Some aspects of village culture in Montgomeryshire in the latter part of the nineteenth century. Ibid., liii, 1954.

### (d) Industrial Wales

> See *The Engineer*, 1856 ff., and *The Iron and Coal Trades Review*, 1866 ff. for weekly summaries of industrial developments in Wales since their inception.

### (i) General

See section J III (*e*).

**3172.** ABERCONWAY, LORD: The basic industries of Great Britain. London, 1927.

**3173.** Census of Great Britain, 1851. Population tables. Vol. i, p. cxxxi: Distribution of the occupations of the people (map).

**3174.** DAVIES, DAVID JAMES: Diwydiant a masnach. Liverpool, 1946.

> DODD, ARTHUR HERBERT: The industrial revolution in North Wales (No. 2342).

**3175.** EDWARDS, NESS: The industrial revolution in South Wales. London, 1924.

**3176.** Industrial survey of South Wales. Made for the Board of Trade by the University College of South Wales and Monmouthshire. London, 1932.

JOHN, ARTHUR HENRY: The industrial development of South Wales (No. 2344).

LERRY, GEORGE GEOFFREY: The industries of Denbighshire from Tudor times to the present day. Part II: The extractive industries (No. 1818).

**3177.** MARQUAND, HILARY ADAIR: South Wales needs a plan. London, 1936.

**3178.** Id.    (ed.): The second industrial survey of South Wales. 3 vols. Cardiff, 1937.

**3179.** MASSEY, PHILIP: Industrial South Wales: a social and political survey. London, 1940.

**3180.** Merthyr Teachers' Association: The story of Merthyr Tydfil. Cardiff, 1932.

**3181.** REES, JAMES FREDERICK: How South Wales became industrialised. In Studies in Welsh history (No. 151).

**3182.** Welsh Reconstruction Advisory Council: First interim report. London, 1944.

**3183.** WILLIAMS, CYRIL RAYMOND: Treffynnon yn 1800. *Lleufer*, vii, 1951.

WILKINS, CHARLES: History of Merthyr Tydfil (No. 707).

WILLIAMS, DAVID TREVOR: The economic development of Swansea and the Swansea district to 1921 (No. 709).

### (ii) Iron, steel, and tinplate

**3184.** ANON.: Pioneers of the Welsh iron industry. *Red Dragon*, iv, 1883.

**3185.** ABBOTT, R: Chronicles of a Caernarvon ironworks. *Trans. Caerns. Hist. Soc.*, 1956.

ADDIS, JOHN PHILIP: The Crawshay dynasty (No. 2369).

BROOKE, EDWARD HENRY: Monograph on the tinplate works in Great Britain (No. 2385).

Id. Chronology of the tinplate works of Great Britain (No. 2386).

Id.    Appendix to the chronology of the tinplate works of Great Britain, 1665–1949 (No. 2387).

**3186.** BURN, DUNCAN LYALL: An economic history of steelmaking, 1867–1939. Cambridge, 1940.

**3187.** BURNHAM, THOMAS HALL, and HOSKINS, GEORGE OWEN: Iron and steel in Britain, 1870–1930. London, 1943.

CHAPPELL, EDGAR LEYSHON: Historic Melingriffith (No. 2373).

**3188.** CLARK, GEORGE THOMAS: The iron manufacture of South Wales. *Westminster Review*, 1848.

**3189.** CRAIG, ROBERT: R. J. Neville and the Llanelly iron shipping company. *N.L.W. Jnl.*, x, 1957–8.

**3190.** DARBY, HAROLD CLIFFORD: Tinplate migration in the vale of Neath. *Geography*, xv, 1929.

**3191.** EVANS, JOHN DAVID: The uncrowned iron king: the first William Crawshay. *N.L.W. Jnl.*, vii, 1951.

EVANS, LESLIE WYNNE: The early iron and coal industries [in Carmarthenshire] (No. 2376).

**3192.** Id.　　The tinplate, steel, and coal industries [in Carmarthenshire]. In A history of Carmarthenshire (No. 605), ii.

**3193.** FAY, CHARLES RYLE: Round about industrial Britain, 1830–1860. Toronto, 1952.
Ch. v: Merthyr Tydfil.

**3194.** FLOWER, PHILIP WILLIAM: History of the trade in tin and tinplates. London, 1875.

**3195.** GRIFFITHS, D.: The tinplate industry in Monmouthshire. *Mon. Rev.*, i, 1933.

**3196.** JEVONS, HERBERT STANLEY: The British steel industry. London, 1932.

JONES, JOHN HENRY: The tinplate industry (No. 2392).

LLOYD, JOHN: The early history of the old South Wales ironworks, 1760–1840 (No. 2381).

MINCHINTON, WALTER EDWARD: The British tinplate industry: a history (No. 2393).

**3197.** SAMUEL, JOHN RHYS: A short history of tin and tinplate. Newport, 1924.

SCRIVENOR, HARRY: History of the iron trade from the earliest records to the present period (No. 2384).

WILKINS, CHARLES: The history of the iron, steel, tinplate, and other trades of Wales (No. 2247).

### (iii) Coal

**3198.** DAVIES, HENRY: The South Wales coalfield, its geology and mines. Pontypridd, 1901.

**3199.** EDWARDS, DAVID: The history of the rise, progress, and present prospects of the coal trade, more particularly steam coal, in South Wales and Monmouthshire. *Trans. Royal National Eisteddfod of Wales,* 1883.

EVANS, EVAN LEWIS (ed.): Braslun o hanes Pontarddulais a'r cylch (No. 594).

**3200.** GRIFFITHS, THOMAS HUGHES: The South Wales anthracite coal industry. *Welsh Outlook,* xiv, 1927.

HARE, ANTHONY EDWARD CHRISTIAN: The anthracite coal industry of the Swansea district (No. 2364).

**3201.** JEVONS, HERBERT STANLEY: The British coal trade. London, 1915.

LERRY, GEORGE GEOFFREY: The collieries of Denbighshire (No. 634).

**3202.** MORRIS, JOHN HENRY, and WILLIAMS, LAURENCE JOHN: R. J. Neville and the early Welsh coal trade. *N.L.W. Jnl.,* x, 1957–8.
  See also CRAIG, ROBERT: R. J. Neville and the early Welsh coal trade—a comment, ibid.; and MORGAN, WALTER THOMAS: A note on Lucy Thomas of Waunwyllt, ibid.

**3203.** Id.    and WILLIAMS, LAURENCE JOHN: The South Wales coal industry, 1841–75. Cardiff, 1958.

**3204.** NORTH, FREDERICK JOHN: Coal and the coalfields in Wales. Cardiff, 1926.

PHILLIPS, ELIZABETH: A history of the pioneers of the Welsh coalfield (No. 2366).

**3205.** PRICE, WATKIN WILLIAM: The history of Powell Duffryn in the Aberdare valley. *P.D. Review,* li–liii, 1942–3.

**3206.** REES, ENOCH: Hanes Brynaman. Ystalyfera, 1880; 2nd edn, 1896.

RHONDDA, MARGARET, VISCOUNTESS (ed.): D. A. Thomas, Viscount Rhondda (No. 2800).

**3207.** THOMAS, DAVID ALFRED (Lord Rhondda): Some notes on the present state of the coal trade. Cardiff, 1896.

**3208.** Id.　　The growth and direction of our foreign trade in coal (1850–1900). Royal Statistical Society, 1903.

**3209.** THOMAS, IVOR: Top Sawyer: a biography of David Davies of Llandinam. London, 1938.

**3210.** VINCENT, JAMES EDMUND: John Nixon, pioneer of the coal trade. London, 1900.

WILKINS, CHARLES: The South Wales coal trade and its allied industries from the earliest days to the present time (No. 2248).

**3211.** WILLIAMS, DAVID TREVOR: Output variation and migration of mining intensity within the western half of the South Wales coalfield, 1906–30. *Procs. of the South Wales Institute of Engineers,* xlviii, 1933.

### (iv) Non-ferrous metals

**3212.** EVANS, LESLIE WYNNE: The non-ferrous metal industries [of Carmarthenshire]. In A history of Carmarthenshire (No. 605), ii.

**3213.** GRIFFITHS, ROOSEVELT: History of non-ferrous industries in South Wales. *Metal Industries,* January, 1942.

HARRIS, JOHN RAYMOND: Michael Hughes of Sutton; the influence of Welsh copper on Lancashire business, 1780–1815 (No. 2402).

HUNT, ROBERT: Notices of the history of the lead mines of Cardiganshire (No. 2403).

LEWIS, WILLIAM JOHN: The Cwmsymlog lead mine (No. 2405).

**3214.** Report of the select committee on copper mines and copper trade. 1799.

**3215.** RICHARDS, THOMAS: Mona mine letters. *Trans. Angl. Antiq. Soc.,* 1946.

**3216.** ROBERTS, ROBERT OWEN: John Hughes, manager of the Upper Bank copper works *circa* 1800. *Gower,* vii, 1954.

Id.　　The development and decline of the copper and other non-ferrous metal industries in South Wales (No. 2407).

### (v) Slate

AMBROSE, WILLIAM ROBERT: Hynafiaethau, cofiannau, a hanes presennol Nant Nanlle (No. 531).

**3217.** DAVIES, DAVID CHRISTOPHER: Treatise on slates and slate quarrying. London, 1876.

DAVIES, WILLIAM LLEWELYN (ed.): The memoirs of Samuel Holland, one of the pioneers of the North Wales slate industry (No. 713).

**3218.** HOBSON, W. D.: Penrhyn quarry. Bangor, 1913.

HUGHES, HUGH DERFEL: Hynafiaethau Llandegai a Llanllechid (No. 535).

**3219.** JONES, JOHN OWEN: Quarrying at Bethesda. *Wales,* i, 1894.

**3220.** NORTH, FREDERICK JOHN: The slates of Wales. Cardiff, 3rd edn, 1946.
Contains bibliography.

**3221.** OWEN, ELIAS: The Penrhyn slate quarry. *Red Dragon,* vii, 1885.

**3222.** Parliamentary papers relating to the Penrhyn and Brynhafod-y-wern quarries, 1819–23.

PARRY, GRIFFITH TECWYN: Llanberis, ei hanes, ei phobl, a'i phethau (No. 544).

**3223.** PARRY, WILLIAM JOHN: Chwareli a chwarelwyr Cymru. Caernarfon, 1897.

**3224.** PRITCHARD, DAVID DYLAN: The slate industry of North Wales. Denbigh, 1946.

**3225.** Id.    The expansionist phase in the history of the Welsh slate industry. *Trans. Caerns. Hist. Soc.,* 1949.

**3226.** Id.    Aspects of the slate industry, etc. *The Quarry-Managers' Jnl.,* July, 1942—October, 1946.
A valuable series of articles on the North Wales slate industry.

**3227.** SMITH, T. C.: Slate quarries in Wales. *Mining Jnl.,* 1860.

WILLIAMS, GRIFFITH JOHN: Hanes plwyf Ffestiniog (No. 727).

**3228.** Welsh slate industry, The: Report by the committee appointed by the Minister of Works. London, 1947.

### (vi) Miscellaneous

**3229.** BASSETT, THOMAS: Braslun o hanes Hughes a'i Fab, cyhoeddwyr, Wrecsam. Oswestry, 1946.

**3230.** FISHER, W. STANLEY: Swansea porcelain. *Apollo,* 1953.

**3231.** JOHN, WILLIAM DAVID: Nantgarw porcelain. Newport, 1948; supplement, 1956.

Id.     Pontypool and Usk japanned wares (No. 2391).

**3232.** Id.     Swansea porcelain. Newport, 1958.

**3233.** MESSHAM, J. E.: The Buckley pottery industry. *Flints. Hist. Soc. Pubns.*, xvi, 1956.

      See also BARTON, K. J.: Excavations at Prescot's pottery, 1954. Ibid.

**3234.** NANCE, E. MORTON: The pottery and porcelain of Swansea and Nantgarw. London, 1942.

**3235.** SHORTER, ALFRED H.: Paper-mills in Monmouthshire. *Arch. Camb.*, 1953.

**3236.** WILLIAMS, ISAAC JOHN: The Nantgarw pottery and its products. *Arch. Camb.*, lxxxvi, 1932.

### (vii) Social conditions: industrial

See sections K II (*g*) and (*m*); III (*b*) (*i*).

**3237.** BESSBOROUGH, THE EARL OF (ed.): Lady Charlotte Guest; extracts from her journal, 1833–1852. London, 1950.

**3238.** Id.     (ed.): Lady Charlotte Schreiber (formerly Lady Charlotte Guest). Extracts from her journal, 1853–1891. London, 1952.

**3239.** BRENAN, TOM, and COONEY, E. W.: A handbook of the social statistics of south-west Wales. Swansea, 1950.

**3240.** Id. and id. and POLLINS, HAROLD: Social change in south-west Wales. London, 1954.

**3241.** BRUCE, HENRY AUSTIN (Lord Aberdare): The present condition and future prospects of the working classes in South Wales. 1851; reprinted in id.: Lectures and addresses, London, 1896.

**3242.** Id.     Letters of . . . Lord Aberdare. Ed. anon. 2 vols. Oxford, 1902.

**3243.** COLLINS, WILLIAM JOHN TOWNSEND: A history of the Silurian lodge, holden at Newport, Mon. Newport, 1941.

**3244.** JONES, GLYN PENRHYN: Cholera in Wales. *N.L.W. Jnl.*, x, 1957-8.

      JONES, THOMAS: Rhymney memories (No. 745).

**3245.** RAMMELL, T. W.: Report on the sanitary condition of the town of Cardiff. Cardiff, 1850.

**3246.** Report on the state of elementary education in the mining district of South Wales (Seymour Tremenheere). Minutes of the Committee of Council on Education, 1839–40, Appendix II. London, 1840.

**3247.** Reports of the royal commission on the employment of children in mines. 1842–3.

**3248.** Reports of the commissioner (Seymour Tremenheere) on the operation of the Mines Act (State of population in the mining districts). 1844–59. (See particularly the reports for 1846, 1847, 1850, 1851, 1856, 1857–8.)

**3249.** Reports of the inspectors of mines, 1852–3, *et seq.*

**3250.** Report of the Commissioners appointed to enquire into the several matters relating to coal in the United Kingdom. 1871.

**3251.** Report of the commission of enquiry into industrial unrest: Wales including Monmouthshire. 1917.

### (e) Communications and transport

### (i) Roads

DODD, ARTHUR HERBERT: The industrial revolution in North Wales (No. 2342).
Ch. iv.

**3252.** GIBB, SIR ALEXANDER: The story of Telford. London, 1935.

**3253.** HARPER, CHARLES GEORGE: The Holyhead road. London, 1902.

**3254.** HOWELL, ABRAHAM: Roads, bridges, canals, and railways of Montgomeryshire. *Mont. Coll.*, viii, 1875; ix, 1876; xv, 1882; xvi, 1883.

**3255.** HOWELLS, CLARENCE S.: Transport facilities in South Wales and Monmouthshire. Cardiff, 1911.

**3256.** JACKMAN, WILLIAM T.: Development of transport in modern England. 2 vols. Cambridge, 1916.

**3257.** LAVENDER, F.: Bishop's Castle turnpike trustees. *Mont. Coll.*, lii, 1951–2.

**3258.** LLOYD, GEORGE: Flintshire packhorse bridges. *Flints. Hist. Soc. Pubns.*, xvii, 1957.

**3259.** PRITCHARD, R. T.: The post road in Caernarvonshire. *Trans. Caerns. Hist. Soc.*, 1952.

**3260.** Id.      The history of the post road in Anglesey. *Trans. Angl. Antiq. Soc.*, 1954.

**3261.** Id.    The Caernarvonshire turnpike trust. *Trans. Caerns. Hist. Soc.,* 1956.

**3262.** RICHARD, T. BRYN: An outline of the history of road and bridge construction, with particular reference to South Wales and Monmouthshire. *Structural Engineer,* 1946.

**3263.** Reports from committees on Holyhead roads, harbour, etc. 1810–22.

**3264.** Reports from Holyhead road commissioners, 1816–45.

**3265.** Report of the royal commission into the state of the roads in England and Wales. 1840.

**3266.** ROLT, LIONEL THOMAS CASWALL: Thomas Telford. London, 1958.

**3267.** WILLIAMS, DAVID: A report on the turnpike trusts. *N.L.W. Jnl.,* viii, 1953–4.
> See also id.: The Rebecca riots (No. 2878), ch. vi.

### (ii) Canals

**3268.** POLLINS, HAROLD: The Swansea canal. *Jnl. of Transport History,* i, 1954.

**3269.** PRIESTLEY, JOSEPH: Historical account of the navigable rivers, canals, and railways through Great Britain. London, 1831.

### (iii) Railways

**3270.** AHRONS, E. L.: Locomotive and train working in the latter part of the nineteenth century. Cambridge, 1953.
> Ch. iv–xi, Railways in Wales.

**3271.** ALLCHIN, M. C. V.: Locomotives of the Taff Vale railway. Portsmouth, 1944.

**3272.** BARRIE, DEREK STIVEN MAXWELTON: The railways of South Wales. *Railway Magazine,* lxxxv, 1939.

**3273.** Id.    The Taff Vale railway. 2nd edn. South Godstone, 1950.

**3274.** Id.    Historical notes on the railways of the western region in South Wales and Monmouthshire. *Procs. of the South Wales and Monmouthshire Railways and Docks Lecture and Debating Soc.,* 1950–1.

**3275.** Id.    The Rhymney railway. South Godstone, 1952.

**3276.** Id.    The Brecon and Merthyr railway. Lingfield, 1957.

**3277.** Id.    and LEE, CHARLES EDWARD: The Sirhowy Valley and its railways. London, 1940.

**3278.** BOURNE, JOHN: The Burry Port and Gwendraeth Valley railway. *Railway Mag.*, xcix, 1953.

**3279.** BOYD, JAMES IAN CRAIG: Narrow-gauge rails to Portmadoc. A historical survey of the Festiniog Welsh Highlands railway and its ancillaries. South Godstone, 1949.

**3280.** Id.    Narrow gauge rails in mid-Wales. South Godstone, 1952.

**3281.** Id.    The Ffestiniog railway. Vol. i, 1800–1889. Lingfield, 1956.

**3282.** Britannia tubular bridge: centenary. *Railway Mag.*, xcvi, 1950.

**3283.** CHURTON, E.: The railway book of England. London, 1851.

**3284.** CLARK, EDWIN: The Britannia and Conway tubular bridges. 2 vols. London, 1850.

**3285.** COZENS, LEWIS: The Tal-y-llyn railway. Sutton, 1948.

**3286.** Id.    The Corris railway. Sutton, 1949.

**3287.** Id.    The Vale of Rheidol railway. Sutton, 1950.

**3288.** Id.    The Welshpool and Llanfair light railway. Sutton, 1951.

**3289.** Id.    The Van and Kerry railways with the Kerry tramway. London, 1953.

**3290.** Id.    The Mawddwy railway. London, 1954.

**3291.** Id.    The Plynlimon and Hafan tramway. London, 1955.

**3292.** Id.    Aberayron transport. London, 1957.

**3293.** DAVIES, ARTHUR STANLEY: Early railways of the Ellesmere and the Montgomeryshire canals. *Trans. Newcomen Soc.*, xxiv, 1943–5.

**3294.** DUNN, JOHN MAXWELL: The Chester and Holyhead railway. South Godstone, 1948.

**3295.** ELLISON, F. B.: The Hay railway, 1810–1863. *Trans. Newcomen Soc.*, xviii, 1937–8.

EVANS, LESLIE WYNNE, and OWEN, GERAINT DYFNALLT: The development of communications [in Carmarthenshire] (No. 2414).

**3296.** GARRAWAY, A. G. W.: The Ffestiniog railway. *Trans. Caerns. Hist. Soc.*, 1955.

**3297.** GASQUOINE, CHARLES PENRHYN: The story of the Cambrian. Oswestry, 1922.

**3298.** GRESHAM, COLIN A.: William Fairbairn and the Conway tubular bridge. *Trans. Caerns. Hist. Soc.,* 1948.

**3299.** HUMPHREYS, C. NEWMAN: A hundred years of transport: the Welshpool and Llanfair light railway. *Mont. Coll.,* li, 1950.

**3300.** JONES, RICHARD BAGNOLD: British narrow-gauge railways. London, 1958.
> Vol. iv, Welsh railways.

**3301.** KIDNER, R. W.: The Cambrian railways. South Godstone, 1955.

**3302.** KLAPPER, CHARLES F., and RICHENS, F. G.: The Welshpool and Llanfair light railway. *Railway Mag.,* lxxxv, 1939.

**3303.** LEE, CHARLES EDWARD: The Sirhowy valley and its railways. *Railway Mag.,* lxxxv, 1939.

**3304.** Id.    Narrow-gauge railways in North Wales. London, 1945.

**3305.** Id.    The Swansea and Mumbles railway. 2nd edn. South Godstone, 1954.

**3306.** LERRY, GEORGE GEOFFREY: Henry Robertson, pioneer of railways into Wales. Oswestry, 1949.

**3307.** MACDERMOT, EDWARD TERENCE: The history of the Great Western railway. London, vol. i, parts 1 and 2, 1927; vol. ii, 1931.

**3308.** MARSHALL, CHARLES FREDERICK DENDY: A history of British railways down to the year 1830. Oxford, 1938.
> Ch. v, Early railways in Wales.

**3309.** MASON, W. W.: Trevithick's first rail locomotive. *Trans. Newcomen Soc.,* xii, 1931–2.

**3310.** MERCER, STANLEY: Trevithick and the Merthyr tramroad. *The Engineer,* April, 1948.

**3311.** Id.    Trevithick and the Merthyr tramroad. *Trans. Newcomen Soc.,* xxvi, 1947–9.

**3312.** MORRIS, E. H., and ELLISON, F. B.: The Hereford and Abergavenny tramroad. *Woolhope Trans.,* 1941.

**3313.** OLIVER, R. C. B.: Railways and Radnorshire. *Trans. Rads. Soc.,* xviii, 1948.

**3314.** PARRY, EDWARD: Railway companion from Chester to Holyhead. London, 1848; 2nd edn, 1849.

**3315.** ROBERTS, O. GLYNNE: The Britannia bridge. *Trans. Angl. Antiq. Soc.*, 1946.

**3316.** ROBERTSON, ANDREW: A chapter in bridge engineering a century ago (Britannia tubular bridge). *Engineering,* 1950.

**3317.** ROLT, LIONEL THOMAS CASWALL: Railway adventure (Talyllyn). London, 1956.

**3318.** SANDS, T. B.: Talyllyn: a rural Welsh junction. *Railway Mag.,* xcvii, 1951.

**3319.** SCRIVENOR, HENRY: Railways of the United Kingdom. London, 1849.

### (iv) Shipping

**3320.** ANON.: The shipping of Wales. *Cambrian Register,* i, 1797; ii, 1799; iii, 1818.

A review of the records of the Conway and the Menai ferries (No. 130 (8)).

CHAPPELL, EDGAR LEYSHON: History of the port of Cardiff (No. 666).

**3321.** CRUBELLIER, M.: Le développement de Cardiff au cours, du xix$^e$ siècle et jusqu' à la crise actuelle. *Annales de Geographie,* xiv, 1936.

DAWSON, JAMES WILLIAM: Commerce and custom; a history of the ports of Newport and Caerleon (No. 737).

HUGHES, HENRY: Immortal sails; a story of a Welsh port [Portmadoc] and some of its ships (No. 252).

LLOYD, ROBERT JOHN HERBERT: Henry Leach (1770–1848), collector of taxes at Milford (No. 2282).

LLOYD, WYNNE L.: Trade and transport: an account of the trade of the port of Swansea and the transport facilities and industry in the district (No. 2421).

MORGAN, DAVID WILLIAM: Brief glory: the story of a quest (No. 720).

**3322.** OWEN, DAVID JOHN: The ports of the United Kingdom. London, 1948.

Ch. xxiii, The North Wales ports; ch. xxiv, The South Wales ports.

REES, JAMES FREDERICK: The story of Milford (No. 787).

**3323.** Reports of select committees on communication between England and Ireland by Milford Haven. 1826–27.

**3324.** RICHARDS, WILLIAM MORGAN: Some aspects of the industrial revolution in south-east Caernarvonshire. I, Y Traeth Mawr; II, Portmadoc. *Trans. Caerns. Hist. Soc.*, 1942–3 and 1944.

**3325.** THOMAS, DAVID: Anglesey shipbuilding down to 1840. *Trans. Angl. Antiq. Soc.*, 1932.

**3326.** Id.    Llechi a llongau: cyfraniad sir Gaernarfon at y chwyldro diwydiannol ym Mhrydain. *Trans. Caerns. Hist. Soc.*, 1939.

> Id.    Hen longau a llongwyr Cymru. Bilingual. (No. 258).

> Id.    Hen longau sir Gaernarfon (No. 259).

### (f) Trade and commerce

#### (i) Trade directories

**3327.** NORTON, JANE ELIZABETH: Guide to the national and provincial directories of England and Wales, excluding London, published before 1856. Royal Historical Soc. London, 1950.

#### (ii) Banking

> See PRESNELL, L. S.: Country banking in the industrial revolution. Oxford, 1956.

**3328.** CRICK, WALFORD FRANK, and WADSWORTH, J. E.: A hundred years of joint stock banking. London, 1936.

> For a translation of the chapter on the North and South Wales Bank, see JENKINS, ROBERT THOMAS: Canrif o hanes banc gogledd a deheudir Cymru. Llundain, 1936.

**3329.** DAVIES, ARTHUR STANLEY: The early banks of mid-Wales. Welshpool, 1935.

**3330.** GREEN, FRANCIS: Early banks in west Wales. *W. Wales Hist. Rec. Soc. Pubns.*, vi, 1916.

**3331.** HODGES, THOMAS MANSEL: Early banking in Cardiff. *Econ. Hist. Rev.*, series I, xviii, 1947.

**3332.** Id.    The history of the Newport and Caerleon savings bank (1830–1888). Ibid., series II, ii, 1950.

**3333.** INGMAN, JOHN: Early Bangor banks. *Trans. Caerns. Hist. Soc.*, 1947.

**3334.** ROBERTS, ROBERT OWEN: Bank of England branch discounting, 1826–59. *Economica*, Aug., 1958.

**3335.** Id.    Bank advances for Welsh drovers in the early nineteenth century. *Bankers' Mag.*, October, 1958.

**3336.** Id.    The operations of the Brecon old bank of Wilkins and Co., 1778–1890. *Business History*, i, I, 1958.

### IV. EDUCATION

For the general background, see ADAMSON, JOHN WILLIAM: English education, 1760–1902, London, 1930; BARNARD, HOWARD CLIVE: A short history of English education, 1760–1944, London, 1947; BIRCHENOUGH, CHARLES: A history of elementary education in England and Wales from 1800 to the present day, London, 1929; LOWNDES, GEORGE ALFRED NORMAN: The silent social revolution: an account of the expansion of public education in England and Wales, 1895–1935, London, 1937.

See also section K II (*j*).

#### (a) Government publications

**3337.** Board (now Ministry) of Education: Welsh Department. Annual reports, 1907 ff.

**3338.** Id.    Education in Wales, 1847–1947. Bilingual. London, 1948.

A useful conspectus with a short list of books.

**3339.** Id.    The future of secondary education in Wales: Report of the Central Advisory Council for Education (Wales). Bilingual. London, 1949.

Useful for the historical background.

**3340.** Hansard: Parliamentary debates (Commons and Lords), 1889.

Debates on the Intermediate and Technical Education Bill (Wales).

**3341.** Minutes of the Committee of Council on education, 1839–40.

Reports of the commissioners of enquiry into the state of education in Wales, 1847 (No. 2894).

**3342.** Reports of the commissioners concerning charities. 1819 ff.

**3343.** Report of the committee on intermediate and higher education in Wales, 1881.

**3344.** Report of the committee on the working of the education Acts, 1886–8.

**3345.** Report of the royal commission on the University of Wales, 1918.

**3346.** Report of the departmental committee appointed to enquire into the position of the Welsh language ('Welsh in education and life'), 1927.

### (b) Sunday schools

**3347.** ANON.: Crybwylliad am ffurfiad a sefydliad ysgolion Sabbothol. London, 1821.

**3348.** EVANS, DAVID: The Sunday schools of Wales. London, 1883.

EVANS, JOHN JAMES: Morgan John Rhys a'i amserau (No. 2512).

**3349.** GILBERT, J.: Life of the late Rev. Edward Williams. London, 1825.

GRIFFITH, DOROTHI MARY: Nationality in the Sunday school movement (No. 2589).

**3350.** GRIFFITH, G. WYNNE: Yr ysgol Sul. Caernarfon, 1936.

**3351.** LEWIS, HOWELL ELVET: Dr. Edward Williams. *Y Traethodydd*, 1907.

**3352.** LEWIS, W.: Canmlwyddiant yr ysgol Sabbothol. Dolgellau, 1886.

**3353.** SHANKLAND, THOMAS: Dechreuad yr ysgolion Sabbothol yng Nghymru. *Cymru*, 1902.

**3354.** THOMAS, BEN BOWEN: Datblygiad yr ysgol Sul yng Nghymru. *Y Cyfarwyddwr*, Mai-Mehefin, 1930.

### (c) Primary and elementary education

**3355.** ANON.: The Welsh education question and the bishop of St. David's. Bristol, 1861.

**3356.** BOWSTEAD, J.: Letters concerning education in South Wales. Stroud, 1861.

**3357.** CRONIN, JOHN M.: Catholic education in Cardiff [1836–47]. *St. Peter's Mag.* Cardiff, June and July, 1922.

**3358.** DAVIES, DAVID JACOB: Ysgol Llanwrin. *Yr Ymofynnydd*, 1954.

**3359.** DAVIES, EBENEZER THOMAS: Monmouthshire schools and education to 1870. Newport, 1957.

**3360.** DAVIES, J. CUNLLO: Ffrwd-fâl. *Cymru*, 1899 and 1900.

**3361.** DAVIES, W. EMLYN: The national schools, Oxford Street in the parish of Swansea St. Mary, 1848–1948. Swansea, 1948.

**3362.** DODD, CHARLES: Wrexham schools and scholars. Wrexham, 1924.

**3363.** EVANS, GWILYM JOHN: Dyddlyfrau ysgol Bethel. *Trans. Caerns. Hist. Soc.*, 1950.

**3364.** EVANS, LESLIE WYNNE: Ironworks schools in Wales, 1784–1860. *Sociological Review*, xliii.

**3365.** Id.    Schools established by industrial undertakings in Caernarvonshire and Merionethshire during the nineteenth century. *Trans. Caerns. Hist. Soc.*, 1954.

**3366.** Id.    Bron-y-foel school, Caernarvonshire. Ibid., 1955.

**3367.** Id.    Sir John and Lady Charlotte Guest's educational scheme at Dowlais in the mid-nineteenth century. *N.L.W. Jnl.*, ix, 1955–6.

**3368.** EVANS, THOMAS: History of the navigation school, Abercynon, 1875 to 1945. Cardiff, 1946.

**3369.** [GABB, JAMES ASHE]: A brief account of James Davies, master of the national school of Devauden-Hill, London, 1833.

> See also id.: Davies of Devauden. A brief memoir of James Davies . . . to which is appended a small tract written by himself, London, 1841; and PHILLIPS, SIR THOMAS: Life of James Davies, a village schoolmaster, London, 1850; 2nd edn, 1852.

**3370.** JONES, EVAN DAVID (ed.): The journal of William Roberts ('Nefydd'), 1853–62. *N.L.W. Jnl.*, viii, 1953–4; ix, 1955–6; x, 1957–8.

**3371.** JONES, EVAN KENFFIG: The story of education in a Welsh border parish, or the schools of Cefnmawr, 1786–1933. Cefnmawr, 1933.

> JONES, IDWAL: The voluntary system at work (No. 2880).
> The appendix contains a list of British schools to 1852. See also review by LLOYD, DAVID TECWYN: Datblygiad addysg, *Y Llenor*, 1944-5.

**3372.** JONES, JAMES RHYS ('Kilsby'): Adgofion am ysgol Neuaddlwyd. *Y Traethodydd*, 1848.

**3373.** Id.    Yr ysgol yn ei pherthynasau â'r wladwriaeth, yr eglwys, a'r gynulleidfa, sef esboniad ar gofnodau Pwyllgor y Cynghor ar addysg. London, 1848.

**3374.** JONES, JOHN CLIFFORD: St. Matthew's school, Buckley, 1849–1949: a centenary booklet. Buckley, 1949.

**3375.** Id.    A history of the schools and education in Buckley. *Flints. Hist. Soc. Pubns.*, xv, 1954–5.

**3376.** JONES-ROBERTS, KATE WINIFRED: Education in the parish of Ffestiniog. *Jnl. Mer. Hist. and Rec. Soc.*, ii, 1956.

**3377.** KAY-SHUTTLEWORTH, JAMES: Public education as affected by the minutes of the committee. London, 1853.

**3378.** LEWIS, HENRY: Ysgolion Brutanaidd Arfon. *Cymru*, 1912.

**3379.** LLOYD, D.: Letter to J. Bowstead. Carmarthen, 1861.

**3380.** OLLIVANT, ALFRED (Bishop of Llandaff): Letter to the clergy in reference to the report of H.M. Inspector of Schools. London, 1856.

**3381.** Pontypool town school: Centenary, 1838–1938. Pontypool, 1938.

**3382.** PRICE, WATKIN WILLIAM: Park schools centenary (Canmlwyddiant ysgol y Comin): its history, with brief references to the history of education in the Aberdare valley. Aberdare, 1948.

**3383.** ROBERTS, OWEN OWEN: Church and education, being an address to the Welsh. Carmarthen, 1843.

**3384.** ROBERTS, ROBERT OWEN: Ysgol weithfaol yr Hafod gan mlynedd yn ôl. *Yr Athro*, Mehefin-Gorffennaf, 1952.

**3385.** ROWLANDS, DAVID ('Dewi Môn'): Ysgol genedlaethol o'r hen-ffasiwn. *Y Geninen*, 1902.

**3386.** SAMUEL, DAVID: Hen ysgolfeistri Cymru. *Cymru*, 1892.

**3387.** Id.     Ystrad Meurig. Ibid., 1893.

**3388.** Id.     Ysgol Llanfihangel Geneu'r Glyn. Ibid., 1894.

**3389.** Id.     Neuadd Lwyd. Ibid., 1895.

SMITH, FRANK: Life of Sir James Kay-Shuttleworth (No. 2900).

**3390.** THIRLWALL, CONNOP (Bishop of St. David's): Letter to J. Bowstead. London, 1861.

**3391.** THOMAS, H.: Father and son. London, 1898.

**3392.** TROTT, ARTHUR LUTHER: Aberystwyth school board and board school, 1870–1902. *Ceredigion*, ii, 1, 1952.

**3393.** Id.     Church day schools in Aberystwyth during the nineteenth century. Ibid., ii, 2, 1953.

**3394.** Id.     Elementary day schools for children of the working classes in Cardiganshire in 1847. Ibid., ii, 3, 1954.

**3395.** VAUGHAN, BETTY C.: The log book of Llansannan school. *Trans. Denbs. Hist. Soc.*, vi, 1957.

**3396.** WALKER, THOMAS G.: Hanes ysgol Henblas, 1841–1943. Llangefni, 1943.

**3397.** WILLIAMS, MRS. A. BAILEY: Education in Montgomeryshire in the late nineteenth century. *Mont. Coll.*, lii, 1951–2.

**3398.** WILLIAMS, JAMES: On religious instruction in national schools in Wales: a letter to the bishop of Bangor. Bangor, n.d.

**3399.** WILLIAMS, WILLIAM: An examination of the principles on which the British and Foreign School Society is established. London, 1823.

**3400.** WILLIAMS, WILLIAM MOSES: Anglesey schools a century ago. *Trans. Angl. Antiq. Soc.,* 1946.

### (d) Welsh in the schools

**3401.** DAVIES, DAN ISAAC: Tair miliwn o Gymry dwy-ieithawg. Dinbych, 1885–6.

**3402.** EVANS, ELLEN: The teaching of Welsh. Cardiff and London, 1924.

**3403.** HUGHES, JOHN: Sir Henry Jones and the Cross commission. *Aberystwyth Studies,* v, 1923.

**3404.** SOUTHALL, J. E.: Bilingual teaching in Welsh elementary schools. Newport, 1888.

**3405.** Id.     Wales, her language, etc. Newport and London, 1892.

### (e) Intermediate and secondary education

See also section A V (*c*) (ii).

**3406.** AARON, RICHARD ITHAMAR: The Central Welsh Board as an examining and servicing agency for primary, secondary, and further education in Wales. Jubilee pamphlet, May, 1896–May, 1946.

**3407.** ARCHER, RICHARD LAWRENCE: Secondary education in the 19th century. Cambridge, 1928.
> Ch. xi, Education in Wales.

**3408.** Central Welsh Board: Annual reports (to 1948).

**3409.** Id.     To-day and to-morrow in Welsh education. Cardiff, 1916.

**3410.** Christ's College, Brecon: The Act of 1853 and the scheme for [its] establishment and regulation. London, 1855.

**3411.** Conferences of the joint education committees of North Wales. Wrexham, 1890.

**3412.** Conferences (general) of the joint education committees of Wales and Monmouthshire. Wrexham, 1890–3.

**3413.** ELLIS, THOMAS EDWARD, and GRIFFITH, ELLIS JONES: Intermediate and technical education (Wales). London, 1889.
> An explanation of the 1889 Act.

**3414.** ELLIS, THOMAS IORWERTH: The development of modern Welsh secondary education. *Trans. Cymmr.,* 1932–3.

**3415.** Id. The development of higher education in Wales. Wrexham, 1935.

**3416.** EVANS, DAVID EMRYS, WHEELER, OLIVE, and WILLIAMS, WILLIAM MOSES: The Welsh Intermediate Education Act, 1889. Addresses. *Trans. Cymmr.,* 1939.

HAMER, FREDERICK EDWARD (ed.): Personal papers of Lord Rendel (No. 2781).

**3417.** JONES, ABEL S.: John Morgan, first headmaster of Narberth county school. Llandysul, 1939.

**3418.** OWEN, PRYS EIFION: The beginnings of the county schools in Caernarvonshire. *Trans. Caerns. Hist. Soc.,* 1957.

**3419.** REICHEL, HARRY RUDOLF: The university in Wales. Newtown, 1920.

**3420.** WATKINS, PERCY EMERSON: A Welshman remembers. Cardiff, 1944.

**3421.** WEBSTER, JOHN ROGER: The first reports of Owen M. Edwards on Welsh intermediate schools. *N.L.W. Jnl.,* x, 1957–8.

WILLIAMS, MRS. A. BAILEY: Education in Montgomeryshire in the late nineteenth century (No. 3397).

**3422.** WILLIAMS, WILLIAM MOSES: A case for the Central Welsh Board (Welsh version by EVANS, ELSBETH OWEN: Gair dros y Bwrdd Canol). Cardiff, 1947.

### (f) Training colleges

**3423.** Bangor Normal College: Statement of position, and appeal. 1860.

**3424.** Id. First report, 1863.

**3425.** HALLIWELL, THOMAS: Trinity College, Carmarthen, 1848–1948. Carmarthen, 1948.

**3426.** MEREDITH, R.: Early history of the North Wales training college. *Trans. Caerns. Hist. Soc.,* 1946.

**3427.** REES, LLEWELYN MORGAN, ROBERTS, THOMAS, and BASSETT, THOMAS MERFYN: Bangor Normal College, 1858–1958. Conway, 1958.

**3428.** SALMON, DAVID: History of the Normal College for Wales. Swansea, 1902.

**3429.** WILLIAMS, JOHN LLOYD: Atgofion tri chwarter canrif. Cyf. iii a iv. Aberystwyth, 1944; Llundain, 1945.

### (g) University education

**3430.** ARCHDALL, HENRY KINGSLEY: St. David's College, Lampeter: its past, present, and future. Lampeter, 1952.

> For further works relating to the college, see EVANS, GEORGE EYRE: Lampeter (No. 566); HARFORD, JOHN SCANDRETT: Life of the bishop [Thomas] Burgess (No. 3457); JONES, WILLIAM BASIL TICKELL (bishop of St. David's): the charters and statutes of St. David's College, etc., Oxford, 1829 (see also Statutes of St. David's College adopted . . . July 12 . . . 1910; and The charters, special statutes and ordinary statutes of St. David's College . . . 1913); R[ICHARDS], R. H., and M[ORRIS], A. E. (archbishop of Wales): The history of St. David's College, *Lampeter Mag.*, xvi, 1938; TREE, RONALD: Laying the foundation stone of St. David's College, Lampeter, *Jnl. Hist. Soc. Church in Wales*, iv, 1954; WILLIAMS, ELLEN (ed.): Life and letters of Rowland Williams, 2 vols., London, 1874; WILLIAMS, ROWLAND: [Twenty sermons], with some account of the work of St. David's College, London, 1857.

**3431.** DAVIES, W. CADWALADR, and JONES, WILLIAM LEWIS: The University of Wales and its colleges. London, 1905.

**3432.** DAVIES, W. E.: Sir Hugh Owen: his life and life-work. London, 1885.

**3433.** ELLIS, THOMAS IORWERTH: Thomas Charles Edwards, letters. Aberystwyth, 1952–3.

Id. The development of higher education in Wales (No. 3415).

**3434.** EVANS, DAVID EMRYS: The University of Wales: a historical sketch. Cardiff, 1953.

**3435.** Id. Universities, past and present: lecture delivered at University College, Swansea, October 8, 1953. London, 1954.

GRUFFYDD, WILLIAM JOHN: Owen Morgan Edwards: cofiant (No. 2780).

**3436.** HARDY, E. G.: Jesus College, Oxford. London, 1899.

**3437.** HETHERINGTON, H. J. W.: The life of Sir Henry Jones. London, 1924.

**3438.** JONES, HENRY: Old memories. London, 1924.

**3439.** JONES, JOHN VIRIAMU: The University of Wales. *Trans. Liverpool Welsh Nat. Soc.*, 1895–6.

**3440.** JONES, KATHERINE VIRIAMU: Life of Viriamu Jones. London, 1915.

**3441.** JONES, THOMAS: Leeks and daffodils. Newtown, 1942.

**3442.** LLOYD, JOHN EDWARD (ed.): Sir Harry Reichel, 1856–1931. Cardiff, 1934.

**3443.** MASTERMAN, NEVILLE: J. Viriamu Jones, 1856–1901, pioneer of the modern university: an appreciation. Llandybïe, 1957.

**3444.** MORGAN, IWAN J. (ed.): The college by the sea: a record and a review. Aberystwyth, 1928.

**3445.** OWEN, HUGH: Letter to the Welsh people. London, 1843.

**3446.** POULTON, E. B.: John Viriamu Jones and other Oxford memories. London, 1911.

REICHEL, HARRY RUDOLF: The university in Wales (No. 3419).

**3447.** TROW, A. H., and BROWN, D. J. A.: A short history of the University College of South Wales, Cardiff, 1883–1933. Cardiff [1933].

### (h) Adult education

**3448.** EVANS, DAVID EMRYS: Adult education in Wales. *Trans. Cymmr.*, 1926–7.

**3449.** Survey of adult education in Wales. Cardiff, 1940.

**3450.** THOMAS, BEN BOWEN: R. D. Roberts. In *Harlech Studies*. Cardiff, 1938.

**3451.** WILLIAMS, CYRIL RAYMOND: Fifty years of adult education in South Wales. W.E.A. jubilee pamphlet. Cardiff [1957].

## V. RELIGION

Theological controversy was, during a very large part of this century, one of the main preoccupations of Welshmen. It would be impossible to print here a bibliography of these debates; reference may, however, be made to chapter xi of THOMAS, OWEN: Cofiant y Parch. John Jones, Talsarn (No. 2837), and to EDWARDS, THOMAS CHARLES: Religious thought in Wales, in WILLIAMS, D. D.: Thomas Charles Edwards, Liverpool, 1921. An inadequate guide to the subsequent period is EVANS, W.: History of Welsh theology, London and Newport, 1900. See also JENKINS, ROBERT THOMAS, in A history of Carmarthenshire (No. 605), ii, chapter III (B), and especially the bibliography on pp. 253–63; EDWARDS, G. A.; and JONES, JOHN MORGAN: Diwinyddiaeth yng Nghymru, *Traethodau'r Deyrnas,* iv, Wrexham, 1924; JOHNES, ARTHUR JAMES: An essay on the causes which have produced dissent . . . in Wales (No. 2925); JONES, P. J.: Welsh theology in the last eighty years, in *The Treasury*, 1927–9; PETER, DAVID: Hanes crefydd yng Nghymru (No. 2474).

The files of Y Traethodydd, Yr Efrydydd, and the magazines of the various Christian denominations in Wales should also be consulted, and valuable statistical and other evidence will be found in the minutes of evidence presented to the royal commission on the Church in Wales (No. 2937).

Of the numerous clerical biographies and local denominational histories, only those of more general historical importance are listed below.

### (a) The (Anglican) Church in Wales

The report of the Church in Wales publications commission appointed in 1949 (Cardiff, 1951) contains a section on church periodicals in the nineteenth century and onwards. The files of Yr Haul (monthly from 1836, quarterly since 1946) and of Y Llan (weekly since 1883) contain useful contemporary material, and since 1944 articles on church life and leaders during and since the nineteenth century have appeared in Cymru'r Groes, Y Gangell, and Province. See also Report of the royal commission on the Church in Wales (No. 2937), the Directory and year book (Cardiff, 1924–9), Official handbook of the Church in Wales (Cardiff, 1930 ff.), and the Minutes of the governing body (1920 ff.), together with the runs (of varying dates since circa 1870) of diocesan calendars, clerical directories, gazettes, etc., and reports of diocesan conferences. The episcopal charges, especially those of bishops Ollivant and Thirlwall (1851 and thenceforth triennially) should be consulted.

**3452.** COPLESTONE, WILLIAM: Memoir of Edward Coplestone, bishop of Llandaff. London, 1851.

EDWARDS, ALFRED GEORGE (Archbishop of Wales): Memories (No. 2884).

**3453.** EVANS, ALBERT OWEN: Minutes and proceedings of an old tract society of Bangor diocese. Bangor, 1918.

**3454.** Id.     A chapter in the history of the Welsh book of common prayer. 3 vols. Bangor, 1922.

**3455.** EVANS, D. D. LLWYD: Thomas Price, 'Carnhuanawc', 1787–1848. Yr Haul, xxxvi, 1934.

**3456.** FOWLER, JOHN COKE: The late lord bishop of Llandaff [Ollivant]. Red Dragon, iii, 1883.

See also memorial notice by J. E. Ollivant. Ibid.

**3457.** HARFORD, JOHN SCANDRETT: Life of bishop [Thomas] Burgess. London, 1840.

**3458.** HARRIS, W. H.: Mudiad Rhydychen (1833–1933), Y Traethodydd, 1933.

For contemporary Welsh reaction to the Oxford movement see articles by OWEN THOMAS et al. in Y Traethodydd, 1845, 1846, 1852, and 1874. See also DAVIES, JOHN HUMPHREYS (ed.): Life and opinions of Robert Roberts

(No. 2836); Evans, D. Eifion: Mudiad Rhydychen yng ngogledd sir Aberteifi,
*Jnl. Hist. Soc. Church in Wales*, iv, 1954; vi, 1956; viii, 1958; James, H. L.:
Yr hen lwybrau, *Yr Haul*, 1932–3; Lewis, H. J.: Mudiad Rhydychen a phlwyf
Llangorwen, ibid., 1933; Williams, D. D.: The Oxford movement and
Wales (1833–45), *Cylch. Cymd. Hanes M.C.*, xviii, 1933.

**3459.** Jones, John: Dean Edwards. *Red Dragon*, vi, 1884.

**3460.** Morgan, John: Four biographical sketches. London, 1892.

> Includes lives of bishops Ollivant and Thirlwall.

> Ollivant, Alfred (Bishop of Llandaff): Some account of the
condition of the fabric of Llandaff cathedral (No. 837).

> Owen, C. E. Vaughan: The vicars of Trefeglwys, 1574–1902
(No. 1706).

**3461.** Owen, Eluned E.: The early life of bishop Owen. Llandysul,
1958.

**3462.** Perowne, J. J. Stuart: Remains, literary and theological, of
Connop Thirlwall, bishop of St. David's. Episcopal charges. 2 vols. London,
1877.

**3463.** Thirlwall, J. C.: Connop Thirlwall. London, 1936.

> See also Huntington, George: Lighter phases of a great mind. *Temple
Bar*, lxxvi, 1886 (Thirlwall at Abergwili).

**3464.** Waldron, C.: Richard Watson, bishop of Llandaff. *Red Dragon*, ix,
1886.

**3465.** Williams, Isaac: Autobiography. Ed. G. Prevost. 1892.

> Williams, Ellen (ed.): Life and letters of Rowland Williams
(No. 3430).

**3466.** Williams, Rowland: Methodism in Wales. *Quarterly Review*,
lxxxv, 1849.

**3467.** Id.      The Church and education in Wales. Ibid., lxxxvii, 1850.

> See also Owen, John: Dr. Rowland Williams and his place in contemporary
thought. *Contemporary Review*, 1870.

**3468.** Id.      Rational godliness. Cambridge, 1855.

> See also Jones, Owen W.: Rational godliness—a Welsh controversy.
*Theology*, lxi, 1958.

**3469.** Id.      Lampeter theology. Carmarthen, 1856.

**3470.** Id.      Christian freedom . . . [with review of bishop Ollivant's
charge]. Cambridge, 1857.

**3471.** Id.    An earnestly respectful letter to the lord bishop of St. David's. Cambridge, London, Carmarthen, 1860.

### (b) The older dissent

#### (i) General

EMMANUEL, HYWEL DAVID: Dissent in the counties of Glamorgan and Monmouth (No. 2472).

**3472.** EVANS, ELWYN (ed.): Some documents relating to non-conformity in Montgomeryshire. *Mont. Coll.*, li, 1949–50; lii, 1951–2.

#### (ii) The Independents

See, generally, the denominational journals: *Y Dysgedydd* (1822 ff.), *Y Diwygiwr* (1835–1911), *Y Cronicl* (1843–1910), *Yr Anybynwr* (1856–1864), *Y Tyst* (1869 ff.), and *Y Cofiadur* (No. 323). See also Undeb yr Annibynwyr Cymreig: reports of meetings and other literature issued in connection with the annual gathering.

In addition to the biographies listed below, see also Nos. 2739, 2756, 2764, and 2768.

**3473.** DAVIES, T. EIRUG, *et al.*: Y Prifathro Thomas Rees—ei fywyd a'i waith. Llandysul, 1939.

DAVIES, THOMAS: Bywyd ac ysgrifeniadau D[avid] Rees (No. 2751).

See also WILLIAMS, GLANMOR (ed.): David Rees, Llanelli; detholion o'i weithiau (No. 2752).

EMMANUEL, HYWEL DAVID: Dissent in the counties of Glamorgan and Monmouth (No. 2472).

**3474.** EVANS, ROBERT (ed.): The church covenant of Yr Hen Gapel, Llanbrynmair [1798]. *Mont. Coll.*, lii, 1951–2.

**3475.** HUGHES, HUGH: Wesleyaeth ac Annibyniaeth. 2 books. Llanelli, 1852 and 1853.

**3476.** JAMES, JOHN LLOYD: Cymanfaoedd yr Annibynwyr, eu hanes a'u llythyrau. Dolgelley, 1867.

**3477.** JONES, DAVID SAMUEL: Cofiant darluniadol y Parchedig William Williams o'r Wern. Dolgellau [1894].

**3478.** JONES, LEWIS DAVIES ('Llew Tegid'): Y tadau Annibynol. 2 vols. Bangor, 1895–8.

**3479.** LEWIS, HOWELL ELVET: Cofiant y Parch. E. Herber Evans. Gwrecsam, 1901.

**3480.** LEWIS, THOMAS: Coleg Annibynol Bangor. *Y Traethodydd,* 1887.

OWEN, GERAINT DYFNALLT: Ysgolion a cholegau yr Annibynwyr (No. 2481).

**3481.** PEATE, IORWERTH CYFEILIOG: Helynt y cyfansoddiadau. *Y Llenor,* 1933, 1934, 1936.
On the controversy concerning the Independent colleges see ANON.: Athrofa y Bala—At yr eglwysi, no imprint, 1871; ANON.: A letter to S. Morley, M.P., Bala, 1880; JONES, EVAN PAN: Y dydd hwn. Oswestry [1880]; id.: Gargantua, Ystalyfera, 1883. See also JONES, EVAN PAN: Oes a gwaith Michael Daniel Jones (No. 2740); and THOMAS, OWEN, and REES, JOHN MACHRETH: Cofiant John Thomas (No. 2770).

REES, THOMAS: History of Protestant Nonconformity in Wales (No. 178).

Id.    and THOMAS, JOHN: Hanes eglwysi Annibynol Cymru (No. 179).

ROBERTS, SAMUEL ('S.R.'): Gweithiau (No. 2766).

**3482.** Id.    Annibyniaeth a Henaduriaeth. Dolgellau, 1840.

**3483.** THOMAS, ROBERT ('Ap Vychan'): Gwaith Ap Vychan. *Cyfres y Fil.* Llanuwchllyn, 1903.
See also JONES, MICHAEL DANIEL, a THOMAS, D. V. (gol.): Cofiant a thraethodau diwynyddol R. Thomas [1882].

**3484.** WILLIAMS, D. G. (ed.): Llythyrau a hanes cymanfaoedd de-orllewin a de-ddwyrain yr Annibynwyr, 1845–1860. Llanelli, 1927.

**3485.** WILLIAMS, R. PERIS: Hanes athrofa Bala-Bangor. *Cymru,* 1914.

### (iii) The Baptists

See the denominational journals: *Seren Gomer* (1818 ff.), *Greal y Bedyddwyr* (1827–37), *Y Gwir Fedyddiwr* (continued as *Y Bedyddiwr*) (1842–59 and 1861–7), *Y Tyst Apostolaidd* (continued as *Y Greal* (1846–1918), *Seren Cymru* (weekly, 1851 ff.), and *Trafodion Cymdeithas Hanes Bedyddwyr Cymru* (No. 321). See also Undeb y Bedyddwyr: reports and annual handbooks (Llawlyfrau'r Undeb). On the Scotch Baptists, see *Yr Ymwelydd* (1877–1933).

**3486.** BASSETT, THOMAS MERFYN: Y Bedyddwyr a mudiad addysg Llanymddyfri. *Traf. Cymd. Hanes Bed.,* 1955.

DAVIES, J. D.: Y Bedyddwyr Albanaidd a'r Bedyddwyr Campbelaidd yng Nghymru (No. 2510).
See also DAVIES, D.: Cofiant J. R. Jones o Ramoth, Llangollen, 1899; 'GLASLYN': Yr ail ymraniad o Ramoth, *Cymru,* 1907; JONES, JOHN RICHARD: Crynhodeb, etc., 1802. Several edns. (reprinted in WILLIAMS, DAVID: Cofiant J. R. Jones o Ramoth (No. 2677)); ROBERTS, R. G.: Y Bedyddwyr Albanaidd yng Nghymru, *Seren Gomer,* 1894.

**3487.** DAVIES, OWEN: Cofiant y Parch. John Prichard, D.D., Llangollen. Caernarfon, 1880.

**3488.** ELLIS, ROBERT ('Cynddelw'): Cofiant y diweddar Barch. E[llis] Evans, Cefnmawr. Llangollen, 1866.

**3489.** GEORGE, IRENE: Llawysgrifau a chofysgrifau'r Bedyddwyr yn Llyfrgell Genedlaethol Cymru. *Seren Gomer*, 1935 and 1936.

JAMES, JAMES SPINTHER: Hanes y Bedyddwyr yng Nghymru (No. 172).

**3490.** JONES, D.: Hanes y Bedyddwyr yn neheudir Cymru. Caerfyrddin, 1839.

**3491.** JONES, E. CEFNI: Hanes coleg y Bedyddwyr yng ngogledd Cymru, 1862–1927. Ffestiniog, 1928.

**3492.** Id.       Gwili: cofiant a phregethau. Llandysul, 1937.

**3493.** JONES, JOHN THOMAS: Christmas Evans. Llandysul, 1938.

See also DAVIES, OWEN (gol.): Gweithiau y Parch. Christmas Evans, cyf. i, Caernarfon, 1898; and HOOD, EDWIN PAXTON: Christmas Evans, the preacher of wild Wales: his country, his times, and his contemporaries, London, 1883.

JONES, W.: Hanes cymanfa[oedd] y Bedyddwyr Neillduol yng Nghymru (No. 2524).

OWEN, BOB: Bedyddwyr Cymraeg yr Unol Daleithiau, 1795–1894 (No. 3081).

**3494.** OWENS, BENJAMIN GEORGE: Llythyrau o gymanfa'r gorllewin, 1818. *Traf. Cymd. Hanes Bed.*, 1957.

**3495.** RHYS, W. J.: Penodau yn hanes y Bedyddwyr Cymreig. Swansea, 1949.

**3496.** RICHARDS, THOMAS: Somerset House: Cofnodion y Bedyddwyr. *Traf. Cymd. Hanes Bed.*, 1952–3.

**3497.** Id.       Bedyddwyr Môn, 1825–1925. Ibid., 1954.

**3498.** Id.       Brwydrau'r tri choleg, 1888–1898. Darlith flynyddol Coleg y Bedyddwyr, Bangor, 1955. [Bangor, 1955.]

**3499.** Id.       Hen Fedyddwyr sir Gaernarfon. *Traf. Cymd. Hanes Bed.*, 1958.

**3500.** WILLIAMS, D.: Cofiant y Parch. Robert Ellis ('Cynddelw'). Caerfyrddin, 1935.

WILLIAMS, J. RUFUS: Hanes athrofeydd y Bedyddwyr yn sir Fynwy, Hwlffordd, a Llangollen (No. 2482).

### (iv) The Society of Friends

See sections H, Nos. 2155–78, and J, No. 2533.

### (v) The Unitarians

See section J, Nos. 2534–45, and the denominational journal, *Yr Ymofyn[n]ydd* (1847–54, 1859 ff.).

### (c) The Methodists
### (i) Calvinistic
### (The Presbyterian Church of Wales)

The denominational journals are : *Y Drysorfa* (1831 ff.), *Y Goleuad* (weekly, 1869 ff.), and *Cylchgrawn Cymdeithas Hanes Methodistiaid Calfinaidd Cymru* (No. 325). For a general bibliography of local history, see DAVIES, JOHN HUMPHREYS (and DAVIES, DANIEL); local histories of Welsh Methodism (No. 2554); titles of major works dealing with Methodism in various localities which have appeared since the compilation of this bibliography appear below. See also the minutes of the general assembly and of the associations, and *Y Blwyddiadur* (year book) (1897 ff.).

**3501.** DAVIES, EDWARD OWEN: Ein cyffes ffydd. Caernarfon, 1923 (from *Cylch. Cymd. Hanes M.C., 1923*).

For other works relating to the Confession of Faith, Church policy, etc., see id.: Ffydd, trefn, a bywyd, Caernarfon, 1930; id.: The Calvinistic Methodist or Presbyterian Church of Wales Bill: 'Proof of evidence' prepared for Parliament, *Cylch. Cymd. Hanes M.C.,* xviii, 3, 1933; id.: Dociwmentau ynglŷn â'r weithred seneddol, ibid., xix, 2, 1934; DAVIES, K. MONIKA: Awduriaeth erthyglau'r gyffes ffydd; Llunio'r gyffes ffydd yn Aberystwyth, ibid., xix, 3, 1934; EDWARDS, THOMAS CHARLES: Diwinyddiaeth y Cyfundeb, *Y Goleuad,* December 22, 1893 (see also *Cylch. Cymd. Hanes M.C.* for 1923); JONES, E.: Y Gymdeithasfa, Caernarfon, 1891.

**3502.** DAVIES, JOHN E.: James Hughes, sef cyfrol goffa. Dinbych [1911].

EDWARDS, THOMAS CHARLES: Bywyd a llythyrau Lewis Edwards (No. 2830).

**3503.** ELLIS, GRIFFITH: Cofiant y Parchedig Edward Morgan, Dyffryn. Dinbych, 1906.

**3504.** ELLIS, HUGH: Hanes Methodistiaeth Gorllewin Meirionydd. Cyf. iii, 1885–1925. Dolgellau, 1928.

**3505.** HOBLEY, WILLIAM: Hanes Methodistiaeth Arfon. 6 chyf. Caernarfon, 1910–24.

JENKINS, DAVID ERWYD: Life of the Rev. Thomas Charles of Bala (No. 2590).

Id.      Calvinistic Methodist Holy Orders (No. 2560).

JONES, JONATHAN: Cofiant Thomas Jones, Dinbych (No. 2833).

**3506.** JONES, MORGAN HUGH: Canmlwyddiant ordeiniad 1811. *Y Traeth-odydd*, 1911.

> For other works relating to the 'Secession' of 1811, see JENKINS, DAVID
> ERWYD: Life of Thomas Charles (No. 2590); id.: Calvinistic Methodist Holy
> Orders (No. 2560); JONES, IDWAL: Notes on the ordination controversy,
> 1809–10, *Cylch. Cymd. Hanes M.C.*, xxix, 4, 1944; JONES, JONATHAN: Cofiant
> Thomas Jones, Dinbych (No. 2833); OWEN, J.: Ordeiniad 1811, *Y Geninen*,
> 1911; ROBERTS, GOMER MORGAN: Trannoeth yr ordeinio, 1811, ym Morgan-
> nwg, *Y Traethodydd*, 1950; ROBERTS, R.: Mr. Charles ac ordeiniad 1811, ibid.,
> 1900.

**3507.** JONES, R. W.: Y ddwy ganrif hyn. Caernarfon, 1935.

**3508.** JONES, W. P.: Coleg Treveca, 1842–1942. Llandysul, 1942.

> For other works and articles on the Calvinistic Methodist colleges, see
> *Cylch. Cymd. Hanes M.C.*, 1930 (i) (on Trevecka); EDWARDS, G. A.: Athrofa'r
> Bala, Bala, 1937; No. 2830 above; MATTHEWS, E., and JONES, J. C.: Cofiant
> J. Harris Jones, Llanelli, 1886; PRITCHARD, J.: Rhamant bywyd athro, Bala,
> 1927.

**3509.** MORGAN, J. J.: Hanes Dafydd Morgan, Ysbyty, a diwygiad '59.
Privately printed [Caernarfon], 1906.

**3510.** Id.      Cofiant Edward Matthews, Ewenni. Privately printed,
1922.

**3511.** Id.      Cofiant Evan Phillips, Castell Newydd Emlyn. Lerpwl,
1930.

**3512.** MORRIS, JOHN HUGHES: Hanes Methodistiaeth Liverpool. 2 gyf.
Liverpool, 1929 a 1932.

**3513.** OWEN, HUGH: Braslun o hanes M.C. Môn (1880–1935). Liverpool,
1937.

**3514.** OWEN, PRICE: Hanes Methodistiaeth Dyffryn Clwyd: dosbarth
Rhuthyn. Cyfarfod misol Dyffryn Clwyd, 1921.

PRITCHARD, WILLIAM: John Elias a'i oes (No. 2835).

**3515.** ROBERTS, JOHN JOHN ('Iolo Carnarvon'): Cofiant y Parchedig
Owen Thomas, D.D., Liverpool. Caernarfon [1912].

ROBERTS, JOHN: Methodistiaeth Galfinaidd Cymru (No. 181).

**3516.** THOMAS, OWEN: Cofiant y Parchedig Henry Rees. 2 gyf. Wrexham,
1890.

> See also DAVIES, ANNIE MARY: Life and letters of Henry Rees. Privately
> printed. Bangor, 1914.

Id.    Cofiant John Jones, Talsarn (No. 2837).

### (ii) Wesleyan

See the denominational journals: *Yr Eurgrawn* (1809 ff.), *Y Gwyliedydd* (weekly, from 1877) continued as *Y Gwyliedydd Newydd* (weekly, 1910 ff.), and *Bathafarn* (No. 320). *The Transactions of the Wesley Historical Society* contain valuable material on the Welsh movement.

For the dissident Welsh Wesleyans ('Y Wesle Bach') see *Blaguryn y Diwygiad* (1842) and *Gedeon, neu Ddiwygiwr Wesleyaidd* (1853–6).

**3517.** BRETHERTON, F. F.: Early Methodism in and around Chester. Chester, 1903.

**3518.** CROWTHER, JONATHAN: The life of the Rev. Thomas Coke, LL.D. Leeds, 1815.

> See also DAVIES, SAMUEL: Thomas Coke, LL.D., *Y Geninen*, 1886; ETHERIDGE, J. W.: The life of the Rev. Thomas Coke, D.C.L., London, 1860; EVANS, W. O.: Thomas Coke, y Cymro a'r cenhadwr, Bangor, 1912.

**3519.** DAVIES, EDWARD TEGLA: Welsh Wesleyan Methodism. Being ch. v in The Methodist Church: its origins, divisions, and reunion. London, 1932.

**3520.** Id.    Troedigaeth efengylaidd John Wesley a'i dylanwad ar Gymru. Bangor, n.d. [? 1938].

**3521.** DAVIES, SAMUEL: Y Parch. Samuel Davies, 1af, a'i amserau, yn cynwys hanes ei fywyd. Bangor [1866].

**3522.** Id.    Cofiant [a phregethau] y Parch. Thomas Aubrey. Cyf. i. Bangor, 1887.

**3523.** DAVIES, WILLIAM: John Bryan a'i amserau. Bangor, 1900.

**3524.** EVANS, ISHMAEL: Wesleyaeth yng Nghymru. *Y Traethodydd*, 1878.

**3525.** EVANS, JOHN (Eglwys-bach) (gol.): Hanes William Aubrey a'i oes, yn nghyda rhai o'i bregethau. Rhyl, 1882.

**3526.** Id.    Pregethau a darlithiau. Bangor [1898].

**3527.** EVANS, J. HUGH: Pregethau, darlithiau, a thraethodau gan y Parch. Rowland Hughes . . . yng hyd a darlith ar ei fywyd a'i athrylith. Caernarfon, 1877.

**3528.** EVANS, WILLIAM: Hanes bywyd a marwolaeth y Parch. E[dward] Jones, Bathafarn. Machynlleth, 1850.

**3529.** EVANS, W. H. (ed.): Cyfrol goffadwriaethol Cynfaen. Holywell, 1888.

**3530.** Id.      Canmlwyddiant y Wesleaid yng Nghymru. *Y Geninen*, 1896–1901.

**3531.** HUGHES, JOHN: Perthynas y Wesleyaid a llenyddiaeth Gymreig. *Y Geninen*, 1896.

**3532.** Id.      Bywyd y Parch. Isaac Jones. Liverpool, 1898.

**3533.** Id.      Cenhadaeth arbenig Methodistiaeth Wesleyaidd yng Nghymru. *Y Geninen*, 1899.

**3534.** HUMPHREYS, JOHN: John Evans, 'Eglwys Bach'. London, 1913.

**3535.** HUMPHREYS, T. J.: Y rheoliadur. Coedpoeth, 1909.

Id.      Hanes Methodistiaeth Wesleyaidd yng Nghymru (No. 2688).

**3536.** JENKINS, ISAAC (gol.): Bywyd a gweinidogaeth y Parch. Hugh Hughes . . . wedi ei ysgrifenu ganddo ei hun. Caerfyrddin, 1856.

**3537.** Id.      Cambrian religious sketches. *City Road Mag.*, 1871.

**3538.** JONES, D. GWYNFRYN, and HUGHES, H. MALDWYN: Cofiant Glanystwyth, sef bywyd y diweddar Barch. John Hughes, D.D. Bangor, 1904.

**3539.** JONES, HUGH: Cofiant y diweddar Barch. Samuel Davies. Bangor, 1904.

Id.      Hanes Wesleyaeth yng Nghymru (No. 175).

**3540.** JONES, JOHN ('Humilis'): Y bywgraffydd Wesleyaidd. Machynlleth, 1866.

A biographical dictionary of sixty-one Welsh Wesleyan ministers and thirty-one English.

**3541.** JONES, R. LLOYD: Neillduolion athrawiaethol y Trefnyddion Wesleyaidd. Rhosymedre, 1889.

**3542.** Id.      Cychwyn Wesleyaeth yng Nghymru. *Y Traethodydd*, 1900.

**3543.** JONES, T. WYNNE: Wesleyan Methodism in the Brecon circuit. Brecon and London, 1888.

**3544.** MORGAN, W. ISLWYN. Wesleaeth yn neheudir Cymru, 1872–88. *Bathafarn*, xiii, 1958.

**3545.** OWEN, BOB: Methodistiaid 1811 ac 1814: esgobaeth Bangor. In Er clod (No. 2575).

**3546.** PRITCHARD, R.: Trefnyddiaeth Wesleyaidd. *Y Traethodydd*, 1847.

**3547.** ROBERTS, G. BEDFORD: Teyrnged o barch i goffa'r Parchedigion David Young, Thomas Morgan, John Evans (Eglwysbach), Rice Owen, T. J. Pritchard. Llandilo, 1937.

**3548.** ROBERTS, GRIFFITH THOMAS: Defnyddiau Crai: Llyfrgell Genedlaethol Cymru. *Bathafarn*, ix, 1954.

**3549.** ROBERTS, O. MADOC: Cofiant y Parch. Hugh Jones, D.D. Bangor, 1934.

**3550.** ROWLANDS, WILLIAM ('Gwilym Lleyn'): Cofiant y Parch. John Davies. Llanidloes, 1847.

**3551.** Id.    Annibyniaeth a Wesleyaeth. Llanidloes, 1852.

**3552.** Id.    Dadleniad Annibyniaeth. Caernarfon, 1853.

> The subsequent rejoinder to HUGHES, HUGH: Wesleyaeth ac Annibyniaeth (No. 3475).
>
> See also WILLIAMS, DANIEL: Gwilym Lleyn (1802–1865). *Bathafarn*, viii, 1953.

WILLIAMS, ALBERT HUGHES: Welsh Wesleyan Methodism, 1800–1858 (No. 2701).

**3553.** Id.    The journal of the Rev. John Hughes. *Bathafarn*, xi, 1956; xii, 1957.

YOUNG, DAVID: Origin and history of Methodism in Wales, etc. (No. 2705).

### (d) The latter day saints
### (The Mormons)

The journals of the Mormon mission in Wales are: *Prophwyd y Jubili* (1846–8) and *Udgorn Seion* (1849–61).

LEWIS, THOMAS HARRIS: Y Mormoniaid yng Nghymru (No. 3077).

> Contains a full bibliography. See also WILLIAMS, DAVID: The Welsh Mormons. *Welsh Review*, vii, 1948.

### (e) Religious revivals
### (i) General

**3554.** HUGHES, HENRY: Hanes diwygiadau crefyddol Cymru. Caernarfon [1906].

**3555.** PARRY, EDWARD: Llawlyfr ar hanes y diwygiadau crefyddol yng Nghymru. Corwen, 1898.

20

### (ii) The Beddgelert revival of 1817

**3556.** [GRIFFITH, RICHARD ('Carneddog')]: Diwygiadau Beddgelert. *Y Llenor.* Ed. O. M. Edwards, i, 1895.

### (iii) The revival of 1859

MORGAN, J. J.: Hanes Dafydd Morgan, Ysbyty, a diwygiad '59 (No. 3509).

**3557.** Id.    The '59 revival in Wales: some incidents in the life and work of David Morgan, Ysbytty. Mold, 1909.

**3558.** PHILLIPS, THOMAS: The Welsh revival: its origin and development. London, 1860.

### (iv) The revival of 1904–5

**3559.** ELLIS, ROBERT: Living echoes of the Welsh revival, 1904–5. London [1951].

**3560.** EVANS, SIDNEY, a ROBERTS, GOMER MORGAN (goln.): Cyfrol goffa diwygiad 1904–1905. Caernarfon, 1954.

**3561.** FRANCIS, THOMAS, *et al.*: Y diwygiad a'r diwygwyr: hanes toriad gwawr diwygiad 1904–05. Dolgellau, 1906.

**3562.** FURSAC, J. ROGUES DE: Un mouvement mystique contemporain: le réveil religieux du Pays de Galles (1904–1905). Paris, 1907.
   An eyewitness account by a French observer.

**3563.** LEWIS, HOWELL ELVET: With Christ among the miners: incidents and impressions of the Welsh revival. London, 1906.

**3564.** MORGAN, JOHN VYRNWY: The Welsh religious revival, 1904–5: a retrospect and a criticism. London, 1909.

**3565.** PHILLIPS, D. M.: Evan Roberts a'i waith. Dolgellau, 1912.

### (f) The (Roman) Catholic Church

For the general background, see BECK, J. A. (ed.): The English Catholics, 1850–1950, London, 1950; Catholic directory (annual), 1837 ff.; GWYNNE, DENIS: A hundred years of Catholic emancipation, 1829–1929, London, 1929.

ATTWATER, DONALD: The Catholic Church in modern Wales (No. 1749).

BESSBOROUGH, THE EARL OF (ed.): Lady Charlotte Guest: extracts from her journal, 1833–1852 (No. 3237).
   Ch. xiii and xiv.

**3566.** BURTON, AMBROSE (Bishop of Clifton): Catholicity a hundred years ago in Glamorganshire and Monmouth. Cardiff, 1914.

**3567.** CANNING, JOSEPH HERBERT: A brief history of St. Mary's, Newport, 1840–1940. Newport, 1940.

**3568.** Id.     (ed.): Catholic registers of Abergavenny, Mon., 1740–1838. *Cath. Rec. Soc. Pubns.,* Miscellanea [xiv], 1927.

**3569.** *Cennad Catholig Llanrwst* continued from April, 1911, as *Cennad Catholig Cymru* (with continuous pagination). Bilingual. Llanrwst, 1910–12.

> Vol. i: The Church in Wales in 1846 (p. 106); St. Mary's, Holyhead (p. 153); Father John Jones, 1843–1911 (p. 177); St. Mary's College, Holywell (p. 373); St. Mary's pro-cathedral, Wrexham (pp. 445, 469).
>
> Vol. ii: J. H. Matthews, Father John Hughes (pp. 267, 199, 231).

**3570.** CRONIN, J. M.: Articles on South Wales Catholicism in *St. Peter's Mag.* Cardiff, 1922–9.

> The Catholic Church in Wales in 1841 (1922, 1923); Catholicism in Porthcawl a century ago (1925); Some notes on the Irish in South Wales, 1825–47 (1925) [see also *South Wales News,* March 16, 1925]; Father Portal, 1825–35 (1926–7); Father Jones—an Oxford convert of the Tractarian movement (1927); A review of Catholicism in Wales in 1827 (1928); A survey of the beginnings of modern organization of Catholicism in Cardiff and Swansea (1929).
>
> *St. Peter's Mag.* also contains articles relating to Catholic emancipation in the issues of 1924, 1926, 1928, and 1929; on the growth of Catholicism since that date in Cardiff in those of 1922, 1923, 1924, 1926, and 1928; in Dowlais (1843–63) in that of 1925; and in Newport in those of 1925, 1926, and 1929.

**3571.** EDWARDS, LEWIS: Maynooth. In Traethodau llenyddol (No. 2886). Wrexham, n.d.

**3572.** HEMPHILL, BASIL: Bishop Joseph Brown, c.s.b. (1798–1890), the apostle of modern Wales. *Studies,* 1950.

HOOK, PAUL (ed.): Catholic registers of Holywell, Flintshire, 1698–1829 (No. 2710).

MATTHEWS, JOHN HOBSON: The Vaughans of Courtfield (No. 2205).

Id. (ed.)     Catholic mission register of Perthir (No. 2713).

Id. (ed.)     Catholic registers of Llanarth (No. 2714).

Id. (ed.)     Some records of the Monmouth mission (No. 2715).

O'BRIEN, J.: Old Afan and Margam (No. 2716).

**3573.** WILSON, A. P.: Letter on South Wales parishes. *The Tablet,* March, 1867.

**3574.** WILSON, DOM ANSELM: Life of bishop Hedley. London, 1930.

# GENERAL INDEX

NOTE. This index is intended as a supplement to the list of contents, and should be used in conjunction with it.

The numerals, except those in brackets, refer to the full numbered titles; no attempt has been made to include cross-references. The numerals enclosed in brackets [ ] refer to pages.